Penelope Nash

Empress Adelheid and Countess Matilda

Medieval Female Rulership and the Foundations of European Society

Penelope Nash
Honorary Associate
Medieval and Early Modern Centre
The University of Sydney, Australia

Queenship and Power
ISBN 978-1-137-59088-6   ISBN 978-1-137-58514-1   (eBook)
DOI 10.1057/978-1-137-58514-1

Library of Congress Control Number: 2016962819

© The Editor(s) (if applicable) and The Author(s) 2017
This work is subject to copyright. All rights are solely and exclusively licensed by the Publisher, whether the whole or part of the material is concerned, specifically the rights of translation, reprinting, reuse of illustrations, recitation, broadcasting, reproduction on microfilms or in any other physical way, and transmission or information storage and retrieval, electronic adaptation, computer software, or by similar or dissimilar methodology now known or hereafter developed.
The use of general descriptive names, registered names, trademarks, service marks, etc. in this publication does not imply, even in the absence of a specific statement, that such names are exempt from the relevant protective laws and regulations and therefore free for general use.
The publisher, the authors and the editors are safe to assume that the advice and information in this book are believed to be true and accurate at the date of publication. Neither the publisher nor the authors or the editors give a warranty, express or implied, with respect to the material contained herein or for any errors or omissions that may have been made.

Cover illustration: "Donizo Offers his Poem to Matilda" Image from Rare Books & Special Collections Library, The University of Sydney (Vita Mathildis, 1115. Vatican: Biblioteca apostolica Vaticana, Cod. Vat. Lat. 4922, fol. 7v. From the Facsimile Edition of the Codex, Jaca Book, Milan 1984)

Printed on acid-free paper

This Palgrave Macmillan imprint is published by Springer Nature
The registered company is Nature America Inc.
The registered company address is: 1 New York Plaza, New York, NY 10004, U.S.A.

Empress Adelheid and Countess Matilda, Sant'Agostino, Modena, Italy (La chiesa di S. Agostino Modena. Archivio fotografico del Museo Civico d'Arte di Modena [photography Penelope Nash])

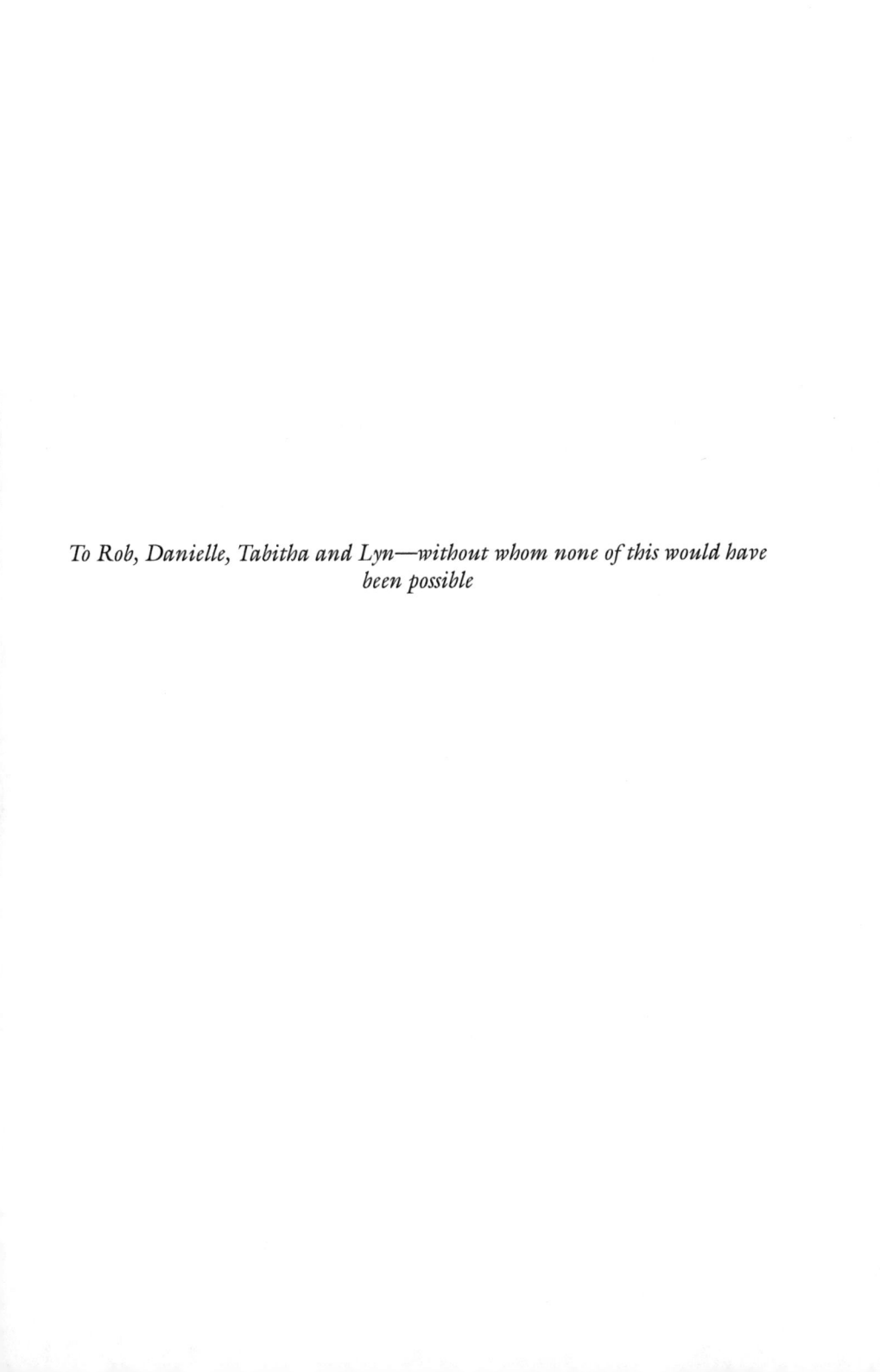

To Rob, Danielle, Tabitha and Lyn—without whom none of this would have been possible

Foreword

Adelheid of Bourgogne (Adelaide di Borgogna) and Matilda of Tuscany (Matilde di Canossa) have been each in turn the subject of several studies in recent decades on the anniversaries of their deaths: 999/1999 for Adelheid; 1115/2015 for Matilda. No one, however, has compared their lives, their politics and their role in history. A comparison was made between Adelheid and another Mathilda, the saint, mother of Otto I (*Queenship and Sanctity. The* Lives *of Mathilda and the* Epitaph *of Adelheid*, ed. by S. GILSDORF, Washington, D.C., 2004), but they lived in the same century and in very proximate locations. In contrast Adelheid and Matilda lived in different centuries and differed in social standing (*status*). One is an empress, the other a countess; the first a wife, widow, mother and grandmother, while the second one was substantially a lonely woman; and, above all, they pertained to different historical contexts: the foundation and establishment of the Holy Roman Empire of the Germanic people for the age of Adelheid, the period of the struggles over investiture, with all the conflicts that ensued, for the age of Matilda.

Nevertheless the comparison is clearly stated, and it is focused in the three parts of the book: *Kin and Kith, Land, Rule*. Yet this is not a book that deals totally with gender studies, even though the feminine aspect is, of course, constantly present. This is a historical study that is broadened from a comparison between the two women to a detailed examination within a wider analysis of the whole Medieval society of the tenth and eleventh centuries. It debates crucial themes dealt with by contemporary historiography, such as imperial power and its underlying ideology, as well as the patrimonial system always linked to the exercise of public power, the role of the powerful woman in time of conflicts or war, the importance of parental bonds and of spirituality as seen in the author's choice of life models (even Biblical ones) and reflected in the acquaintances they established during their daily lives and also in their actions.

Greatly relevant is the attention that the author dedicates to the Latin terminology used by the sources, always subtly analyzed in order to seek in the connotations of the documentary and literary sources, often written according to the patterns of formulaic language, the legal differences in the established roles, or to detect even a hint of the slightest differences between relatives. And of note is also the attention dedicated throughout to iconographic display and to the locations where the historical events took place, with maps. The sources are carefully put to good use and the author is perceptive and full of observations, which demonstrates her vast knowledge of the bibliographical material, especially in English. So the author can discuss themes that go far beyond the simple comparison between the two historical figures and examine many different facets of her topic.

The relationships of Adelheid and Matilda with relatives and friends (*Kin and Kith*) are carefully described, but more interesting is the anthropological contrast between introductions by people nowadays ('What do you do for a living?') compared with those in traditional societies like the Arrernte people ('To whom are you related?') to underline the importance of belonging to a certain family or clan. The comparison becomes even more persuasive about the spirituality of the two women, both vowed to the cloister, compelled to live politically active lives and devoted to military action (Matilda).

As regards the part concerning the *Land*, the three case studies (Melara, Hochfelden, Canossa) are persuasive about three different attitudes in the course of time. The in-depth research on 'the Choice of Law' is highly significant, even though, at the end, historical reasons (that is, the wielding of power) prevail over the legal or juridical ones. As far as the existing difference between the greater freedom of noblewomen in Italy in questions of heredity compared with the ones in 'Germany' is concerned, the reason might be found, perhaps, in the more highly structured organization of the Germanic power system.

In the third part (*Rule*), the differences in status between the two women are well developed, one an empress, the other a countess, but while the second (Matilda) could act directly, even by leading an army (as DAVID J. HAY, *The Military Leadership of Matilda of Canossa 1046–1115*,

Manchester and New York, 2008, argued convincingly), the former (Adelheid) relied mostly on the men who were close to her for direct military action, but participated actively in matters of policy and planning.

The conclusions are broadly shared with the observation that probably Matilda was not the one who chose 'a *masculine* model' for herself, but this is precisely the notion of a male Middle Ages (as Georges Duby wrote), as well as a long-lasting historiography, that is attributed to her. In another perspective while Adelheid chose the monastery at the end of her life, Matilda preferred to follow her religious ideal, supporting Pope Gregory VII, rather than her political interests (as vassal of the emperor). This choice, and the consistency she showed, although against her own interests, is, from my point of view, an intrinsic characteristic of her gender. The problem is more extensive, and it concerns the loss of freedom that the Church Reform of the eleventh century brought to women, as Jo Ann MacNamara stated (Jo Ann McNamara, *Canossa and the Ungendering of the Public Man*, in *Medieval Religion. New Approaches*, ed. by C. HOFFMAN BERMAN, New York—London, 2005, pp. 102–122).

In any case the actions of Adelheid, fully described in the poem by Donizone so that she becomes a model for Matilda, are the most important connection between the two women, who both distinguished themselves among their contemporaries, and are worthy of study, as well as celebration, as this intriguing book shows.

Paolo Golinelli
Full Professor of Medieval History
University of Verona
www.paologolinelli.it

Acknowledgements

I take great pleasure in thanking the many people for their help in the project which produced my dissertation and then this book. In the writing of my doctoral thesis at The University of Sydney, many people provided thoughtful suggestions, advice and corrections. I am particularly grateful to Lynette Olson and to John Gagné, my supervisors, and for the insightful and useful comments by Paolo Golinelli, Chris Wickham and John O. Ward on the submitted thesis from which this book was developed.

I owe a special debt of gratitude to Lynette Olson, who encouraged me in many things and wisely discouraged me in others. Henrietta Leyser inspired me about restructuring, inclusions and exclusions on one memorable summer day at Winchester. Paolo Golinelli gave valuable comments as Reader of the complete manuscript and has been supportive over many years in several ways, including inviting me to Garda to present at *Matilde nel Veneto*, taking me to San Benedetto Po and, with Rita Severi, showing me Frassinoro and their home town of Verona. Lynette Olson and Lola Sharon Davidson spent time on the drafts and imparted their wisdom to me. Beverley Firth and Valerie Eads travelled joyfully with me through Adelheid's and Matilda's territories. Margaret Barrett, Alison Creber, Dexter Hoyos, Jann Hoyos, John Hirst, Penny Russell, David Warner, Chris Wickham, Beverley Firth, Valerie Eads, Jane Ross, Danielle Pryke, Juanita Feros Ruys, Hilbert Chiu, Thomas Bisson, Susan Barrett, James Drown, Robin Appleton, Robert Aldrich, Genevra Kornbluth, Cynthia Kaye, Nada Maio and Jan Roberts made valuable suggestions at various times before or during the manuscript's development.

Many people improved my translations and added other insights, especially Lynette Olson, John O. Ward, Alison Waters, Deirdre Stone, Lola Sharon Davidson, John Scott, Dexter Hoyos, Jann Hoyos, Frances Muecke, Anthony Alexander, Brian Taylor and members of the German Reading Group, Michael Nelson, Tomas Drevikovsky and Pia Ottavian. Lola Sharon Davidson, John O. Ward and Nada Maio redirected their valuable time to review the Author's proofs.

John Watson encouraged with poetry.

Thanks are due also to the staff of Fisher Library, always helpful, especially Rena McGrogan, Aleksandra Nikolic and Julie Price. Several libraries and museums gave permission to use their images, not all of which could be included because of limitations of space. I thank formally the copyright holders for permission to reproduce the images that are included in this book and informally all of the individuals who helped in obtaining them. Linda Huzzey of Koolena Mapping prepared the maps according to my specifications. I thank my friend Ian Jackson for introducing me to Linda.

I thank The University of Sydney, Department of History, School of Philosophical and Historical Inquiry and the Medieval and Early Modern Centre at The University of Sydney, the Sydney Medieval and Renaissance Group, the Australian Early Medieval Society, the Australian and New Zealand Association for Medieval and Early Modern Studies, the Australian National University, Monash University, the University of Western Australia and the Australian Government. Members of these institutions gave me financial and other support.

I am grateful for the encouragement to explore ideas over the years by editors and publishers associated with the *Journal of the Australian Early Medieval Society*, *Storicamente*, *Basileia*, and *Medieval Feminist Forum* and with Palgrave Macmillan ('Empress Adelheid's Vulnerabilities', in *Royal Mothers and Their Ruling Children*), Brepols ('Reality and Ritual', in *Understanding Emotions in Early Europe*) and Pàtron ('L'imperatrice e la contessa', in *Matilde nel Veneto*).

Thanks are owing to Charles Beem and Carole Levin, the general editors of the Queenship and Power series at Palgrave Macmillan, for their early interest in my work. Rachel Crawford, Jessie Wheeler, Michelle Smith and Kristin Purdy gave me good and speedy advice along the way. Ganesh Kannayiram, Joshua Raj and the team from Springer helped me patiently through the production process.

I am indebted to many other friends and colleagues for their ongoing friendship, support and love. I thank them all.

Finally I could not have done anything without Rob and Danielle, who carried the bags and the baggage literally and figuratively throughout.

Note on Names

The following table lists those people whose names are apt to be confused:

Preferred usage	Elaboration	Dates
Empress Adelheid or Queen Adelheid	Wife of King Lothar I of Italy and then of Emperor Otto I. Originally Adelheid of Burgundy; one of the two main subjects of this book	d. 999
Abbess Adelheid of Quedlinburg	Granddaughter of Empress Adelheid and daughter of Otto II and Empress Theophanu	d. 1043
Queen Adelaide of Aquitaine	Queen of the Franks; wife of King Hugh Capet	d. 1004
Countess Adelaide of Turin	Mother of Empress Bertha; Adelaide is sometimes referred to as Adelaide of Susa to distinguish her from her daughter Adelaide of Savoy (d. 1081)	d. 1091
Bishop Anselm (I, the Elder) of Lucca	Uncle of Bishop Anselm the Younger of Lucca; became Pope Alexander II; his successor was Pope Gregory VII	d. 1073
Bishop Anselm (II, the Younger) of Lucca	Countess Matilda's confessor; supporter of Gregorian reforms	d. 1086
Archbishop Anselm of Canterbury	Supporter of Gregorian reforms; a spiritual advisor to Countess Matilda	d. 1109
Countess Beatrice of Tuscany	Mother of Matilda of Tuscany; Countess, *dux*, Marchioness; also known as Beatrice of Lotharingia, Beatrice of Bar (and Beatrice of Canossa)	d. 1076
Queen Bertha of Italy	Married King Rudolf II of Italy; Mother of Empress Adelheid; later wife of King Hugh of Italy	d. 966

(*continued*)

xv

(continued)

Preferred usage	Elaboration	Dates
Empress Bertha	Daughter of Adelaide of Turin; first wife of Emperor Henry IV	d. 1087
King Conrad I of Burgundy	Brother of Empress Adelheid	d. 993
Emperor Conrad II	First of the Salian dynasty; married Gisela of Swabia, granddaughter of King Conrad I of Burgundy	d. 1039
Duke Conrad of Lower Lotharingia	Eldest surviving legitimate son of Emperor Henry IV and Empress Bertha; initially the heir	d. 1101
King Henry I of East Francia (Henry the Fowler)	First of the Ottonian dynasty	d. 936
Duke Henry I of Bavaria	Second surviving son of King Henry I of East Francia	d. 955
Duke Henry II of Bavaria (Henry the Wrangler)	Son of Duke Henry I of Bavaria	d. 995
Emperor Henry II (Duke Henry III of Bavaria)	Son of Duke Henry II of Bavaria; last of the Ottonian dynasty	d. 1024
Emperor Henry III	Son of Emperor Henry II	d. 1056
Emperor Henry IV	Son of Emperor Henry III and Empress Agnes	d. 1106
Emperor Henry V	Second surviving legitimate son of Emperor Henry IV and Empress Bertha; last of the Salian Dynasty	d. 1125
Abbot Hugh of Cluny	Expanded the power of Cluny; supporter of Pope Gregory VII and Gregorian reforms; godfather of Emperor Henry IV	d. 1109
Bishop Hugh of Die, then Archbishop of Lyons	Papal legate in France; supporter of Gregorian reforms	d. 1106
Abbot Hugh of Flavigny	Abbot of Flavigny; possibly abbot of Saint-Vanne later; initial supporter of Gregorian reforms	d. betw. 1114 and late 1140s
Queen Mathilda	Wife of King Henry I of East Francia; mother-in-law of Empress Adelheid	d. 968
Abbess Mathilda of Quedlinburg	Daughter of Empress Adelheid	d. 999
Mathilda of West Francia	Second wife of King Conrad I of Burgundy; daughter of Louis IV of West Francia (d'Outremer) and Gerberga, daughter of King Henry I of East Francia	d. 981–990/992
Countess Matilda of Tuscany	*marchionissa, comitissa, dux, ducatrix*; sometimes known as Matilda of Canossa; one of the two main subjects of this book	d. 1115

Chronology

Empress Adelheid

912		Otto I born
919		Otto's father, Henry of Saxony, elected king of the East Franks at Fritzlar (King Henry I)
926		Hugh of Arles, count of Provence, becomes king of Italy, ousting King Rudolf II
c. 930		Otto I marries Edith, daughter of King Edward and granddaughter of Alfred the Great
c. 931		Adelheid born to Bertha, daughter of Duke Burchard I of Swabia, and King Rudolf II of Burgundy
933	Mar 14	Henry I defeats Magyars at Riade
936		Otto I is acknowledged successor at Erfurt
	July 7	King Henry I dies
	Aug 8	Otto I crowned king at Aachen
937		Adelheid's father, King Rudolf II, dies
		Hugh marries Rudolf's widow, Bertha
	Dec 12	Adelheid and Hugh's son, Lothar, are betrothed; Adelheid receives extensive estates from Hugh and Lothar
		Adelheid and her mother brought up in the Italian court at Pavia
946		Edith dies
947		Lothar, son of Hugh, becomes co-ruler of Italy with his father; Adelheid marries Lothar who grants her more estates
c. 948		Hugh dies and Adelheid and Lothar become queen and king of Italy

(continued)

(continued)

950	Nov	Lothar dies; Adelheid inherits more estates on his death
951	Apr 20	Adelheid is captured by Berengar II and imprisoned
	Aug 20	Adelheid escapes and Adalbert Atto shelters her at his castle of Canossa
		King Otto I's brother Henry of Bavaria escorts Adelheid to Otto at Pavia
	Oct 9	Adelheid and Otto marry at Pavia and are crowned queen and king; Adelheid brings the kingdom of Italy to Otto
952 / 953?		Adelheid gives birth to two sons, Henry and Brun, who die in childbirth or very young
954 / early 955		Adelheid gives birth to Mathilda, the future abbess of Quedlinburg
955 and later		Otto rewards Adalbert Atto with the counties of Reggio, Modena and later Mantua
955		Henry I, duke of Bavaria, dies
	Aug 10	Otto I defeats Magyars at Lechfeld
	Late	Adelheid gives birth to first surviving son, the future Otto II
961	May	Otto II elected co-ruler with Otto I at Worms and crowned at Aachen
962	Feb 2	Adelheid and Otto I crowned and anointed as empress and emperor by Pope John XII
966		Adelheid's mother, Bertha, dies leaving extensive properties to her daughter. Adelheid's daughter Mathilda becomes abbess of Quedlinburg
967	Dec	Otto II crowned co-emperor with his father
968	Mar 14	Death of the dowager queen mother, Mathilda
968–971		Adelheid and Otto I in Italy; Abbess Mathilda of Quedlinburg acts as regent in Germany
972	early	Bishop Dietrich of Metz escorts Theophanu from Benevento to Rome
	Apr 14	Otto II marries Theophanu
973	Mar	Assembly at Quedlinburg
	May 7	Otto I dies
973–974	From May 7—Jun 974	Adelheid acts as regent for Otto II and Theophanu
974		First revolt of Henry the Wrangler
975		The first daughter, the future Abbess Sophie of Gandersheim, was born to Theophanu and Otto II
977		Second revolt of Henry the Wrangler
	July	The second daughter, the future Abbess Adelheid of Quedlinburg and Gandersheim, was born to Theophanu and Otto II
978		Adelheid and Otto II quarrel and Adelheid goes to Lombardy

(continued)

980	July	Birth of Otto III to Theophanu and Otto II
981		Bishopric of Merseburg merged with Magdeburg
		Otto II campaigns in Southern Italy
982	Jul 13	Otto II's army defeated by the Emir of Sicily and his men near Crotone
983	May	Assembly at Verona elects the young Otto III joint king with his father
	Dec 7	Otto II dies
	Dec 25	Otto III crowned king at Aachen; after the ceremony news of Otto II's death reaches Aachen
984	early	Henry the Wrangler abducts Otto III
	Easter	Henry the Wrangler claims kingship
	Jun 5	Duke Charles of Lower Lotharingia accuses Bishop Dietrich of Metz of disloyalty to Otto III
	Jun 9	Gerbert of Aurillac urges Bishop Dietrich of Metz to support Otto III
	Jun 29	Henry the Wrangler hands over Otto III to Theophanu, Adelheid and Mathilda Abbess of Quedlinburg, at Rohr; the three *dominae imperiales* act as regents
985	July	Adelheid moves to Pavia; steadies political matters in northern Italy
986	Easter	General recognition of Otto III as king at Quedlinburg
987	May	Louis V of West Francia dies; Hugh Capet succeeds
988 or after		Death of Emma, daughter of Adelheid and Lothar
990	After May	Adelheid leaves Italy to stay in Burgundy with her brother King Conrad I of Burgundy
991	Jun 15	Theophanu dies; Adelheid becomes sole regent for young Otto III
		Adelheid founds a monastery at Selz on lands Otto I had given her in 968
993		Death of Adelheid's brother King Conrad I of Burgundy
994		Otto III comes of age
995		Henry the Wrangler dies
996	May 21	Adelheid's grandson Otto III is crowned emperor at Rome
999	c. Feb 6	Death of Adelheid's daughter Abbess Mathilda of Quedlinburg
	Apr 9	Gerbert of Aurillac becomes Pope Sylvester II
		Adelheid travels to Burgundy to negotiate with the unruly magnates on behalf of her nephew, the newly acclaimed King Rudolf III
	Dec 16/17	Adelheid dies

Countess Matilda

1037		Beatrice of Bar and Lotharingia marries Boniface of Canossa, grandson of Adalbert Atto
1046		Matilda of Tuscany/Canossa born to Beatrice of Lotharingia and Margrave Boniface of Tuscany/Canossa
1050		Birth of Henry IV to Empress Agnes and Emperor Henry III
1052		Boniface is assassinated
1054		Beatrice marries her second husband, Duke Godfrey 'The Bearded' of Lotharingia, who is her cousin
c. 1054 / 1055		Matilda's older siblings Frederick and Beatrice die
1055		Henry III takes Beatrice and Matilda prisoner in Italy and brings them to Germany
1056		Henry III releases Beatrice and Matilda, who return to Italy; Henry III dies; Empress Agnes assumes the regency for her son the young King Henry IV
1069 / 1070		Matilda's stepfather Godfrey the Bearded dies; Matilda marries her stepbrother Godfrey III, 'the Hunchback', of Lower Lotharingia
1070 / 1071		Matilda gives birth to a daughter Beatrice
1071	Jan 29	Matilda's little daughter dies
1072	Jan 19	Matilda begins the government and administration of possessions in Middle and Upper Italy. She issues her first diploma with Beatrice
1073	Apr 22	Hildebrand becomes Pope Gregory VII
1074		Beatrice and Matilda attend the Roman Lenten Synod
	By 2 Feb	Matilda is estranged from her husband Godfrey the Hunchback
1076	Feb 22	Pope Gregory excommunicates King Henry IV at a Lenten Synod
	Feb 26	Godfrey the Hunchback is murdered
	Apr 18	Matilda's mother, Beatrice, dies
	Dec	Henry IV, his mother-in-law Countess Adelaide of Turin, her son Armadeus, Queen Bertha and others cross the Alps into Italy
1077	Jan 24–28	Henry IV, Gregory VII, Matilda, Abbot Hugh of Cluny and Countess Adelaide of Turin at Canossa. Henry begs the pope to absolve his sins and remove the excommunication. Matilda negotiates between Henry and the pope
1079		Matilda may have given all her property to Pope Gregory VII and his successors
1080	Mar 7	Matilda attends the Lenten Synod where Gregory VII excommunicates Henry IV for the second time
1080 / 1081		Matilda and her army defeated by Henry IV's Lombard allies at Volta near Mantua

(continued)

1081	Mar	Henry IV enters Italy. Bishop Anselm (II) of Lucca vows loyalty to Pope Gregory VII and takes refuge with Matilda at Canossa
From 1082		Under an imperial ban by Henry IV Matilda loses much of her lands
1084	Mar 21	Rome surrenders to Henry IV
	Mar 24	Antipope Clement III (Wibert) crowns Henry IV emperor at Rome
	Jun 17	Henry IV leaves Italy, but his eldest son and heir, Conrad, stays behind
	Jul 2	Matilda's army defeats Henry's Lombard allies at Sorbara
1085	May 25	Pope Gregory VII dies in Salerno
	Jun 1	Henry IV confiscates Matilda's estates in Lotharingia
1086	Mar 18	Bishop Anselm (II) of Lucca dies at Mantua. Matilda is present At Canossa Matilda possibly receives and rejects a proposal of marriage from Robert Curthose, the eldest son of William the Conqueror
1089		Following the advice of Pope Urban II Matilda marries again, this time to Welf V of Bavaria
1090	March	Henry IV returns to Italy
	May	Welf V defends Mantua against the siege of Henry IV
1091	Apr 10	Mantua falls to Henry IV
	Winter	At Tricontai Matilda's troops are betrayed and overwhelmingly defeated by Henry IV and his allies
	End of the Year	Henry holds the region north of the Po, except for Nogara and Piadena
1092	Summer	Henry IV's siege of Monteveglio
	Sep– early Oct	Matilda convenes a council of her supporters at Carpineti to discuss terms of surrender to Henry IV but decides to fight on
	Oct	Matilda's troops defeat Henry IV's at Canossa
	End of Year	Matilda regains Gubernola and Ripalta
1093	Mid-March to late July	Henry IV's son Conrad defects with his troops to Matilda's side
1094	Early	Henry IV's second wife, Praxedis, separates from him; Matilda rescues her from Verona
1095	Mar 1–7	Matilda at the Council at Piacenza presided over by Pope Urban II
		Matilda and Welf V separate
1096–1097		Henry IV reconciles with Welf IV, Matilda's father-in-law and, by doing so, gains access to the Brenner Pass. Henry restores Matilda's lands to her and returns to Germany after being stranded for seven years in Italy

(*continued*)

(continued)

1097		Matilda attends the Roman Synod of 1097. Empress Adelheid canonized by Pope Urban II at a Roman Synod in either 1097 or 1099
1099		Guido Guerra is noted as the adopted son of Matilda between 1099 and 1108
1100–1115	Jun 7	Matilda holds court numerous times and issues diplomata, judging cases and donating land
1102	Nov 17	At Canossa Matilda reputedly renews her donation of her property to the papacy
1103	Nov–Dec	Matilda in Tuscany where she makes donations and escorts Archbishop Anselm of Canterbury on the road to Rome
1105	Dec 23–31	Henry IV is imprisoned by his son Henry V and abdicates
1106	April	Matilda at Modena cathedral for the translation of the bones of St Geminanus to the new cathedral
	Aug 17	Death of Henry IV, who is buried at Speyer
	Oct	Matilda in Modena for the dedication of the cathedral with Pope Paschal II
	Oct 20–27	Matilda at the Council of Guastalla presided over by Pope Paschal II
1111	May 6–8	At Bianello, Matilda receives Henry V as her guest Matilda may have made Henry V her heir
1111–1115		Matilda continues to hold court and make donations to monasteries especially to San Benedetto Po
1114	Oct	Matilda pardons the Mantuans who, believing her dead, had burned down her castle
1115	July 24	Matilda dies and is buried in the monastery of San Benedetto Po
1116		Henry V descends into Italy to take possession of Matilda's inheritance

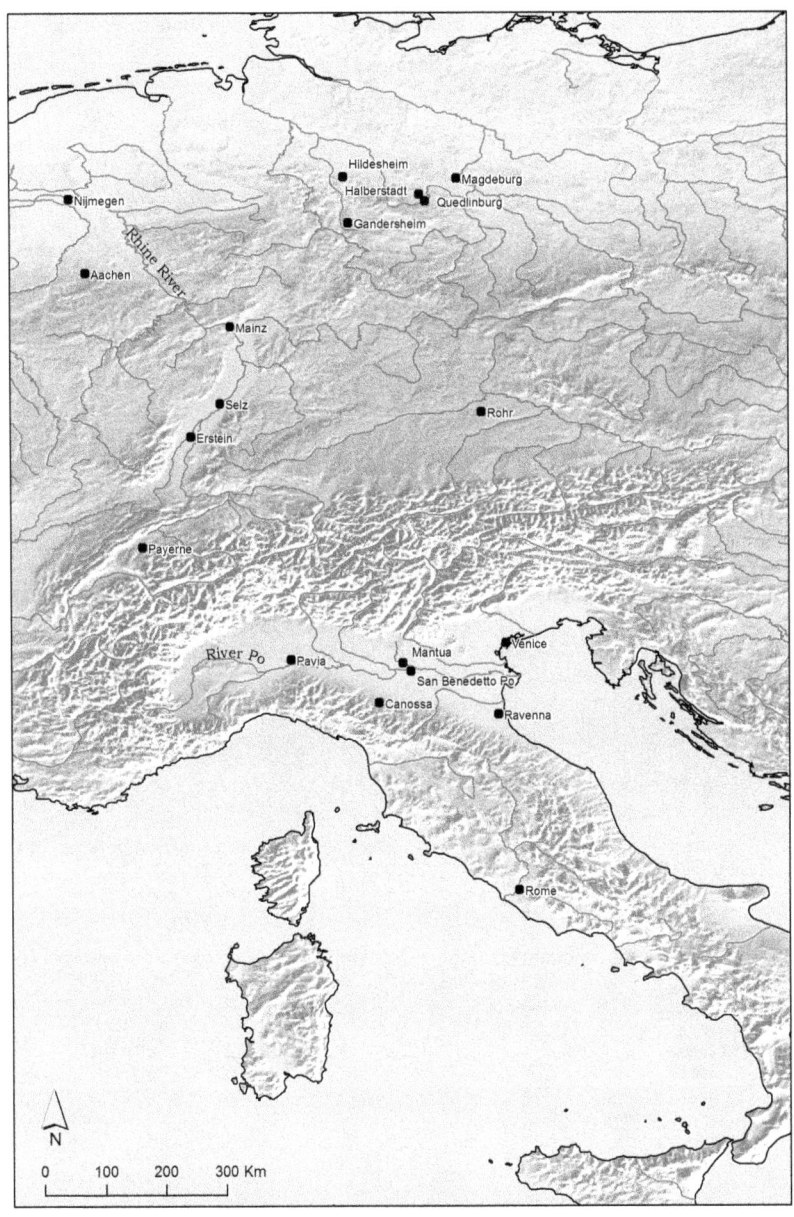

Map 1 'Adelheid's and Matilda's World' (Map specified by Penelope Nash. Map prepared by Koolena Mapping)

Table 1 Adelheid's and Matilda's Family Connections and the Burgundian Rudolfings

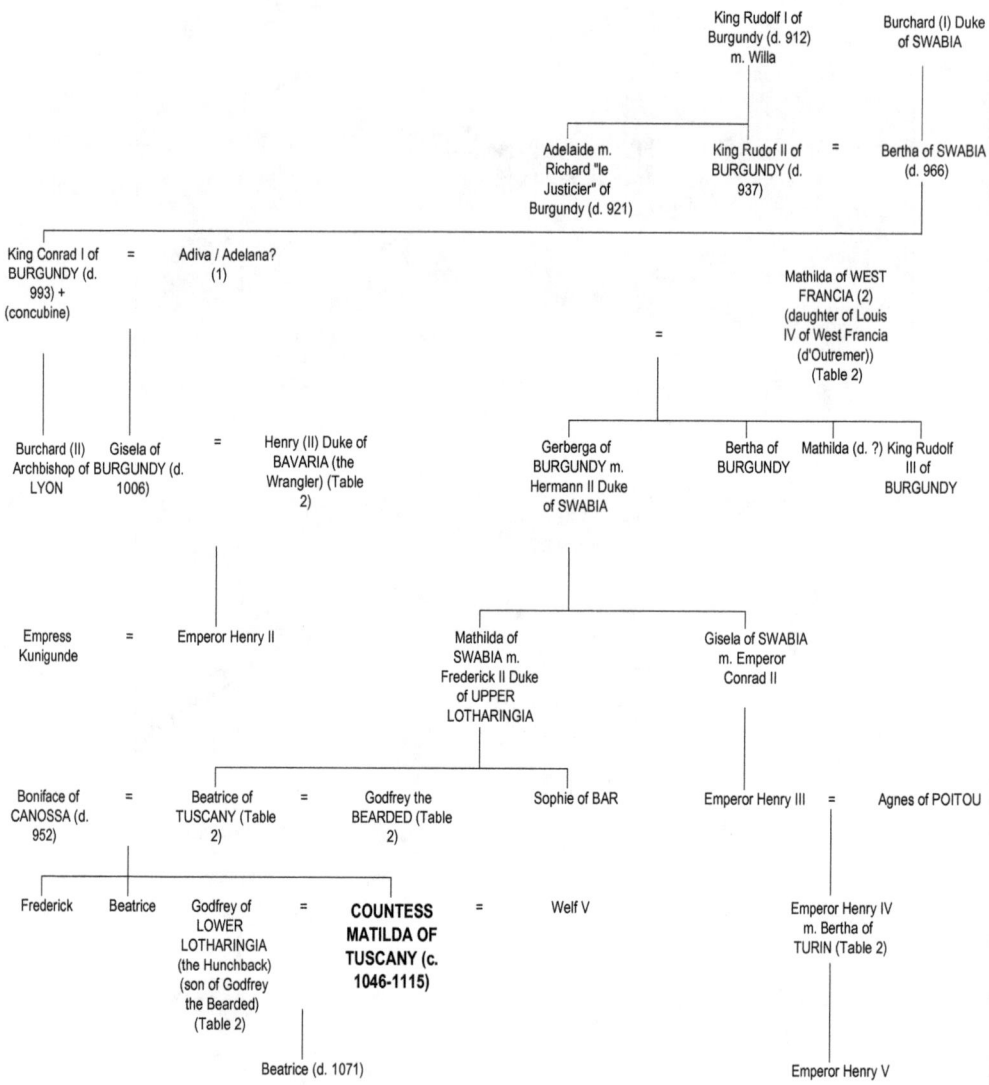

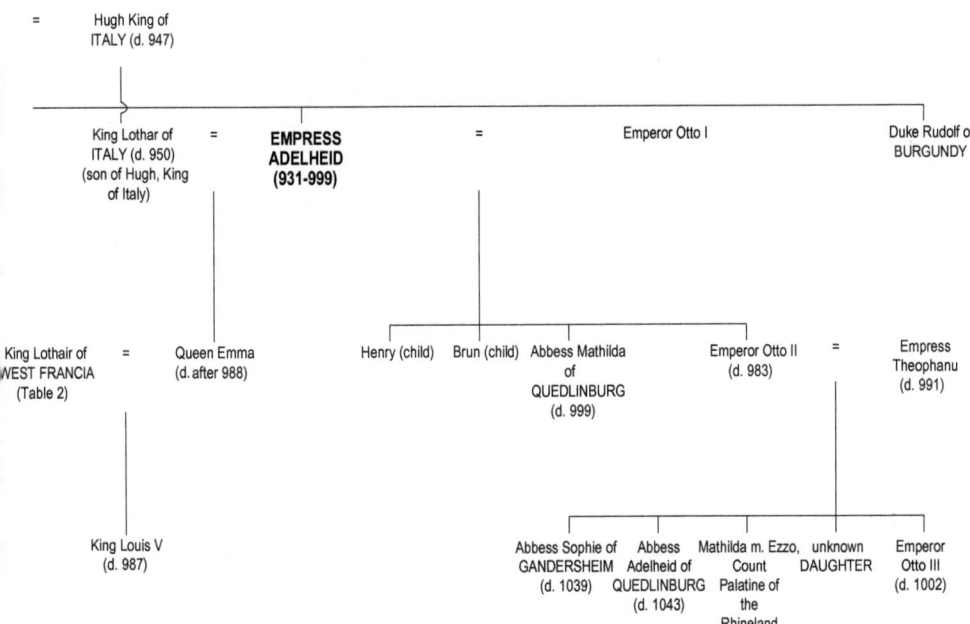

Table 2 Adelheid's and Matilda's Family Connections and the Liudolfings

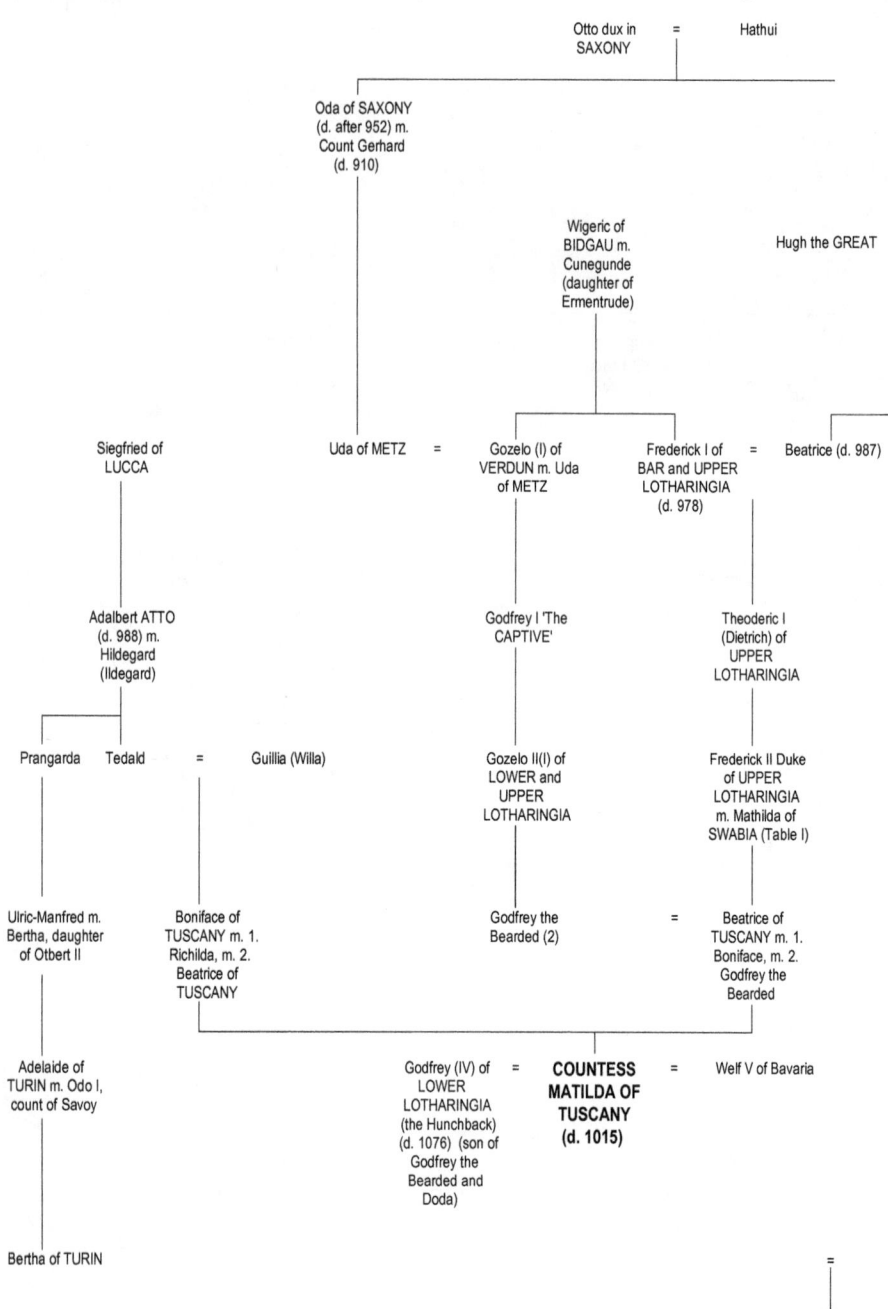

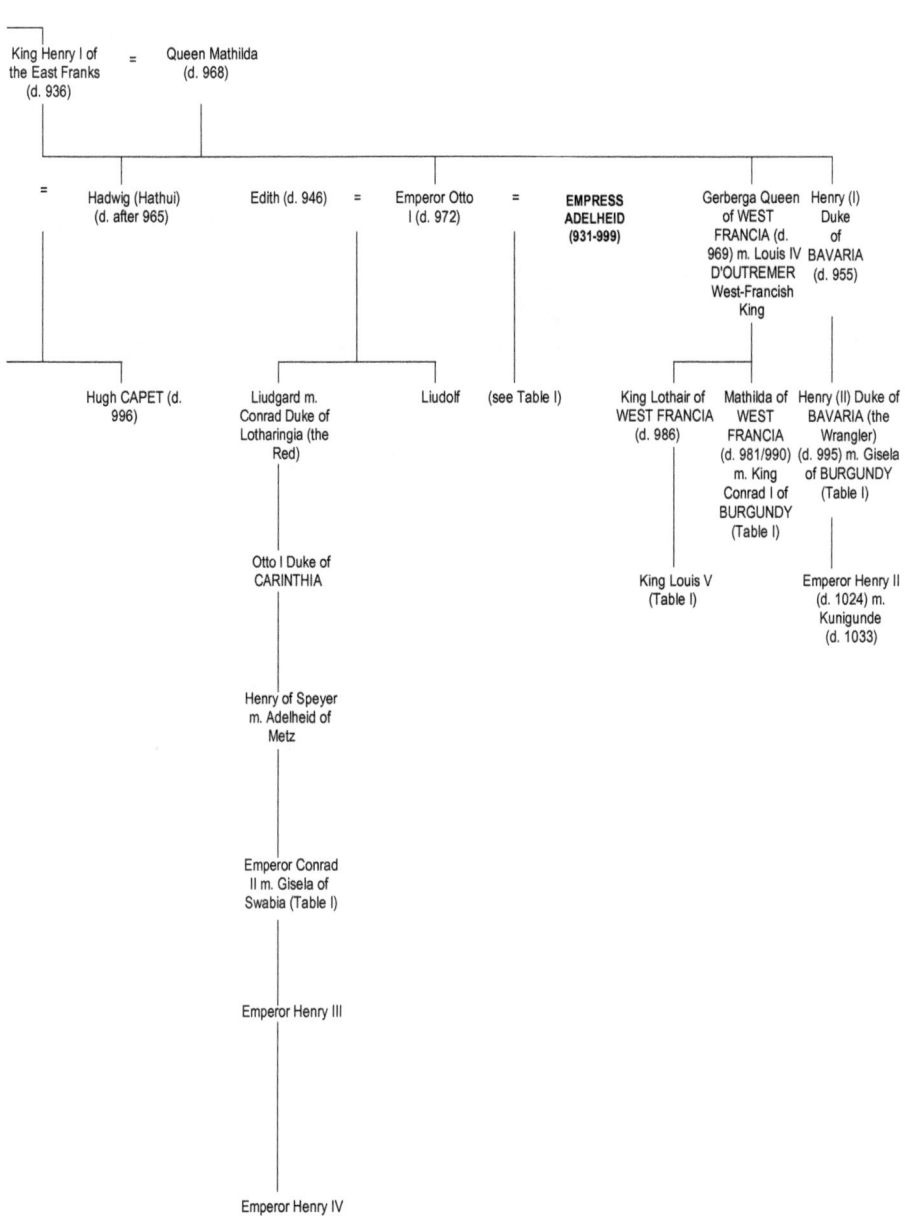

CONTENTS

1 Introduction: Masterful and Formidable Ladies — 1

2 Kin and Kith: Keeping Friends and Placating Enemies — 15

3 Land: Building and Maintaining a Property Portfolio — 95

4 Rule: Models of Rulership and the Tools of Justice — 129

Epilogue — 223

List of Abbreviations — 231

Notes on Sources and Translations — 237

Bibliography — 239

Index — 271

List of Maps

Map 3.1	Old and New Routes between the East-Frankish Kingdom and Italy (Map specified by Penelope Nash. Map prepared by Koolena Mapping)	101
Map 4.1	Adelheid's interventions with Otto I (Map specified by Penelope Nash. Map prepared by Koolena Mapping)	144
Map 4.2	Adelheid's sole interventions in Otto III's diplomata—15 June 991–December 994 (Map specified by Penelope Nash. Map prepared by Koolena Mapping)	147
Map 4.3	Matilda's centers of power (Map specified by Penelope Nash. Map prepared by Koolena Mapping)	165
Map 4.4	Matilda's diplomata (Map specified by Penelope Nash. Map prepared by Koolena Mapping)	170
Map 4.5	Matilda—number of diplomata—after Spring 1097–July 1115 (Map specified by Penelope Nash. Map prepared by Koolena Mapping)	174

CHAPTER 1

Introduction: Masterful and Formidable Ladies

In the spring of 951 Berengar II, margrave of Ivrea, who claimed the kingship of Italy, imprisoned the nobly born Queen Adelheid in the castle of Garda on the shore of the lake of the same name in the province of Verona. Since Adelheid was the recent widow of King Lothar of Italy (d. 950), Berengar wished to compel her to marry his son, thus consolidating for himself the kingship of Italy. After several months in captivity, Adelheid with her maidservant and the help of a priest dug a tunnel beneath the earth and escaped the guards under cover of night. The chroniclers report that as day broke Adelheid hid in caverns and in the furrows of grainfields to avoid the pursuers. Berengar followed her, passed through the field in which she was concealed under the blades of the tall grain and tried to part the surrounding stalks with his spear, but he did not find her. Bishop Adelhard of Reggio accompanied Adelheid with her maidservant and priest to the castle of Canossa in northern Italy where his vassal, the rising castellan Adalbert Atto, took her in and defended her against Berengar's troops. Adelheid's position as bearer of the kingdom under ancient Lombard custom meant that those within her inner circle had access to her riches and influence: if Atto gained her favor, he could benefit greatly from the wealth and power of the widowed queen.

At about nineteen years of age Adelheid was young, beautiful and a wealthy widow, even more desirable for her ability to enhance a new husband's claim to the kingship of Italy. At Adelheid's invitation the East

© The Author(s) 2017
P. Nash, *Empress Adelheid and Countess Matilda*,
DOI 10.1057/978-1-137-58514-1_1

1

Frankish king, Otto I, descended from Germany into Italy. Berengar fled without a fight, and Otto seized and occupied Pavia, the capital of the Italian kingdom. Otto sent his brother Henry, duke of Bavaria, to cross the River Po and to escort Adelheid to him in the captured city. After testing her faithfulness with gold—how Otto did this we are not told—Otto married her. They were crowned at Pavia before Christmas 951, Otto with the ancient iron crown of the Lombards, while the northern Italian magnates hailed them as king and queen of the Franks and the Lombards. Adalbert Atto was richly rewarded for his service—Otto gave him the lands of Reggio, Modena and Mantua—and thus the upstart Canossan family solidified their holdings around the Apennine Mountains. Atto's great-granddaughter Matilda would bring his actions to fruition.

One hundred and twenty years later, during the especially cold January (1077), Canossa was the scene of another momentous event. Pope Gregory VII had disagreed with King Henry IV of Germany about who should appoint the new archbishop to the see of Milan. The dispute escalated into a battle over rival claims of authority. At Worms on 24 January 1076 Henry IV had Pope Gregory VII declared powerless, and the pope retaliated by excommunicating the king at the Lenten Synod the same year. Gregory released everyone from his fealty to the king and consequently few of Henry's vassals chose to obey him. Henry and the royal party crossed the winter Alpine Passes from Germany to Italy, the men creeping on hands and knees or clinging to the shoulders of guides while the queen and her ladies were drawn on sledges of ox skin. They arrived at fortress Canossa, over which Countess Matilda presided, one of many properties that she inherited from her great-grandfather Adalbert Atto. The chroniclers report that Abbot Hugh of Cluny, Henry's godfather, urged Henry to seek Matilda's help as negotiator. As chief power broker in northern Italy and Henry's cousin, Matilda succeeded in obtaining Pope Gregory's clemency for Henry, provided that Henry promised to be faithful to the see of the Romans. Every day for three days Henry, clothed in the woolen garment of a penitent with frost and snow burning his bare feet, climbed the cliff of Canossa, prostrated himself in the form of a cross in front of the pope and swore fidelity to him. When Gregory accepted the king back into the Christian fold, three days after Henry's initial request for forgiveness, Henry had saved his crown but had acknowledged the superiority of the pope over the bishops and their flocks in his realm. Though illustrious in this world, the king was now merely one of the many owing obedience to the pope. Together Countess Matilda, Abbot Hugh of Cluny, Pope Gregory VII and Henry IV met at a great feast at castle Canossa in celebration of the reconciliation, but Henry sat with a grim demeanor, not eating and drumming his fingernails on the wooden table. And so began in earnest the great conflict between the papacy and the empire that changed their relationship and the governance of Europe forever.

***

Lives of Two Women

Since the activities of its two main subjects, Empress Adelheid and Countess Matilda of Tuscany, are presented thematically rather than chronologically in this book, it is useful to give here an overview of their lives. In brief the first woman under consideration, Adelheid, was born in about 931 in Burgundy. Her parents were Rudolf II, king of Burgundy (912–937) and king of Italy (922–926), and Queen Bertha, originally from Swabia. After Rudolf's death, Bertha married King Hugh of Italy and at the age of sixteen Adelheid married her stepbrother, Lothar. When Hugh died in 948, Lothar and Adelheid became king and queen of Italy. Their daughter, Emma, was born in 949. After Lothar's death in November of the following year, Berengar, margrave (marquis) of Ivrea, who wished to strengthen his claim to the kingship of Italy, imprisoned Adelheid at Garda in northern Italy. She escaped and in September 951 married Otto I, the leading man in Saxony at that time (The details of her capture, escape and flight to Otto at the royal city of Pavia opened this chapter).

During the first four years of their marriage, the rebellions against Otto I by close relatives threatened his authority, but after the deaths of most of his troublesome protagonists and his victory over the Magyars at Lech near Augsburg in 955, Otto asserted his primacy in Germany. Between 951 and 956 Adelheid bore four children, two of whom survived until adulthood: Mathilda, who became abbess of the monastery at Quedlinburg, and the heir, Otto II. The royal couple ruled by traveling around the kingdom and administering justice from their peripatetic court, as was then customary. On 2 February 962 Pope John XII anointed and crowned Adelheid and Otto I empress and emperor at Rome. The extant diplomata or charters (records of the declarations and orders of the king/emperor) for that year were all issued from northern Italy, mainly from Pavia, the traditional capital of Italy. Adelheid ruled with Otto I for twenty-two years.

On 14 April 972 Otto II married the Byzantine princess, Theophanu, at Rome, and a year later Otto I died at Memleben, leaving the empire to his son. Adelheid was now the dowager empress, but she acted as regent for the young couple for the next year and then operated mostly independently in Italy, Germany and Burgundy, where she attended certain key imperial events, endowed monasteries and visited her brother and sister-in-law, King Conrad and Queen Mathilda of Burgundy. Theophanu and Otto II had five children, four of whom survived to adulthood. When Otto II died at only twenty-eight on 7 December 983, the successor, Otto III, was only three. Empress Adelheid (his grandmother), Empress Theophanu (his mother) and Abbess Mathilda of Quedlinburg (his aunt) were given the regency of the empire, after other claimants were dismissed. Theophanu was active mainly in Germany while Adelheid was active in Italy. On Theophanu's unexpected death in June 991, Adelheid took on the regency alone, ruling the empire, although in her grandson's name, until Otto III reached his majority in 994. She died in December 999 at the monastery of Selz in Alsace, and Pope Urban II canonized her at the Lenten Synod of either 1097 or 1099.

Countess Matilda of Tuscany (sometimes known as Matilda of Canossa) was born in northern Italy, probably at Lucca or Mantua, to Beatrice of Bar, also known as Beatrice of Lotharingia, and Margrave Boniface of Tuscany in about 1046, nearly fifty years after Adelheid's death. There were a number of connections between the two women that began with Adalbert Atto, Matilda's great-grandfather, who sheltered Adelheid in his castle of Canossa in 951. Atto's son Tedaldo left the castle-fortress of Canossa to his son Boniface in 1012. After Boniface was assassinated in 1052, Beatrice married her cousin Duke Godfrey, 'The Bearded', of Lotharingia. However, they married without the permission of the emperor, Henry III, whose authority the new couple threatened because of their power in northern Italy and the close familial connections. Duke Godfrey the Bearded fled, and Henry ordered Beatrice and Matilda to Germany. In 1056 Henry III released Beatrice and Matilda, who returned to Italy; only after Henry III died, did Godfrey the Bearded come back to Tuscany. As a consequence of the death of her brother and sister at about this time, Matilda became the sole direct heir of her parents.

To consolidate the new familial connections, Matilda was engaged to her stepbrother, Godfrey III, 'The Hunchback', the son of Godfrey the Bearded and his first wife, Doda. After the couple married in 1069 Matilda gave birth to a daughter, who died young in 1071. Godfrey the Bearded died, Matilda and Godfrey the Hunchback separated and in early 1072 at the age of twenty-five, Matilda began the government and administration of extensive possessions in middle and upper Italy jointly with her mother. By 2 February 1074 Matilda was estranged from her husband. On 22 February 1076 Pope Gregory VII excommunicated the new king of Germany, Henry IV, son of Emperor Henry III and second cousin of Countess Matilda, for questioning the pope's authority. Four days later Godfrey the Hunchback was murdered. On 18 April Beatrice died but not before she had guided Matilda in how to operate as an effective ruler as Beatrice herself had done. Matilda was now in possession of extensive assets inherited from her father, mother and husband and was the undisputed ruler of territories that stretched from Lake Garda in the north of Italy to Tarquinia in the south. The fortress Canossa, where her grandfather, Adalbert Atto, had sheltered Adelheid, was also now in her sole possession.

A year later King Henry IV needed to have Pope Gregory VII's excommunication lifted because he rightly feared that his men would not continue to obey an excommunicated king and that therefore he would be unable to rule. Henry traveled south across the Alps in the northern winter of 1076/1077 with an extensive entourage in order to negotiate with the pope, to whom Countess Matilda had offered safety at Canossa. As a result of the successful negotiations that Matilda and others had facilitated between the pope and the king, Gregory lifted Henry's excommunication and the king could once again command his men (Those events are described earlier in this chapter in more detail). In March 1080 Pope Gregory VII excommunicated Henry IV again, but on this occasion Henry took little notice. From that time Henry IV was in conflict with Gregory VII and the pope's ally Matilda. On the one hand Matilda was the vassal of her cousin Henry IV and owed him allegiance. On the other hand she was dedicated to papal reform and to papal centrality. When king and pope were in conflict she sided with the papal contingent, serving seven popes with obedience and devotion.

Matilda spent the period from 1080 until October 1092 in intermittent warfare against Henry IV. After Henry's Lombard allies defeated Matilda's troops at Volta near Mantua, Henry conquered Rome and was crowned emperor by the Antipope Clement III in March 1084. In June Henry left Italy, leaving his son and heir, Conrad, in charge. In July 1084 Matilda's army defeated Henry's allies at Sorbara. A year later Henry confiscated her estates in Lotharingia. In 1089 on the advice of Pope Urban II, who wanted to strengthen his support by uniting two allied houses, Matilda married Welf V of Bavaria, whose father Welf IV of the house of Este was an opponent of Henry IV. Henry returned to Italy in early 1090. During that year and the next Henry won many victories against Matilda and her troops in Italy, but in October 1092 she forced him to withdraw at Canossa. Sometime in the first half of 1093 Henry's heir, Conrad, and Conrad's troops changed to Matilda's side and in the following year Henry's second wife, Praxedis, left him and Matilda rescued her from Verona. In 1095 Matilda separated from her second husband. Henry IV was confined to a small area around the north of Italy until 1097, when he reconciled with Welf IV, and consequently the Alpine Passes and the route to the north, which the Este family controlled, became accessible to the emperor again. Henry IV never returned to Italy.

From about 1093 Matilda had greater freedom to operate. She issued the majority of her diplomata, which show her allocating lands and other property and resolving disputes throughout her territory. She attended papal councils and Roman synods. She was present in April 1106 at the translation of the bones of St. Geminianus to the new cathedral at Modena, and at the dedication of the cathedral with Pope Paschal II in October later the same year. In 1111 she received the new Salian king, Henry V, as her guest at Bianella near Canossa. She continued to hold court and make donations to monasteries until her death on 24 July 1115 at or near the monastery of San Benedetto Po, where she was buried. Pope Urban VIII organized the theft of her remains from San Benedetto Po in 1633 and had them interred in St. Peter's at Rome, where they remain under a statue of her by Bernini.

***

The comparison of two powerful medieval elite women against the background of the changes in the eleventh century, which saw the shift from the early to the later Middle Ages, is the subject of this book. The analysis of how and why Empress Adelheid, in a relatively benign environment, and Countess Matilda of Tuscany, against the grain, seized opportunities and overcame obstacles to retain and to increase their wealth and to exercise power foregrounds the study. While the chroniclers accorded the two women immense praise, modern medievalists, with a few exceptions, have paid them narrow or comparatively scant attention. Patricia Skinner laments that little attention has been paid to Matilda as a ruler.[1] Thomas Bisson regrets that, although her power as an heiress and an ally is well understood, 'she remains virtually unknown as a *lord prince* in the greatest age of that species' [my italics].[2] Going further, despite the recognition by Matilda's chroniclers of the concordance between the lives of Matilda and Adelheid, detailed comparisons to date have been rare. Nevertheless François Bougard recognized the power of the comparison of these two women when he stated:

> Like [empress] Adelheid before her, she [Theophanu, the daughter-in-law of Adelheid] was even granted an imperial coronation, and because of this she was bestowed with the same sacred quality ... Theophanu and the others set the scene for equally important rulers in the eleventh century, such as Beatrice of Canossa, *ductrix et marchionissa* of Tuscany, and her daughter Mathilde.

However, Bougard sounds a warning, without perhaps fully identifying the pull of the changes across the eleventh century:

> Yet even though the position of the female sovereign in Italy was stronger than elsewhere ... it was also ambiguous, because it lacked clear institutional definition and ultimately depended on the support of the aristocracy of the kingdom.[3]

Although women in the earlier period had relatively better access to wealth and power (they could have done better but they could have done a lot worse too), the opportunities were not wonderful. They still had to watch their step; they were still under men's control. Neither Adelheid, who lived in a more ambiguous, less clearly articulated society, nor Matilda, who lived in one transforming into a community of more institutionalized structures and of greater organization, could be totally secure—angst about position and the trustworthiness of alliances encouraged both to act with vigilance.

The real history of the opportunities for women to gain and to retain wealth is a history of the change in scarcity and in plenty. Because of low population at the beginning of the eleventh century, women had value for their labor and as bearers of children. Marriage, supposedly an indissoluble personal union and a social instrument, structured patrimony within families through dowries and marriage settlements, alliances and exchanges of land. Combined with the availability of plentiful land, the reverse dowry—the major marriage payment whereby the future husband gave the future wife property (often lands and movable goods)—provided for the maintenance of the future widow. Often the reverse dowry remained in the possession and the control of the woman on her husband's death, enabling her to live independently.[4] Sometimes, however, the widow had to fight for her entitlements.[5]

As the eleventh century progressed, increased population ensured that land became less abundant for both men and women and so means were found to redistribute what remained. Karl Leyser cites the evidence of the demise of the lavish endowments of Ottonian monasteries to show one way in which possessions were snatched back and how the newly released wealth helped support the rise of the comital holdings: 'the Saxon princes became somewhat less tolerant of wealthy widows disposing of great inheritances. Instead they forced them to remarry and used their possessions to build up those competitive territorial lordships which the prolonged impotence of the later Salian emperors in Saxony made possible.'[6] As competition intensified, so too did the inheritance customs and the purpose of marriage change, the consequence being that women's inheritance suffered more than men's. The fragmentation of the tenth-century estates caused by the division of the inheritance among all children gave way to a rise in primogeniture (inheritance by the firstborn son). In replacing partible inheritance by women and men with primogeniture, families sought to 'preserve, build up and consolidate the patrimony'.[7] The rise of the castellans and knights as progenitors of the later patrilinear dynasties of the high Middle Ages ousted earlier family structures.[8] Ownership within the family patrimony shifted:

> Women no longer serve as the nodules through which pass the surest kinship ties. The daughter is treated as a marginal member of her father's lineage, and after her marriage, her children will leave it entirely; their allegiance passes to her husband's line. Women also lose the claim to a full (or at least fair) share with their brothers in the family patrimony.[9]

By the early twelfth century, the sacramental ideal of marriage had become a distinct concept to ensure dynastic survival. In discussing Philip I of France's second marriage in 1092, Georges Duby wrote that marriage 'overt, public, ceremonious, surrounded by special words and deeds, is at the center of any system of values, at the junction between the material and the spiritual'.[10] In such a reorientation of the nature of marriage as both dynastic and sacramental, the wife's ownership and control of land gave way to ownership by the husband. Younger sons were now forbidden to marry or were required to marry later and fewer lands were available for brides. Alternatively the adoption of stricter Germanic rules of incest was used to exclude them. The stricter rules encouraged a culture of initiation via tests and trials before breeding and an emphasis on the knight's ultimate goal as marriage. The reluctant groom had to be coaxed to marry; the reverse dowry declined and all but disappeared by the end of the twelfth century.[11] The rise of the knight and the obligations of male vassal to male lord further excluded women and limited their opportunities to retain wealth. The rise of the fief, given primarily for military service, and passed undivided to the eldest son, excluded people who could not give military service, that is, women.[12] In 1037 Emperor Conrad II issued the *Constitutio de feudis*, which barred women specifically from the inheritance of fiefs in Italy.[13]

In the same way as an aristocratic woman had greater opportunities to acquire wealth at the beginning of the eleventh century rather than at its end, so too she could avail herself of comparatively more opportunities to exercise power in the earlier period. We have seen above the ability of the queen to wield power in the earlier period. So too educated abbesses, usually from the royal families (and especially in Ottonian Germany), in heading the great foundations, minted coins, held markets, set up their abbeys as key stopping points for the itinerant royal retinue, presided over the Saxon assemblies, on occasions ruled in the king's absence and generally exercised significant power and managed great wealth obtained from endowments.[14] In consequence, certain noble women were privileged (for example, the women of the Saxon aristocracy in late tenth and early eleventh centuries) because of longevity and relatively greater freedom to inherit property, to control great wealth and to wield great power.[15]

As the eleventh century progressed, the occasions for women to exercise power diminished. Concomitant with the rise of nobles and the development of more circumscribed governmental structures, the power of the king was called into question and consequently so was that of his queen, especially in Italy and Germany. Although the king/emperor still maintained a court and his household, he and his retinue became less central to power as other structures formed. As the machinery of government became more impersonal, aristocratic men were able to exercise public power as administrators of the new institutions, but this opportunity was not open to noble women who were relegated to private power in a shrinking sphere as the household became increasingly marginalized while other power structures gained prominence. England was an exception in that the public institutions under the king never completely died out. On the Continent, especially in France, public institutions eventually re-emerged. Altogether everywhere the growth of a more organized society consigned family, household and women to the periphery.[16]

As well as changes in the secular sphere, changes in the ecclesiastical domain affected women to their detriment in different ways. With the enforcement of celibacy of the clergy, the opportunity for clerical wives to exercise power as part of the 'parish' disappeared.[17] Not only women's power but women's status itself reduced.[18] So too the rise of the importance of the sacraments, especially the Eucharist, disadvantaged the abbesses, canonesses and nuns who, while they had always been dependent on priests, now found themselves privileging those ordained men for bearing the sacrament to them. No one has summarized the situation better than R. W. Southern. The tenth-century elite women 'were masterful and formidable ladies and they did not forget that they belonged to a ruling caste ... These ladies of the Dark Ages have some remarkable religious and literary achievements to their credit'. Nevertheless by the late eleventh century times had changed. '[T]heir period of splendid independence did not last long. As society became better organized and ecclesiastically more right-minded, the necessity for male dominance began to assert itself.' [19]

The changes in society of the eleventh century did not go unnoticed by a later generation. Following Emperor Frederick Barbarossa's announcement of his imperial rights at Roncaglia in northern Italy in 1158, Archbishop Eberhard of Bamberg, in considering the emperor to be getting above himself in deeming all civil administration to be derived from and consequently subject to imperial authority, looked back to the tenth century:[20]

> The records of another time are consulted, the imperial titles are read perhaps in the form which suited that age and the goodness as well as the simplicity of those times ... But now all things are changed.[21]

Based on such sources written by the educated elite, scholars have been in general agreement about the scope and multiplicity of changes which occurred in Europe in the eleventh century.[22] In essence, the eleventh century saw the rise of a more organized and centralized society in Western Europe where the secular and ecclesiastical governance functions were beginning to separate from each other, the results of which in general advantaged men but disadvantaged women.

This is the accepted paradigm. Successful women operated in the period before the changes of society in the later eleventh century under a less structured society where women could do better. A century later women who succeeded did so in spite of the disadvantages of the society that in the latter half of the eleventh century was growing more rigid and authoritarian. Whether the two women under examination were severely constrained by the restrictions imposed on them by their society in different ways or whether they operated in much the same way because women just continued on as before is not clear-cut. Did Matilda succeed in spite of the paradigm or because the paradigm is wrong and she continued in much the same way as women always had, coping with or escaping from the straitjackets of their societies? This book tests the veracity of the paradigm by examining the lives of Empress Adelheid and Countess Matilda.

Notes

1. Patricia Skinner, *Women in Medieval Italian Society, 500–1200* (Harlow: Pearson Education, 2001), 138.
2. Thomas N. Bisson, 'Review of *Die Urkunden und Briefe der Markgräfin Mathilde von Tuszien* by E. Goez and W. Goez', *Speculum* 76, no. 2 (April 2001), 457.
3. François. Bougard, 'Public Power and Authority', in *Italy in the Early Middle Ages: 476–1000*, ed. C. L. Rocca (Oxford: Oxford University Press, 2002), 43–44.
4. David Herlihy, 'The Medieval Marriage Market', in *Medieval and Renaissance Studies* (Durham, NC: Duke University Press, 1976), 2–7, 9.
5. Janet Nelson, 'The Wary Widow', in *Courts, Elites, and Gendered Power in the Early Middle Ages: Charlemagne and Others*, ed. Janet Nelson (Aldershot: Ashgate, 2007), II.82–113; Henrietta Leyser, *Medieval Women: A Social History of Women in England, 450–1500* (London: Weidenfeld and Nicolson, 1995), 168–86.
6. Karl Leyser, *Rule and Conflict in an Early Medieval Society: Ottonian Saxony* (London: Edward Arnold, 1979), 70–71.
7. Lynette Olson, *The Early Middle Ages: The Birth of Europe* (Houndmills: Palgrave Macmillan, 2007), 172.
8. *Contra* Constance Brittain Bouchard, *'Those of My Blood': Constructing Noble Families in Medieval Francia* (Philadelphia: University of Pennsylvania Press, 2001), 175–80.
9. David Herlihy, *Medieval Households* (Cambridge, MA: Harvard University Press, 1985), 82.
10. Georges Duby, *The Knight, the Lady and the Priest: The Making of Modern Marriage in Medieval France* (Harmondsworth, UK: Penguin, 1985), 18–19.

11. Herlihy, 'Marriage Market', 9, 19; Helen M. Jewell, *Women in Dark Age and Early Medieval Europe c. 500–1200* (Basingstoke: Palgrave Macmillan, 2007), 77–78. Contra Herlihy, *Medieval Households*, 98–103; John B. Freed, *Noble Bondsmen: Ministerial Marriages in the Archdiocese of Salzburg, 1100–1343* (Ithaca, NY: Cornell University Press, 1995), 149–50.
12. Herlihy, 'Marriage Market', 9; Olson, *Early Middle Ages*, 171–72.
13. See Herlihy *contra* its effectiveness in Germany: David Herlihy, 'Land, Family and Women in Continental Europe, 701–1200', in *Women in Medieval Society*, ed. Susan Mosher Stuard (Philadelphia: University of Pennsylvania Press, 1976, repr. 1977), 22–23.
14. Sean Gilsdorf, *Queenship and Sanctity: The Lives of Mathilda and the Epitaph of Adelheid* (Washington, DC: Catholic University of America Press, 2004), 27; Gerd Althoff, 'Saxony and the Elbe Slavs in the Tenth Century', *NCMH* 3 (1999), 271, 275, 290–91.
15. Leyser, *Rule*, 49–73.
16. Jo Ann McNamara and Suzanne Wemple, 'The Power of Women through the Family in Medieval Europe, 500–1100', in *Women and Power in the Middle Ages*, ed. M. C. Erler et al. (Athens, GA: University of Georgia Press, 1988) 83–93; Jo Ann McNamara, 'Women and Power through the Family Revisited', in *Gendering the Master Narrative: Women and Power in the Middle Ages*, ed. Mary Carpenter Erler et al. (Ithaca, NY: Cornell University Press, 2003), 17–30; Elizabeth Haluska-Rausch, 'Transformations in the Powers of Wives and Widows near Montpellier, 985–1213', in *The Experience of Power in Medieval Europe: 950–1350*, ed. Robert F. Berkhofer, Alan Cooper and Adam J. Kosto (Aldershot: Ashgate, 2005), 153–68; K. R. Dark, *Civitas to Kingdom: British Political Continuity 300–800* (London: Leicester University Press, 1999), 94–6, 136, 169, 255–57; Kathryn L. Reyerson and Thomas Kuehn, 'Women and Law in France and Italy', in *Women in Medieval Western European Culture*, ed. Linda Elizabeth Mitchell (New York: Garland, 1999), 131–41; Olson, *Early Middle Ages*, 197, 199; Pauline Stafford, '*La Mutation Familiale*: A Suitable Case for Caution', in *The Community, the Family, and the Saint: Patterns of Power in Early Medieval Europe.*, ed. Joyce Hill and Mary Swan (Turnhout: Brepols, 1998), 124–25; Penelope Nash, 'Maintaining Elite Households in Germany and Italy, 900–1115:

Finances, Control and Patronage', in *Elite and Royal Households in Later Medieval and Early Modern Europe*, ed. Theresa Earenfight (Leiden: Brill, forthcoming 2017).
17. Jo Ann McNamara, 'Canossa and the Ungendering of the Public Man', in *Medieval Religion: New Approaches*, ed. Constance Hoffman Berman (Routledge, 2005), 102; Dyan Elliott, 'The Priest's Wife: Female Erasure and the Gregorian Reform', in Berman, *Medieval Religion*, 123–26, 145.
18. Skinner, *Women*, 152–53.
19. Although Southern was referring to women in religious life, his remarks are applicable to all ruling women at that time: R. W. Southern, *Western Society and the Church in the Middle Ages*, vol. 2 (London: Hodder and Stoughton, 1970), 310.
20. Brian S. Pullan, ed., *Sources for the History of Medieval Europe: From the Mid-Eighth to the Mid-Thirteenth Century* (Oxford: Blackwell, 1966), 179; Brenda Bolton, '*Totius christianitatis caput*. The Pope and the Princes', in *Adrian IV The English Pope (1154–1159): Studies and Texts*, ed. Brenda Bolton et al. (Aldershot: Ashgate, 2003), 135.
21. Rahewin, *Gesta Friderici imperatoris, libri III et IV*, ed. G. Waitz and B. von Simpson, *MGH SSrG* [46]:162–346 (1912), 4.22, trans. Charles Christopher Mierow, *The Deeds of Frederick Barbarossa* (New York: Norton, 1966), 257.
22. R. I. Moore, 'Review article: Duby's Eleventh Century', *History* 69 (225) (1984), 46; R. I. Moore, *The Origins of European Dissent* (Oxford: Blackwell, 1977), 9–18.

CHAPTER 2

Kin and Kith: Keeping Friends and Placating Enemies

In 2009 Diane J. Austin-Broos wrote about the sociocultural changes experienced by the Arrernte people of Central Australia, focusing on the strong mutual obligations to family that weakened as people aged and lost the capacity to fight or to negotiate. The waning of power in old age holds particularly true of the women of the Arrernte. Mutual obligations between families require members to reciprocate in elaborate ways. If someone perceives the interaction with him or her to be inadequate, disharmony, feuds, fighting and the employment of elaborate procedures to regain equilibrium are the result. The Arrernte have lived a nomadic lifestyle whose values comprise strong concepts of property and place. Property, which encompasses both knowledge and relatedness, gives either access to or authority over place. In the past century the Arrernte largely abandoned their nomadic existence, as Christian missionaries and government intervention promoted settlement. A more recent state-sponsored 'return to country' superseded the missions but continued to support a settled way of life.[1] Austin-Broos reports that the Arrernte, despite such momentous changes in their lifestyle, 'still ask, "To whom are you related?" whereas nonindigenous Australians ask, "What do you do (for a living)?"'[2]

A thousand years earlier, in the late tenth century, the aristocratic culture of the communities of medieval Europe would seem to function completely differently from the nomadic culture of the Arrernte tribe. Whereas the Aboriginal inhabitants of Australia experienced almost complete isolation from other societies from when they arrived on the Australian continent until European settlement began in the late eighteenth century, Western European aristocratic families about the turn of the first millennium experienced almost ceaseless contact with their neighbors. For them property did not embrace a separate concept of knowledge that could be applied to place; it encompassed well-defined geographical locations and movable goods. Despite these differences, what unites the Arrernte and the medieval dynasties was the way that property represented and reinforced social obligations, and the way it served as the ground in which family and friendship ties were planted. Land and kinship supported each other.

Both the Arrernte communities and the medieval families of Europe demanded rigorous norms and performed elaborate rituals to settle disputes and to maintain harmony, all based firmly on family ties. Consequently, although the nobility of early medieval Europe might obtain and express their wealth and power through acquisition of land and ruling actions, rules and regulations would not control such a community unless ties between kin and kith bound society together in harmony. It is difficult for modern analysts to understand exactly the relationships and expectations of kin to each other at that time, but there is no doubt that they were strong and that, if they failed, society fell apart.

Who Were 'Kin' in the Middle Ages?

The primary sources show that people set more store on some kinship relationships than on others. There has been much debate among medieval historians about the extent of the relationships, their strength among families and the consequent effects on thoughts and actions, especially in the tenth and eleventh centuries. What 'family' meant in practice remains a key question not easily answered. Karl Leyser notes the fluidity of the noble kins of the Carolingian and post-Carolingian world, who 'present to the historian an oddly horizontal rather than vertical aspect, very different from the later dynasties of counts, castellans and, by the twelfth century, even knights'.[3] Marc Bloch's important analysis of kindred groups and kinship ties in the Middle Ages highlights the long pre-medieval history of the ties based on blood relationships with its concomitant lack of documentation until approximately the thirteenth century. In medieval Europe words that described those interrelationships often overlapped with terms meaning 'friends', with occasional clarification such as 'friends by blood'. Toward the end of the eleventh century a male leader whose followers were drawn from his kin and who were also bound by the new ties of vassalage formed the strongest bond.[4] Gerd Althoff used the term 'family', broadly associating it with 'kindred' and 'relatives'—expressions difficult for modern historians to apply accurately to past individuals and groups but 'characterized by mutual obligations'.[5] The importance of the ties of blood, and 'family', meaning those related by a common ancestor, cannot be overstated. When the term *familia* was used in the Middle Ages it meant a household including servants and attendants, wider in meaning than a modern nuclear family but narrower than an extended family. The concepts of 'family' and 'kin' were very fluid. Moreover a woman might make major changes of affiliation in moving into her husband's household. Consequently she would need to decide which of those related by blood she would regard as 'family'.[6]

Ancestors were acknowledged whether they originated in either the male or the female lines. The terms *agnatio* and *cognatio*, however, have been used with a variety of meanings.[7] Karl Leyser argues persuasively for the term *agnatio* to be used for descendants through the male line and *cognatio* for descendants through the female line. He supports his arguments directly from the medieval sources, particularly Isidore of Seville, for definitions, but focuses on tenth-century examples. Acknowledging inconsistencies in the medieval sources, Leyser notes, however, that *cognatio* was not always used for descendants through the female line, citing the example of Hildegundis, abbess of Geseke in Westphalia (part of Saxony in the tenth century), who used the word to mean her direct descent through her father and paternal grandfather. In addition the maternal uncle had a special role in relation to his nephews.[8] Modern usage of the term *cognatio* encompasses maternal kin alone or else all kin traced through both father and mother (the classical Latin usage).[9] Consistent with Leyser's recommendations and to maintain clarity, here *cognatio* is used to mean maternal kin alone in discussions about the value of the male and the female influences on the noble families of the medieval period. Consequently the terms 'agnates' and 'cognates' and their corresponding adjectives 'agnatic' and 'cognatic' refer to descendants through the male line and descendants through the female line respectively.

In addition to being very conscious of their antecedents, medieval nobles indicated their relationship to one another by the use of particular terms. While *consanguinei*, as the word implies, signified those who shared blood, *parentes* and *propinqui* were used with a range of meanings. Those who shared blood or were otherwise 'close'—who were either related by marriage or were more distant relatives, such as a great-uncle, a great-nephew or a second cousin—could all be referred to as *parentes* or *propinqui*, or even more confusingly as *amici*. *Consanguinei* were involved in important decisions such as selection of a marriage partner.[10] Sometimes sons were distinguished from others who were also closely related by blood. Salvian gives one such example in the fifth century: 'It is hard when anybody bequeaths little to his children and *relatives*.'[11]

Who Were 'Kith' in the Middle Ages?

In contrast, those persons who were known, taken collectively, as friends, fellow-countrymen, neighbors or acquaintances and who had no common ancestry were consequently not kin. The term 'kith', with its origins in Old High German and Middle English, denoted those who were known but who were less familiar.[12] Referring particularly to the Middle Ages, Althoff notes that 'kith', occasionally in use as a contrast to 'kin', might include 'friends' and 'followers' if they were not related by blood.[13] In a society where the state as we know it was not fully formed, those who were not kin nor bound in other ways treated each other more warily and with more reserve.

Nonetheless in the close relationships of the tenth century, it was difficult to find people who did not have some blood in common in their ancestry. The Capetian kings, for example, had trouble finding queens whose consanguinity was acceptable. If no one was available, the solution was to defy the consanguinity prohibitions or to marry into a lower social group. On the other hand, ambitious leaders with 'practical power' could and did enhance their own status and power by marrying women with fine lineages.[14] None was more aware of this than Otto I in his choice of his first wife, Edith, and then, after her death, his second, Adelheid.

Adelheid and Her Kin

Liudolf (d. 866), the founding father of the successful kin-group that came to be called the Liudolfings, married a Frankish woman from the highest aristocracy, Oda (d. 913). Their descendants consciously married only into ruling families.[15] Otto I, their great-grandson, a proven victor on the battlefield and so one possessed of 'practical power', first chose a daughter of the deceased King Edward (the Elder) of the nation of the Angles.[16]

The Importance of Lineage

Liudprand of Cremona notes Edith's exalted lineage through the male line as the daughter of King Æthelstan's brother 'regis Hadelstani fratris filiam' (erroneously, as she was Æthelstan's half-sister, not his niece).[17] Widukind of Corvey records her accurately as daughter of Edward, king of the Angles, and sister of King Æthelstan.[18] Those two contemporary chroniclers distinguished neither the fact that Æthelstan and Edith had different mothers nor considered their cognatic lineages. Hrotsvitha of Gandersheim, however, records Edith as descended from 'a most illustrious mother' and 'from an eminent family of great kings', besides being 'born of the blessed stock of Oswald the king'.[19] Edith's grandfather through her father, King Edward (the Elder), was Alfred the Great, although Hrotsvitha does not name him.[20] In contrast Hrotsvitha denigrates Edith's half-brother, Æthelstan, born of an unnamed 'woman of greatly inferior descent'.[21] That woman was not a worthy *consors regni*: 'an unrenowned *consors regni* bore him [Æthelstan] to the king [Edward]'. In contrast Edith and Adelheid were worthy by inference to be *consors regni* of another king, Otto I.[22] (See Chap. 4 on Adelheid's rule for the meaning of *consors regni* and the history of the imperial term 'inclita'.) Æthelstan, despite his inferior lineage on his mother's side, held the royal power in the kingdom of the Angles.[23] Even though Edith and her brother were born of the same father, Hrotsvitha highlights her exceptional lineage through her mother over that of her father.[24] Although too much self-awareness should not be attributed to particular kindreds,[25] Hrotsvitha's emphasis on Edith's cognatic rather than her agnatic ancestors together with her striking foregrounding of the female protagonists in her *Gesta* strongly endorse Edith's worthy female ancestry over her inferior male ancestry.

For Otto's second marriage, Hrotsvitha emphasizes his choice of an even more distinguished future wife. Hrotsvitha salutes Adelheid as the daughter of the mighty King Rudolph ('Regis Rothulfi ... magni') and descendant of a long line of renowned monarchs, with the nobility of her parents so illustrious that she was given the name 'Æthelheitham',[26] variously 'Adelheid' or 'Adelaide' in English and 'Adalheid', 'Addeida', 'Hadeleida', 'Alheydis' or other variations in the Latin charters.[27]

'Adel' comes from the old High German word *adal*, meaning 'noble' or 'nobility', and *heit* has the meaning 'type' or 'character' or '-ness' or '-hood'.[28] Her great-aunt Adelaide was the daughter of Waldrada and Count Conrad of Auxerre and sister of King Rudolf I. She married Richard le Justicier, grandson of Boso the Elder (d. c. 855) and brother of King Boso of Provence (d. 887), and accordingly joined the Bosonid family. Another connection to the Bosonids occurred when the future Empress Adelheid married her first husband, Lothar, who was also descended from Boso the Elder but through a different son Hubert.[29] Perhaps Hrotsvitha is here giving a nod to the agnatic side of the family but placing all the emphasis on an eminent female member. Hrotsvitha stresses that Adelheid's deeds confirmed her truly regal lineage that clearly derived from her mother's and father's lines.[30] Through at least three generations of female antecedents and possibly four, Adelheid's ancestor Gisela was a daughter of Emperor Louis the Pious.[31] Although her father and her paternal grandfather were kings of High Burgundy, Hrotsvitha regarded Adelheid's mother's cognatic lineage more highly. These examples illustrate Karl Leyser's further point about the noble kins of the Carolingian and post-Carolingian world, mentioned above, that some of that apparent fluidity 'can be explained by the importance of maternal relatives and descent. They ranked as high as and even higher than paternal kin, if they were thought to be nobler and had better things to offer.'[32]

Blood Relations and Mutual Obligations

Despite her exalted lineage, from an early age Adelheid had surprisingly few close kin to support her. When her father died in 937, Hugh, formerly count of Arles and afterwards king of Italy, married Adelheid's mother, Bertha, to secure the Burgundian throne for himself. While the six- or seven-year-old Adelheid accompanied her mother to the court of Pavia, her older brother Conrad remained under the protection of Otto I at the German court.[33] Later Hugh sent Bertha back to Burgundy.[34] By 937 Adelheid's three grandparents had died. Only her maternal grandmother, Reginlind, remained, her whereabouts not easily determined but unlikely to be with her granddaughter in Pavia.[35] Thus Adelheid, although privileged in being brought up in the Pavian court and betrothed to her stepbrother, Lothar, the king of Italy in waiting, had no close kin with her for much of the time. The activities of one of her three brothers, Duke Rudolf of Burgundy (d. 986), remain somewhat obscure[36]; her youngest brother Burchard (d. 956/7) became a cleric and eventually archbishop of Lyons[37]; and her older brother Conrad succeeded his father as king of Burgundy.

'[F]ew European rulers of any period can have left as little trace in the record after reigning for nearly sixty years as has Conrad the Pacific of Burgundy.'[38] Karl Leyser refers to his 'long shadowy reign'.[39] Conrad's loyalty to the Ottonian kingship did not waver from the time that Otto I put him under guard at a very young age,[40] no doubt for the strategically political reason of keeping track of the kingdom of Burgundy. Count Hugh of Arles, the rival of Conrad's father King Rudolf II, had rudely stripped the kingship from Rudolf and their ongoing rivalry rent Italy in pieces. Meanwhile Conrad, king from about the age of twelve on his father's death in 937 until his own on 19 October 993, appears to have managed serious political upheavals with aplomb, imposing good law within the kingdom and peacefully expanding into Provence. Conrad played an ongoing role in Adelheid's life. Conrad's second wife, Mathilda of West Francia, as the daughter of King Louis IV (Louis d'Outremer) and Otto I's sister Gerberga, was twice tied to Adelheid: as niece by marriage and as sister of Adelheid's son-in-law King Lothair of France.[41] In times of trouble Adelheid retreated to the Burgundian kingdom of her brother Conrad and her sister-in-law, Mathilda of West Francia.

Hrotsvitha of Gandersheim in a long exposition placed Adelheid as clear initiator and solver of her first major problem that began in 950 after the death of her first husband, King Lothar.[42] Adelheid's capture by Berengar II, escape from imprisonment and marriage to Otto I has already been discussed in Chap. 1. A second major problem arose between Adelheid and her son Otto II in 978 as a consequence of which Adelheid left the court. Her brother King Conrad of Burgundy performed the role of negotiator, probably with Abbot Maiolus of Cluny.[43] There may have been two disagreement-reconciliation incidents that Abbot Odilo of Cluny appears to have conflated: one disagreement in 978 and a reconciliation by 17 February 980; and a second disagreement after that date with another reconciliation later in 980. The evidence for the first of these incidents is a report by the Saxon Annalist for 978: 'Empress Adelheid with her [grand]daughter Abbess Adelheid departed for Italy on account of certain disagreements caused between her and her son [Otto II].'[44] A charter of 17 February 980, in which Adelheid intervened with her son, shows that by that time the two were in harmony again.[45] The second of these disagreement-reconciliation incidents occurred sometime after the charter intervention, but before another reconciliation, this being the one mediated by Conrad and Maiolus later in that same year.[46] Whether there was one disagreement and reconciliation or two, Conrad, as maternal uncle of Otto II, had the ability to exercise extra influence. Further inconclusive but suggestive evidence for his power is provided by Odilo of Cluny, who describes Otto II as approaching first 'his uncle the king' (King Conrad of Burgundy) and then Abbot Maiolus to negotiate a peaceful settlement between himself and his mother.[47]

Conrad's influence appears again in the crisis after Otto II's unexpected death in May 983. Duke Henry II of Bavaria (known to history as Henry the Wrangler), son of Otto I's brother, Duke Henry I of Bavaria, abducted his nephew, Otto III, and attempted to usurp the throne. Adelheid, her daughter-in-law, Theophanu, and her daughter, Abbess Mathilda of Quedlinburg, forgave Henry the Wrangler. The *Quedlinburg Annals* attribute Henry's pardon to the intervention of Conrad, a probable example of the influence of family ties: Henry the Wrangler was married to Conrad's daughter Gisela.[48] That Conrad ruled resolutely is confirmed by the speedy revolt of the counts against his son King Rudolf III within a year of the latter's taking up the rulership of Burgundy after Conrad's death. Indeed Rudolf's aunt Empress Adelheid, then more than sixty, arrived to quell the riots, something her nephew Rudolf was incapable of doing.[49]

Not all appeals to kinship were successful. Two petitions by Emma, Adelheid's daughter by her first husband, King Lothar of Italy, apparently remained unanswered or, at least, unresolved. Emma, widow of Lothair, West Frankish king, intended to act as regent for her son. The son, now King Louis V of West Francia, quarrelled with his mother, who fled to Reims.[50] Shortly afterwards Louis V died, and Lothair's brother, Charles of Lower Lotharingia, intriguing for the vacant throne, held Emma captive. Emma, in two letters to her mother and one to her sister-in-law, Theophanu, begged them to use their influence to either restore her to office or to release her.[51] Adelheid received copies of all three letters. Emma's appeals did not succeed. There is no record of any reply from either recipient. Adelheid's relationship with her daughter by King Lothar of Italy, Emma, remained fraught. Emma's marriage to King Lothair of West Francia did not bring the anticipated peace between the West-Frankish and Ottonian dynasties. Caught up in the struggle for rulership in the West-Frankish kingdom, Emma failed to retain the allegiance of the leading men.

Friends and Followers

Like many noble women of the time, Adelheid moved to the locality of her successive husbands and their families. Her early experience stood her in good stead later in life as she negotiated her way through the critical situations in which she found herself. When her widowed mother married King Hugh of Italy, the very young Adelheid learnt to negotiate relationships outside her kin, surrounded by unfamiliar faces and courtly customs. She used her expertise gained in the Italian court during her brief marriage to Hugh's son, Lothar, and their rulership of Italy. When Lothar died, she selected as her second husband the most likely man to become chief ruler, Otto I. Although marriage placed her in powerful positions, the uncertain situations of inheritance and the fragility of state practice provided plenty of opportunities for her to use her well-honed negotiating skills.

Two relationships linked warriors to their lords—those of kinship and those of vassalage.[52] Both kinds of tie often applied to the same person. In 757 Duke Tassilo submitted to his lord king by commending himself 'with his hands to vassalage'.[53] At that time vassalage was still primarily owed to kings. By the later eleventh century, the greater the number of castles owned by a lord and the greater the number of people related by kinship and by vassalage that the lord could call upon, the greater his power.[54] When Hrotsvitha wrote in the mid-tenth century, between those two periods, she was aware of obligations between people that were not strictly speaking based on kin relationships but called into action the ties of vassalage. Three such men assisted Adelheid at various times. Their examples, taken one after another, illustrate the ties of loyalty in the period when Carolingian governance still operated.

Henry I of Bavaria, Brother of Otto I

Hrotsvitha describes the special, although short-lived, bond that Adelheid developed with Duke Henry I of Bavaria, Otto I's brother and thus her brother-in-law. Henry's daughter, Abbess Gerberga of Gandesheim, had instructed Hrotsvitha to write the *Gesta Ottonis*, but their close relationship as abbess and canoness in the same convent and the sensitivity to criticism of the royal household made Hrotsvitha's task very difficult. Accordingly Hrotsvitha's careful explanation of the establishment of the relationship between Henry and Adelheid takes on especially subtle meaning. In the past Otto I had suppressed serious rebellions by Henry (939,

941).⁵⁵ Hence Henry's relationship with Otto's new wife needed ratification. Hrotsvitha detailed Henry's obligations to his brother King Otto I:

> Meanwhile, in Italy, Duke Henry, the esteemed brother of the king, with the utmost endeavour of his heart performed the tasks required of his obedience to the king, of fulfilling in his kindly zeal *not only his office as a well-loved brother, but rather the duty of a servant.*⁵⁶

Although Duke Tassilo in the eighth century had commended himself 'with his hands to vassalage.... and promised fidelity to King Pippin ... as a vassal',⁵⁷ the translation of the word 'servi' as 'vassalage' is usually premature in tenth-century usage. Hrotsvitha chose her words carefully and she may have meant vassalage or else she may have intended that Henry sought to position himself as a subject to his king in the same way that Charlemagne asked all his subjects to swear an oath of loyalty to him as king, not as a vassal to a lord.⁵⁸ Nevertheless *servus* ('servi') is the word Hrotsvitha chose. In the same passage Hrotsvitha listed Henry's obligations to Adelheid as Otto's wife, naming his relationship to her as that of a brother, and her reciprocal care for him.

> Hence, he greatly pleased the king [Otto] himself and likewise was joined in brotherly love to the queen and esteemed with respectful affection by her.⁵⁹

Hrotsvitha's narrative, apparently straightforward but carefully contrived, confirms the harmonious bond of sister-in-law to brother-in-law. A mere sixty lines later Hrotsvitha attests to Henry's perfect harmony with Otto by citing Adelheid's love for and faithfulness to him, the brother of the king.⁶⁰ Adelheid in this case had negotiated the tricky relationship with her new brother-in-law, who had not always been in harmony with his own brother, her husband. Henry finally committed himself to Otto and died in 955 in his favor, due in large part to his service to Adelheid and her approval of his efforts.

Gerbert of Aurillac

Although Adelheid's marriage to Otto I had joined her to the family of the Liudolfings, she had no familial relationship with Gerbert, monk of Aurillac in the Auvergne, abbot of Bobbio, archbishop of Reims and, finally, Pope Sylvester II appointed by Otto III. '[B]orn of poor but free parents', Gerbert was placed while young in the monastery of St Gerald in Aurillac. This gave him the opportunity to favorably impress Count Borrell II of Barcelona on the latter's visit there in 967. Borrell facilitated Gerbert's studies in Spain and introduced him to Pope John XIII who, captivated by his intelligence, sent him to Emperor Otto I; in turn, Otto engaged Gerbert as tutor for his son. The orderliness and the power of the Ottonian court impressed Gerbert, exposed previously to strong petty nobility who were antagonistic to the weak kingship in his home region.[61] In consequence from the time of his introduction to the Ottonian court Gerbert never wavered in his support for both the court and Adelheid right up to her death in 999, despite one letter of minor complaint.[62] He supported her as strongly as he did the three emperors whom he served in turn until he died in 1003, shortly after the selection of the last Ottonian king, Henry II.

Of Gerbert's 264 extant letters, nine are addressed to Adelheid or refer to her, either from Gerbert or written by him on behalf of another.[63] None of Gerbert's letters from Otto I's lifetime exists, and only twenty during Otto II's independent reign after his father's death.[64] Since the first letter to Adelheid is dated to the second half of 982, Gerbert was addressing her as Otto I's widow and thus dowager empress, no longer first lady in the kingdom as that position now resided with her daughter-in-law, Theophanu. Gerbert's only criticism occurs in one letter in which he accuses Adelheid of over-allocating funds to charity as she had assigned the same lands to more than one person, perhaps showing her need for supporters at that time.[65] By 22 January 984 Gerbert knew that Henry the Wrangler, son of Otto I's brother, Duke Henry I of Bavaria, was plotting to take over the kingdom.[66] In a letter to Adelheid dated in early 984, when the fate of the kingdom hung in the balance because of the death in December 983 of Adelheid's son Emperor Otto II, Gerbert's tone changed from admonitory to conciliatory: he begged her forgiveness for granting her land to others only on terms favorable to his own monastery of San Colombano at Bobbio, although broadly at her instigation.[67] Gerbert, originally appointed abbot there by Otto II shortly after November 980, would have taken an oath to the king as one of his *fideles*.[68] In that oath he would very likely have promised to be a faithful helper, offering aid and counsel in accordance with his office and person.[69] In 984 Gerbert reminded Adelheid of the oath and confirmed his loyalty to her; he would maintain the same fidelity toward Adelheid as he had to her son, the now deceased Otto II.[70]

Gerbert may also have encouraged Otto III to reconcile with Adelheid. Thietmar, bishop of Merseburg, notes the disagreement between Adelheid and her grandson Otto III, which occurred after the death of her brother Conrad in 993. Odilo of Cluny either had discounted it or was unaware of that event, which Thietmar explains as happening in a similar manner to Adelheid's previous disagreement with her son Otto II: corrupt men, this time young ('iuvenum depravatus'), persuaded Otto III to drive his grandmother away.[71] The exact process by which Otto III and Adelheid became reconciled is not known. The evidence resides in a most conciliatory letter from Otto to her in 996, written by Gerbert of Aurillac on Otto's behalf after his coronation as emperor.[72] Otto addressed Adelheid as 'always August Lady Empress' ('Dominae imperatrici semper augustae'), thus recognizing her political role. He acknowledged that God conferred the 'rights of empire' ('iura imperii') upon him in accordance with her wishes ('secundum vota et desideria vestra'); that he knew and experienced her 'maternal affection' ('maternum affectum'), thus demonstrating the importance of the ties of kinship; and that her 'zeal and piety' ('studia, pietatem') had given him spiritual guidance. So Adelheid had weathered a number of serious disagreements with close male kin or near-kin. These were recorded at the time but were resolved in all accounts.

Willigis of Mainz

Archbishop Willigis of Mainz, the most important churchman of the empire, also featured in Gerbert's correspondence.[73] He had not always held such an elevated position. According to Thietmar, Willigis rose from low family connections as a result of the goodness of his mother, whose vision of miraculous signs at his birth predicted his future greatness. Thietmar reports that her child became equal to and in some cases superior to those who came from more noble families.[74] He might have had ancestors with fewer aristocratic connections but may have considered himself to be of the *nobiles*.[75] In a period of considerable sensitivity to the supposed inherent connection between great office and noble birth, Willigis achieved the highest clerical position at court under the first two Ottos. Otto I conferred the office of chancellor on him in 970 or 971, when Willigis was about forty, and in 975 Otto II made him Archbishop of Mainz (the most prestigious see in the empire) and Archchancellor (primate) of Germany.[76] Willigis crowned Otto III and Henry II king, the former in 983 at Aachen and the latter in 1002 at Mainz.[77]

Both the length of his life (930–1011) and his faithful and attentive service to the mainstream Ottonian dynasty, whether its members were male or female, helped Willigis to achieve and to retain high office. Records of Willigis's relationship with Adelheid are not found in correspondence between them; rather, the evidence for their association lies in the more formal accounts of the kingdom and empire contained in the diplomata (the legal written instruments of government), the records of the great court meetings over which they presided in their respective positions and, to a lesser extent, in the chronicles of the time. The current understanding of the relationship between Adelheid and Willigis must remain therefore less certain than that between Gerbert and Adelheid.

Adelheid first encountered Willigis some time after her wedding to Otto I in late 951, perhaps not until 969 when Bishop Folkold recommended that the thirty-nine-year-old cleric replace him as teacher of Otto II, then about thirteen. We know that Willigis was capable of great loyalty, at least to this one episcopal colleague. He did not forget Folkold's recommendation to the Ottonian Court when Duke Boleslav II of the Bohemians drove Folkold out of Meissen in 992: Willigis welcomed the aged bishop, ensuring that he was cared for in every way.[78]

Could Willigis's loyalty to the three *dominae imperiales* (Empress Adelheid, Empress Theophanu and Abbess Mathilda of Quedlinburg) in the crisis over the succession of Otto III be questioned? Although Willigis crowned Otto III king on Christmas Day 983, in March of the following year he may have shown his reluctance to take sides by sending only observers to Saxony rather than confronting Henry the Wrangler's claim to the throne directly. Consequently Archbishop Adalbero (in a letter written by Gerbert) urged him to support the two empresses, Adelheid and Theophanu.[79] Thereafter, and as a result of Adalbero's letter, Willigis wrote his own letter to the women advising them as to when they might safely return to Germany from Italy.[80] Adalbero's letter to Willigis was only one of a spate of letters Gerbert wrote to a number of significant people in support of the two women.[81] Thietmar presents Willigis's interaction with Henry the Wrangler as energetic. Unlike other great men of the duchy, who sent envoys to scrutinize Henry's actions, Willigis did not despatch mere observers: he ordered his own *milites* from Mainz to attend, a far more active involvement.[82] Willigis joined his own forces from outside Saxony with those of Henry's Saxon enemies against Henry the Wrangler.[83] Willigis and the chancellor Hildibald of Worms may have really saved the throne for Otto III.[84] Surely prudence and insight, not reluctance, prompted Willigis's absence from Saxony in March 984. Willigis's sending of *milites* should be regarded as positive and active support for the young king Otto III, not hesitancy. His later actions indicate committed support for the Ottonian royal house.

Willigis's aid and advice to the Ottonian court continued while Theophanu remained regent for Otto III and, although at a distance, extended to Adelheid during her exercise of royal authority in Italy that began shortly after the confirmation of Otto III as ruler.[85] On Theophanu's death in 991 Willigis supported Adelheid's sole regency for Otto III (see Chap. 4). When Adelheid moved from the court to undertake almsgiving and travel on Otto III's coming of age, Willigis lost influence. After the emperor's death in early 1002, Willigis strongly supported bestowal of the kingship on Henry the Wrangler's son, Henry (III) duke of Bavaria. As the great-grandson of Henry I, king of the East Franks, he remained the only eligible living Ottonian.[86] Thus Willigis decisively aided and abetted the continuation of the Ottonian dynasty.

Willigis's number of appearances as witness in the charters reveals the extent of his favorable position at court. Adelheid's and Willigis's presence in the diplomata, Adelheid as intercessor and Willigis as witness, and their attendance together at the court gatherings show that they met each other on at least formal occasions. Adelheid and Willigis attended the meetings at Verona in 983 and at Rohr in 984, the final reconciliation assembly at Quedlinburg in 986, and the consecration of the cathedral at Halberstadt.[87] In the last month of her life, Adelheid's regard for Willigis showed itself in her request for him to say masses for her dead son, Otto II.[88] While Willigis's title as senior archbishop would have placed him in a suitable position to undertake that spiritual role, Adelheid would not have entrusted it to him without believing in his worthiness. Willigis had proved loyal to the royal house time and again.

Spiritual Family

Five men, forming a spiritual family, championed Adelheid's official sanctification, achieved after a period of one hundred years. To be considered a candidate for sainthood it was not sufficient for a woman to lead a pious life. Declarations that led to a person's canonization depended on the favorable reportage of men influential in the church. Five such men with connections to the monasteries of Selz or Cluny supported Adelheid during her life and after her death, and all contributed to her official canonization. Those were her confessor Ekkeman, the first abbot of Selz; the peacemaker Maiolus, the fourth abbot of Cluny (964–994); her biographer Odilo, the fifth abbot of Cluny (994–1049); Bishop Otto of Strasbourg (1085–1100); and the prior of Cluny, later Pope Urban II (1088–1099).[89] Adelheid's special relationship with Cluny was strengthened because the mother house was located in Burgundy, the region where Adelheid was born and where her brother Conrad ruled. Moreover from Adelheid's lifetime until her canonization there is steady but intermittent evidence of support for her from outside that ecclesiastical circle. For example the last Ottonian, King Henry II, honored her and fifty years later, a list of her miracles was compiled.

The first influential man, Ekkeman, Adelheid's chaplain and confessor, is known from two contemporary writers: Gerbert of Aurillac and Odilo of Cluny. In a letter dated 984 Gerbert requested Ekkeman, a monk of the imperial court, to speak favorably about him there: Ekkeman continued in high standing with 'an admirable woman' ('admirabilis feminę'), possibly Adelheid, whose 'household' ('domus') considered him 'illustrious' ('clarum').[90] He may have been in the chancelleries of Otto I and Otto II.[91] Odilo recorded Adelheid's influence in the establishment of Ekkeman as both abbot of Selz and her confessor. 'She appointed there an abbot, Ekkeman by name, a man of good repute, learned in human knowledge and divine wisdom, whom she wished always to have as her instructor in holy writ.'[92] In the *Miracula* written in the later part of the mid-eleventh century, in the section describing King Henry II's visit to Adelheid's tomb, Ekkeman is mentioned by function but not by name.[93]

The necrology lists at Marcigny (a subsidiary Cluny house), refer to a monk called 'Ekkeman', whom some writers have identified with Adelheid's confessor. This suggests he may have made his vows at Cluny.[94] However, a variety of people were listed in the necrologies: members of other Cluniac houses (who may or may not have been monks but who were listed as though they were), non-Cluniac monks, and lay benefactors and familiars.[95] This Ekkeman may be Adelheid's confessor because the necrology includes members of the imperial family: 'Adelaida imperatrix', 'Otto imperator' (Adelheid's son Otto II) and 'Berta regina' (Adelheid's mother).[96] Ekkeman's association in the same document with these illustrious people implies that this Ekkeman had court contacts. Despite his eminence at the court and his imperial patron, the first abbot of Selz remains an elusive historical figure—unlike Abbot Maiolus of Cluny.

In 954 charters of the abbey of Cluny record the election of Maiolus as abbot in a grand ceremony before named bishops, the abbot of St Peter of Cavaillon (or Chalon-sur-Saône),[97] and 132 other monks.[98] While the frail third abbot Aymard lived (d. 964), Maiolus acted as coadjutor rather than abbot. According to the *Life* of Maiolus, Adelheid was devoted to him. Its author Syrus of Cluny thought her approval important: 'as if the finest of handmaids, [she] was wishing to devote loyalty to him [Maiolus], since through the prayers of the blessed Maiolus to the most generous one [that is God, who provided all abundantly], she was hoping to be visited herself by the grace of the divine presence.'[99] Maiolus was so trusted that 'the emperor had this man as his intimate counsellor, a trustworthy mediator between separate parties.'[100] In 972 Adelheid handed San Salvatore over to Abbot Maiolus, to be ordered by the rule of St Benedict. In 973 Adelheid and Otto I thought so highly of him that they wanted to nominate him for pope, but he declined.[101] Maiolus continued the regal alliance with their son; he has already been noted as instrumental in making peace between Adelheid and Otto II earlier in this chapter. Although Adelheid 'was wont to love all other good men', she loved Maiolus more than any other monk.[102] The combination of Adelheid's affection for him and Maiolus's influence meant that his impact on her reforming zeal was significant.

After Maiolus died, Odilo became the fifth abbot of Cluny. A monk of Souvigny named Jotsaldus wrote a biography of Odilo between about 1049 and 1053. According to Jotsaldus, Adelheid in her love and admiration for Odilo agreed with princes and powerful Christians, other notables such as Robert, king of the Franks, and Emperor Henry II. In the same passage Jotsaldus accords Adelheid the title 'mother of the Ottos' ('mater Ottonum'), that is, mother of Otto II and Otto III.[103] Odilo of Cluny's *Epitaph* presented a 'humiliation-exaltation schema' for Adelheid, modeled on the life of Christ who overcame the humiliating death on the cross to achieve a triumphant victory.[104] Odilo placed himself in his biography of Adelheid toward the end of her life in an incident where she bade him a tearful farewell, predicting her imminent death. Although somewhat formulaic, Odilo's comment contains personal elements:

> There was in her presence a certain monk, who was called an undeserving abbot [that is, Odilo], but who nevertheless was considered by her to be of some importance. When she [Adelheid] turned her gaze on him [Odilo],

and he looked back at her, both began to weep copiously. *I would say that she did more then than if I said she had cured many people.* For she humbly observed the quite rough clothing in which he was dressed, and pressed it to her most holy eyes and serene mouth as she kissed it, saying to him in a low and familiar voice.[105]

That passage, where Odilo chose to remain anonymous (not an unusual action by monks to demonstrate their modesty), testifies to Adelheid's regard for Odilo and his for her, and to their close personal relationship. His brief but remarkable *Epitaph* about her set a new standard for biographies of female rulers.

Odilo died too soon to become the chief architect of the list of Adelheid's posthumous thirteen miracles. The honor of carrying forward her case appears to belong to a bishop on friendly terms with the emperor, who became the fourth clerical influence in Adelheid's sanctification.[106] Before Bishop Otto of Strasbourg's involvement in the late eleventh century, Henry II visited Adelheid's grave at Selz (either in 1002 as king or in 1014 as emperor), as reported in the later *Miracula*.[107] It was not permitted for Henry to celebrate her merits there without apostolic (that is, papal) decree and clerical consent, by which is meant that the idea of a formal sanctification process was in mind.[108] The list of Adelheid's miracles was probably composed at Alsace in the diocese of Strasbourg in 1057 in order to provide evidence for her canonization. Progress toward Adelheid's sanctification could not proceed at that time, purportedly because the turbulent era of the Investiture Dispute followed immediately. Later in a somewhat less agitated period Otto, bishop of Strasbourg from 1085 until 1100 and consequently responsible for the tomb of the empress as a diocesan obligation, initiated the canonization of the empress on seeing the relevant documents.[109]

The fifth churchman to influence Adelheid's official sanctification was Pope Urban II. Toward the end of the eleventh century, when the immediate problems of the Investiture Controversy had abated, Pope Urban canonized Adelheid in accordance with three criteria: the testimony of a good life, a list of miracles and the processes of the church. Urban was pope for eleven years, during which period Matilda of Tuscany's activities, starting with domination and harassment by King and later Emperor Henry IV, ended with Henry's defeat, the defection of his wife and elder son Conrad to the faction of Matilda and the pope, and Matilda's settlement into a stable period of effective lordship.[110] The above five clerical men together brought about Adelheid's canonization over a period of one hundred years. These men can truly be considered her spiritual family although she did not know all of them.

Good relationships, such as Adelheid maintained with friends and followers, could never be guaranteed with all kith. Yet considering the power Adelheid wielded as queen of Italy and of East Francia and later empress, the sources report remarkably few enemies. Unsurprisingly she clashed with the dowager queen, her mother-in-law (Otto I's mother, Queen Mathilda), and the new queen, her daughter-in-law (Otto II's wife, Theophanu). Like those of her predecessor Edith, Adelheid's disagreements with Queen Mathilda most probably arose out of the difficulties of living with a powerful queen, demoted but still in the palace. It is well known that Adelheid and her own daughter-in-law, Theophanu, had disagreements. Odilo of Cluny's alleged statement by Theophanu about Adelheid, 'If I live another year, Adelheid's power in this world will be small enough to fit in the palm of my hand,'[111] remains a mere trifle in the management of the empire. Their significant alliances far outweighed their disagreements.[112] After the uprising of the Slavs in the summer of 983 and Otto II's unexpected death on 7 December that same year, further dangers from the northeast threatened the empire. In the West, King Lothair, his son King Louis V, Duke Charles of Lower Lotharingia (977–c. 992), and Duke Hugh Capet of West Francia (960–987) competed at various times for the West-Frankish throne. The women resolved these matters either by energetic warfare or by fine negotiation. Although the sources are sparse it can be ascertained that Hugh, margrave of Tuscany from 969 until 1001, and the Slavic Miesco I, ruler of Poland from about 950 until 992, were present with Theophanu and Otto III at Quedlinburg for the Easter celebration in 991, where they exchanged gifts.[113] The women worked together remarkably well in difficult times to resolve or to smooth over conflicts.[114]

***

Almost all Adelheid's close kin predeceased her. Three of her grandparents died before her birth and one of her grandmothers and her parents died before she was ten. Two husbands, five children and two brothers predeceased her. Her two remaining daughters were dedicated to their monasteries at a young age. The long periods Adelheid spent in Italy and the necessity for her to travel often and widely so as to rule the kingdom hindered her ability to visit them frequently. Of her close kin only her youthful grandson, Otto III, lived beyond her, he who had not always been available or in harmony with her. For those reasons Adelheid had no choice but to forge her ties where she could outside her *consanguinei*. Consequently the people in relationships with Adelheid and Otto I involving mutual obligations assumed a greater importance. Nevertheless, she emerged triumphant both in majesty and in credibility with the empire intact and her grandson assured in his role as emperor.

Adelheid experienced great conflict four times during her life. On the initial occasion, Adelheid's first husband, King Lothar, died; Berengar II imprisoned her, but she escaped. Otto I's brother Duke Henry I of Bavaria met and escorted her to Otto, and she and Otto married.[115] Next, on the death of Otto I she took up the rulership of the empire as regent for a period on behalf of her son Otto II, but he, at the instigation of hostile men ('viri iniqui'), chafed at her control.[116] Then her son died unexpectedly and she, after a period of harmony with her daughter-in-law, Theophanu, and the crisis of the succession conflict with her nephew-by-marriage, Henry the Wrangler, quarreled with Theophanu.[117] On the fourth occasion her grandson, Otto III, approaching his coming-of-age, sent her away.[118] (It is striking that there was never any criticism about Adelheid's conduct in sexual matters, a most unusual situation when that was a common method of discrediting ruling women.) On all four occasions Adelheid gained, or eventually regained, the favor of each new ruler, Otto I, Otto II and Otto III, and preserved the dynasty and the empire.[119]

The Family Connections of Adelheid and Matilda

Adelheid's important connections included ties with the ruling family of the territories that were to become France. Mathilda of West Francia, the wife of Adelheid's brother Conrad, was the daughter of King Louis IV d'Outremer. Emma, Adelheid's daughter by her first husband, King Lothar of Italy, married King Louis IV's son King Lothair. Adelheid's brother-in-law by marriage was Hugh the Great, who married Otto I's sister Hadwig (also known as Hathui). They initiated the long-lasting Capetian dynasty, founded by their son Hugh Capet. Adelheid was rightly called 'mother of kingdoms' and 'mother of all kingdoms' and addressed as 'exalted lady, cherisher of kings and kingdoms'.[120]

Just as Adelheid and her contemporaries were aware of her antecedents, so certain of Matilda of Tuscany's connections to Adelheid would have been known to Matilda and to her contemporaries. Hrotsvitha carefully noted Adelheid's noble ancestry, and Donizo recorded Countess Matilda's

Canossan ancestors as well as highlighting the association of Adelheid with the early Canossan family. Matilda of Tuscany was a direct descendant of Adelheid's Ottonian mother-in-law, Queen Mathilda of Ringelheim, and father-in-law, King Henry I. Their daughters, Gerberga and Hadwig, were Matilda of Tuscany's ancestors via two different lines.[121] In addition through the marriage of Adelheid's brother, King Conrad of Burgundy, to Gerberga's daughter, Mathilda of West Francia, Adelheid became an aunt through several generations to Matilda of Tuscany. Empress Gisela, wife of Emperor Conrad II, acknowledged family ties by bringing up her nieces, Beatrice (mother of Matilda of Tuscany) and Sophie (aunt of Matilda of Tuscany), on the death of their father in 1033.[122] So Matilda of Tuscany's ancestors, the sisters Gerberga and Hadwig, daughters of the first members of the Ottonian dynasty (King Henry I and Queen Mathilda of Ringelheim), as sisters-in-law of Adelheid gave Empress Adelheid and Countess Matilda a clear dynastic connection.

Although Matilda of Tuscany's cognatic lineage was more impressive than her agnatic lineage, Donizo focused on her paternal ancestry, but included her great-grandmother (Hildegard), grandmother (Guillia or Willia) and mother (Beatrice) in the illuminations in his manuscript of the *Life* of Matilda.[123] Donizo's aim in his family history, written in the early twelfth century, was undoubtedly to promote the house of Canossa, when encastellation had already changed the physical landscape and power structures were shifting in favor of the comital class. In the first half of the eleventh century Matilda's father, Boniface, ruled and built up the property side of the Canossan inheritance in northern Italy. However, the extensive female contributions cannot be ignored. Boniface married twice into fortune and fine lineage: his wives Richilda and Beatrice brought wealth and Beatrice also brought the kudos of royal familial connections. Beatrice inherited in turn from Boniface. Her second husband, Godfrey the Bearded, also appreciated her wealth and connections. One diagram of the House of Verdun (Ardennes) shows Godfrey the Bearded's agnatic lineage—a valuable chart as the connections between each of the participants in this house are not easily available—but omits important Matildine female relatives.[124]

Adelheid and Matilda of Tuscany could trace their ancestry to Louis the Pious (d. 840), Charlemagne's son, mostly through the female line. Adelheid's cognatic ancestry leads to Gisela (d. 918), a direct descendant of Louis the Pious.[125] Matilda's ancestor, Wigeric of Bidgau, was married to Cunegund, whose mother Ermentrude was also a direct descendant of

Louis the Pious.[126] The interest here is the part that the women played in the lineage. We should note the custom for families to name their daughters after important female ancestors. Empress Adelheid and her first husband, King Lothar of Italy, appear to have named their daughter, Emma, an unusual name at that time, after her distant aunt, the wife and Carolingian queen of Louis II the German (d. c. 806), a son of Louis the Pious.[127] From the late tenth century onwards into the mid-eleventh century there was an emphasis at the various courts on the Continent on naming the daughters after prominent female ancestors from the cognatic side: 'it was common by the mid-eleventh century to name a daughter for her maternal relatives (at least when naming her Mathilda or Gerberge).'[128] Despite the evidence for contemporary emphasis on the importance of females from the cognatic side, male ancestry continues to be relatively easily found and followed in many modern histories, while the female antecedents, sometimes often considered more significant in their time, are rarely given appropriate weight.

Notwithstanding the efforts by Hrotsvitha, active in the latter half of the tenth century, and by other contemporary writers, the real decline in the status of the queen and especially in her importance as mediator between 'rulers and rebels' became evident in the last third of the eleventh century in Germany. Empress Agnes and Queen Bertha participated little if at all in such consultations. Agnes did not travel to Canossa and so avoided the role of dowager-empress negotiator unlike Empress Adelheid, who had performed it with her nephew's troublesome magnates. Apparently Henry IV's queen Bertha did not participate as a negotiator at Canossa either, unlike the countesses Matilda of Tuscany and Adelaide of Turin.[129]

Matilda's Kin

Matilda of Tuscany's interactions with her cousin, the king and later emperor, Henry IV, became a source of reciprocal dissatisfaction until death parted them. As they were of much the same age and lived much the same length of time, their mutual provocation lasted almost all of Matilda's lifetime. In contrast, Matilda's relationships with other kin remained demonstrably amiable. For example, after Henry IV died in 1106 the countess lived in harmony with his son, now King Henry V, for the following nine years.

In Matilda's early life her mother was undoubtedly a great source of support and leadership. Growing up with her stepsister Ida, Matilda developed in common with her a strong spiritual side.[130] She forged political and spiritual connections with various religious communities and popes, especially Gregory VII and the six popes who followed. Her ruling life also brought her into contact with numerous nobles and other privileged individuals and the peasantry. We have less information about the latter because the extant records consist of diplomata, formal letters and a *Vita*, all emanating from a literate elite and recording details mostly about land rights and entitlements of direct interest to them rather than their underlings.

Personal connections were important to Matilda just as they had been to Empress Adelheid. Matilda had to contend with a society changing in structure, one that looked back less to the Carolingian modes of operation under which Adelheid functioned and instead operated with roles that were more prescribed. As the daughter of a duchess and duke and then later as a lord herself, she owed duties to the vassals whose expectations of her and hers of them became more fully defined over her lifetime. While Matilda forged tight bonds with her vassals during her political life, the personal relationships with her family formed her—especially the early ties with her mother.

Growing Up

Matilda's mother, with her eminent aristocratic origins, enhanced by two strategic marriages, became her greatest political influence. Beatrice of Lotharingia, descended from the first Ottonian king, Henry I, retained close connections with the Salian empire as niece of the empress: Gisela, sister of Beatrice's mother, Mathilda of Swabia (d. 1033), had married Emperor Conrad II.[131] On Conrad's death in 1039 Beatrice's connections with royalty continued as first cousin to Gisela's and Conrad's son, the new king and later emperor Henry III. Henry married Agnes of the House of Aquitaine: their son (later Henry IV) and Matilda of Tuscany were consequently second cousins. In contrast the direct personal influence of Matilda's father Boniface can only have been brief since he died in 1052 when Matilda was about six years of age. His widow, Beatrice, remarried in 1054, perhaps for strategic reasons, to guarantee the inheritance of her children.

There were two problems with Beatrice of Lotharingia's second marriage to Godfrey the Bearded. First, the Lateran Synod of 1057, summoned by Pope Nicolas II shortly after their wedding, forbade marriages up to the seventh degree.[132] Godfrey and Beatrice were kindred within the prohibited degree: Beatrice as a descendant of King Henry I (Henry the Fowler) through five generations and Godfrey the Bearded as a descendant of Oda of Saxony, sister to Henry I, through four generations. Consequently Henry and Oda's parents (Duchess Hathui of Saxony and Duke Otto of Saxony) were ancestors in common to Beatrice and Godfrey the Bearded.[133] There was an even closer connection: Beatrice and Godfrey were both part of the house of (Verdun) Ardennes and descended from Wigeric of Bidgau in four generations.[134] Even though Beatrice and Godfrey's wedding occurred before the Synod of 1057, they addressed any potential consanguinity issues by vowing to live chaste lives and by financially supporting foundations to a church.[135] Peter Damian, in a letter to Beatrice in 1057, praised their actions.[136]

The second problem was not so easily fixed. Since Beatrice was both a vassal and closely related to Emperor Henry III, her marriage to Godfrey needed Henry's permission.[137] The triangle of relationships between Beatrice, Godfrey and Henry III could not be resolved easily: Beatrice and Godfrey's marriage threatened Henry III's landed power, combining as it did the large landholdings of Canossa and Lotharingia. Godfrey the Bearded's father had held the lands of Upper Lotharingia (1033–44) and Lower Lotharingia (1023–44). Godfrey, having ruled the lands of Upper Lotharingia with his father, expected Henry to give him, as elder son, those of Lower Lotharingia too on his own father's death. Henry, however, gave Lower Lotharingia to Godfrey's brother, Gozelo III.[138] Like Lantbert, an obscure count who fell out with Emperor Otto III nearly fifty years earlier, Godfrey became a fierce opponent of Emperor Henry III. Otto had deprived Lantbert of his lands and made him a public enemy.[139] Similarly Godfrey too became a public enemy of Henry III.

Beatrice's conflict with Henry III had direct consequences for her children. While Beatrice's son Frederick lived, she could rule the March of Tuscany in his name. Frederick and Matilda's older sister, Beatrice, died within two years of the death in 1052 of their father, Boniface. There is debate about the exact dates of the deaths of two of the children, Beatrice and Frederick, and where they died. The souls of all three children were mentioned in a donation by Beatrice to the monastery of St Mary in Badigulsula on 17 December 1053. Since Matilda was alive then, the deaths of the two older children cannot be assumed from that information. Two schools of thought exist about the dates of their deaths, especially

Frederick's. Either Frederick was alive in 1053 when Countess Beatrice was still a widow and imperial inheritance laws would have required property to be left away from her son if Beatrice remarried: Beatrice would not have done so in those circumstances. Frederick must have died soon after, but before Beatrice married Godfrey the Bearded, sometime in 1054.[140] Alternatively Beatrice remarried because she could not rule the March of Tuscany without a male heir, and at that time, Frederick was underage. Consequently she remarried to retain the March. In that case the deaths of the two older children are therefore likely to have occurred after the wedding.[141] In addition if the deaths of the two children occurred in Italy, then Robinson's statement that all three children went to Germany with Beatrice must be incorrect and Lazzari's proposed date of 1055 for the deaths of the children is late.[142] Frederick died in particularly obscure circumstances with some inconclusive evidence that he had been murdered by Emperor Henry III.[143] Since Beatrice had dared, without asking the emperor, to contract a marriage 'with a public enemy', as punishment Henry descended into Italy, forced Beatrice and her remaining child Matilda north over the Alps to Germany and imprisoned them there from 1055 to 1056.[144] Henry III's rage undoubtedly made an impression on a young Matilda.

Her mother's remarriage brought Matilda into new relationships. Ida of Boulogne, the daughter of Godfrey the Bearded and Godfrey's first wife, Doda, became Matilda's stepsister. Both Matilda and Ida had to deal with the new spouses of their parents, Matilda with a stepfather and Ida with a stepmother. The two young women had about three years to become acquainted with each other before Ida's wedding to Eustace II of Boulogne in 1057. Ida's life (1040–1113) was roughly contemporaneous with Matilda's (1046–1115). Nevertheless for children a difference of six years matters, and when the families were amalgamated, Matilda was about eight and Ida, about fourteen. Where Ida spent her childhood and hence the exact influences of Matilda and Ida on each other remain unknown, although it is possible that Ida traveled extensively with her father during that period.[145] Nevertheless opportunities for the stepsisters to become acquainted must have presented themselves. Not only did Matilda form a new relationship with her stepsister, Ida, but she also met a new stepbrother, Godfrey the Hunchback, whom she married.[146] The exact date of the wedding is not known: documentation of the event survives from the record at the deathbed of Matilda's stepfather, Godfrey the Bearded, in 1069.[147] The proposed connection of the houses of Verdun and Canossa/Lotharingia, however, did not last: Matilda separated from Godfrey the Hunchback in 1071. In contrast, the early familial papal networks worked well and the bonds that Matilda made with later popes held. The early papal connection to the House of Canossa set a lasting pattern. Godfrey the Bearded's brother Frederick, formerly abbot of Monte Cassino, became Pope Stephen IX, holding office from 2 August 1057 until 29 March 1058.[148] With a background of close family papal connections that leaned toward the reform faction, Matilda developed strong personal links, not only with later reforming popes, bishops and other clerics but also with political powerbrokers of the royal house and comital aristocrats.

Such a combination of contacts among her kin and kith during childhood and early adulthood set the direction for Matilda's later life. The violent deaths of her father and stepfather occurred while she was still young. After two further key events—her separation from her husband and the death of their little daughter—Matilda put aside intimate family life and copied her mother in taking up the cudgels of political life. The premature deaths of her brother and sister had propelled Matilda into an unanticipated role since Frederick had been expected to take on the mantle of his father the duke. Instead, Matilda, the youngest and only remaining child of the Canossan dynasty, became the sole heir. Three significant public events in Matilda's life reveal intricate and important interactions with her kin and kith. The first, concerned with issuing her initial diploma, describes an important stage in the development of an active public political life.

1. Mantua, 19 January 1072: The Beginning of Rule

The first charter that Matilda jointly issued with her mother's experienced guiding hand contained information illustrative of the familial connections of the young Matilda at about twenty-six years of age. The original charter was signed by Beatrice and Matilda. Of this earliest diploma only copies remain, the first dating from 1272; four witnesses attest to its accuracy.[149]

Beatrice had no doubt selected the witnesses to this first diploma. The references to both Beatrice's father and Matilda's father very early in the charter place the two women in their kindred relationships confirmed by their assurance that they lived by Salic Law, under which Beatrice's marriage to Godfrey the Bearded and Matilda's to Godfrey the Hunchback had placed them.[150] Toward the end of the document Beatrice and

Matilda twice again refer to themselves as mother and daughter: in the first reference, without names; in the second as 'mother and daughter' ('mater et filia') at the beginning of the list of penalties to be imposed—fifty pounds in weight of gold and fifty pounds in weight of silver. The actions to confirm the diploma recorded within the document include a formal raising of the parchment with the ink from the ground and offering it to the judge of the sacred palace.[151]

The actions described and the wording at the end of the document are reminiscent of Empress Adelheid's similar wording in the description of three donations about land in documents issued from Erstein in Alsace and dated to the first half of April 999.[152] Like Adelheid, Matilda and Beatrice in this their first diploma confirmed their gifts with promises and rituals such as the formal raising of the parchment from the ground, the use of the 'festuca' (stalk or stick) and other ritualistic actions that recalled strongly those of the empress some seventy years before. Adelheid, situated at Erstein, acted on her own initiative since her grandson Emperor Otto III was issuing his own diplomata in Rome at the same time. She called upon Lombard Law for her document, which dealt with gifts to locations in northern Italy issued by a northern Italian notary of the palace, John of Pavia. Matilda and Beatrice invoked Salic Law, not well understood in Italy at that time. Despite Adelheid's diploma calling upon Lombard Law, in contrast with Matilda and Beatrice's invocation of Salic Law, both sets of charters included remarkably similar formulaic words and actions. Written more than seventy years apart, the documents follow similar northern Italian imperial charter traditions, but in Matilda and Beatrice's document the locus of power had shifted from imperial palaces to comital fortifications.

Conclusions about the followers of Matilda and Beatrice and their relationships with the two women can be deduced from the men named as either present at or signatories to the diploma.[153] Algiso, Razo and Beatus, all from Fornigada, appear only in this diploma, then all three vanish from Matilda's charter record.[154] Issued from Mantua but about property and possessions in Fornigada, the diploma records the gifts from Matilda and Beatrice to the monastery of Sant'Andrea at Mantua that included the chapel of St George and other appurtenances in Fornigada—a place containing a cluster of houses in the villa Pietole (or Pletule) of the parish Virgilio, about five kilometers southeast of Mantua.[155] A reasonable conjecture is that Algiso, Razo and Beatus had a local interest in the gifts contained in this charter, and there was no further reason to involve them in others.

Another signatory to Matilda and Beatrice's first diploma was Ingo of Fornigada who later appears in one more of Matilda's diplomata, that time for Matilda alone after Beatrice's death and more than six years after the first diploma.[156] Matilda issued the 1078 charter from Puntiglo, in the southeast of Tuscany, probably in the county of Chiusi, sixty kilometers southeast of Siena, a long way from Fornigada and Mantua. Since his name appears within a charter that refers to *comites* ('counts') and a *vicecomes* ('delegate of a count') and among the names of judges and an abbot, it would be reasonable to assume that Ingo occupied a position of some consequence. Since he witnessed the second charter so far from the place of issue of his first appearance he might also be presumed to be a man of some means, able to travel. Another witness to the charter, Crescentius, appears in two later diplomata, temporally and geographically removed from the first. Crescentius features in the body of two consecutive charters, both issued in late 1080 (numbers 31 and 32).[157] No more is known of Crescentius in Matilda's diplomata. Another witness to the charter was Rogerius who had ties to Reggio: he was referred to as 'of the Regio community' for this first charter and 'of Regio' for diploma number 9, his only other Matildine charter.[158]

Two other signatories of special interest, Paganus of Corsena and Iohannes, complete the list of participants of interest in the first diploma. Paganus of Corsena features nineteen times, the most often of all witnesses or signatories in Matilda's diplomata. He witnessed or appeared in the first four extant genuine documents issued by Matilda with her mother Beatrice and then a further three in their early rule together.[159] In number 14, the final document of the seven, Roland, the son of Paganus, appears for the first time. We next see Paganus in diploma number 19, dated 27 May 1076, the first (extant) one issued by Matilda after her mother's death on 18 April 1076. Paganus appears at the head of an illustrious list of witnesses in a document that invested the (unnamed) abbess of the Benedictine monastery at San Sisto at Piacenza with property at Cortenuova.[160] The history of the monastery is relevant here. San Sisto was established in 874 by Emperor Louis II the Younger and Empress Angelberga. Part of Angelberga's reverse dowry from Louis and other property was also appropriated to San Sisto. Shortly after her wedding to Otto I in late 951, the future Empress Adelheid strengthened Abbess Berta of San Sisto's access to the abbey's allied properties, by intervening in a diploma on behalf of the abbess in February 952.[161] Those interventions and Countess Matilda's instructions in 1076 in her diploma number

19, witnessed by Paganus and a particularly eminent set of men as mentioned above, show how powerful lay women as well as men took care of church women and were alert to the threats to properties associated with their monasteries.

Diploma number 20, dated 1 June 1077, was the first extant diploma that Matilda issued after the Canossan events of January 1077. Including that appearance, Paganus acted as either a signatory to Matilda's diplomata or was listed in the body, with his son Roland, a total of six times until 1083.[162] From then until 1100 there is no mention in the diplomata of the Corsena family as acting in any capacity. On 3 April 1100 Roland's name appears in the body of a charter for the first time without his father, and again in the next extant charter, issued seven days later.[163] In 1105 Matilda extended her practical benefaction of the Corsena family to another son of Paganus. Hildebrand had died, leaving a number of possessions to the monastery of San Pietro at Pozeuli (Badia Pozzeveri), which was located approximately eleven kilometers southeast of Lucca.[164] Matilda confirmed in the court, through her right of ban, the goods that Hildebrand had donated to the monastery.[165] From the record of Hildebrand's wealth and the earlier prominence of his father in Matilda's charters, it is reasonable to assume that Hildebrand, his brother Roland, and their father, Paganus, were a family from the wealthier echelons of society in comital service to Matilda.

The final person of interest in the first diploma, Iohannes, is listed under the title 'iudex sacri palatii', a person whose role encompassed the duties of public notary and solicitor.[166] From the end of the tenth century the office had developed separately from the 'judices et missi domni regis (imperatoris)' ('judges and *missi* of the lord king (emperor)') and the incumbent owed his appointment to the count palatine, a local official who reported to the emperor.[167] For Matilda, Iohannes signed as 'iudex sacri palatii' in a further five documents ranging from 1072 to 1107.[168] According to the evidence in the extant diplomata Iohannes traveled across Matilda's territory, from Mantua (1071) to as far south as the county of Volterra, just south of Livorno (1107). His travels followed no obvious pattern except that they covered a wide spread of locations. Numbers 52 and 53, the former issued in 1099 from near Lucca and the latter nearby at Poggibonsi four days later, may have been witnessed by Iohannes because the closeness of the location was convenient, rather than of any great import. The same Iohannes may also be the writer of five or six more of Matilda's documents, since the editors specifically name 'Pfalzrichter Iohannes' ('palatinus iudex Iohannes') as the writer of those further diplomata in their comments on diploma number 1.[169]

Iohannes 'palatinus iudex' was already experienced in the processes involved in the development of diplomata. He was present when Matilda's mother, Beatrice, issued two charters: at Florence in 1070 and at Frassinoro in 1071.[170] Whether the Iohannes 'iudex sacri palatii', 'palatinus iudex et advocatus' and 'palatinus iudex' were one and the same remains unclear, although very likely, even allowing for Iohannes being a common name. A not completely conclusive argument in support of two titles belonging to the same person can be adduced from document number 55, where both Iohannes 'iudex sacri palatii' and Iohannes 'palatinus iudex et advocatus' appear within the body and at the end of the document, both apparently performing similar if not the same functions.[171] Furthermore the editors seem to equate Iohannes 'palatinus iudex' with Iohannes 'iudex sacri palatii' and Iohannes 'palatinus iudex et advocatus' when, in their comments on document number 1, they refer the reader to document number 55, identifying him as *advocatus* of the monastery at Brescello.[172] The example of Iohannes highlights the difficulties in understanding exactly the number and identity of Matilda's followers. Nevertheless the interactions of those who can be identified provide a contrasting mixture of backgrounds and occupations.

Many of Matilda's followers appear together more than once in her diplomata. Within two years of the issuing of Matilda's first diploma, Paganus and Ingo met again. Ingo is listed in the body of a diploma at Puntiglo with Paganus on 19 February 1078. In that document Matilda, now ruling alone after her mother's death, appeared in court to oversee the waiver by Count Hugh, son of a certain Hildebrand (deceased by 1078, and consequently not the same Hildebrand discussed above in document number eighty-seven, dated to 1105), of all claims on the castle Mons Niger (Montenero) and the villa Limignana in favor of the monastery of San Salvatore of Monte Amiata.[173] Paganus and Crescentius met again at Ferrara on 23 November 1080.[174] Matilda, as shown by the sequence and continuity of the appearance of the main players in these diplomata, firstly with her mother and then independently, exhibited loyalty to families over a long period with apparent reciprocal fidelity. Matilda's interest in collegiality became evident shortly after she issued her first diploma and launched herself on her political life. She carried her interest into the crucial events leading up to the historic meeting at Canossa in 1077 and during the meeting itself. The second series of events, the negotiations between Pope Gregory VII and King Henry IV at Matilda's stronghold of Canossa, describes interactions between key players who argued for or against the papal reform movement.

2. *Going to Canossa, January 1077: A Crucial Negotiator*

Matilda's year before the meeting at Canossa had been a tumultuous one. After the Council of Worms of 24 January 1076 Pope Gregory VII had excommunicated King Henry IV because Henry had offended on a number of counts: by his condemnation of Gregory, his continuing association with excommunicates, his unwillingness to promise or to perform penance and his divisive disrespect for the church.[175] At the council certain German bishops had railed against 'this new senate of women'('hunc feminarum novum senatum'), whose members consisted of Matilda of Tuscany, her mother, Beatrice, and Henry IV's mother, Agnes (although not Henry's wife Bertha).[176] Matilda's estranged husband, Godfrey the Hunchback, had been assassinated in late February.[177] Matilda then began the long fight with Godfrey's nephew, Godfrey of Bouillon, over the lands in Lotharingia that her husband had left to his nephew rather than to her.[178] Her mother died on 18 April 1076. In late May, Matilda issued her first diploma after her mother's death.[179] By January 1077, the year of Henry's excommunication was drawing to a close. Gregory had documented the excommunication at the Synod of 14–22 February in the *Record of the Lent synod of 1076*.[180] A year later Henry took action. He sought 'to avert deposition by the [dissident princes]' and a reconciliation with the pope that would restore normal relations with the German bishops.[181] The two disagreed over the meeting place for their proposed reconciliation. Henry wanted Gregory's absolution to be granted at Rome. Gregory, however, refused to negotiate there. He traveled north, aiming for Augsburg, where a faction hostile to Henry would have given the pope an advantage. Henry, however, reached Italy before Gregory had managed to obtain the promised escort for the journey. Gregory was trapped in Italy, indeed in danger of capture by Henry's troops. He called on his faithful daughter in Christ to harbor him and Matilda invited him to take refuge in her castle at Canossa. In late January 1077 Henry arrived at Reggio, twenty miles northeast of Canossa.[182] Many in his entourage were Matilda's kin.

Henry IV and Matilda were second cousins. They shared common great-grandparents in Hermann II of Swabia and Gerberga of Burgundy.

Hermann and Gerberga's daughter, Mathilda of Swabia, was maternal grandmother to Countess Matilda, and their other daughter, Gisela, was paternal grandmother to Henry IV. On the death of Henry IV's father, Emperor Henry III, on 5 October 1056, the magnates had confirmed the young heir in the kingship, albeit with his mother Agnes acting as regent. (Henry was born on 11 November 1050.)[183] Subjected to power struggles among the court hierarchy and even being kidnapped at the age of eleven by certain bishops, he had endured uncertainty and fear during the years before he reached his majority.[184] In mid-1076 the Saxons rose in rebellion again. Henry's great victory over them in 1075 had turned to vulnerability, very much assisted by his strife with the papacy. Henry ruled his leading men, who were divided among themselves, more by their enmity toward each other rather than by their loyalty to him.[185] The meeting at Canossa was a make-or-break event. Henry crossed the Alps into Italy through the pass of Mount Cenis with the blessing of his kinsman Count William of Burgundy, who was a cousin of Henry's mother, Agnes.[186]

Henry IV brought with him to the meeting at Canossa his young son and heir, Conrad, Matilda's second cousin once removed. Like Emperor Otto II and Theophanu, who had taken their little son Otto III at an even younger age south over the Alps in winter in a parade of splendor, supremacy and pride to the Italian kingdom in 980/981,[187] Henry brought his wife Bertha and little Conrad, the latter born on 12 February 1074 and accordingly not yet two years old. King Henry, excommunicate and not yet emperor, could not exhibit splendor, supremacy and pride on his first visit to Italy in 1077, even though Conrad's presence promised continuing kingship and the likelihood of further progeny to strengthen the Salian dynasty. Henry's view, at least according to his later words and actions, appears to have been that he merely required absolution and that he never considered that his kingship had been at issue. Timothy Reuter argues convincingly that Henry merely sought a *deditio* ('a ritualised surrender').[188] The evidence on Pope Gregory's side remains contradictory: the text of the oath of 28 January 1077 and Gregory's letter of March 1080, three years later, contain areas of ambiguity.[189] Henry had much to lose if he could not have his first excommunication lifted by the pope, since otherwise his magnates might not obey him.

Accompanying Henry IV to Canossa was Countess Adelaide of Turin (not to be confused with Empress Adelheid, one of the two subjects of this book). As his mother-in-law, Adelaide had become, by her daughter's marriage to Henry, part of the family of Matilda. Yet an earlier even stronger kin tie bound the two women together: Adelaide's grandmother Prangarda was the sister of Matilda's grandfather Tedaldo. Consequently Matilda stood in the same relationship to Adelaide as she did to Henry IV, that is, as second cousin. By 1077, Adelaide of Turin, a powerful woman thrice-widowed, ruled (sometimes alone and at other times with her sons) important lands on both sides of the mountain passes: the Mark of Turin, territory inherited from her father (who died in about 1034), and Savoy, territory gained from the marriage with her third husband (Otto I, count of Savoy, who had died by May 1060).[190] Between them Matilda and Adelaide controlled vast territories, especially strategic for Henry IV.[191] Adelaide of Turin's territorial control rivaled Matilda's, yet contemporary documents do not appear to record any difficulties between them. At Canossa Adelaide formed part of the contingent that mediated between Henry and Gregory.

Bertha, Henry IV's queen and Adelaide of Turin's daughter by her third husband, Count Otto I of Savoy, was Matilda's second cousin once removed, via Adelaide. The bishops had not railed against Bertha, however, at the Council of Worms in 1076. Less important politically than the earlier German queens/empresses Kunigunde (wife of Emperor Henry II) and Gisela (wife of Emperor Conrad II), she wielded little power in the negotiations at Canossa.[192] Another important nobleman present at Canossa in 1077 was Margrave Adalbert Azzo II of the Este family, an eminent layman in his late seventies or eighties at that time. Although he supported Henry IV's request for release from excommunication he later became no more than a vacillating supporter of the king.[193] The clerical contingent included Abbot Hugh of Cluny, godfather to Henry.[194] It has been argued that Bishop Anselm (II) of Lucca (d. 1086) was also present at Canossa, although no sources mention that.[195] Matilda, a close colleague of Anselm, her confessor, protected him when he was evicted from his see of Lucca in 1081.[196] Nevertheless it is unknown if Anselm would have joined the contingent of negotiators. We do know that Abbot Hugh's secretary Odo (Eudes), prior of Cluny at Mâcon and later Pope Urban II, was present.[197] The foremost cleric in attendance was Pope Gregory VII. His origins remain obscure. It is likely that he came from outside Rome and he is not known to have been related to Matilda.[198] At the negotiations at Canossa in 1077 he accepted the pleas of Matilda and others from the negotiating contingent to be reconciled with Henry.

Gregory's pardon of Henry did not have a long-lasting effect: his second excommunication of the king in 1080 only strengthened Henry's resolve to rid himself of that meddlesome pope.

The roles of the mediators at Canossa in 1077 were established: Adelaide of Turin as queen mother, her son Amadeus as close kin and heir presumptive of the March of Turin, Abbot Hugh of Cluny as godfather and church representative, Margrave Adalbert Azzo II of Este and other princes as eminent nobles, and Matilda of Tuscany as relative of Henry and hostess. The method they employed was intercession on behalf of the king to the pope. What is without question is the important role that Matilda as both host and kin played in resolution of the conflict. It was Matilda whom Hugh of Cluny asked to negotiate between the pope and Henry.[199] Her biographer Donizo wrote that Hugh of Cluny turned to Matilda to negotiate without naming anyone else. Donizo's remark is not conclusive, given his partiality and what must be hearsay at that time rather than his direct witness[200]; nevertheless his report gives information not available elsewhere about the roles of the various people at Canossa.

3. Quistello, 9 January 1106: Mature Lordship

It was in 1106, twenty-nine years later, that the third significant development in Matilda's political life occurred. By this date Donizo had been a monk at Canossa for approximately twenty years, with the opportunity to hear from first-hand witnesses, and the scenario was completely different. By then Matilda had supported a total of seven reforming popes. In 1106, Pope Paschal II reigned in Rome.[201] Henry IV's antipope, Wibert (Pope Clement III), a distant relative of Matilda and a thorn in the side of the papal reformers, had died (1100).[202] In 1091 another Canossan encounter between Henry and Matilda, this time a military one, had resulted in Henry's decisive defeat in Italy and his later departure, never to return to Italy. Henry IV's heir, Conrad, and second wife, Praxedis, had defected to Matilda (in 1093 and 1094).[203] Conrad died suddenly in 1101. His younger brother Henry V, nominated as new heir at twelve or fourteen years of age, deposed his father on 31 December 1105 at Ingelheim.[204] By 1106 the now experienced Matilda dispensed justice widely in northern Italy. The places from where she issued all her extant diplomata that can be located are widely distributed, especially north and south of the Apennines.

The differences between her first and ninety-third extant diplomata are remarkable for the scope of their coverage, the sophistication of argument, and the growth in the number and variety of witnesses and signatories. Her ninety-third charter, issued from Quistello, is examined in Chap. 3 as an example of how Matilda managed her landholdings and exercised justice. The charter is examined here below to reveal her involvement and interactions with the people whom she gathered around her in her maturity, forming a network of relationships operating under her authority.

Ubaldus 'iudex' appears twice in Matilda's diploma of 9 January 1106, once as Judge of Carpineti and once as signatory. It is not certain if the references are to the same person or to two different people. Ubaldus 'iudex' features in at least seventeen Matildine documents,[205] and possibly a further five more if the Ubaldus mentioned in those documents is the same person.[206] The likelihood is high since 'Ubaldus' is frequently mentioned as from Carpineti, situated twenty-nine kilometers southsouthwest of Reggio.[207] If the charters refer to the same person, Matilda used his services once in 1078 and then extensively between 1092 and 1114. The proliferation of the name 'Ubaldus' associated with the location Carpineti supports the idea that it is the same 'Ubaldus' witnessing to those charters. What can be said confidently is that the number and variety of Matilda's followers had grown enormously since her first venture into public life.

Matilda's chancery support had also increased since her first diploma. For diploma number 93 Matilda nominated her archpriest and chaplain Frugerius to craft the words.[208] As 'capellanus' Frugerius may have acted as head of Matilda's chancery.[209] Frugerius, first coming to notice in Matilda's charters in 1100, fashioned eleven documents for the countess.[210] Frugerius exercised much spiritual and lay responsibility: 'archpriest and chaplain, priest, erstwhile chaplain of the distinguished prelate Reginus'.[211]

As with Matilda's first charter, a number of apparently local men feature only once in diploma number 93, or only a few times elsewhere.[212] In contrast Albericus of Nonantola features in eight authentic diplomata and in one lost document.[213] The remnants of the lost document include the names of Albericus and Tebertus of Nonantola, who attended a meeting at Vignola on 8 November 1109.[214] All the diplomata that feature Albericus come from Matilda's period of stable success. The eight complete charters show a steady rise in the status of Albericus from October 1102 until his last appearance in May 1115. There appears to be a distinct hierarchy in the names, which is repeated in other charters. Since Albericus's name is high on the list, his place in society is clearly important. In a diploma dated 24 January 1107, Matilda confirmed goods in and near Campitello, including the church of Santa Maria del Bosco for the monastery of San Paolo at Parma. The marks of Count Albert, Arialus of Melegnano, Gerard (son of Bosonis), Albert (son of Manfred) and Belentionis of Uarstalla precede that of Albericus, but are followed by those of Ardericus of Campitello, then Sigefredus of Campitello, Hugh son of Ragimunus, Bontempus, Viscovellus and several others.[215] Finally Albericus appears in Matilda's second to last extant document, issued about one month before her death in early May 1115.[216] In this long document, obviously important to her, Matilda confirmed her gifts and those of her ancestors to the monastery of San Benedetto Po.

The family and follower connections recorded in diploma number 93 were reinforced in other diplomata. The name of Bosolinus, son of Guizolus, appears once in Matilda's charters, in number 93, although his father's does not reappear in any of them. The same Guizolus, however, might have had another son, Boso, who features in two of Matilda's charters.[217] In the first, a long diploma dated to 1099, Matilda renewed and extended, with the approval of her purported adopted son, Guido Guerra, the donation of her forebears to the monastery of Brescello.[218] The second issued in 1107 demonstrates Matilda's relationship with the pope: with the permission of Pope Paschal II she gave goods in Stenay and Mouzay to the bishopric of Verdun.[219] Paganus (not further identified), who appears in diploma number 93, cannot be convincingly identified with Paganus of Corsena, who appears in many of Matilda's earlier diplomata and was examined above in the section 'Mantua, 19 January 1072: the beginning of rule'.[220] These are only some examples of Matilda's followers. Many others not named were present at the issue of charter 93 ('et reliqui plures').

Matilda's ninety-third extant charter shows a sophistication well beyond that of the first one written with her mother. A cultured and highly educated chancery, developed by Matilda, now managed her lands. She demonstrated a clear authority in her commands. Most of all, as this section set out to show, she had gathered around her a loyal following, the core of whom appeared regularly in diplomata. They too interacted with each other as they met time and again to witness and execute her commands. These faithful did not include all who were close to the countess, however. A second marriage, another possibly in prospect, an adopted son and a young daughter occupied her.

Family Matters

For some time modern writers have debated whether Matilda had a female or male child with her first husband, Godfrey the Hunchback. Elke Goez states that Matilda bore him a son.[221] Convincing evidence for a daughter lies in a document of Beatrice's dated 29 August 1071. This document records Beatrice's foundation of the monastery at Frassinoro, located in the Modena-Reggio Apennines on a convenient route for the Canossans to travel between their southern and northern properties, and refers to the burial there of a very young daughter, named Beatrice.[222] Modern writers agree that Matilda had no further children.

The rumor of an interest by Robert Curthose in a marriage with Matilda lacks concrete evidence but it has been suggested that sometime between January 1084 and September 1087 Matilda may have received and rejected a proposal of marriage from Robert, the eldest son of William the Conqueror. A marriage between Matilda and Robert potentially advantaged Robert for the troops she could bring him to support his father. What is certain is that Robert married Sibyl (or Sybil) of Conversano, and Matilda married Welf V in 1089.[223] Welf V was the son of Welf IV (Welf the Elder), who was himself the half-brother of Hugh of Maine. Welf the Elder and Hugh were sons of Margrave Adalbert Azzo II of Este through different mothers.[224] In the winter of 1091–92, when Henry IV was trapped on the Este family lands that included Tricontai, family connections heightened the interests of Matilda, Welf V and Hugh of Maine in the situation.[225] As close kith to Matilda, Hugh's betrayal of her, by informing Henry IV of her impending attack and tricking her troops into remaining where they were, was devastating. Donizo named the traitor Hugh as someone who should have behaved nobly because of both his ancestry and his upbringing but did not. To Donizo nobility was not only an inheritance but a state of mind that implied noble actions. Anyone who was truly noble would not commit a disgusting crime.[226]

Between the end of 1089 and the first half of 1090, that is, about six months to a year before the battle of Tricontai, in a diploma in memory of her father Matilda granted Welf V extensive lands around Campitello and several other places, including courts, woods and fishing rights.[227] Later marital difficulties between Welf V and Matilda explain why Donizo does not mention Welf by name. (Donizo avoids mentioning either of Matilda's husbands.) Welf V certainly continued to support Matilda's and the pope's agenda of reform, unlike the ignoble traitor Hugh of Maine (and unlike Matilda's first husband, Godfrey the Hunchback). Welf V remained faithful to church reform until 1094 when his father, seeking to possess Matilda's lands, sought a rapprochement between the couple. On failing in that matter, Welf the Elder and Welf V were reconciled with Henry IV. Henry was finally able to leave Italy, since Welf the Elder could provide him with access to the pass over the Alps.[228] The two Welfs left with Henry in 1095.

It is not clear why Matilda's second marriage foundered almost as quickly as her first. Welf's marriage to Matilda, when he was about seventeen or eighteen and she was about twenty-six years older, did not draw significant comments from contemporary writers on their age difference.[229] According to Bernold of Constance (also known as Bernold of St Blasien) the marriage that united the two most powerful houses in northern Italy was encouraged by Pope Urban II as a political convenience against Henry IV and his allies.[230] Control of both sides of the Alpine Brenner Pass certainly shifted to the anti-imperial party, since Welf V's father owned extensive lands in Italy.[231]

Instead of age or status differences, changes in circumstances that made the marriage no longer necessary to either party probably explain the failure of Matilda and Welf V's marriage. Instead of initial mutual convenience between the two parties, Matilda wanted support against Henry IV with a family powerful in southern Germany, and Welf the Elder coveted her lands to supplement his in Emilia and Lombardy. By 1094 Welf the Elder had failed in his attempt to reconcile Matilda and his son and Matilda no longer needed the alliance since she had defeated Henry. Bernold of Constance's report supports such an explanation.[232] Henceforth Matilda abandoned marriage and instead attempted to secure her succession.

Many ruling women have felt the pressure to nominate an heir. From Brescello on 12 November 1099, at about age fifty-three, Matilda renewed and extended, with the consent of her purported adopted son, Guido Guerra, the gift of her forefathers to the monastery of Brescello.[233] That was an important event, recorded in one of her longest diplomata. Matilda's choice was politically astute, because Guido belonged to a suitable family, the house of Guidi.[234] However, only five of Matilda's authentic documents were issued with Guido Guerra as beneficiary, associated issuer or witness.[235] Another three were either false or doubtful or a lost fragment.[236] Guido Guerra died in 1124.

Matilda also welcomed to her side the elder son, Conrad, of her cousin Henry IV, in 1093, Henry IV's second wife, Praxedis, in 1094, and ultimately Henry IV's younger son, the future Emperor Henry V.[237] Conrad, according to Henry IV's supporters,

> was won over by the persuasions of Mathilda – for whom may not womanly guile corrupt or deceive? – and joined his father's enemies.... When a running report brought this news to the enemies of the Emperor, they [that is, Matilda's supporters] were exultant, they applauded, they sang, they praised the deed of the son, [and they praised] especially the woman who was the chief mover of the deed.[238]

Matilda's enemies portrayed 'the situation as one of a vulnerable young man fallen into the clutches of an astute woman', whereas Donizo painted 'Matilda's support of ... Conrad's defection as kin solidarity'.[239] Since Henry IV's grandmother and Matilda's grandmother were sisters, Conrad, as Henry's son, was Matilda's second cousin once removed. Donizo's actual phrase remains instructive: 'She [Matilda] soon received him assuredly as a worthy and beloved kinsman ('carumque propinquum').'[240] After Conrad's defection to Matilda but before his death, Henry IV nominated his surviving legitimate son, the future Henry V, as heir: desertion by that son too must have been a grievous blow for the king. So Matilda won over her kin, also close kin of Henry IV, and even his wife, Praxedis. As well as defeating him on the battlefield, Matilda had inflicted a personal wound.

A Philosophical Salon

From about 1090 Matilda concentrated her energies on philosophical polemics. *Fideles* of Matilda in tune with her ideas of church reform gathered around her. Bishop Anselm (II, the Younger) of Lucca, Bishop Rangerius of Lucca (Anselm's successor), John of Mantua, Bishop Bonizo of Sutri, the anonymous writer of the *Vita Anselmi* and others were members of the 'only princely court in the *regnum* before the last decades of the twelfth century'.[241] They formed a political salon of intellectuals and scholars.[242] Matilda's ability to attract such an intelligent and faithful gathering gives some idea of the influence she wielded. The members wrote eulogistic accounts of the countess and her manly mind and deeds[243] and educated her in the polemics of the Gregorian ideology.[244] The instruction of the laity by the clergy was not uncommon: Count Frederick of Mömpelgard from the Burgundian-Lotharingian nobility, a kinsman of Matilda, and Count Robert I of Flanders were two of those coached in anti-imperial polemics.[245] Matilda is the best documented and arguably the one with most influence. Additional followers of what are often called Gregorian ideals included the canonist Bernold of Constance, the biographer Paul of Bernried, Cardinal Deusdedit and the political theorist Manegold of Lautenbach.[246] Anselm of Lucca the Younger, John of Mantua and Bishop Bonizo of Sutri are of special interest in their interactions with Matilda.

Three *Lives* survive of Anselm of Lucca (d. 1086): one by his successor, Rangerius of Lucca (died c. 1112), written approximately between 1096 and 1099,[247] and two attributed to Pseudo-Bardo, one written c. 1086–1087, possibly at Mantua,[248] and the other a shorter, later life.[249] Anselm's own book against Wibert (antipope Clement III)[250] and a collection of canons (*Collectio canonum*),[251] which later formed part of Gratian's *Decretum*, promulgated his Gregorian views.[252] Anselm's relationship with Matilda reflected his dual roles, as a supporter of church reform and as her confessor. The section 'Spiritual Family' below enlarges on their relationship.

Very little is known about John of Mantua, the second writer of interest in Matilda's intellectual coterie. His explication of the sheathing of the apostle Peter's sword is allegorical rather than literal. According to John, the sheathing of the sword meant to put it in its rightful place rather than not to use it. Such an interpretation gave Matilda the moral right to wage war on behalf of Pope Gregory VII and later popes, and paved the way for Bernard of Clairvaux's 'two swords theory' of 1146.[253] Two document fragments remain of Matilda's request for commentaries from John, which she received between 1081 and 1084 (a difficult time for Matilda in the struggle with Henry IV in Italy).[254] John addressed his *Tractatus Cantica Canticorum* (*Tract on the Song of Songs*) and *de Sancta Maria* to Matilda—'ad semper felicem Matildam' and 'ad comitissam Matildam'.[255] He developed arguments which legitimized Matilda's continuation of the war against Henry IV.

Bishop Bonizo of Sutri (died after 1090, possibly as late as 1094) was the third polemicist, among the many, of special interest in relation to Matilda.[256] His writings relating particularly to her are *Liber ad amicum*[257] and *Liber de vita Christiana*.[258] The former, a polemical history of the church written in about 1085 or 1086, praised armed combat in defense of the faith. The latter supported holy war in a collection of canons, written sometime between 1089 and 1094.[259] In the *Liber ad amicum*, addressed to an unknown friend, sometimes identified as Matilda but more likely to have been a close vassal of hers,[260] Bonizo attempted to answer two questions:

> why in this time of calamity does mother church lie groaning on the earth, why does she cry out to God and her prayers are not heard, why is she oppressed and is not set free? Why do the sons of obedience and peace [the Gregorian supporters] lie prostrate, while the sons of Belial rejoice with their king [Henry IV], especially since He who orders all things is also He who judges with equity?

and

> whether it was and is lawful for a Christian to engage in an armed struggle for the sake of the faith.[261]

The second question, the more interesting of the two in an analysis of Matilda, addressed the same problem identified by Anselm of Lucca. Like Anselm and John of Mantua, Bonizo argued for the validity of righteous battle as well as lauding Matilda's many brave military deeds.[262] He summed up his views at that time in the final paragraph of his book, particularly referring to her opposition to heretical views:

> Let them ['the most glorious knights of God'] endeavor to equal in goodness the most excellent Countess Matilda, the daughter of St Peter, who with a virile mind, neglecting all worldly considerations, is prepared to die rather than to break the law of God and to oppose the heresy that now rages in the Church in every way, as far as her strength permits.[263]

She became the embodiment of a righteous anti-heretical figure based on female Old Testament models. After such a resounding tribute to Matilda it seems surprising that in the later *Liber de vita Christiana*, Bonizo took a completely contrary attitude. Although his argument for the Gregorian reforms remained, he no longer supported Matilda. His vitriolic attack on her in that polemic echoed those of the supporters of Henry IV. Why he turned can only be guessed at but the answer may lie in his opinion of Matilda's treatment of those supporters of Henry IV who changed to Matilda's side.

By 1082 Henry IV's supporters had ejected Bonizo from his see of Sutri. Henry then captured him. After his release Bonizo successfully sought sanctuary with Matilda. It was under her patronage shortly after these events that he wrote his *Liber ad amicum*.²⁶⁴ There are two probable reasons for Bonizo's later animus toward Matilda. First, Bonizo's intense support for church reform clashed with the more lenient attitudes that Matilda and Pope Urban II held toward those who turned away from Henry toward them. Second, Matilda and Urban only gave Bonizo partial support for his episcopacy in Piacenza, leaving him vulnerable to Henry and his troops.²⁶⁵

Another set of factors contributed to Bonizo's turning against Matilda. Matilda had a history of attempting to avoid direct conflict if possible. She had moved from place to place in the long fight with Henry over a number of years, rather than meet him directly on the battlefield. Matilda and Pope Urban II gathered into the fold those who asked for leniency including the schismatic or imperially invested bishops, Archbishop Anselm III of Milan and Bishop Daimbert of Pisa. Pope Urban undermined Bonizo's position by querying the election of the more radical Bonizo to the see of Piacenza and by doubting the support of many of the clerks and laymen there. They expelled Bonizo from the city in 1089, having brutally maimed him. They plucked out his eyes and scarcely left his limbs attached to his body. Bonizo, perceiving lukewarm support from Matilda and Urban, turned against her in his *Liber de vita Christiana,* written after his disfigurement. Subsequently, in 1094, according to Bernold of Constance, Bonizo received the martyr's crown.²⁶⁶

Spiritual Family

As well as fostering a philosophical salon Matilda maintained extensive contacts with clergy and spiritual advisers. They were not related by blood but formed a select family to which she also turned for secular advice and whose members in turn consulted her. Archbishop Anselm of Canterbury and Bishop Anselm (II) of Lucca, among others, provided her directly with spiritual guidance. The monk Donizo praised her secular and her spiritual actions in his *Life* of her, but probably did not have much direct contact with her. Just as the Cluniac foundation and reforms had influenced Adelheid's life, a hundred years later the actions and words of Hugh, abbot of Cluny, contribute to the modern discussion on how Cluny's influence affected Matilda. Another Hugh, archbishop of Lyons and a keen reformer, eagerly informed Matilda about and requested her involvement in church matters. Above all the first and most influential connection was formed between Matilda and the great supporter of church reform Pope Gregory VII. Their contact began early in her life.

Pope Gregory VII

From Rome on 4 March 1074 Pope Gregory VII wrote a letter to Countess Beatrice and her daughter Matilda. He began by asking the mother and daughter to resolve a dispute between a bishop and a count: 'we ask you and urge you as most dear daughters ('karissimas filias') that you bring to a perfect end the good thing that you have begun.'[267] He reiterated his direction to them to continue with an active public life.

> In truth, from love of God and by holding dear one's neighbour to help the wretched and to assist the oppressed – this is something that I place before prayers, fasts, vigils, and other good works however many they may be, for I do not hesitate with the Apostle to set true charity before all virtues.[268]

Gregory had earlier ordered his 'daughters most beloved of St Peter' ('dilectissimę sancti Petri filię'),[269] who were considering taking the veil as nuns, to imitate the life of Martha, not the life of Mary.[270] The exigencies of the political situation in which he found himself outweighed the actions he might have wished to approve in agreement with Christ, who stated that Mary, rather than her sister, had chosen the better part. Gregory had supported his argument with words from St Paul[271] and continued by urging their ongoing participation in the world: he wished them to work with him in church politics.

> Because if this [that is, charity], the mother of all virtues, which compelled God to come from heaven to earth that he might bear our misery, did not instruct me, and if there were someone who in your stead would come to the aid of wretched and oppressed churches and would be of service to the universal church, I would be at pains to advise that you should leave the world with all its cares ('ut speculum relinqueretis cum omnibus eius curis').[272]

Despite Gregory's injunction to continue to work in the world, Matilda again considered becoming a nun, after being widowed in early 1076.[273] Later that year Gregory reported to Bishop Hermann of Metz: 'in what state of life she should continue under God's direction, I do not yet grasp for certain.'[274] There were two pulls on people living in medieval times, particularly strongly felt in the time of the reform agenda: 'two features … are found in every part of medieval life: a strong grasp on the things of this world, and an ardent desire for the rewards of eternity.'[275] Gregory urged on Matilda the necessity for her salvation to be achieved as a layperson. Deeply committed to the reform church, Matilda allowed the pope to persuade her.

Of the seven popes whom Matilda supported unstintingly, Pope Gregory VII seems to have been her greatest inspiration. They appear to have had a genuine human and spiritual alliance. Gregory's letters to Matilda and her mother, Beatrice, contain affectionate phrases, although they are firmly grounded in religious tenets. In February 1074 the pope sent Matilda his most focused letter about matters important for her spiritual development. Unlike others he wrote to her, that letter contained conspicuously less worldly business. He made three points: he confirmed briefly the importance of her ongoing work in the world, he urged her to receive the Eucharist frequently, and he asked her to put her confidence in the Mother of God.[276] In a total of twelve surviving letters Gregory either urged Matilda directly to be active in the world or discussed her work with others.[277] Odilo of Cluny's *Epitaph*, written toward the end of Empress Adelheid's life in the late tenth century, also contains no encouragement for her to enter a monastery (although she lived in one for her last years); nor does it hint that her life would have been more appropriately spent in one. By the late tenth century ruling women, if they were competent, politically useful, and had no capable rivals, were encouraged to maintain their secular positions. By the late eleventh century their place had become less certain. Empress Agnes ultimately found court politics too full of intrigue: she was forced to retire from the court in 1062 shortly after her eleven-year-old son, Henry IV, was kidnapped by the archbishop of Cologne and other leading men. Gregory encouraged her and Matilda's support for church reform and asked for their prayers. Matilda, urged on by later popes, succeeded in pursuing an active life, grounded in comital rather than royal or imperial authority.

Gregory's second piece of advice in his February 1074 letter coincided with a new emphasis in church theology: the heightened interest in the laity's regular and frequent reception of the Eucharist.[278] The pope justified his recommendation of the former with quotations from three church writers: Ambrose of Milan, Pope Gregory the Great and John Chrysostom. Ambrose argued in one passage that Christ's shedding of his blood was linked to the remission of sins; in another that, since bread is 'daily', partaking of the consecrated bread once a year was inappropriate. He too linked frequent communion to remission of sins. Pope Gregory the Great contended that the celebration of the Passion resulted in absolution and salvation. John Chrysostom reasoned that Christ nourishes with his blood those individuals whom he has regenerated.

Gregory's third piece of advice was in tune with a general increasing interest in Mary, the Mother of God.[279] Consequently he advised Matilda to pay attention to her as intercessor with God: 'as she is higher and better and more holy than every mother, so she is more merciful and more gentle towards sinful men and women who repent.' In addition she is 'more responsive than a natural mother and more mild in her love for you'.[280] Gregory gave this advice to Matilda while her mother was alive. The closeness between Matilda and Gregory created rumors that their friendship with each other was more than it should have been. Lampert of Hersfeld reported the rumors but vigorously rejected them; Gregory's subsequent correspondence became more circumspect.[281]

Anselm of Canterbury

Two Anselms contributed to Matilda's spiritual direction—Anselm of Canterbury and Anselm of Lucca. Anselm, archbishop of Canterbury from 1093 until 1109, wrote letters of spiritual advice to a number of women, including Matilda. Two letters from Anselm to Matilda and one from Matilda to Pope Paschal II about Anselm are extant. In the first letter Anselm advises her to carry a veil, which she could put on quickly in case death suddenly came upon her. In mentioning the veil Anselm was referring to her long unfulfilled wish to enter a convent: 'I always preserve in my heart the memory of your holy desire through which your heart yearns to hold the world in contempt; but the holy and unwavering love which you have for mother Church lovingly holds you back.'[282] Seemingly Gregory VII and Anselm were aware of her wishes. Anselm thanked the countess for arranging for her people to give him protection on his journey through her territories when he was traveling to and from Rome in 1103. (He may have visited her at that time.) He promised to send her his completed *Orationes sive meditationes* (*Prayers and Meditations*).[283] The second letter followed very soon after the first, since in it he stated that he had enclosed the *Prayers and Meditations*. He included all the prayers, even though some may not be appropriate because they may be pleasing to someone else. He advised that they should be read a little at a time with intense and lingering meditation and just enough to encourage the wish to pray.[284]

It is highly likely that Matilda took Anselm of Canterbury's advice on how she should read his *Prayers and Meditations* because of her long acquaintance with Benedictine monks, her literacy, and, above all, because it was she who requested them: 'It pleased your highness that I send her the Orationes.'[285] At the monastery of Admont in Styria in Upper Austria highly educated women recited or sang the *Prayers* from a mid-twelfth-century manuscript, a copy of Anselm's original to Matilda (which does not survive).[286] The opening image shows Anselm giving Matilda the prayer book. A second image shows them kneeling with eyes raised in prayer to Christ.[287] Those images provide evidence of how her prayerful and powerful persona was viewed by literate nuns a short time after her death.

The third letter, dated 1105, is a carefully worded missive from Matilda to Pope Paschal II, asking for clemency for the archbishop.[288] Anselm of Canterbury had left Rome, impatient with the pope's slowness in excommunicating the English king, Henry I, who had refused to conform to the papal strictures on clerical homage to laypersons and lay investiture. King Henry I had expelled Anselm from England because he and Anselm had been in dispute after Pope Urban II had banned the investiture of bishops by kings at the Lenten Synod of 1099. Urban's successor, Pope Paschal II, had upheld the ban and threatened to excommunicate Henry I, who had banished Anselm from England. Anselm believed Paschal to be responding too slowly.[289] Matilda asked Paschal to take into account 'the tribulations and wretchedness' that Anselm bore.[290] Matilda's petition succeeded, or at least contributed to the resolution of Anselm's troubles, since, about the time of or just after Matilda's request, the pope sent two letters to England, one to King Henry I and one to his queen, Mathilda, asking the king to receive Anselm back and his queen to intercede with the king for him.[291] Shortly afterwards King Henry I of England canceled his banishment of Anselm, who returned to England and resumed his role as archbishop there.

Anselm of Lucca

Abbot Ekkeman of Selz was Adelheid's spiritual confessor; Bishop Anselm II of Lucca, encountered above as a member of Matilda's philosophical salon, was Matilda's. Bishop Anselm I of Lucca (Pope Alexander II from

1061) recommended his nephew Anselm, who had been trained by the Benedictines, after Matilda requested a teacher and spiritual director. Anselm II undertook those tasks from 1061, when Matilda was sixteen, until 1069.[292] In 1073 Pope Gregory VII wrote of him to Beatrice and Matilda when he became bishop-elect of Lucca. Gregory hoped that Anselm would choose the right hand rather than the left, that is, that he would run his bishopric free of simony.[293] Anselm did and became Matilda's confessor, which he remained until his death in 1086.[294] In 1101 Paschal II appointed Bernard of Vallombrosa, later bishop of Parma, as Matilda's confessor.[295] In 1104, Matilda was instrumental in his successful taking up of the bishopric after his initial imprisonment by the citizens for making remarks in his sermon against the king: she sent her vassals to rescue him. The leading citizens of Parma supported Matilda's adherents in the city, thereby turning Parma to the reform party.[296]

More information about Matilda and Anselm II of Lucca's relationship is available than about that between Empress Adelheid and her confessor Ekkeman. Eleven of Matilda's diplomata, eight of them genuine and three of dubious authenticity, refer to Anselm. Two early documents issued together with Beatrice list Anselm as either taking part in the work or in attendance. By the time of the promulgation of the second diploma in 1075 Anselm had become Bishop of Lucca.[297] Two from the period of Matilda's early independence involve her directive to hand over property in Montecatini Alto to the bishop, an order somewhat unwillingly obeyed by the men involved.[298] Three further diplomata mention Matilda and Anselm in the text. In the first Matilda was present when Bishop Leo of Pistoia lent Anselm one hundred pounds, since at that time (1084/1085) Anselm was a dispossessed vicar.[299] In the second, shortly afterwards, Anselm conveyed Matilda's thanks to Bishop Hermann of Metz for his involvement in the penance that the people of Briey were to undertake for a homicide.[300] The third, dated between 1116 and 1118, after Matilda's death, is associated with another diploma, not one of the twelve linked directly with Anselm, and of uncertain authenticity. Together they refer to the treasure and its compensation that Matilda and Anselm took from and repaid to the monastery of Sant'Apollonio at Canossa to support Pope Gregory VII against Henry IV.[301] One document of 1100, concerned with dealings about housing the bishop's men, mentions Rangerius, by then bishop of Lucca, and commemorates Anselm, as 'cum Anselmo beate memorie Lucensi episcopo'.[302] A second document, a letter from Matilda to Archbishop Hugh of Lyons, can be inferred from one by him to her. Hugh's letter, dated between 1085 and 1087, must refer to previous letters from Matilda and 'to blessed Anselm of most reverent memory', urging him to return to Rome.[303] (Hugh's letter is discussed further below in the section about Hugh of Cluny and Hugh of Lyons.) Two other documents are patently false because they include his purported activities at dates after his death in 1086. However, it is of note in the second, a document created in the fifteenth century, that Anselm's function as confessor has been remembered more than three hundred years after Matilda's death.[304] Those examples, with the variety of references to Anselm, show the extent of Matilda's involvement in the spiritual and temporal needs of the church and of the community.

Anselm II of Lucca appears to have provided active advice. Like Anselm of Canterbury, Anselm of Lucca gave Matilda a set of prayers that he had composed for her.[305] Copies from the thirteenth century of five prayers remain, apparently given to Matilda by Anselm of Lucca before Anselm of Canterbury sent his. Three prayers (numbers 1, 2 and 5) concern the Eucharist and two are directly addressed to Mary, the Mother of God (numbers 3 and 4). They draw extensively on references to the Old and New Testaments, especially the Psalms and the Gospels of Matthew and Luke, and call on Mary's powers of intercession with God, of which Matilda should avail herself.[306] In both respects Anselm's advice to Matilda concurs with that of Pope Gregory VII.

One further connection of Matilda with Anselm contributes to an understanding of her spiritual outlook. She was associated with a miracle performed at his tomb through Adelasia, one of the few women to be associated with Matilda and Anselm's circle. On a certain night when staying with Matilda Adelasia experienced great pain in her stomach. Matilda arranged for a cushion on which Anselm was accustomed to sit to be placed on Adelasia's body where the pain was located. Adelasia shortly afterwards found she was free of all pain.[307] Two matters relating to Matilda are pertinent in this narrative. The first is the current and subsequent history of the association of Matilda with Adelasia that the above narrative provides. Adelasia was the daughter of Margrave Adalbert Azzo II of the Este family, who features above for his attendance at Canossa in 1077 and for his ownership of land at Tricontai, near where Matilda's and Henry IV's armies fought. Azzo's wife, Gercendis of Maine, acted as a count in the dispute at Le Mans of

1069. (Gercendis is discussed further in Chap. 4.) Adelasia was probably a friend or companion of Matilda, since she was staying in a room belonging to the countess during the above incident. Adelasia's half-brother was Hugh of Maine, named in Donizo's *Vita Mathildis* and already discussed as the betrayer of Matilda's troops. Adelasia's mother is unknown. Adelasia's and Hugh's half-brother, Welf IV, was the father of Welf V, who became Matilda's second husband in 1089, a few years after Anselm's death.[308] The described incident may or may not have taken place before or after the wedding. Consequently it is not known if Matilda was acquainted with Adelasia before Matilda's second marriage. The above discussion shows that the interconnections between church, religion, and lay life could not easily be separated, even during that period when church and lay structures were parting ways.

Donizo, a Monk from Sant'Apollonio

Donizo probably came to the monastery of Sant'Apollonio at Canossa as a child about 1087. He states that he had lived at the same locality for twenty-five years before Matilda translated the remains of some of her ancestors to Canossa. There are only three certain dates when the countess visited Canossa: 1077, 1092 and sometime between 1110 and 1111. The latest period was the one when she was most likely to have placed the bodies of her ancestors in the sarcophagi in the crypt of the chapel.[309] It is unlikely that Donizo met Matilda frequently since he was bound to an oath of 'stability'. That oath did not mean that Donizo could not travel but that he needed a reason to leave Canossa, and would have been unlikely to travel with her. Donizo was not her chaplain or confidant and would have known only the external outline of the facts or, at most, the sentiments and opinions prevailing at the court of the countess.[310] He was at Canossa in 1092 when Henry IV unsuccessfully besieged the castle, although he was possibly not a direct witness to the battle.[311] He was also there between 1110 and 1111 when Henry V visited the area and Matilda traveled to Canossa and the nearby castles.[312] Despite the apparent lack of opportunities for Donizo to have been intimately acquainted with Matilda, the devotion he showed in writing the *Vita Mathildis* and the emphasis he places on her spiritual actions as well as on her other activities warrants his inclusion in her spiritual family.

Pope Paschal II, the Cathedral of Modena and the Bones of St Geminianus

In late 1106 Matilda accompanied Pope Paschal II to a council at Guastalla[313] where, in 1102, she had transferred the ownership of the site of an important Canossan property to the female monastery of San Sisto of Piacenza.[314] On the way she participated with the pope in the translation of the body of the early Christian bishop, St Geminianus,[315] at Modena cathedral, and then travelled with the pope as far as Verona.[316] Matilda had gained the confidence of the clerics, citizens, canons, and nobles seven years earlier in 1099. As a result they agreed to build a new cathedral at a time when the city of Modena had been without a bishop for three years. Matilda's achievement of consensus among this diverse range of people was no mean feat, considering the complicated religious and civic interconnections within society at the time. Dodo had been nominated bishop of Modena, but not consecrated until the deaths of Pope Urban II in July 1099 and of the antipope Clement III (Wibert) in the autumn of 1100 ended the schism. Dodo, supported by Matilda for the bishopric, became a beneficiary of Matilda's largesse on a number of occasions, receiving gifts of property and other goods.[317] That alliance was another example of her ability to form close ties with senior reform-minded clergy.

The translation of the relics of St Geminianus from the old crypt to the new cathedral of Modena is depicted in images illustrating the *Relatio* in a thirteenth-century copy of an early twelfth-century manuscript, written by a cathedral canon between 1096 and 1110.[318] The first image shows Matilda standing with an authoritative air on the right. Two women and five male workers stand behind her on her left. On her right stand three clerics wearing miters (with two of them holding their staffs of office), an abbot and four monks. They are gathered around the grave of the saint. The image depicts the debate that took place in spring 1106 between Bishop Dodo of Modena, who wanted to display the relics of the saint to the pilgrims before translation, and the citizens of Modena who, protective of the holy remains, were opposed to the idea. They sought Matilda's advice and agreed to her proposal that the decision be held over for Pope Paschal II's arbitration on his way to Guastalla in October of that year. The second image shows the opening of the saint's sarcophagus at the later date. In that picture, Matilda is on the viewer's left, holding her gift of an altar cloth. In front of her the architect Lanfranc holds the lid of the sarcophagus, while two male workers stand behind him and the countess.

On the right Bishop Bonsenior of Reggio Emilia stands, also supporting the lid of the casket. Behind him stand Bishop Dodo of Modena and two clergy. Below, soldiers and armed citizens are deployed to defend the holy relics.[319] By that time the countess held vast amounts of property in the Reggio Emilia region. In its words and imagery the *Relatio* acknowledges the key role taken by Matilda. Her power in the region is demonstrated by her presence at the two events and her prominent position in the two images in company with the citizens, the episcopacy, the workers and the architect; by her knowledge of papal movements; and by her influence on the pope.

Hugh of Cluny and Hugh of Lyons

Two Hughs, one an abbot and one a bishop, had significant interactions with Matilda. Hugh, sixth abbot of Cluny, was godfather to Henry IV, who was close kin to Matilda as cousin. After the death of her husband, Emperor Henry III, Empress Agnes wrote to Abbot Hugh to ask him to safeguard her little son, now heir ('haeredem').[320] Hugh continued to associate with his godson, even after Henry IV's first excommunication by Pope Gregory VII. Consequently Hugh fell under the pope's ban, which was lifted only a few days before the reconciliation meeting of January 1077 at Canossa.[321] Abbot Hugh was presented with a dilemma: whether to be loyal to his godson or to his church. According to some sources, Henry did place his right hand in that of his godfather Hugh, when confirming his oath to the pope after the resolution at Canossa, probably because Hugh was Henry's *paterfamilias*.[322] Nevertheless Donizo wrote in his *Vita* that Hugh had deferred to Matilda, reputedly saying it was not his place to involve himself in such matters.[323] While Hugh appears to have been a signatory to the final document of agreement between the papal and royal parties, Donizo's reservations about the strength of his earlier participation should be noted. His account of Matilda's decisive role at Canossa balances the German chronicles.[324]

Only one of Matilda's diplomata touches on her association with another Hugh, the archbishop of Lyons. The fragment, tentatively dated between 1085 and 1087, refers to Bishop Anselm II of Lucca and has already been discussed in relation to Matilda's association with Anselm and Archbishop Hugh.[325] The fragment appears to be part of a letter from Matilda to the archbishop, in which she directs him to come to Rome. It in turn seems to be a reply to an earlier letter from the archbishop to her, included in Abbot Hugh of Flavigny's *Chronicon* and dated to between 1085 and March 1086.[326] It is clear that Archbishop Hugh of Lyons sent a letter to Matilda in which he severely criticized Desiderius, Abbot of Monte Cassino (Pope Victor III of short tenure, 24 May 1086, and then 9 May–16 September 1087), for his procrastination, indecision and boasting, and for his conniving with Henry IV.

A second letter from Archbishop Hugh of Lyons to Matilda condemns Abbot Hugh of Cluny. The letter complains that Abbot Hugh continued to say prayers at Cluny for the excommunicated Henry IV, that the abbot had been evasive when the archbishop raised the issue with him and that he had excused himself by saying that he was praying for whatever emperor there might be.[327] The letter mentions the abbot of Monte Cassino and also alludes to orders to the Cluniac monks to refrain from contact with Abbot Richard of Saint-Victor, and indeed with the writer himself. (Pope Victor III, formerly abbot of Monte Cassino, excommunicated Abbot Richard and Archbishop Hugh of Lyons in 1087.[328]) Therefore there appear to be at least two extant letters from Hugh of Lyons to Matilda concerned with the perfidy of abbots in maintaining their support for Henry IV: Abbot Desiderius of Monte Cassino (briefly Pope Victor III) and Abbot Hugh of Cluny.[329] Archbishop Hugh of Lyons was part of a small but vigorous group who opposed Desiderius's election to the papacy. Despite Hugh's grievances aired in his letter to her, Matilda persuaded Victor to return to Rome, apparently ignoring Hugh's complaints.[330] Matilda had had influence with Desiderius previously in 1085. As executor of Pope Gregory VII's last wishes, Desiderius had asked the cardinals to undertake three actions: to consider how to fill the imminent vacancy, to write to Matilda to request Gregory's nominees of his successors and to add Matilda's other suggestions to the list to be conveyed to Rome.[331] The correspondence examined briefly above shows the extensive consultation undertaken, the amount of information exchanged between senior clergy and Matilda and her ability to negotiate with people with whom she did not always agree.

Gregory VII addressed only two people with 'personal warmth and feeling', Matilda and Archbishop Hugh of Lyons.[332] Hugh exerted immense influence over the pope, who made him permanent papal legate in France.[333] Several extant letters to or about him from Gregory contain very high praise.[334] Hugh was one of only three people whom Gregory nominated as capable of succeeding him.[335] In his two letters to Matilda did Archbishop Hugh of Lyons expect her to inform anyone of Abbot

Hugh of Cluny's purported betrayal or to act in any other way? His letters are testimony to Matilda's power and influence with prominent bishops.

***

Superficially Adelheid and Matilda followed similar paths as young women growing up in wealthy families. Each of them when very young suffered the death of her father, with her mother remarrying shortly afterwards. Subsequently both young women were taken to foreign courts, the former to the Italian court of Pavia and the latter to the German court.[336] When still young, both married a stepbrother. Matilda soon renounced her political marriage. Questions of consanguinity featured strongly in the lives of Matilda's relatives but did not appear to be such an issue with Adelheid's family. The aristocrats of the eleventh century traced their lineage if they could to the Carolingian kings and queens but were especially bound by a culture that censured close marriage.

Not long after Adelheid and Matilda married their first husbands, the stepfathers of both died, leaving their mothers widowed again. The stepbrothers/husbands of the women disappeared comparatively rapidly from the scene—Adelheid's husband through his early death and Matilda's through her rejection of her husband and his subsequent death. Thereafter both widow mothers ruled with their widow daughters. However, although the primary reason for the two young women to marry their stepbrothers—the consolidation of possessions in the form of property—was the same, the status of each of the stepbrothers differed in important ways. Adelheid's marriage to Lothar brought her the kingdom of Italy; Matilda's to Godfrey the Hunchback raised him to the position of duke. This had a remarkable effect on the lives of the two women. Adelheid operated within the not well-defined boundaries of the later half of the tenth century; the boundaries that did exist gave her structure but not major constriction. She worked within what was there. Matilda stretched the boundaries of her times and made new rules about how she—as female margrave, count and duke—would preside over her inherited lands. Both Adelheid and Matilda contracted second marriages. Adelheid's was highly successful in terms of increase in power and in wealth. Matilda's second, strategic marriage finished after she and her husband no longer had interests in common. While Adelheid might well have believed that the Ottonian succession would be secure after her death, Matilda did not have a direct descendant as successor. She had tried various forms of patronage and protection, first with her kin Conrad, son of Henry IV, who died early, then with her purported adopted son, Guido Guerra, who only appears briefly in the historical record.[337] Finally she made peace with her kin, Henry IV's second son and heir, Henry V. In 1116, after Matilda's death, Henry V descended into Italy to claim the Matildine lands.

Toward the end of their lives both Adelheid and Matilda turned their minds more directly to spiritual matters: Adelheid after handing over the government of the empire to her grandson and Matilda still firmly in control politically, until illness forced her to consider her approaching death. Nevertheless neither woman totally abandoned her political empire. Adelheid toured sites in Burgundy and France where her family originated, and Matilda forcefully subdued the rebellious Mantuans after the rumor spread among them that she had died. Both women ultimately settled near their spiritual homes, Adelheid at the monastery at Selz and Matilda at San Benedetto Po.

Notes

1. Diane J. Austin-Broos, *Arrernte Present, Arrernte Past: Invasion, Violence, and Imagination in Indigenous Central Australia* (Chicago: University of Chicago Press, 2009), 2–4, 130–53.
2. Austin-Broos, *Arrernte Present*, 6.
3. Karl Leyser, 'Maternal Kin in Early Medieval Germany. A Reply', *P&P*, no. 49 (1970), 126 (reprinted with expanded footnotes as Karl Leyser, 'Maternal Kin in Early Medieval Germany', in *Communications and Power in Medieval Europe: The Carolingian and Ottonian Centuries*, ed. Timothy Reuter (London: Hambledon Press, 1994), 181–88).
4. Marc Bloch, *Feudal Society*, trans. L. A. Manyon, 2nd ed. (London: Routledge & Kegan, 1962), 123–24.
5. Gerd Althoff, *Family, Friends and Followers: The Political Importance of Group Bonds in the Early Middle Ages* (New York: Cambridge University Press, 2004), 23–41.
6. Bouchard, *Those of My Blood*, 2–4, 180; Constance Brittain Bouchard, *Sword, Miter, and Cloister: Nobility and the Church in Burgundy, 980–1198* (Ithaca, NY, and London: Cornell University Press, 1987), 29.
7. D. A. Bullough, 'Early Medieval Social Groupings: The Terminology of Kinship', *P&P*, no. 45 (1969), 7–18; Leyser, 'Maternal Kin. Reply', 126–34). The original paper on which the discussion centered is Karl Leyser, 'The German Aristocracy from

the Ninth to the Early Twelfth Century: A Historical and Cultural Sketch', *P&P*, no. 41 (Dec., 1968), 25–53.
8. Leyser, 'German Aristocracy', 35–36; Régine Le Jan, *Famille et Pouvoir dans le Monde Franc (VIIe–Xe siècle): Essai d'Anthropologie Sociale* (Paris: Publications de la Sorbonne, 1995), 226–28; Leyser, 'Maternal Kin', 181, 185–86, 188; Bloch, *Feudal Society*, 137.
9. Jack Goody, *The Development of the Family and Marriage in Europe* (Cambridge: Cambridge University Press, 1983), 222–26; Le Jan, *Famille*, 162–63.
10. Bouchard, *Those of My Blood*, 5; Bouchard, *Sword*, 29; Bullough, 'Early Medieval Groupings, 12.
11. 'Durum est ab aliquo filiis ac *propinquis* parum relinqui [my italics]', Salvian of Marseille, *Salviani presbyteri Massiliensis libri qui supersunt*, ed. C. Halm, *MGH AA* 1.1 (Berlin: Weidmann, 1877), *Ad ecclesiam*. 3.12.51, p. 152.
12. *OED Online*, s.vv. 'kin', 'kith', 'uncouth.' 'Kith' is mainly of interest in contrast to 'kin'.
13. Althoff, *Family*, 65–101.
14. Bouchard, *Those of My Blood*, 32, 49.
15. Eduard Hlawitschka, *Die Ahnen der hochmittelalterlichen deutschen Könige, Kaiser und ihrer Gemahlinnen: Ein kommentiertes Tafelwerk*, 2 vols, *MGH*, Hilfsmittel, 25 (Hanover: Hahn, 2006), 1.1, Table VI. For evidence of the prestige in which the Ottonian lineage was held, see the abundance of the Ottonian names transmitted through the female line in Le Jan, *Famille*, 221–23.
16. Hrotsvitha, *Gesta*, lines 75–77. For discussion of Edgiva, the sister whom Otto did not choose, see Simon MacLean, 'Making a Difference in Tenth-Century Politics: King Athelstan's Sisters and Frankish Queenship', in *Frankland: The Franks and the World of the Early Middle Ages. Essays in Honour of Dame Jinty Nelson*, ed. Paul Fouracre and D. Ganz (Manchester: Manchester University Press, 2008), 168, 173, 179.
17. Liudprand, *Antapodosis*, 4.17.
18. Widukind, *Res*, 1.37.
19. 'genitrix clarissima … magnorum summo de germine regum … natam de stirpe beata / Oswaldi regis', Hrotsvitha, *Gesta*, lines 81, 86, and 95–96.

20. 'Aedwardi regis natam ... Eaditham', ibid., lines 77, 206. David Pratt, *The Political Thought of King Alfred the Great* (Cambridge: Cambridge University Press, 2007), 106; Sean Gilsdorf, *Queenship*, 6.
21. 'generis mulier satis inferioris', Hrotsvitha, *Gesta*, line 82.
22. 'Quem peperit regi consors non inclita regni', ibid., line 80.
23. Ibid., line 79.
24. For the well-born mother, see Le Jan, *Famille*, 230–31.
25. Leyser, 'Maternal Kin', 188n33.
26. 'Edita magnorum longo de stemmate regum; / Cui nomen clarum dictavit summa parentum / Nobilitas, illam digne vocitans Æthelheitham', Hrotsvitha, *Gesta*, lines 472–74.
27. *DO* I, Index, 673.
28. *Old High German (ca. 750–1050) English Dictionary online*, s.v. 'adal', http://glosbe.com/goh/en/, date accessed 20 August 2016; *Deutsch-Englisch-Wörtenbuch*, s.v. 'heit', http://www.dict.cc/, date accessed 20 August 2016; Régine Le Jan, 'Adelheidis: le nom au premier millénaire. Formation, origine, dynamique', in *Adélaïde de Bourgogne: Genèse et représentations d'une sainteté impériale*, ed. Patrick Corbet, Monique Gouillet and Dominique Iogna-Prat (Dijon: Université de Dijon, 2002), 29–42.
29. Bernard, *Chartes*, vol. 1, no. 379, 358–61; Constance Brittain Bouchard, 'The Bosonids or Rising to Power in the Late Carolingian Age', *French Historical Studies* 15, no. 3 (1988), 407–31.
30. Hrotsvitha, *Gesta*, line 477.
31. Hlawitschka, *Ahnen* 1.1, Table VIII, Reference 61 or 63, 'Gisela'. Empress Adelheid's mother's great-great-great-grandmother, Gisela, was a daughter of Louis the Pious.
32. Leyser, 'Maternal Kin. A Reply', 126.
33. Herbert Zielinski, 'Konrad', *LMA* 5, 1342; Bouchard, 'Burgundy and Provence, 341–42.
34. Gilsdorf, *Queenship*, Introduction, 6.
35. In about 907 Reginlind (d. 958 or later) married Burchard of Swabia (d. 926), variously called Burchard I (he was the first duke) or Burchard II (his father was Count Burchard, d. 911). For terminology that uses Burchard II, see Hlawitschka, *Ahnen* 1.1, Tables VIII, XI. See also Winfrid Glocker, *Die Verwandten*

der Ottonen und ihre Bedeutung in der Politik. Studien zur Familienpolitik und zur Genealogie des sächsischen Kaiserhauses (Cologne and Vienna: Böhlau, 1989), 286.
36. Gilsdorf, *Queenship*, 192n74.
37. Adelheid's brother Burchard I was archbishop of Lyons (949–956/7). Brother Burchard I should not be confused with Adelheid's nephew, Burchard II, archbishop of Lyons (979–1031), the bastard son of Conrad and his concubine, Aldiud. *Die Urkunden der burgundischen Rudolfinger*, ed. T. Schieffer and H. E. Mayer, *MGH, Regum Burgundiae e stirpe Rudolfina Diplomata* (Munich: 1977), Nr. 74; 17n10; Janet Nelson, 'Tenth-Century Kingship Comparatively', in *England and the Continent in the Tenth Century: Studies in Honour of Wilhelm Levison (1876–1947). Studies in the Early Middle Ages*, eds David Rollason, Conrad Leyser and Hannah Williams (Turnhout, Belgium: Brepols, 2010), 307; Barbara H. Rosenwein, *To be the Neighbor of Saint Peter: The Social Meaning of Cluny's Property, 909–1049* (Ithaca, NY: Cornell University Press, 1989), 154 and 189n144.
38. Timothy Reuter, 'Introduction: Reading the Tenth Century', in *NCMH* (1999), 3.
39. Karl Leyser, "The Ottonians and Wessex," in *Communications and Power in Medieval Europe: The Carolingian and Ottonian Centuries*, ed. Timothy Reuter (London: Hambledon Press, 1994), 84.
40. Flodoard of Reims, *Les Annales de Flodoard de Reims*, ed. Philippe Lauer (Paris: Picard, 1905), s.a. 940.
41. Mathilda of West Francia should not be confused with her grandmother, Queen Mathilda, wife of King Henry I (d. 936): Glocker, *Die Verwandten der Ottonen*, 283–84.
42. Hrotsvitha, *Gesta*, lines 467–665.
43. Odilo, *Epitaphium domine Adalheide auguste (Die Lebensbeschreibung der Kaiserin Adelheid von Abt Odilo von Cluny).* ed. Herbert Paulhart, (= *Festschrift zur Jahrtausendfeier der Kaiserkrönung Ottos des Großen*, vol. 2. [MIöG, Ergänzungsband 20/2]) (Graz and Cologne: Böhlau, 1962), ch. 6; Syrus of Cluny, *Vita sancti Maioli*, ed. Dominique Iogna-Prat, in *Agni Immaculati*, 163–285 (Paris: Éditions du Cerf, 1988), 3.2, pp. 263–66.

44. 'Adelheidis inperatrix cum filia Athelheidhe abbatissa in Italiam profecta est propter quasdam discordias inter se et filium factas', *Annalista Saxo*, ed. K. Nass, *MGH SS* 37 (2006), s.a. 978, p. 226. See also *Annales Magdeburgenses*, ed. G. H. Pertz, *MGH SS* 16:105–96 (1859), s.a. 978, p. 154.
45. *DO* II, Nr. 213.
46. Karl Uhlirz, *Jahrbücher des Deutschen Reiches unter Otto II. und Otto III. Otto II. 978–983*, 2 vols, vol. 1 (Leipzig and Berlin: Dunker and Humblot, 1902, repr. 1967), 110–11, 139; René Poupardin, *Le royaume de Bourgogne, 888–1038: Étude sur les origines du royaume d'Arles* (Paris: Champion, 1907, repr. Geneva: Slatkine, 1974), 82.
47. 'regi avunculo', Odilo, *Epitaphium*, ch. 6.
48. *AQ*, s.a. 984, 472; Nelson, 'Tenth-Century Kingship', 301–5; Bouchard, 'Burgundy and Provence', 341–42.
49. Odilo, *Epitaphium*, ch. 12; Guido Castelnuovo, 'L'aristocrazia del Vaud sino alla conquista Sabauda (inizio XI–metà XIII secolo)', *Bolletino Storico-Bibliografico Subalpino* 86 (1988), 491.
50. Harriet Pratt Lattin, *The Letters of Gerbert, with his Papal Privileges as Sylvester II*, (New York: Columbia University Press, 1961), 135n1.
51. Gerbert, *Epistolae (Die Briefsammlung Gerberts von Reims)*, ed. F. Weigle, *MGH Briefe* 2 (Berlin: Weidmann, 1966), Letters 97; 119; 128; trans. Lattin, *Letters*, Letters 100, 128, 137.
52. Bloch, *Feudal Society*, 124.
53. 'in vasatico ... per manus', *Annales Regni Francorum*, ed. F. Kurze, *MGH SSrG* [6] (Hanover: 1895), s.a. 757; David Herlihy, *The History of Feudalism* (London: Macmillan, 1971), 86.
54. Thomas N. Bisson, *The Crisis of the Twelfth Century: Power, Lordship, and the Origins of European Government* (Princeton, NJ: Princeton University Press, 2009), 62–65.
55. Widukind, *Res*, 2. 2; Thietmar, *Chronicon*, 2.34; David A. Warner, *Ottonian Germany: The Chronicon of Thietmar of Merseburg* (Manchester: Manchester University Press, 2001), 32; Karl Leyser, "Liudprand of Cremona: Preacher and Homilist," in *Communications and Power in Medieval Europe: The Carolingian and Ottonian Centuries*, ed. Timothy Reuter (London: Hambledon Press, 1994), 122.

56. 'Interea dux Henricus, regis venerandus / Frater, in Italia cordis conamine summo / Obsequiis operam gessit regalibus aptam, / *Officium non germani solummodo cari,* / *Sed mage ius servi* studio complendo benigni [my italics]', Hrotsvitha, *Gesta,* lines 675–79. Duke Henry I's territories in Bavaria were situated near Italy and consequently it was appropriate for him to intervene there on Otto I's behalf.
57. 'in vasatico ... per manus ... et fidelitatem promisit regi Pippino ... sicut vassus', *Annales Regni Francorum,* s.a. 757; Susan Reynolds, *Fiefs and Vassals: The Medieval Evidence Reinterpreted* (Oxford: Oxford University Press, 1994), 86–89; Olson, *Early Middle Ages,* 88–89, 94.
58. *Capitulare missorum generale,* ed. A. Boretius, *MGH Capitularia regum Francorum, Legum sectio* I:33:91–99 (Hanover: 1883), 91–93; Nicholas Everett, 'Paulinus of Aquileia's *Sponsio episcoporum*: Written Oaths and Ecclesiastical Discipline in Carolingian Italy', in *Textual Cultures of Medieval Italy,* ed. W. Robins (Toronto: University of Toronto, 2011), 173; Levi Roach, 'Submission and Homage: Feudo-Vassalic Bonds and the Settlement of Disputes in Ottonian Germany', *History* 97, no. 327 (2012), 377.
59. 'Hinc non inmerito regi placuit satis ipsi, / Est quoque reginae fraterno iunctus amore / Affectuque pio fuerat dilectus ab illa', Hrotsvitha, *Gesta,* lines 680–82.
60. Ibid., lines 737–38.
61. Richer, *Histories. Richer of Saint-Rémi,* trans. Justin Lake, 2 vols, Dumbarton Oaks Medieval Library (Cambridge, MA: Harvard University Press, 2011), vol. 2, 3.44; Lattin, *Letters,* pp. 3–4.
62. Gerbert, *Epistolae,* Letter 6, trans. Lattin, *Letters,* Letter 13.
63. Gerbert, *Epistolae,* Letters 6, 20, 62, 74, 97, 119, 128, 204, 215, trans. Lattin, *Letters,* Letters 13, 28, 69, 81, 100, 128, 137, 217, 210.
64. The first surviving letter is dated to 976: Lattin, *Letters,* Letter 35.
65. Gerbert, *Epistolae,* Letter 6, trans. Lattin, *Letters,* Letter 13.
66. Gerbert, *Epistolae,* Letter 39, trans Lattin, *Letters,* Letter 24.
67. Gerbert, *Epistolae,* Letter 20, trans. Lattin, *Letters,* Letter 28.
68. Lattin, *Letters,* pp. 6–7 and Letter 8.

69. Gerbert, *Epistolae*, Letters 11, 20, 158, 185, trans. Lattin, *Letters*, Letters 18, 28, 166, 229; Charles Edwin Odegaard, 'The Concept of Royal Power in Carolingian Oaths of Fidelity', *Speculum* 20, no. 3 (Jul., 1945), 279.
70. 'quam fidem filio dominae meae A.[Adelheid] servavi, eam matri servabo', Gerbert, *Epistolae*, Letter 20, trans. Lattin, *Letters*, Letter 28.
71. Thietmar, *Chronicon*, 4.15.
72. Gerbert, *Epistolae*, Letter 215, trans. Lattin, *Letters*, Letter 210. Otto III's coronation as emperor occurred on 21 May 996: Lattin, *Letters*, p. 269n.
73. Gerbert, *Epistolae*, Letters 34, 46, 150, 158, 184, trans. Lattin, *Letters*, Letters 42, 52, 158, 166, 228.
74. Thietmar, *Chronicon*, 3.5.
75. Leyser, 'German Aristocracy', 27; Chris Wickham, *The Inheritance of Rome: A History of Europe from 400 to 1000* (London: Penguin, 2010), 524.
76. *DO I*, Nr. 404; Lattin, *Letters*, 72n1.
77. Thietmar, *Chronicon*, 3.26, 5.11; John M. Jeep, *Medieval Germany: An Encyclopedia* (New York: Garland, 2001), s.v. 'Mainz'.
78. Thietmar, *Chronicon*, 4.5–4.6.
79. Gerbert, *Epistolae*, Letter 27, trans. Lattin, *Letters*, Letter 35.
80. Dominik Waßenhoven, 'Swaying Bishops and the Succession of Kings', in *Patterns of Episcopal Power: Bishops in 10th and 11th Century Western Europe*, ed. Ludger Körntgen and Dominik Waßenhoven (Berlin/Boston: Walter de Gruyter, 2011), 98.
81. Gerbert, *Epistolae*, Letters 30–35, trans. Lattin, *Letters*, Letters, 38–43.
82. Thietmar, *Chronicon*, 4.2.
83. Althoff, 'Saxony', 270.
84. Karl Leyser, '*Theophanu divina gratia imperatrix augusta*: Western and Eastern Emperorship in the Later Tenth Century', in *The Empress Theophano: Byzantium and the West at the Turn of the First Millennium*, ed. A. Davids (Cambridge: Cambridge University Press, 1995), 163.
85. Lattin, *Letters*, 117n6.
86. Eckhard Müller-Mertens, 'The Ottonians as Kings and Emperors', *NCMH* 3 (1999), 254, 256–57, 260; Hlawitschka, *Ahnen* 1.1,

Table XII; Przemyslaw Urbańczyk, *Europe around the Year 1000* (Warsaw: Polish Academy of Sciences Institute of Archaeology and Ethnology, 2001), 482.
87. Thietmar, *Chronicon*, 3.24; 4.4; 4.9; 4.18.
88. Odilo, *Epitaphium*, ch. 20.
89. Franz Staab, 'Liste der Äbte und Pröpste', in *Adelheid: Kaiserin und Heilige, 931 bis 999*, eds Maria Pia Andreola Panzarasa and Liliane Obreiter (Karlsruhe: INFO, 1999), 196.
90. Gerbert, *Epistolae*, Letter 21, trans. Lattin, *Letters*, Letter 29.
91. Josef Fleckenstein, *Die Hofkapelle der deutschen Konige: Die Hofkapelle im Rahmen der ottonisch-salischen Reichskirche*, 2 vols, vol. 2 (Stuttgart: Hiersemann, 1966), 47, 72, 74.
92. 'Abbatem ibi prefecit nomine Eccemagnum, boni testimonii virum, humana scientia et divina sapientia doctum, quem in divinis literis habere voluit assidue preceptorem', Odilo, *Epitaphium*, ch. 10.
93. 'abbatem illius cenobii', *Liber miraculorum sancte Adelaide or 'Der Wunderbericht'*, ed. Herbert Paulhart, in *Die Lebensbeschreibung der Kaiserin Adelheid von Abt Odilo von Cluny*, 45–54 (Graz and Cologne: Böhlau, 1962), ch. 5. See also the edition by Giuliano Sala and Giorgio Vedovelli, *Vita e miracoli di Adelaide di Borgogna. Epitaphium Adalheidae imp. Liber miraculorum* (Torri del Benaco: 1990).
94. Gerald Beyreuther, 'Kaiserin Adelheid: "Mutter der Königreiche"', in *Herrscherinnen und Nonnen: Frauengestalten von der Ottonenzeit bis zu den Staufern*, ed. Erika Uitz, Barbara Pätzold and Gerald Beyreuther (Berlin: Wissenschaften, 1990), 76; Joachim Wollasch, 'Das Grabkloster der Kaiserin Adelheid in Selz am Rhein', *FMSt* 2 (1968), 136–38; Patrick J. Geary, *Phantoms of Remembrance: Memory and Oblivion at the End of the First Millennium* (Princeton, NJ: Princeton University Press, 1994), 61.
95. Giles Constable, 'Cluniac Reform in the Eleventh Century', in *The Abbey of Cluny: A Collection of Essays to Mark the Eleventh-Hundred Anniversary of its Foundation*, ed. Giles Constable (Berlin: LIT, 2010), 96.
96. Joachim Wollasch, 'Cluny und Deutschland', in *SMGB* (St. Ottilien: 1992), 12–13; Giles Constable, 'Liturgical Commemoration', in Constable, *The Abbey of Cluny*, 126–30.

97. For Cabellio as Cavaillon in Burgundy, see A. H. M. Jones, J. R. Martindale and J. Morris, *The Prosopography of the Later Roman Empire*, 3 vols (Cambridge: Cambridge University Press, 1971), vol. 3, s.v. 'Armentaria'. Alternatively for Cabillonum as Chalon-sur-Saône, see Gregory of Tours, *Miracles of the Bishop St. Martin*, ed. Raymond Van Dam, in *Saints and their Miracles in Late Antique Gaul*, 199–303 (Princeton, N.J.: Princeton University Press, 1993), 3.60, p. 283.
98. Bernard, *Chartes*, vol. 2, no. 883, 1–2; Matthew Innes, 'On the Material Culture of Legal Documents: Charters and their Preservation in the Cluny Archive (9th–11th Centuries)', in *Documentary Culture and the Laity in the Early Middle Ages*, eds Warren Brown, Marios Costambeys, Matthew Innes and Adam J. Kosto (Cambridge: Cambridge University Press, 2013), 283–320; Joachim Wollasch, 'Les obituaires, témoins de la vie clunisienne', *CCM* 22, no. 86 (1979), 149–71.
99. 'Imperatrix uero, acsi ancillarum ultima, impendere cupiebat ei deuotionis obsequia, quoniam beati Maioli per preces abundantiori se uisitari diuine presentie sperabat gratia', Syrus of Cluny, *Vita sancti Maioli*, 2.22, 242.
100. 'Hunc imperator habebat auricularium, hunc a secretis fidum internuntium', ibid., 2.22, 242–3. Alternatively, '[he, Maiolus, was] the ear and repository of the imperial secrets': Scott G. Bruce, 'Local Sanctity and Civic Typology in Early Medieval Pavia: The Example of the Cult of Abbot Maiolus of Cluny', in *Cities, Texts, and Social Networks, 400–1500: Experiences and Perceptions of Medieval Urban Space*, ed. Caroline Goodson, Anne Elisabeth Lester and Carol Symes (Farnham, Surrey: Ashgate, 2010), 181–82.
101. Syrus of Cluny, *Vita sancti Maioli*, 3.10.
102. Odilo, *Epitaphium*, ch. 16. Paul Amargier, 'Saint Maïeul et sainte Adélaïde, une amitié', in *Saint Maïeul et son temps. Millénaire de la mort de Saint Maïeul, 4ᵉ abbé de Cluny, 994–1994. Actes du Congrès International (Valensole 12–14 mai 1994)* (Digne-les-Bains: 1997), 185–87.
103. See the shorter and the longer Jotsaldus: Jotsaldus, *Vita Odilonis abb. Cluniacensis*, ed. G. Waitz, *MGH SS* 15/1:812–820 (1887), 1.6, p. 813; and Jotsaldus, *Vita Odilonis de Cluny*, PL 142:879–940, 1.6, p. 902.

104. Gilsdorf, *Queenship*, 55.
105. 'Erat quidam ibi in presentia ipsius monachus, qui licet esset indignus abbas vocitari, ab ea tamen putabatur alicuius esse momenti. Quem cum illa respiceret, et ipse eam esset intuitus, cepit uterque flere uberius. *Dicam eam tunc plus fecisse, quam si dicerem eam multos infirmos sanasse.* Vestem enim satis incultam, qua erat indutus, humiliter apprehendit et sanctissimis oculis et serenissime sue faciei osculando impressit eique familiariter et cum silentio dixit: ... [my italics]', Odilo, *Epitaphium*, ch. 18.
106. Franz Neiske, 'La tradition nécrologique d'Adélaïde', in Corbet, et al., *Adélaïde de Bourgogne*, 90.
107. *Liber miraculorum*, ch. 5; Eric Waldram Kemp, *Canonization and Authority in the Western Church* (London: Oxford University Press, 1948), 68–69. For the dating of this visit to 1014 rather than to 1002, see Wollasch, 'Grabkloster', 140n37.
108. *Liber miraculorum*, chs 5, 13; Wollasch, 'Grabkloster', 139.
109. Patrick Corbet, *Les saints ottoniens: sainteté dynastique, sainteté royale et sainteté féminine autour de l'an Mil* (Sigmaringen: Thorbecke, 1986), 61, Fig. II, 66; Herbert Paulhart, 'Zur Heiligsprechung der Kaiserin Adelheid', *MIöG* 64 (1956), 65–66.
110. *ODP*, s.v. 'Urban II'; I. S. Robinson, *Henry IV of Germany, 1056–1106* (Cambridge: Cambridge University Press, 1999), 292–93, 312.
111. '"Si annum integrum supervixero, non dominabitur Adalheida in toto mundo, quod non possit circumdari palmo uno"', Odilo, *Epitaphium*, ch. 7.
112. Thietmar, *Chronicon*, 4.18.
113. *AQ*, s.a. 991.
114. Johannes Fried, 'Theophanu und die Slawen. Bemerkungen zur Ostpolitik der Kaiserin', in *Kaiserin Theophanu: Begegnung des Ostens und Westens um die Wende des ersten Jahrtausands*, ed. Anton von Euw and Peter Schreiner (Cologne: Schnütgen-Museum, 1991), 367–70; Josef Fleckenstein, *Early Medieval Germany*, trans. Bernard S. Smith (Amsterdam: North-Holland Publishing Company, 1978), 167–68; Leyser, *Rule*, 44.
115. Odilo, *Epitaphium*, chs 2–3.
116. Ibid., ch. 5.
117. Ibid., ch. 7.
118. Thietmar, *Chronicon*, 4.15.

119. Odilo, *Epitaphium*, chs 3, 6, 7; Gilsdorf, *Queenship*, 55.
120. 'matrem regnorum', 'omnium ... mater regnorum', Gerbert, *Epistolae*, Letters 74, 128, trans. Lattin, *Letters*, Letters 81, 137; 'Dominę precelsę regum regnorumque altrici nobilissimę', Froumond, *Die Tergernseer Briefsammlung*, ed. Karl Strecker, *MGH Epp. sel.* 3:1–96 (Berlin: Weidmann, 1925, repr. 1964), *Ep.* 1, pp. 2–3.
121. Gerberga (d. 969) and Hadwig/Hathui (sisters of Otto I) were Matilda of Tuscany's great-great-great-grandmothers. The two lines met at the maternal grandparents of Countess Matilda. Matilda's grandmother was a direct descendent of Gerberga (d. 969). Matilda's grandfather was a direct descendent of Hadwig (d. perhaps after 965). The first line went through Beatrice's maternal grandmother, Gerberga of Burgundy (d. after 1016), and then through the maternal line to Gerberga (d. 969). The second line went through Beatrice's paternal grandfather, Duke Theoderic (I) of Upper Lotharingia (d. 1026/7), and then through the maternal line to Hadwig. (Note that other versions of the name Theoderic are Theodoric, Dietrich or Thierry.) See also Leyser, *Rule*, betw. 92 and 93; Margherita Giuliana Bertolini, "Note di genealogia e di storia canossiana," in *Margherita Giuliana Bertolini: studi canossiani*, ed. Ovidio Capitani and Paolo Golinelli (Bologna: Pàtron, 2004), Table 2, p. 26.
122. The line that linked Adelheid to Matilda of Tuscany as great-great-great-great-aunt started with her brother Conrad and his wife Mathilda of West Francia. Their daughter, Gerberga of Burgundy (d. after 1016), was Adelheid's niece. The line continues through Gerberga's daughter, Mathilda of Swabia (d. 1031–1033), to her daughter, Beatrice (d. 1076), who was Matilda of Tuscany's mother. Empress Gisela's obligation to her nieces, Beatrice (d. 1076) and Sophie (d. some considerable time after her sister), arose because they were the daughters of Empress Gisela's sister, Mathilda of Swabia, and Frederick II of Upper Lotharingia (d. 1033). Empress Gisela was also Beatrice's godmother. Joan Ferrante, *To the Glory of Her Sex: Women's Roles in the Composition of Medieval Texts* (Bloomington: Indiana University Press, 1997), 236n46. See also Elke Goez, *Beatrix von Canossa und Tuszien: Eine Untersuching zur Geschichte des 11. Jahrhunderts* (Sigmaringen: Jan Thorbecke, 1995), 11–12.

123. Donizo, *VM*, Figs 3–6, between pp. 16 and 17.
124. Patrick Healy, *The Chronicle of Hugh of Flavigny: Reform and the Investiture Contest in the Late Eleventh Century* (Aldershot: Ashgate, 2006), Appendix 2, p. 235.
125. Gisela (d. 918) was Adelheid's great-grandmother: Hlawitschka, *Ahnen*, 1.1, Table VIII.
126. Ermentrude's father was Louis the Stammerer (Louis II, d. 879), son of Charles the Bald (d. 877), son of Louis the Pious. Bouchard, *Those of my Blood*, 79. See also Le Jan, *Famille*, 184, 456; Marios Costambeys, Matthew Innes, and Simon MacLean, *The Carolingian World* (Cambridge: Cambridge University Press, 2011), xx, xxi; Hlawitschka, *Ahnen*, 1.1, Table XIII.
127. Emma was the great-great-great-great niece of Adelaide, wife of Richard le Justicier (d. 921): Bouchard, *Those of My Blood*, 127–29; for further discussion of the migration of women's names in the upper nobility, see also 120–34. Louis the German (d. 876) was the third son of Louis the Pious and his first wife, Ermengard (d. 818): Costambeys, Innes and MacLean, *Carolingian World*, xx, xxi.
128. Bouchard, *Those of My Blood*, 117.
129. Timothy Reuter, 'Peace-Breaking, Feud, Rebellion, Resistance: Violence and Peace in the Politics of the Salian Era', in *Medieval Polities and Modern Mentalities*, ed. Janet Nelson (Cambridge: Cambridge University Press, 2006), 384.
130. I am grateful to Professor Sally Vaughn for drawing to my attention the opportunity for Matilda to develop a strong relationship with her stepsister Ida, pers. comm., 11 July 2012.
131. Robinson, *Henry IV*, 24.
132. Mairi Cowan, 'The Spiritual Ties of Kinship in Pre-Reformation Scotland', in *Finding the Family in Medieval and Early Modern Scotland*, ed. E. Ewan and J. Nugent (Aldershot: Ashgate, 2008), 116; Amy Livingstone, *Out of Love for my Kin: Aristocratic Family Life in the Lands of the Loire, 1000–1200* (Ithaca, NY: Cornell University Press, 2010), 165.
133. The connections for Beatrice went through her mother, Mathilda of Swabia, then Gerberga of Burgundy, Mathilda of West Francia, Gerberga to King Henry I and also through her father, Frederick II of Upper Lotharingia, then Theoderic I of Upper Lotharingia, Beatrice, Hadwig to King Henry I. The connection of Godfrey

the Bearded went through his father, Gozelo II of Lower and Upper Lotharingia, then through Godfrey I 'The Captive', Uda of Metz to Oda of Saxony, sister of King Henry I (d. 936).
134. David J. Hay, *The Military Leadership of Matilda of Canossa 1046–1115* (Manchester: Manchester University Press, 2008), xvi; Healy, *Hugh of Flavigny: Reform*, Appendix 2, 235.
135. Even well before that Synod, churchmen were concerned about consanguinity issues to the seventh degree. Owen J. Blum, *Letters of Peter Damian*, 6 vols (Washington, DC: Catholic University of America Press, 1989), vol. 1, Letter 19.
136. Peter Damian, *Epistolae*, ed. K. Reindel, 4 vols, *Die Briefe des Petrus Damiani, MGH Briefe* (Munich: 1983–93), vol. 2, Letter 51, s.a. 1057.
137. Beatrice and Henry III had a grandmother in common, Gerberga of Burgundy (d. after 1016), daughter of Mathilda of West Francia and King Conrad I of Burgundy (Empress Adelheid's brother).
138. Godfrey the Bearded's father and brother were Gozelo II and Gozelo III (sometimes confusingly numbered Gozelo I and Gozelo II). Robinson, *Henry IV*, 20; Sally N. Vaughn, *St. Anselm and the Handmaidens of God: A Study of Anselm's Correspondence* (Turnhout: Brepols, 2002), 126–27; Healy, *Hugh of Flavigny: Reform*, Appendix 2, 235.
139. David A. Warner, 'Ideals and Action in the Reign of Otto III', *JMH* 25, no. 1 (1999), 10.
140. Goez, *Beatrix*, 20–21.
141. Tiziana. Lazzari, 'Goffredo di Lorena e Beatrice di Toscana', (paper presented at the La reliquia del Sangue di Cristo. l'Italia e l'Europa al tempo di Leone IX, Convegno Internazionale di Studi Mantova (I), Mantua, 23–26 novembre 2011); Tiziana Lazzari, 'Before Matilde: Beatrice of Lorena "Dux et Marchio Tusciae"', (paper presented at the International Medieval Congress, Leeds, England, July, 2012), 4. I am grateful to Dr. Lazzari for her generosity in sending copies of these two papers to me.
142. Goez, *Beatrix*, 21; Robinson, *Henry IV*, 24.
143. Landulf Senior, *Historia Mediolanensis*, ed. L. C. Bethmann and W. Wattenbach, *MGH SS* 8:32–100 (1848), 3.31, p. 97; Goez, *Beatrix*, 20; Lazzari, 'Goffredo', 13; Lazzari, 'Before Matilde', 4;

Paolo Golinelli, *Matilde e i Canossa*, 2nd ed. (Milan: Mursia, 2004), 172–73.
144. 'hosti publico', Lampert, *Annales*, 67; Lazzari, 'Goffredo', especially 8–12.
145. Vaughn, *St. Anselm*, 128.
146. I have used Robinson and Vaughn's numbering system for the house of Verdun (Ardennes), wherein Godfrey the Bearded is Godfrey II and Godfrey the Hunchback, after succeeding his father appears as Godfrey III of Lower Lotharingia. In Healy's system Godfrey the Bearded is Godfrey III and Godfrey the Hunchback appears as Godfrey IV. Robinson, *Henry IV*, 401; Vaughn, *St. Anselm*, 296, 323; Healy, *Hugh of Flavigny: Reform*, 235. See also Emmanuel J. Mickel, ed., *Les Enfances de Godefroi and Le retour de Cornumarant*, vol. 3, The Old French Crusade Cycle (Tuscaloosa, Alabama: University of Alabama Press, 1999), 60–61, 70.
147. Valerie Eads, 'The Geography of Power: Matilda of Tuscany and the Strategy of Active Defense', in *Crusaders, Condottieri and Cannon: Medieval Warfare in Societies around the Mediterranean*, ed. L. J. Andrew Villalon and Donald J. Kagay (Leiden: Brill, 2002), 361.
148. *ODP*, s.v. 'Stephen IX (X)', Robinson, *Henry IV*, 33; Hay, *Military Leadership*, xvi.
149. *DD MT*, Nr. 1.
150. Ibid. Nr. 28; Goez, *Beatrix*, 76; Tiziana Lazzari, 'Miniature e versi: mimesi della regalità in Donizone', in *Forme di potere nel pieno medioevo (secc. VIII–XII). Dinamiche e rappresentazioni*, ed. G. Isabella (Bologna: 2006 (Dpm quaderni–dottorato 6)), 73.
151. *DD MT*, Nr. 1.
152. Böhmer, *RI* 2.3, Nr. 1307b, Erstein, early April 999, 712–13 and Nrs 1308a, and 1309a, 1309b, 1309c, 713–14.
153. Lino Lionello Ghirardini, *Storia critica di Matilde di Canossa: problemi (e misteri) della più grande Donna della storia d'Italia* (Modena: Aedes Muratoriana, 1989), 53–114.
154. *DD MT*, Nr. 1, and s.vv. 'Algiso', 519; 'Razo', 543 and 'Beatus of Fornicata', 522.
155. Ibid., s.vv. 'Fornicata', 566; 'Pletule', 577.
156. Ibid., Nrs 1; 25; s.v. 'Ingo', 534.

157. Ibid., Nrs 31, 32; s.v. 'Crescentius', 526.
158. Ibid. Nrs 1, 9; s.v. 'Rogerius', 544.
159. Ibid., Nrs 1–4, 10–11, 14.
160. Ibid., Nr. 19.
161. Roberta Cimino, 'Angelberga: il monastero di San Sisto di Piacenza e il corso del piume Po', in *Il patrimonio delle regine: beni del fisco e politica regia fra IX e X secolo*, ed. Tiziana Lazzari, *Reti Medievali Rivista* 13, no. 2 (Firenze University Press, 2012): 141–42, 144, 146, 149, 150–54, 156, 158, doi: 10.6092/1593-2214/365); *DO I*, Nr. 141; Paolo Golinelli, *Adelaide. Regina Santa d'Europa*, Donna d'Oriente e d'Occidente (Milan: Jaca Book, 2001), 83.
162. *DD MT*, Ibid., Nrs 20, 25, 30–32, 36.
163. Ibid., Nrs 58, 59.
164. Ibid., Nr. 87; s.vv. 'Ildebrandus', 534; 'Pozeuli', 578.
165. The locations of those properties today are as follows: Corsena (Corsena), Cocila (Cocciglia), Cuculagium (Cocolaio), Munianum (Borgo a Mozzano), Bulianum (Buliano), Uilla (Monti di Villa), Granaiolum (Granaiola), Piscolle (Biscolle), Lulianum (Luliano), Munte Figatese (Montegegatesi), Galicanum (Gallicano), Mulazana (Molazzana), Col de Melo (Melo a Conio), Munte Altissimo (Monte Altissimo), Calumine (Calomini) and Saxi (Sassi). Ibid. Locations Index, 555–89.
166. Niermeyer, *Lexicon*, s.v. 'judex', 563.
167. Robinson, *Henry IV*, 5.
168. *DD MT*, Nrs 16, 52, 53, 55, 70.
169. See ibid., p. 32 and Nrs 55, 99, 100; 112, 113, and possibly 70.
170. Goez, *Reg. Bea.*, Nrs 23, 25; *DD MT*, p. 32; Goez, *Beatrix*, 111, 127.
171. *DD MT*, Nr. 55.
172. Ibid., Nr. 1, p. 32.
173. Ibid. Nr. 25.
174. Ibid., Nr. 32.
175. Robinson, *Henry IV*, 143–49, 246.
176. *Quellen zur geschichte Kaiser Heinrichs IV*, ed. Franz-Josef Schmale and Irene Schmale-Ott, 2nd ed., *AQDG* 12 (Darmstadt: Wissenschaftliche Buchgesellschaft, 1968), Appendix A, 474.15; Patrick Healy, '*Merito nominetur virago*: Matilda of Tuscany in the Polemics of the Investiture Contest', in *Studies on Medieval*

and *Early Modern Women 4: Victims or Viragos?*, ed. Christine Meek and Catherine Lawless (Dublin: Four Courts Press, 2005), 55n33.
177. Either 22 or 24 or 26 February, see: Robinson, *Henry IV*, 147; Vaughn, *St. Anselm*, 140; H. E. J. Cowdrey, *Pope Gregory VII, 1073–1085* (Oxford: Clarendon Press, 1998), 142 and H. E. J. Cowdrey, *The Register of Pope Gregory VII, 1073–1085: An English Translation* (Oxford: Oxford University Press, 2002), 211n27.
178. Jonathan Riley-Smith, *The First Crusaders, 1095–1131* (Cambridge: Cambridge University Press, 1997), 96.
179. *DD MT*, Nr. 19.
180. Gregory VII, *Registrum*, 3.10a.
181. Robinson, *Henry IV*, 163, 164.
182. Lampert, *Annales*, s.a. 1077; Robinson, *Henry IV*, 159–61; Timothy Reuter, 'Contextualising Canossa: Excommunication, Penance, Surrender, Reconciliation', in *Medieval Polities and Modern Mentalities*, ed. Janet Nelson (Cambridge: Cambridge University Press, 2006), 163–64.
183. *Chronica monasterii Casinensis: (Die Chronik von Montecassino)*, ed. H. Hoffmann, *MGH SS* 34 (1980), 2.91, p. 345; Robinson, *Henry IV*, 19, 26.
184. Robinson, *Henry IV*, 42–65.
185. Ibid., 63–104, especially 104; Stefan Weinfurter, *The Salian Century: Main Currents in an Age of Transition*, trans. Barbara M. Bowlus (Philadelphia: University of Pennsylvania Press, 1999), 137–42.
186. Robinson, *Henry IV*, 159–60.
187. Mathilde Uhlirz, *Jahrbücher des Deutschen Reiches unter Otto II. und Otto III. Otto III. 983–1002*, ed. Karl Uhlirz and Mathilde, 2 vols, vol. 2 (Leipzig and Berlin: Dunker and Humblot, 1954), 4.
188. Reuter, 'Contextualising', 147–66, especially 155.
189. Gregory VII, *Registrum*, 4.12a; 7.14a.
190. Adelaide of Turin and Susa, 'Women's Biography: Adelaide of Turin and Susa', in *MWLL*, http://epistolae.ccnmtl.columbia.edu/woman/105.html, date accessed 4 April 2016; Charles William Previté-Orton, *The Early History of the House of Savoy, (1000–1233)* (London: Cambridge University Press, 2011, reprinted in Nabu Public Domain Reprints, 2011), 212.

191. Robinson, *Henry IV*, 287.
192. Reuter, 'Peace-Breaking', 385.
193. Valerie Eads, 'The Last Italian Expedition of Henry IV: Rereading the *Vita Mathildis* of Donizone of Canossa', *JoMMH* 8, no. 2 (2010), 38.
194. Donizo, *VM*, 2.1, lines 91–93. For the complex relationship between Cluny and the papacy at that time, see Giles Constable, 'Cluny and the Investiture Controversy', in Constable, *The Abbey of Cluny*, 179–86.
195. Reuter, 'Contextualising', 161. Anselm II, also known as Anselm the Younger, should not be confused with his uncle Anselm, sometimes known as either Anselm (I) or Anselm the Older of Lucca (d. 1073), who became Pope Alexander II.
196. Paolo Golinelli, '"Non semel tantum sed pluribus vicibus": The Relations between Anselm of Canterbury and Mathilda of Tuscany', (paper read at the International Congress on 'Saint Anselm and His Legacy', Canterbury, 22–25 April, 2009), http://www.paologolinelli.it/1/saint_anselm_725953.html, date accessed 22 August 2016; Healy, *Hugh of Flavigny: Reform*, 104.
197. Skinner, *Women*, 137; Robert H. Rough, *The Reformist Illuminations in the Gospels of Matilda: Countess of Tuscany. (A Study in the Art of the Age of Gregory VII)* (Nijhoff, 1973), 14.
198. Cowdrey, *Pope Gregory VII*, 27–28; Constable, 'Cluny and the Investiture Controversy', 182.
199. Both Reuter and Robinson include Hugh of Cluny as mediator but Donizo is quite explicit that Hugh asked to withdraw. Donizo, *VM*, 2.1, lines 91–93; Reuter, 'Peace-Breaking', 384–5; Robinson, *Henry IV*, 161.
200. Donizo was at Canossa by 1086. He died after 1133. Hay, *Military Leadership*, 17; Niermeyer, *Index*, s.v. 'Donizo'.
201. *ODP*, s.v. 'Paschal II'.
202. I. S. Robinson, *Authority and Resistance in the Investiture Contest: The Polemical Literature of the Late Eleventh Century* (Manchester: Manchester University Press, 1978), 100 and 111n76. For Wibert's descent from Gerard, son of Matilda's great-great-grandfather Siegfried of Lucca, I am indebted to Alison Creber, pers. comm., 12 July 2013.
203. Robinson, *Henry IV*, 288, 368, 289–90.

204. Ibid., 300, 266, 336–7.
205. *DD MT*, Nrs 24; 44, 56, 69, 73, 87, 88, 92, 93, 95, 114, 119, 120, 126, 128, 132, 135.
206. Ibid., Nrs 58, 89, 132, A7, A10.
207. Ibid., s.v. 'Carpinetum', 560.
208. 'per manum Frugerii archipresbiteri et capellani', ibid., Nr. 93.
209. Niermeyer, *Lexicon*, s.v. 'capellanus'. For a discussion of Matilda's chancery see Roberto Ferrara, 'Gli anni di Matilde (1072–1115). Osservazioni sulla "cancelleria" canossiana', in *I poteri dei Canossa, da Reggio Emilia all'Europa: atti del convegno internazionale di studi (Reggio Emilia-Carpineti, 29–31 ottobre 1992)*, ed. Paolo Golinelli (Bologna: Pàtron, 1994), 89–98.
210. *DD MT*, Nrs 57, 63, 64, 65, 67, 69, 80, 83, 93, 94, 105.
211. Ibid., s.v. 'Frogerius–archipresbiter et capellanus, sacerdos, quondam Regini presulis egregii cappellanus', 528.
212. Ibid., Nr. 93, and s.vv. 'Adelbertus', 518; 'Albinus', 519; 'Dibertus', 527 (and possibly as Daibertus in Nr. †148); 'Guibertus–filius Gandulfi', 531; 'Paulus', 541; 'Stefanus', 547; 'Ugo', 550.
213. Ibid., Nrs 71, 92, 93, 99, 106, 114, 115, 138, Dep. 79, and s.v. 'Albericus–de Nonantula', 519.
214. Ibid., Nr. Dep. 79.
215. Ibid., Nr. 99.
216. Ibid., Nr. 138.
217. Ibid. s.vv. 'Boso', 'Bosolinus', and 'Guizolus', 525, 533.
218. Ibid. Nr. 55. For doubts about the authenticity of that document and consequently Matilda's adopton of Guido Guerra, see Paolo Golinelli, 'Sul preteso "figlio adottivo" di Matilde di Canossa, Guido V Guerra', in *Medioevo Reggiano. Studi in ricordo di Odoardo Rombaldi*, ed. Gino Badini and Andrea Gamberini (Milan: Franco Angeli, 2007), 123–32; Paolo Golinelli, 'Review of *Die Urkunden und Briefe der Markgräfin Mathilde von Tuszien*, by E. Goez et W. Goez', *CCM* 45, no. 177 (2002), 88–89.
219. *DD MT*, Nr. 100.
220. 'Paganus' is listed in the index in *DD MT*, Nrs 4, 20, 21, 93. The 'Paganus' in Nr. 93 (s.a. 1106) is unlikely to be Paganus of Corsena, identified explicitly in the index in Nrs 4 and 20 and by association in Nr. 21, because of the absence of the name of

Paganus of Corsena from Matilda's diplomata for many years and because his service, if it were he, would be exceptionally long.
221. Goez, *Beatrix*, 30.
222. Goez, *Reg. Bea.*, Nr. 25; Paolo Golinelli, 'Modena 1106: istantanee dal Medioevo', in *Romanica, Arte e liturgia nelle terre di San Geminiano e Matilde di Canossa*, ed. Adriano Peroni and Francesca Piccinini (Modena: Franco Cosimo Panini, 2006), 1–20.
223. Bernold, *Chronicon*, s.a. 1089; William M. Aird, *Robert Curthose: Duke of Normandy (c.1050–1134)* (Woodbridge: Boydell Press, 2008), 96, 191–93, 212.
224. Donizo, *VM*, 168n99; *Act. Pont. Cenom.*, 33.376; Richard E. Barton, *Lordship in the County of Maine, c.890–1160* (Woodbridge: Boydell, 2004), xiii.
225. Donizo, *VM*, 168n98; Hay, *Military Leadership*, 131–32.
226. Donizo, *VM*, 2.6, lines 586–87.
227. *DD MT*, Nr. 42. Niermeyer, *Lexicon*, s.v. 'curtis'. See eighteen separate meanings including 'manor', 'estate', 'fenced-in space containing the house and yard', 'royal residence', 'royal palace' 'the personnel of the king's court' and 'the king's treasury'. *Curtis* not only refers to a physical location but also to the king's personnel and the king's treasury.
228. Bernold, *Chronicon*, s.a. 1095.
229. For comments on eleventh-century pious widowhood, see John A. Dempsey, 'From Holy War to Patient Endurance: Henry IV, Matilda of Tuscany, and the Evolution of Bonizo of Sutri's Response to Heretical Princes', in *War and Peace: Critical Issues in European Societies and Literature 800–1800*, ed. Albrecht Classen and N. Margolis (Berlin/Boston: Walter de Gruyter, 2011), 237–38.
230. 'contra excommunicatos', Bernold, *Chronicon*, s.a. 1089.
231. Dempsey, 'Holy War', 237.
232. For analysis of the marriage, see Penelope Nash, 'Empress Adelheid and Countess Matilda Compared' (PhD diss., University of Sydney, 2014), 216–17; Bernold, *Chronicon*, s.aa. 1089, 1095.
233. *DD MT*, Nr. 55. For doubts about the authenticity of the Brescello document, see Golinelli, 'Review of *Die Urkunden*', 88–9.

234. William Heywood, *A History of Pisa: Eleventh and Twelfth Centuries* (Cambridge: Cambridge University Press, 1921, repr. 2010), 94; George W. Dameron, *Episcopal Power and Florentine Society, 1000–1320* (Cambridge, MA: Harvard University Press, 1991), 71.
235. *DD MT*, Nrs 55, 57, 76, 79, 92.
236. Ibid., Nrs †141, Dep. †67, Dep. 100.
237. Hay, *Military Leadership* 144–45, 220.
238. 'á [sic] Mahtilde persuasus – quem enim astucia feminea non subvertat aut decipiat? – iunctus inimicis patris.... Quod ubi ad hostes imperatoris currens fama pertulit, exultabant, plaudebant, cantabant, laudabant factum filii, praecipue feminam ducem facti', *Vita Heinrici IV. Imperatoris*, ed. W. Eberhard, *MGH SSrG* [58] (Hanover and Leipzig: 1899), 7, s.a. 1093, trans. T. E. Mommsen and K. F. Morrison, *Imperial Lives and Letters of the Eleventh Century* (New York: Columbia University Press, 1962), 118–19; Tilman Struve, 'Matilde di Toscana – Canossa ed Enrico IV', in *I poteri dei Canossa, da Reggio Emilia all'Europa: atti del convegno internazionale di studi (Reggio Emilia-Carpineti, 29–31 ottobre 1992)*, ed. Paolo Golinelli (Bologna: Pàtron, 1994), 449.
239. Skinner, *Women*, 140.
240. Donizo, *VM*, 2.11, lines 849–50.
241. Ronald G. Witt, *The Two Latin Cultures and the Foundation of Renaissance Humanism in Medieval Italy* (New York: Cambridge University Press, 2012), 292.
242. I. S. Robinson, 'The Friendship Circle of Bernold of Constance and the Dissemination of Gregorian Ideas in Late Eleventh-Century Germany', in *Friendship in Medieval Europe*, ed. Julian Haseldine (Stroud, UK: Sutton, 1999), 185–98; Mario Nobili, 'La cultura politica alla corte di Mathilde di Canossa', in *Le sedi della cultura nell'Emilia romagna. L'alto-medioevo*, ed. Ovidio Capitani (Milan: Silvana, 1983), 217–36; Giuseppe Vecchi, 'Temi e momenti di scuola nella "*Vita Mathildis*" di Donizone', in *SM* I, 210–17.
243. 'virilis animi', Hugh of Flavigny, *Chronicon Hugonis monachi Virdunensis et Divionensis Abbatis Flaviniacensis*, ed. G. H. Pertz, *MGH SS* 8:280–502 (1848), s.a. 1084, 2.462, line 12; 'tanto virilius … subvenire' ('to assist … with so much more manly vigor'); 'viriliter contendit' ('hastened with manly vigor'); 'virili-

ter fugavit' ('she drove out with manly vigor'), Bernold, *Chronicon*, s.aa. 1089, 1090, 1097. For further discussion of 'viriliter' and derivatives as applied to Matilda, see Chap. 4.

244. Anke Holdenried, *The Sibyl and her Scribes: Manuscripts and Interpretation of the Latin Sibylla Tiburtina c. 1050–1500* (Aldershot: Ashgate, 2006), 5; John France, 'Holy War and Holy Men: Erdmann and the Lives of the Saints', in *The Experience of Crusading, Volume 1: Western Approaches*, ed. Marcus Graham Bull and Norman Housley (Cambridge: Cambridge University Press, 2003), 193–208.

245. Frederick of Mömpelgard (d. 1091) was a son of Matilda's maternal aunt, Sophie. Mömpelgard, currently known as Montbéliard, lies within the Doubs department of France: Dr. Michael Nelson, pers. comm., 7 September 2012. See also Robinson, *Authority*, 101–2; Previté-Orton, *Early History*, 244; Donizo, *VM*, 125n7.

246. Paul of Bernried, *Vita Gregorii VII papae*, ed. J. B. M. Watterich, in *Pontificum Romanorum vitae* 1:474–545 (Aalen: Scientia Verlag, 1966); Deusdedit, *Libellus contra invasores et symoniacos et reliquos schismaticos*, ed. E. Sackur, *MGH Ldl* II: 292–365 (1892); Deusdedit, *Collectio canonum. Die Kanonessammlung des Kardinals Deusdedit*, ed. Victor Wolf von Glanvell, vol. 1 (Aalen: Scientia, 1967); Manegold of Lautenbach, *Liber ad Gebehardum*, ed. K. Francke, *MGH Ldl* I: 308–430. See also Alex Novikoff, 'Licit and Illicit in the Rhetoric of the Investiture Conflict', in *Law and the Illicit in Medieval Europe*, ed. Ruth Mazo Karras, Joel Kaye and E. Ann Matter (Philadelphia: University of Pennsylvania Press, 2008), 186.

247. Rangerius of Lucca, *Vita metrica sancti Anselmi Lucensis episcopi*, ed. E. Sackur, G. Schwartz and B. Schmeidler, *MGH SS* 30/2:1152–1307 (1929); Niermeyer, *Index*, s.v. 'Rangerius episcopus Lucensis'.

248. Pseudo-Bardo, *Vita Anselmi episcopi Lucensis*, ed. R. Wilmans, *MGH SS* 12:13–35 (1856); Niermeyer, *Index*, s.v. 'Vita et miracula Anselmi episc. Lucensis'.

249. Pseudo-Bardo, *Anselmi episcopi Lucensis vitae primariae fragmenta*, ed. W. Arndt, *MGH SS* 20:692–96 (1868).

250. Anselm of Lucca, *Liber contra Wibertum*, ed. E. Bernheim, *MGH Ldl* I:517–28.

251. Anselm of Lucca, *Collectio canonum una cum collectione minore*, ed. F. Thaner (Aalen: Scientia, 1915, rev. 1965).
252. Cowdrey, *Pope Gregory VII*, 303–6; H. E. J. Cowdrey, 'Christianity and the Morality of Warfare during the First Century of Crusading', in Bull, *Experience of Crusading*, 179–87.
253. John of Mantua, *Iohannis Mantuani in Cantica canticorum et de sancta Maria Tractatus ad Comitissam Matildam*, ed. B. Bischoff and B. Taeger, Spicilegium Friburgense 19 (Freiburg: Universitätsverlag, 1973), p. 52; Healy, '*Merito nominetur virago*', 51–52; I. S. Robinson, 'Gregory VII and the Soldiers of Christ', *History* 58, no. 193 (1973), 184–86.
254. *DD MT*, Nrs Dep. 44; Dep. 45.
255. John of Mantua, *Cantica*, pp. 25, 156.
256. I. S. Robinson, *The Papal Reform of the Eleventh Century: Lives of Pope Leo IX and Pope Gregory VII* (Manchester: Manchester University Press, 2004), 42.
257. Bonizo of Sutri, *Liber ad amicum*, ed. E. Dümmler, *MGH Ldl* I:568–620
258. Bonizo of Sutri, *Liber de vita Christiana*, ed. E. Perels (Berlin: Weidman, 1930); Dempsey, 'Holy War', 217–52.
259. Niermeyer, *Index*, s.v. 'Bonizo episcopus Sutrinensis'; Hay, *Military Leadership*, 220; Robinson, 'Gregory VII and Soldiers', 189–90.
260. Hay, *Military Leadership*, 210; Robinson, *Papal Reform*, 43–44.
261. 'Quid est, quod hac tempestate mater ęcclesia in terris posita gemens clamat ad Deum nec exauditur ad votum, premitur nec liberator; filiique obedientie et pacis iacent postrati, filii autem Belial exultant cum rege suo; presertim cum qui dispensat omnia ipse sit qui iudicat ęquitatem' and 'Si licuit vel licet christiano pro dogmate armis decertare', Bonizo of Sutri, *Liber ad amicum*, 1, p. 571, trans. I. S. Robinson, *Book to a Friend*, in Robinson, *The Papal Reform of the Eleventh Century*, 158. The children of Belial abandoned the true God and led others from their city to serve other (false) gods, Deuteronomy 13:13.
262. Bonizo of Sutri, *Liber ad amicum*, 6.599, 7.602, 7.605, 7.606, 8.609, 8.610, 9.612, 9.613, 9.620.
263. 'Emulenter [gloriossissimi Dei milites] in bonum excellentissimam comitissam Matildam, filiam beati Petri, que virile animo, omnibus mundanis rebus posthabitis, mori parata est potius quam

legem Dei infringere et contra heresim, que nunc sevit in ecclesia, prout vires suppetunt, omnibus modis impugnare, ibid., 8.620.
264. Hay, *Military Leadership*, 210.
265. David J. Hay, 'The Campaigns of Countess Matilda of Canossa (1046–1115): An Analysis of the History and Social Significance of a Woman's Military Leadership' (PhD diss., University of Toronto, 2000), 134.
266. Bernold, *Chronicon*, s.a. 1089.
267. Gregory VII, *Registrum*, 1.50
268. Ibid., 1.50.
269. Ibid., 1.11.
270. Giles Constable, *Three Studies in Medieval Religious and Social Thought* (Cambridge: Cambridge University Press, 1995), 44–92.
271. I Cor. 13:13.
272. Gregory VII, *Registrum*, 1.5.
273. Matilda's estranged husband, Godfrey the Hunchback, was killed in February 1076: Cowdrey, *Register*, p. 211n27.
274. Gregory VII, *Registrum*, 4.2.
275. Southern, *Western Society*, 216.
276. Gregory VII, *Registrum*, 1.47.
277. Ibid., 1.47; 1.50; 2.9; 2.30; 3.5; 3.8; 4.12; 6.12; 6.18; 6.22; 9.3; 9.11.
278. Elizabeth Saxon, 'Carolingian, Ottonian and Romanesque Art and the Eucharist', in *A Companion to the Eucharist in the Middle Ages*, ed. Ian Christopher Levy, Gary Macy and Kristen Van Ausdall (Leiden and Boston: Brill, 2012), 279–80.
279. Adam S. Cohen, *The Uta Codex: Art, Philosophy, and Reform in Eleventh-Century Germany* (University Park: Pennnsylvania State University Press, 2000), 46–49, 185–90; Mary Clayton, *The Cult of the Virgin Mary in Anglo-Saxon England* (Cambridge: Cambridge University Press, 1990); Stephen J. Shoemaker, 'Mary at the Cross, East and West: Maternal Compassion and Affective Piety in the Earliest *Life of the Virgin* and the High Middle Ages', *JTS* 62, no. 2 (2011), 570–606.
280. 'quia, quanto altior et melior ac sanctior est omni matre, tanto clementior et dulcior circa conversos peccatores et peccatrices' and 'promptiorem carnali matre ac mitiorem in tui dilectione', Gregory VII, *Registrum*, 1.47.

281. Lampert, *Annales*, s.a. 1077; *Liber de unitate ecclesiae conservanda*, ed. W. Schwenkenbecher, *MGH Ldl* II: 173–291 (1892), 2.36, lines 15–18; Cowdrey, *Pope Gregory VII*, 300–301.
282. Anselm of Canterbury, *Sancti Anselmi Cantuariensis archiepiscopi opera omnia*, ed. Franciscus Salesius Schmitt, 6 vols (Edinburgh: Thomas Nelson, 1946–63), vol. 5, ep. 325, trans. Walter Fröhlich, *The Letters of Saint Anselm of Canterbury*, 3 vols (Kalamazoo: Cistercian Publications, 1990, 1993, 1994), vol. 3, 38–41, at 39.
283. Benedicta Ward, *The Prayers and Meditations of St. Anselm*, Penguin Classics (Harmondsworth: Penguin, 1973).
284. Anselm of Canterbury, *Sancti Anselmi opera omnia*, 3.4, trans. Joan Ferrante, 'Anselm of Canterbury to Matilda of Tuscany, Prologue to the Prayers', http://epistolae.ccnmtl.columbia.edu/letter/236.html, date accessed 16 May 2016; Mary Agnes Edsall, 'Learning from the Exemplar: Anselm's *Prayers and Meditations* and the Charismatic Text', *Mediaeval Studies* 72 (2010), 161–96.
285. Anselm of Canterbury, *Sancti Anselmi opera omnia*, 3.4; Rachel Fulton, 'Praying with Anselm at Admont: A Meditation on Practice', *Speculum* 81, no. 3 (2006), 718–22.
286. Orationes sive meditationes (Admont: Stiftsbibliothek, MS 289); Alison I. Beach, *Women as Scribes: Book Production and Monastic Reform in Twelfth-Century Bavaria* (Cambridge: Cambridge University Press, 2004), 83.
287. Otto Pächt, 'The Illustrations of St. Anselm's Prayers and Meditations', *Journal of the Warburg and Courtauld Institutes* 19, no. 1/2 (1956), 71 and plates 16a and 17a; 80–82.
288. *DD MT*, Nr. 84, trans. Fröhlich, *Letters*, vol. 3, Letter 350.
289. See letters between Henry, Paschal and Anselm: Fröhlich, *Letters*, Letters, 318, 319, 338, 348, 351; Sally N. Vaughn, *Anselm of Bec and Robert of Meulan: The Innocence of the Dove and the Wisdom of the Serpent* (Berkeley: University of California Press, 1987), 272–92.
290. *DD MT*, Nr. 84.
291. Fröhlich, *Letters*, vol. 3, Letters 351, 352.
292. Edsall, 'Learning', 165–6.
293. Gregory VII, *Registrum*, 1.11.

294. Donizo, *VM*, 2.2, lines 281–90; Kathleen G. Cushing, 'Events that Led to Sainthood: Sanctity and the Reformers in the Eleventh Century', in *Belief and Culture in the Middle Ages: Studies Presented to Henry Mayr-Harting*, ed. Richard Gameson and Henrietta Leyser (Oxford: Oxford University Press, 2001), 193–96.
295. Donizo, *VM*, 2.14, lines 944–70.
296. Reinhold Schumann, *Authority and the Commune, Parma, 833–1133*, Fonti e studi 2nd ser. 8 (Parma: Deputazione di storia patria per le province parmensi, 1973), 322–23.
297. *DD MT*, Nrs 8, 14.
298. Ibid., Nrs 20, 21.
299. Ibid., Nr. A4.
300. Ibid., Nr. A5.
301. Ibid., Nr. Dep. 41; Nr. A11.
302. Ibid., Nr. 59.
303. Ibid., Nr. Dep. 48. For the connections among Matilda, Anselm of Lucca and Hugh of Lyons, see Edsall, 'Learning', 166–68. For the friendship between the two clergymen see, for example, Hugh's invitation to Anselm to stay with him at Lyons in 1103, and Anselm's reply, in Fröhlich, *Letters*, vol. 2, Letters 260, 261.
304. *DD MT*, Nrs †145, Dep. 87.
305. André Wilmart, 'Cinque textes de prière composés par Anselme de Lucques pour la comtesse Mathilde', *Revue d'ascétique et de mystique* 19 (1938, reedited 1964), 49–72.
306. Rachel Fulton, *From Judgment to Passion: Devotion to Christ and the Virgin Mary, 800–1200* (New York: Columbia University Press, 2002), 225–28; Silvia Cantelli, 'Le preghiere a Maria di Anselmo da Lucca', in *Sant'Anselmo, Mantova e la lotta per le Investiture. Atti del convegno internationale di studi (Mantova, 23–24–25 Maggio, 1986)*, ed. Paolo Golinelli (Bologna: Pàtron, 1987), 291–99; Brian K. Reynolds, *Gateway to Heaven: Marian Doctrine and Devotion Image and Typology in the Patristic and Medieval Periods. Volume 1. Doctrine and Devotion* (New York: New City Press, 2012), 208–9, 270; Kathleen G. Cushing, *Papacy and Law in the Gregorian Revolution: The Canonistic Work of Anselm of Lucca* (Oxford: Clarendon Press, 1998), 4.
307. Pseudo-Bardo, *Vita Anselmi episcopi Lucensis*, ch. 69, p. 32.

308. L. A. Muratori, *Delle antichità estensi ed italiane*, vol. 1 (Modena: 1717), 23–24; Eads, 'Last Expedition', 38.
309. Luigi Simeoni, 'La Vita Mathildis di Donizone et il suo valore storicho-critiche', *Atti e memorie della Deputazione di storia patria per le antiche provincie modenesi* 7, no. 4 (1927), 19–21.
310. Luigi Simeoni, 'Il contributo della contessa Matilde al Papato nella lotta per le investiture', *SG* 1 (1947),368.
311. Eads, 'Last Expedition', 57–58.
312. Simeoni, 'Vita Mathildis di Donizone', 20.
313. Guastalla was located approximately twenty-five kilometers south-southwest of Mantua. *DD MT*, s.v. 'Guarstalla', 568; Uta-Renate Blumenthal, *The Early Councils of Pope Paschal II, 1100–1110* (Toronto: Pontifical Institute of Mediaeval Studies, 1978), 38–42.
314. Donizo, *VM*, 2.17, line 1110. For a brief history of Matilda's involvement with the wayward nuns there and her replacement of them by reformed nuns from Clermont-Ferrand, see Dorothy F. Glass, 'The Bishops of Piacenza', in *The Bishop Reformed: Studies of Episcopal Power and Culture in the Central Middle Ages*, ed. J. S. Ott and A. T. Jones (Aldershot: Ashgate, 2007), 225.
315. St Geminianus was a fourth-century deacon, who became bishop of Modena. The sculptures on the southern side of the cathedral show him expelling a demon from the daughter of Emperor Jovianus and being rewarded by the emperor with gifts: Dorothy F. Glass, *The Sculpture of Reform in North Italy, ca. 1095–1130: History and Patronage of Romanesque Façades* (Farnham, England: Ashgate, 2010), 124; 184, 186–87, and Figs 4.19, 4.20.
316. Simeoni, 'Contributo', 367.
317. Golinelli, 'Modena 1106', 3–5; Giuseppe Russo, 'Modena nel 1106', in *SM I*, 130–32.
318. Relatio translationis corporis sancti Geminiani (Modena: Archivio capitolare, Cod. O.II), fols 10r; and printed copy in *Relatio translationis corporis sancti Geminiani*, ed. G. Bertoni, *RIS2* VI/1 (Bologna: 1907).
319. Glass, *Sculpture*, 139, 142. Golinelli, 'Modena 1106', 3–5; Christine B. Verzar, 'Picturing Matilda of Canossa: Medieval Strategies of Representation', in *Representing History, 900–1300:*

Art, Music, History, ed. Robert A. Maxwell (University Park: Pennsylvania State University Press, 2010), 80–81.
320. *Epistolae diversorum ad S. Hugonem*, *PL* 159:931–946, cols 932C–D; L. M. Smith, 'Cluny and Gregory VII', *EHR* 26, no. 101 (1911), 29.
321. H. E. J. Cowdrey, *The Cluniacs and the Gregorian Reform* (Oxford: Clarendon, 1970), 160.
322. Berthold of Reichenau, *Chronicon: Die Chroniken Bertholds von Reichenau und Bernolds von Konstanz, 1054–1100*, ed. I. S. Robinson, *MGH SSrG* n.s. 14:161–381 (Hanover: 2003), s.a. 1077, 258; Gregory VII, *Registrum*, 4.12, 5.7; Cowdrey, *Cluniacs*, 160–61; Jacques Le Goff, 'The Symbolic Ritual of Vassalage', in *Time, Work and Culture in the Middle Ages*, ed. Jacques Le Goff (Chicago: University of Chicago Press, 1980), 237–87, esp. 256.
323. Donizo, *VM*, 2.1, lines 91–93.
324. Paolo Golinelli, 'Donizone e il suo poema per Matilde', in *Vita di Matilde di Canossa*, ed. Paolo Golinelli (Milan: Jaca Book, 2008), 12.
325. *DD MT*, Nr. Dep. 48.
326. The letter opens: 'Hugo sanctae Lugdunensis aecclesiae servus, dilectissimae in Christo sorori Mathildi divinae consolationis uberrimam gratiam', Hugh of Flavigny, *Chronicon*, 2.466–68, trans. Joan Ferrante, 'Hugh, bishop of Die, archbishop of Lyon, to Matilda of Tuscany', in *MWLL*, http://epistolae.ccnmtl.columbia.edu/letter/231.html, date accessed 15 May 2016. (Note that at the date of viewing, the reference to Hugh of Flavigny's *Chronicon* should be 466–68, not 462–63.)
327. D'Achery, *Spicilegium sive collectio veterum aliquot scriptorum qui in Galliae bibliothecis delituerant*, vol. III (Paris: 1723), 426–27; Smith, 'Cluny', 32; Joseph H. Lynch, 'Hugh I of Cluny's Sponsorship of Henry IV: Its Context and Consequences', *Speculum* 60, no. 4 (1985), 824; Cowdrey, *Cluniacs*, 176n1.
328. H. E. J. Cowdrey, *The Age of Abbot Desiderius: Montecassino, the Papacy, and the Normans in the Eleventh and Early Twelfth Centuries* (Oxford: Clarendon Press, 1983), 261.
329. *ODP*, s.v. 'Victor III', Monika Gude, 'Die *fideles sancti Petri* im Streit um die Nachfolge Papst Gregors VII', *FMSt* 27 (1993), 290–316.

330. Cowdrey, *Desiderius*, 207.
331. Ibid., 186.
332. Cowdrey, *Cluniacs*, 147.
333. Gregory VII, *Registrum*, 4.16; Healy, *Hugh of Flavigny: Reform*, 21, 81.
334. Gregory VII, *Registrum*, 1.69; 2.43; 2.59.
335. Simeoni, 'Contributo', 360.
336. Goez, *Reg. Bea.*, Nr. 11c; Goez, *Beatrix*, 24; Robinson, *Henry IV*, 32.
337. H. E. J. Cowdrey, 'Review of *Die Urkunden und Briefe der Markgräfin Mathilde von Tuszien*, by Elke Goez and Werner Goez', *JEH* 51, no. 3 (2000), 604; Giovanni Tabacco, 'Northern and Central Italy in the Eleventh Century', *NCMH* 4, Part 2 (2004), 88; Golinelli, 'Sul preteso "figlio adottivo"' 123–32.

CHAPTER 3

Land: Building and Maintaining a Property Portfolio

A commonly held paradigm about social changes that occurred between the tenth and eleventh centuries is that inheritance shifted to 'primogeniture in the male line', land began to pass 'normally from father to eldest son in each generation' and marriage became 'an indissoluble personal union, blessed by the church ... whose essential function was to ensure dynastic survival'. In particular, 'women were brought more closely into subjection by diminishing the proportion both of their father's land which it was customary to offer as dowry, and of their husband's as marriage-portion, and by transferring its management, which women had hitherto been accustomed to exercise independently, to the husbands.'[1] The consequence of this proposed paradigm was that women's power through land ownership and inheritance started to decline.

R. I. Moore's forceful assessment of the changes in the eleventh century is supported by scholars and well illustrated by case studies. In the less regulated, chaotic early Middle Ages, wills, chronicles and annals record women inheriting, retaining and transferring land ownership, primarily based on personal relationships. Because 'land was a crucial resource, one of the principal bases of all status, wealth, and power',[2] women's importance and social prominence in the management of family property empowered them. Nevertheless in the field of land management women did not act in isolation. The church looms large in the source material and kin exerted extraordinary pressure on women, although the sources assert the rights and alleged empowerment of early medieval women in reference to property.[3]

Wives, Widows and Land

Throughout all levels of society, a prospective wife or her family might give a dowry to her husband: the wife would equally expect a gift from the husband. From late Roman times the gift from the husband to the wife was the norm (and the major payment), although gifts both ways were named *dos* in the Latin documents. Clear distinctions can be made in English by calling the gift from the wife to the husband the dowry and that from the husband to the wife the reverse dowry. As originally conceived the reverse dowry was given to the wife as usufruct (right of temporary possession): she was able to leave it to her children or, if property, alienate it as she wished. During the late tenth and eleventh centuries the reverse dowry transformed into the dower that was more restrictive: less frequently was the wife given outright ownership and the husband was jointly responsible for the usufruct with his wife, rather than the wife having responsibility alone. Instead of a given piece of property the wife became entitled to a proportion of the income from the husband. In the twelfth century the dower gave the wife usufruct only of a portion of her husband's patrimony, of value on his decease but eliminating her financial independence during his life and restricting it after his death. An additional gift to the bride from her husband after the consummation of their marriage, the *Morgengabe*, could be inherited by the bride's surviving heirs (later the practice of giving the *Morgengabe* faded away).[4] The reverse dowry in Ottonian and Salian Germany reverted to her husband or his heirs, as we shall see. In general inheritance for women in the early Middle Ages was better than in the later Middle Ages. Such distinctions become important in discussing the first woman under review in this book, Empress Adelheid, and her ability to manage her lands in Germany.

Widows above all were subject to predation for their possessions. In the Carolingian period of the early ninth century, when a Frankish noblewoman acquired property by gifts at marriage, inheritance and her endowment in widowhood, she might only have usufruct during her life, be overruled in her donations to the church by her sons and on remarriage lose her reverse dowry to her second husband.[5] Dowagers' lands owned by aristocratic women were especially subject to theft. The ability of even a queen to retain her possessions was still atypical in Carolingian times. Unusually Ermentrude, queen of the Franks in the early ninth century, had the gift of her reverse dowry to the abbey of Corbie (or at least part of her dowry) confirmed by her husband.[6] However, in the late ninth century, Richgard, widow of King Charles the Fat, lost her lands that she had inherited when Charles's successor took over as proprietor of the convent of SS Felix and Regula in Zurich. Those lands, formally attached to the convent, were no longer available to her.[7] Similarly in the eleventh century, Edward, stepson of Queen Emma of England, deprived her of her land and treasures.[8]

Nevertheless Italy was a special case. Even before the late sixth century, kingship could be transmitted through the royal dowagers and consequently there existed a greater opportunity for such dowagers to retain their property. The queen had a special role as 'bearer and transmitter of royalty'.[9] The transfer of rulership was repeated through a number of royal Italian women. In following that historical tradition Adelheid, as royal consort, had title to power in Italy through her first marriage to Lothar, king of Italy, further enhanced by her Carolingian descent from King Pippin of Italy (through her father) and from Judith, the second wife of Louis the Pious (through her mother). The struggle for the kingdom of Italy was played out in a number of contemporary chronicles. On her first widowhood Berengar II wanted his son to marry Adelheid and Otto I wanted to marry her himself. Hrotsvitha records Adelheid's escape from imprisonment by Berengar II to Otto I at Pavia, the ancient Lombard capital (discussed in more detail in Chap. 1 of this book).[10] Consequently by the middle of the tenth century in Italy women continued to be acknowledged as legitimizers of royalty just as male heirs to the throne were recognized by prowess on the battlefield.[11]

Italy, as well as privileging female carriage of rulership, also favored female ownership of lands. Lombard Law allowed daughters to inherit one-third of their father's property if there were no sons.[12] Adelheid brought her Italian land inheritance to the Saxon kingdom. The Saxon royal women of the late tenth century were favored by particular longevity and special freedoms that allowed them to exercise great power.[13] Nevertheless the Saxon dowagers were not immune from harassment. After the death of Henry I, king of the East Franks, the leading men demanded money from his widow, Queen Mathilda, and by much persecution succeeded in driving her into a monastery. Contemporary authors report a similar reason for Queen Mathilda's later estrangement from her sons Otto I and Duke Henry I of Bavaria. They forced her to give up her dotal lands.[14] My brief history of women's ability to obtain landed property by a number of means—including inheritance, marriage and other gifts—shows the limitations with which even privileged women had to contend in order to retain their property.

Empress Adelheid

Adelheid inherited extensive property from all members of her first and second families. On 12 December 937 her then future father-in-law, King Hugh of Italy (originally Hugh of Arles), gave his daughter-in-law-to-be, Adelheid, extensive possessions in northern Italy and around Lake Como, [15] including 4580 manses as well as gifts of property approximately along and around the Via Emilia and south of the Apennines.[16] Adelheid's new property southeast of Pavia stretched as far as the Lambro River and southwest as far as the rivers Bormida and Orba. Other lands were located around Reggio Emilia, Modena and Bologna, and in the county Cornio near Populonia around the cities Empoli, Pisa, Lucca, Pistoia, Luni, Siena and Chiusi. In 947 her new husband, King Lothar, gifted lands in Corana, Cantone and Rivasioli to her.[17] Hugh died in about 948. In 950 on the death of Adelheid's first husband, King Lothar, son of the now deceased King Hugh, Adelheid inherited King Lothar's paternal estates.[18] She took these lands with her to Otto I at their wedding in 951. In 966 Adelheid inherited her mother's estates, which included former gifts of 1160 manses from Kings Hugh and Lothar on 12 December 937[19] as well as Erstein, which Otto I had given to Bertha in 953.[20] Adelheid's widow's portion on Otto I's death in 973 consisted of considerable lands in Alsace, Thuringia, Saxony and Slavonia.[21] As either reverse dowry or additional gifts, Adelheid received five royal estates, including Selz. The other four estates were Hochfelden, Sermersheim, Schweighausen and Morschweiler. Morschweiler is perhaps Merzweiler. After all those gifts and inheritance are totaled up, Adelheid possessed property of 21 royal estates, four abbeys and 6640 manses. As a comparison, the Bishop of Bamberg received 150 manses as compensation to give up his establishment at Bamberg, and Meinwerk of Paderborn's donation of 1100 manses to his church could house a whole diocese.[22]

By late 982 Adelheid controlled more of the crown land of the Lombard kings in northern Italy than did her son, the emperor.[23] On Otto II's unexpected death in late 983, a flurry over the management of the realm ensued. When Adelheid, her daughter-in-law, Theophanu, and her daughter, Mathilda, Abbess of Quedlinburg, had finally and firmly taken the reins as regents for the three-year-old Otto III, the imperial diplomata appeared in his name. With Otto III still under-age, the three women, not the young king, issued those diplomata (the legal written instruments of government), albeit with the necessary concurrence of the royal chancellery and the magnates, including the leading churchmen. The events surrounding this regency are examined further in Chap. 4 on Adelheid's rulership.

In 987 Adelheid's grandson, the child Otto III, still king in name only, reconfirmed Adelheid's lands with the concurrence of Theophanu and the support of the German chancellery. The terms of ownership and rights of donation, sale and exchange used the same form of words in both the diploma of 973 and in the earlier diploma from the Italian chancellery of 937 for her betrothal.[24] Thus the crown publicly affirmed ownership under the same terms. In 991, on the death of Theophanu, Adelheid, now in her sixties, was invited to continue as regent for Otto III, who was still under-age. By late 994 Otto was legally able to take over the empire in his own right,[25] yet Adelheid's influence continued at court, as shown by her appearance on several diplomata as successful intercessor, enabling and facilitating grants of gifts to abbeys, monasteries and convents[26]—a mark of the new emperor's high regard for his grandmother and a demonstration of her ability to share in power in the imperium. Only when she finally retired to the Abbey of Selz did her influence at court wane.

Despite the various diplomata confirming Adelheid's possessions and her right to allocate them to others as she wished, as a dowager herself, her lands were automatically in peril and she was not immune from attack. Syrus noted in his *Life* of Maiolus of Cluny that after her husband's death, the enemies at court accused Adelheid of attempting to '"squander" the kingdom and drive the king [her son Otto II] from power'.[27] Odilo of Cluny, too, attributes Adelheid's breach with her son to 'evil men who only sought to sow discord between them',[28] while Thietmar, bishop of Merseburg, blames the 'advice of impudent young men' for an early rupture with Otto III.[29]

Two factors contributing to such disputes appear to have been at work, especially in Germany. One was a special concern over the imperial rights to land. Although Adelheid's widow's portion from Otto I had been given to her with the same terms as the Italian gifts from her first husband and her former father-in-law, there does not seem to have been the same agreement in the German chancellery as in the Italian one. Susan Reynolds has distinguished between the property of the kingdom and that of the royal family in Germany.[30] Mathilde Uhlirz has argued that a difference existed between the Italian and the German courts in how they viewed the possessions of the dowagers. The German court had a concern about allowing the lands to slip from imperial control. The exercise of law was still dominated by the idea that in the case of a gift from the imperial possessions, the right of transfer could only be given to a restricted extent. The possessions given, tied to the person receiving them, were therefore not transferable and also not hereditary, except in a narrow sense. The power of the German king relied primarily on the extent of the imperial possessions, which was endangered if the widow's portion was disposed of without restriction.[31]

An example of the intense feelings generated in Germany about imperial right to lands appears in the case of Hadwig, the childless widow of Burchard of Swabia (d. 973). Visiting Alemannia in 994, Otto III showed haste to uphold his hereditary right.[32] He changed the legal position of the Abbey of Waldkirch from a private possession belonging to the founder's family (that is Hadwig's property) to an imperial monastery.[33] His deed recalls Richgard's situation in Alsace in the late ninth century, discussed earlier in this chapter. To uphold his action Otto, consciously or unconsciously, drew on the tradition of the German *Morgengabe* with its reversionary rights to the male heirs. The second factor causing dissension about land ownership in Germany was confusion between the meaning of the reverse dowry and the *Morgengabe*. Discord about Adelheid's lands was likely to hark back to the conflation of the meaning of the terms and consequently confusion over the difference in inheritance rights between those two gifts. In Germany the 'disputes over *dos* arose from persisting uncertainties over reversionary rights.'[34] Empress Agnes and Countess Matilda of Tuscany experienced similar difficulties with their property in the latter half of the eleventh century, the complications of which are explored later in this chapter.

Erstein, Burgundy and Selz

Otto I had shown little interest in Alsace, which lay at the edge of his kingdom, until Adelheid brought Erstein and other locations in Alsace to his attention. In 951 Otto gave considerable lands that mainly lay in the north of Alsace to his bride as her widow's portion.[35] In 953 he gifted the abbey of Erstein, closely associated with the royal palace there, to his new mother-in-law, Bertha, and in 959 transferred property in Alsace to his wife's brother, Rudolf, who was made Duke of Alsace.[36] Otto II celebrated Christmas there in 975 and Otto III did the same in 994 with Adelheid and her granddaughter Sophie, and probably with Adelheid's daughter, Abbess Mathilda of Quedlinburg.[37] Alsace became a key center of imperial governance for the Ottonians and the later Hohenstaufen empire.[38] From the middle of the tenth century, Alsace became the main link between the East-Frankish kingdom and Burgundy, and toward the south to the passes into Italy (see Map 3.1).

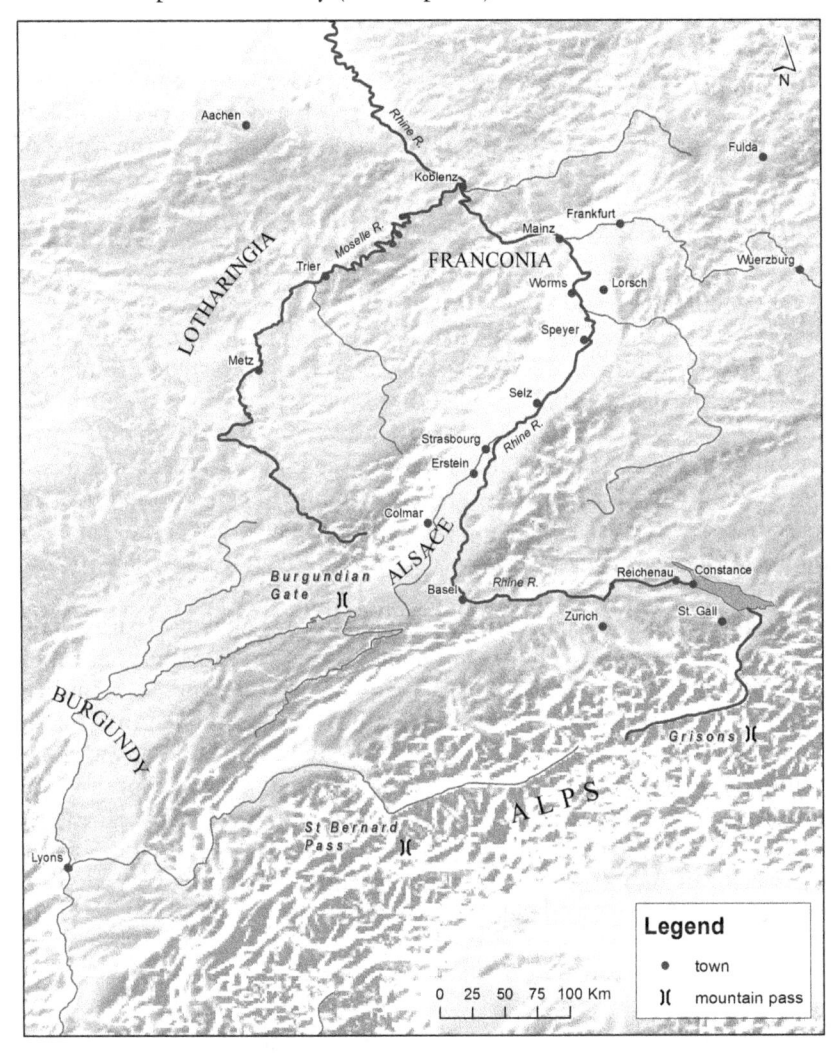

Map 3.1 Old and New Routes between the East-Frankish Kingdom and Italy (Map specified by Penelope Nash. Map prepared by Koolena Mapping)

The Ottonians replaced the Moselle 'Route' with the Rhine 'Route', to the financial and political benefit of the upper Rhine. Instead of traversing the Alps through the Burgundian Gate and the St Bernard Pass, travelers took the Rhine to Basel and then continued their passage through either the Grisons or the St Bernard Pass. Two hundred years later the chronicler Otto of Freising considered the country between Basel to Mainz to be the stronghold of the kingdom.[39]

A second location of significance in Alsace was Selz. Adelheid founded a monastery for men in 991 on land Otto I had given her in 968.[40] Diplomata issued in favor of the Benedictine monastery, in the name of Otto III, but in reality under Adelheid's rule as regent, granted the community royal protection, immunity, the right to elect its own abbot[41] and to hold a market and mint coins.[42] The lucrative grants 'built up the fortress' ('urbem ... edificans').[43] The monastery received great donations of 'estates, buildings, gold and jewels, precious vestments, and other trappings'.[44] Selz fulfilled both a spiritual and a military function. At Christmas 994 Otto III, having only recently reached his majority, issued rich gifts to Selz.[45] Adelheid secured the protection of the pope for Selz and Otto III attended the abbey's consecration on 18 November 996.[46] Significantly, several of the diplomata about Selz were issued after Theophanu's death and before Otto III reached his majority.[47] Consequently it was Adelheid herself as regent (despite the diplomata being issued under the name of the male ruler) who had the power to and did issue those grants of her own land to the monastery.

Burgundy and Alsace were two regions that Adelheid particularly favored, one because of the strong family connections in Burgundy and the other because of her ongoing interest in Erstein and Selz, and in Alsace in general. Adelheid's influence is not usually coupled in modern scholarship with the developments in Burgundy and Erstein. However, by uniting two favorite destinations, she changed the imperial route for the emperors' journeys to and from Italy so that it now ran through Alsace and the Burgundian Gate. The new route significantly increased the status and wealth of Alsace while continuing to enhance Burgundy's prospects through association and trade.[48]

***

Adelheid followed the pattern of early medieval elite women in that she had the opportunity to acquire land and other possessions. However, her retention of such enormous amounts of land was unusual for even privileged women of the ninth and tenth centuries, notwithstanding the added advantage of her Italian connections. Adelheid's accomplishments show what was possible for women in the later tenth century. Nevertheless she had been unusually savvy in converting her opportunities into achievements. More successful than other women in fighting challenges to her possessions, she survived two husbands, a brother, her son, her daughter-in-law and at least one of her two daughters. With the strong support of the bishops and other leading men of the realm, she was appointed joint regent with her daughter-in-law and daughter for her infant grandson. On her daughter-in-law's death she was again invited to become regent for her grandson. Then in her sixties, she ruled without opposition until his coming of age, retiring to the Abbey of Selz, her favorite foundation, until her death on 16 or 17 December 999. At the early death of her grandson Otto III, just a little more than two years later, the kingdom was initially in turmoil. Shortly afterwards Henry, duke of Bavaria, emerged as the successful contender to lead the East-Frankish people, becoming the last king and emperor of the Saxon dynasty to rule.

As Moore so energetically and persuasively argues, by the mid-eleventh century, women's power was diminishing in both their ability to maintain their wealth and in endorsement of their right to rule.[49] Support for the existence of a drastic transformation appears in the change in matronymic charters. The number of such charters, whereby individuals identified themselves with their mothers,[50] was giving way to the emerging patrilineal lineages that deliberately limited the inheritance rights of women.[51] The princes of the realm were flexing their political muscles and the papacy was starting to convert its reform program into a zeal for church autonomy.

The significance of the change from Empress Adelheid's ability to wield extreme power over both her possessions and the kingdom becomes apparent in the history of Empress Agnes in the following century. When, in 1056, Agnes legitimately took on the regency for her five-year-old son, afterwards to become Henry IV, her story did not have the same happy outcome as that of the young Otto III and the female regents acting for him. Whereas Otto III had been restored with the help of the church and support of certain of the princes, Henry IV's kidnapping by the leading men (including possibly Archbishop Anno of Cologne) caused the Empress Agnes to withdraw from the scene and eventually abdicate. The position of the empress as regent was no longer unchallenged; she now relied on the power of the princes.[52]

Countess Matilda of Tuscany

By the late eleventh century, one such great 'prince' was Countess Matilda of Tuscany. She lived a generation after Agnes whose son, King and Emperor Henry IV, was no match for the grand duchess. Owning vast stretches of land in the north of Italy, Matilda was no less concerned with her inherited and acquired property than Adelheid. Three case studies that link the two women being compared show the vagaries of property management in the period under study. These case studies deal with estates at Melara, Hochfelden and Canossa. Adelheid and Matilda held interests in the same two properties (Melara and Canossa) and the other property (Hochfelden) began in Adelheid's possession and passed into the hands of another empress and then a count. The ownership of the first property, the great royal estates around Melara, shifted from Adelheid to that of a religious house, eventually bordering certain lands belonging to Matilda. The changes to ownership of the Melara lands illustrate the different techniques that, as a ruling but not a royal woman, Countess Matilda applied to obtain and profit from her lands while keeping her unruly vassals in order. In the second example the royal lands of Hochfelden passed from the possession of Empress Adelheid to that of Empress Agnes, wife of Emperor Henry III. The Hochfelden case shows a relatively standard progression of royal land through royal hands with an interesting change of possession in Matilda's time. The third example is Canossa. In 951 under the protection of Matilda's great-grandfather (Adalbert Atto), Adelheid sheltered in the great castle of Canossa, which Matilda eventually inherited. Used as living quarters and a fort, it only ever temporarily housed members of the royal German household—it was never in their possession. The example of Canossa shows the increase of land ownership of the rising comital class by careful accretion and manufacture of seignorial and dynastic power.

In their property management the two women took advantage of peculiarities of property laws that had their origins in the barbarian law codes still extant. Adelheid operated under Lombard Law in the kingdom of Italy after her wedding to Lothar but when she married Otto I came under Salic Law. Nevertheless she used aspects of Lombard Law when transferring property at Pavia, as we shall see later in this chapter. Matilda by birth came under Lombard Law. When she married Godfrey the Hunchback of Lower Lotharingia she claimed her authority through right of Salic rather than Lombard Law. Matilda employed her fortresses for military purposes. Adelheid, on the other hand, had fewer opportunities to exercise her power in such a way. The contrasting techniques that Adelheid and Matilda employed to manage their properties are examined against the changing background of the eleventh century.

Matilda and the Rise of Comital Power

In about 940 Hugh, king of Italy and father-in-law of Adelheid, endowed the Lombard family headed by Siegfried of Lucca with property around Parma.[53] Siegfried had always resided south of the Apennines,[54] but as a consequence of Hugh's largesse, Siegfried and his family took the first steps north across the mountains, leaving Tuscany for Emilia.[55] In 951 Adalbert Atto, Siegfried's son, aligned himself with Otto, king of the East Franks, against Berengar II by safeguarding Adelheid in his castle of Canossa and then delivering her to Otto I.[56] Adalbert Atto, Matilda of Tuscany's great-grandfather, sealed his future fortune by his shrewd action: Otto I rewarded him with the counties of Reggio and Modena and later Mantua. Accordingly Adalbert Atto shifted his patrimony northeast across the Apennines into the River Po area. He further increased his landholdings when he inherited the property of his father in 958.[57]

Texts as early as the 770s had recorded a slow but steady movement toward resettlement of the lower Po plain. Because the depopulation of the area in the seventh century relative to the sixth had allowed the marshes to creep back with their concomitant regrowth of vegetation, the encroaching new inhabitants occupied lands needing to be cleared for farming.[58] By the ninth century the polyptychs[59] of the Po plain show an increasingly rigorous lordly oversight.[60] By selling and exchanging, Lord Adalbert Atto combined his scattered estates into aggregated holdings in the River Po valley. His son Tedaldo persisted with the tradition and so too did his son, Boniface, Matilda's father. Both men fanned out from the river to take new land legally or by force.[61] Boniface added plunder, tricks and marriage to acquire further lands and consolidate his power.[62] While land around the Po by its very closeness to a river prone to flooding was less cultivated, more marshy and wooded, and so of limited economic value, the advantage was proximity and the exploitation of the wide resources that such a varied landscape could provide.[63] Country people moved in and worked the land, converting at least some to cultivation.[64] By 1030 Matilda's father, Boniface, was so powerful that he presided over public courts while seated in a boat that paused at numerous points along the

Po.[65] By the mid-eleventh century the house of Canossa had become the foremost establishment between the Apennines and the Alps, while retaining a commanding presence southwest of the Apennines around Tuscany.

Boniface's two wives contributed substantially to the holdings of the house of Canossa. His first wife, the widowed heiress Countess Richilda, daughter of Giselbert, count palatine of Bergamo, brought to her new husband two thousand pounds and vast possessions in northern Italy of more than 40,000 square kilometers.[66] His second wife, Beatrice, had inherited lands in Lotharingia through her father, Frederick, duke of Upper Lotharingia, while her mother's connections to Swabia enabled Beatrice to inherit additional lucrative property. Beatrice's marriage to Boniface in 1037 added the extensive property of her dowry.[67] However, on Boniface's death in 1052, when Beatrice was about thirty-five years of age and her younger daughter five or six, his widow held only a tentative claim on Boniface's properties and power.

The possession of the lands was a point of contention with Emperor Henry III. Beatrice's legal claim to keep Boniface's properties after his death rested only on her role as mother of Frederick, Boniface's heir. It is likely that when Frederick died Beatrice's position was in danger of becoming untenable; she feared that the inheritance from Boniface would not be preserved either for her or for her surviving daughter, Matilda.[68] Only by a speedy marriage with a mighty prince was there any hope of confronting the vagaries of her position. Consequently to strengthen the Lotharingian/Canusian power block, Beatrice married her cousin Godfrey the Bearded, while Matilda was betrothed to Godfrey the Hunchback, his son and now also Matilda's stepbrother. However, Beatrice and Godfrey married without the emperor's permission (Henry III had right of veto as feudal lord and by feudal law[69]). Henry may have had a particularly violent reaction to Beatrice's second marriage because the creation of the power block of Flanders–Hennegau a few years earlier had taken him by surprise. The emperor would not tolerate any power in northern and central Italy inimical to the empire and that would dominate the roads to Rome.[70] However, because Beatrice had the powerful protection of her relative Pope Leo IX, also Henry III's kinsman, Henry did not dare interfere directly in Mantua and Tuscany.[71] After Pope Leo IX died in April 1054, the emperor descended into Italy: Beatrice's new husband, Godfrey the Bearded, fled; her kinsmen and her first husband's vassals failed to defend her.[72] Henry III's men arrested the recalcitrant bride with little Matilda and conveyed them north across the Alps to the German court.[73]

Emperor Henry III died unexpectedly in October 1056 but not before pardoning the penitent Godfrey the Bearded and Beatrice, who returned with Matilda to Italy. In the turmoil of the appointment of Henry III's widow, Empress Agnes, as regent for her son little Henry (Henry IV), Beatrice and Godfrey could now be regarded in practical terms as protectors of the crown's interests south of the Alps. However, because her son, Frederick, had died, Beatrice's hold on the properties remained tenuous while Godfrey had no sanction by imperial law for his position as margrave of Tuscany.[74] Since Matilda's two older siblings had died, as sole daughter she remained the heir to her father's and mother's properties. Despite Beatrice's marriage to Godfrey the Bearded and the marriage of Matilda to Godfrey the Hunchback, the deaths of the two Godfreys (in 1069 and 1076) ensured the legacies from her father and mother would come to Matilda. Note, however, she was unable to inherit her husband's lands because he had already destined them to his nephew, Godfrey of Bouillon. With no living brother, husband or stepfather, Matilda was no longer bound by the restrictions of inheritance to patrimonial stems.[75]

Furthermore Boniface had ensured that many of his properties were granted to him formally as fiefs.[76] To preserve ownership for his family he had acquired much property by a method that allowed his wife and later his daughter to inherit possessions uncontested. The precarial emphyteuse (immovable property that is leased but where the lessor retains ownership and may require the lessee to improve the land)[77] originated in the area of Ravenna and guaranteed the wife and the legitimate children of both sexes the continuation of the fiefdom. Boniface set up a Three-Generation Contract[78] whereby he was able to leave those possessions unchallenged to Beatrice and later to Matilda with the now-concomitant military authority. Beatrice left her daughter numerous farms almost completely intact.[79] Matilda added to her inheritance as well as making restitution for many of the possessions that Boniface had extorted by violence.[80]

To retain possession of her estates and thus her wealth, Matilda required not only to manage them but also needed the wherewithal to increase them, and the experience and nerve in the political field to deal with other comital threats. For the twenty years before her death, the documents show Matilda's mother acting with growing power: evidenced by her increasing use of the terms *dux*, *comitissa* and *marchessa*, her attendance at synods and her donations of properties.[81] During that period Beatrice guided Matilda into becoming increasingly politically active. On her mother's death in 1076 Matilda had already acquired the experience to rule the strong-willed nobility in northern Italy. Matilda's father, Boniface, died in 1052, murdered with a poisoned arrow while out hunting. Matilda's brother, Frederick, and sister, Beatrice, died sometime about 1054. Some modern authors suspect that Frederick was murdered but there is insufficient evidence to confirm this. Matilda's stepfather, Godfrey the Bearded, died in 1069. Matilda's husband, Godfrey the Hunchback, was assassinated in 1076. Wealth from the extensive landholdings inherited from her father, stepfather, brother, sister, husband and mother enabled her to buy allegiance.[82] Until her death in 1115, Matilda's means fluctuated as her possession of the inherited property varied between loss and re-conquest, especially during the battles with the adult Henry IV.

An exact list of Matilda's possessions and their status is impossible to obtain. In the progress from Adalbert Atto to Matilda, distinctions between allodial land (land owned outright) and fiefdoms remain obscure: the Canossans frequently gave allodial property to a monastery or church but then got it back as a fiefdom. Tuscany was a particularly difficult location to categorize: the Canossans, on the one hand, directly regulated margravial possessions but, on the other hand, preserved the whole of Tuscany as an imperial fiefdom and operated as feudal lords over the smaller princes. The Canossans founded or endowed monasteries and hospices and extensive administrative rights were often connected with them. The Canossans owned land, rights and properties at an astounding 854 locations at least, including thirteen in Lotharingia.[83] The status of the Matildine lands, that is, whether Matilda held her possessions as allodial, imperial or church fiefdoms, remained so complex that they were a subject of dispute between the emperor and the pope for two hundred years after Matilda's death.[84]

The History of Three Landholdings

Three landholdings that show the different opportunities for control available to the empress and the countess, serve as case studies. None ever belonged to both women, but two properties were connected to Adelheid and Matilda and the third illustrates the limits of the powers of an empress. The lands of Melara lay beside the River Po to the east of Milan and Pavia and to the west of the great centers of Bologna and Ravenna. Hochfelden was located in Alsace, northwest of Strasbourg. Southwest of the River Po, the high rock of Canossa emerged out of the plain, one of many natural stone formations scattered throughout the valley of the Po.

The Case of Melara

Once again the pigs of Revere were running wild in the neighboring woods of Melara, eating the acorns then escaping and trampling the crops in the nearby fields. Brother Liutharius was driven to distraction. Even though Melara near Ostiglia on the Po was a mere outpost of the mother house, he, as prior, had responsibilities to San Salvatore at Pavia. He had told the people from Revere time and again that they had no right of pannage in the abbey's woods. Finally the prior persuaded the aging Countess Matilda to take action. Three days after Epiphany in the year of our Lord 1106, she issued a diploma forbidding her peasants of Revere to fatten their swine on the farm of Melara, which bordered her land. The countess had responded to the prior's plea and confirmed the abbey's sole prerogative to pannage there.[85] As lord, Matilda's right and duty was to settle the dispute.

The account of the seemingly minor infringement about access to pannage of swine at Melara, described above, combined with information from other sources, reveals an unexpected amount of information about the management of landholdings in northern Italy between the mid-tenth and early twelfth centuries. In 2015 the town of Melara in the Province of Rovigo in the Region of Veneto had a population of 1803.[86] The present small and quiet town does not reflect the imperial history of the area that began for Adelheid when her future first husband and father-in-law gave her the great royal court of Melara near Ostiglia on the Po,[87] as one property among many, on her betrothal in 937.[88]

In 982 Adelheid intervened in a document issued by Otto II from Capua that donated Melara, among other gifts, to the monastery of San Salvatore, originally an ancient Lombard abbey.[89] Adelheid confirmed the gift in 999. In the first half of April 999 she gave thirty-six courts to the Abbey of San Salvatore at Pavia, including the royal court holding of Melara with all its pertaining rights, as an unimpeded freely given gift.[90] Three charters, issued separately on 12 April, record the details of all her donations.[91] The dowager empress chose the Abbey of San Salvatore to receive her bounty of dotal lands from her inheritance from the Italian kingdom. In the records of the dispossession no man was consulted. Adelheid acted in her own right: at the same time as she was authorizing those donations from Erstein, her grandson, the emperor, was at Rome busy issuing his own charters about other matters.[92]

The lands of Melara remain a point in common between Adelheid and Matilda. Although Matilda did not own those lands, in 1106 the dispute arose because her 'men' of Revere nearby had intruded there. Revere was part of the Canossan lands.[93] Boniface and Beatrice retained the possession of Revere and Quistello (among other locations) exclusively but also initiated the development of manses around the area, including at Revere.[94]

In 1106 in the areas of Matilda's lordship, the Po region and Tuscany were at peace with the empire. In the previous year Emperor Henry IV had been forced to abdicate in favor of his son and Matilda had no quarrel with the new king, Henry V. At about fifty-nine years Matilda sported robust health; from the town of Quistello she issued her document with clear intentions. In her account of her judgment, Matilda emphasized that she had consulted extensively and not only with her own people:

> Abiding by the worthy prayers of these people and knowing the matter from the more diligent relation of our faithful, we have found at length from consistent testimony of many, that in that wood ... violence, of which we have spoken above, was unjustly inflicted upon the *curtis* of Melara by our men.[95]

Matilda asserted her authority strongly when rebuking her own men:

> Now we wish to make known to all our loyal people both present and future alike that we have firmly instructed to have removed the aforementioned violence from the *curtis* of Melara, so that no one of our people might dare to keep their pigs nor anyone of ours enter within the above mentioned confines of the aforementioned woods, without the permission of the prior who will be at the time in power in the *curtis* of Melara.[96]

Having tried as best she could to ensure that her order should stand in perpetuity, Matilda gave warnings about breaking the agreement:

> If anyone will be tempted to come now against this our page of arrangement and about this, which we have composed for the remedy of our soul, should wish justly or unjustly to molest the aforesaid *curtis*, he should know himself to incur our wrath and as the penalty of our *bannum* he must pay fifty pounds of silver, half to the aforementioned church of San Salvatore, half indeed to our treasury[97]

Finally Matilda signed the document with her customary wording and a flourish:

> [T]hat this writing always in its strength be permanent. That this be believed as true and in future times be held more firmly, we have strengthened with the subscription of our own hand.[98]

The document was framed with a particular agenda in mind. Although Matilda listed her notary and witnesses she acted alone with full authority. The document is couched in language to express the strong call on the loyalty of Matilda's people, her wide consultation to understand the facts of the case and the very stern orders to her men to refrain from bearing violence to the property attached to the abbey. In the event of a future violation, Matilda had set the penalty at fifty pounds of silver with one half of the penalty to go to the lord, that is, to herself. Matilda used the term 'violence' twice in the diploma. If considered a judgment on violence, her penalty is reminiscent of certain fines exacted under Rothair's Edict of AD 643. In specific laws that appear to be related to the king's interest, including those connected with murder, brigandry, attacks by vigilantes, seizing unlawful pledges and falsifying tree-marks, the king's share of recompense would be half the fine, if his people committed such acts of violence.[99] (In contrast, Rothair's Edict on the compensation for damage to property by runaway pigs carried a maximum penalty of loss of one pig or three siliquae, depending on the permutations of the offence.[100]) Other laws that give half the fine to the king control the violation of women in various ways. In allocating the same penalty, those laws acknowledge the guardianship of the king over the women.[101] The fine to the king was not normal, however, under Salic Law, under which Matilda stated that she operated, but was more common under Lombard Law. Nevertheless by setting the penalty high and her own recompense at half the fine, Matilda condemned the violence and emulated royal authority.[102] She set herself up as ultimate guardian of those to whom the diploma applied.

The history of the holding of Melara records two women controlling their property using the legal means at their disposal—their charters. First, an empress-dowager controlled her property in her own right without male oversight by a testamentary donation of her royal court to a renowned abbey in the late tenth century. Second, a female comital lord exercised her rights over her men in a property matter to exact justice in the manner of a king.

The Case of Hochfelden

The history of Melara is an example of a royal landholding that did not fall into the hands of the rising comital class. The royal court of Hochfelden left the hands of royalty and entered the hands of a count. From the viewpoint of later centuries, to be able to connect ownership of your own property to that of the Ottonians of the tenth century indicated a special relationship of the owner with that glorious dynasty. For the Salian dynasty of the eleventh century, continuity over more than one dynasty in the giving and receiving of property became a source of pride. In particular, to possess proven dotal property specifically from the reverse dowry (that is, property given to the wife by the husband on their marriage that became her own property legally disposable as she wished) should mean that the possessor was free of imperial interference. The property of Hochfelden had such a history.

The villa Hochfelden in Alsace had been part of Empress Adelheid's endowment from Otto I.[103] Approximately eighty years later it appeared as a possession of Empress Agnes in a charter of her son King Henry IV, issued on 20 May 1065.[104] Although Hochfelden belonged to Agnes, only two days later Henry IV granted property there to Count Eberhard of Nellenburg. The reasons for this are convoluted and some background is required. Emperor Henry III, on his deathbed in 1056, had asked his wife Agnes to make restitution of all lands he had appropriated. After his death and on Agnes's petition, their son King Henry IV restored Breme Abbey in about 1061 or 1062 to the cathedral in Como.[105] On 20 May 1065 Henry IV, again on Agnes's petition, added the county of Chiavenna and the Maira Bridge with the bridge toll to the diocese of Como. Chiavenna had probably been taken previously from the diocese by Henry III and enfeoffed to Count Eberhard of Nellenburg. Now the count needed to be compensated in turn for the return of Chiavenna to Como. On 22 May 1065, two days after Henry IV's first charter (noting his mother's ownership of the villa Hochfelden), Count Eberhard of Nellenberg received a document giving him *duas villas*, woods, meadows and other items at Hochfelden: Henry IV conferred on him the *villam Hochwelt nominatam*, Agnes's possession and, in addition, other unnamed lands.[106]

A matter of curiosity is that the second document that gives property to Count Eberhard makes no mention of Hochfelden being part of the empress's lands; that is, there was no distinction between the imperial possessions that Henry IV disposed of and the possessions that Agnes had power over. The charter states merely that Hochfelden contained *duas villas* together with descriptions of woods, meadows and so on. Were the lands given away not part of her son's property but Agnes's own? That is, Henry IV had taken it upon himself to dispose of his mother's property.

Although Agnes's rule as regent for her under-age son Henry IV had ceased in 1062 on his abduction by the princes of the realm, she may have been at court toward the end of 1062 since she appears in a royal diploma in November. During 1063 she did not intervene, and only four times in 1064. After Henry IV's coming of age in March 1065, Agnes became once more the most frequent intervener in the royal charters for two months. After May she departed for the Abbey of Fruttuaria and then Rome. Her apparent intention was to renounce the world, which she did probably in summer or autumn of 1065.[107] The question therefore arises about how conscious Agnes was of the status of her possessions at the time that she agreed to their dispersal. She was in all likelihood aware of her ownership—dotal lands were particularly notable because of their special properties. Alternatively, she was willing to give the lands away, without caring too much about the niceties, because she intended to renounce the world. A third possibility arises that depends on the choice and application of the laws in the German kingdom, discussed later in this chapter.

The Case of Canossa

The two landholdings of Melara and Hochfelden discussed above belonged to Adelheid, though neither of them was ever in Matilda's possession. While Melara became a place of direct interest to Matilda in exercising her lordship, Hochfelden illustrates the slippage of royal property to comital possession (although not to Matilda's), the increasing precariousness of the retention of property by royal women and the rise in wealth and independence of the comital class during the eleventh century. The third landholding, the castle and fort of Canossa, has a history that parallels the rise of the comital lords in the tenth and eleventh centuries, especially in northern Italy. The fortunes of the house of Canossa became directly connected with the royal court, initially through Adelheid. Before the Canossan family obtained the patronage of the royal house, however, Matilda's great-grandfather, Adalbert Atto, a vassal of Bishop Adelhard (or Adalardo) of Reggio Emilia, had joined the army of the bishop, who rewarded him by giving him Canossa.[108] The family historian, Donizo, speaking through the voice of the locality of Canossa itself, wrote that

Count Atto found a bare rock and erected a great castle and fortress upon it.[109] Donizo employed rhetorical flourishes to write about the rock of Canossa; the building development clearly depended on the wealth of its founder. Then 'growing rich, Atto raised my defence walls on high'.[110] Although at Canossa there was a plentiful supply of local stone, marble was transported with immense efforts across the Apennine passes. Later Matilda 'renewed me continually in having made more modern towers'.[111]

After Adalbert Atto's protection of Adelheid at the castle of Canossa in 951, Otto I made him Count of Canossa. Matilda's ancestors, the Attonidi, tapped into a general trend toward family self-consciousness: they put the private castle in the center of the operations of their family, which achieved official recognition of its power and became a dynasty at the same time, taking its name from the castle.[112] Donizo wrote his history of the Canossan family between the years 1111 and 1115, some 165 years after Adalbert Atto's building spree at Canossa. The text is commonly known as *Vita Mathildis* (*The Life of Matilda of Canossa*) and was probably commissioned by Matilda. At the time of writing Donizo, already imbued with an interest in the history of the lineage of the Canossa family, had entitled his full work *De Principibus Canusinis*. The poem is divided into two books, the first dedicated to Matilda's ancestors, the second to Matilda. Each book is twenty chapters long, and according to the author's intentions, each should contain 1400 verses. The first contains 1385 verses that became 1400 with the miniature's captions, while to the second he added the song *De insigni obita memorandae Comitissae Mathildis* (verses 1401–1535), when he heard of the countess's death in 1116, and the *Exhortatio Canusii de adventu imperatoris* (verses 1536–1549) to welcome the arrival of Henry V at Canossa.[113]

The development of the Canossan fortress is described in other documents too. A papal bull of 975 speaks of the monastery of Sant'Apollonio as 'in the rock which is called Canuxia'. The next attestation for Canossa is a *roca Kanosia* in 1007. In 1255 Salimbene de Adam recorded in his chronicle that a city army from Reggio Emilia had attacked Canossa, stormed it and destroyed it.[114] Nowadays the tower is gone and only the ruins of the church of Sant'Apollonio are clearly visible. Although only about one-third of the original surface area of the Canossa rock of about 6000 square meters remains,[115] it is not difficult to imagine the courtyard where Matilda and Pope Gregory VII walked.

Interestingly the episode describing Adelheid's escape from prison and arrival and presence at Canossa forms a major part of Book 1 in Donizo's

Life. Since his *Life* contains an image of himself and Matilda, in which he presents his book to her for her approval and acceptance, it must be presumed that her influence on its contents was substantial. In that case we can reasonably assume that Matilda thought so highly of the presence of Adelheid at Canossa, under the protection of Matilda's great-grandfather, that Matilda influenced what and how much Donizo included about Adelheid. Having worked closely with the sources I am convinced that such emphasis is no accident. The contents have so many details in common with Hrotsvitha's *Deeds of Otto* that Donizo's *Life* was either directly based on her work or on a source or sources heavily influenced by it.

Adelheid emerged from the castle of Canossa in 951 to wed Otto I, king of the East Franks, thus allying herself with the German Reich. One hundred years later Matilda affiliated herself with the reform party of the church against the king Henry IV. In 1077 Canossa became the locus of great humiliation for Henry IV when, after mediation initiated by Matilda, he reputedly waited three days in the snow outside the castle for the pope, a guest in Matilda's castle, to lift his ban of excommunication.[116] As a result the castle of Canossa stands as an emblem for the change from support for the king and the acceptance of royal governance in northern Italy to independence, the rise of the comital class to power and, shortly afterwards, the rise of the communes.

THE SIGNIFICANCE OF LAW

Two of the three properties under study illustrate how the women used aspects of the barbarian laws for their property management and disposal. The Lombard and Salic legal codes developed out of the legacies of the waves of migration of the various tribal groups into Europe in previous centuries. The Lombard Laws were striking in that, unlike any other law codes except those of the Anglo-Saxons, almost every decree claimed royal responsibility for its issue from the time of the Edict of Rothair (AD 643).[117] By the tenth century fines under the Lombard Laws often passed to the king, rather than the *civitas*, and judicial officials also answered to him, not to the people. Contrary to the Lombard Laws, fines under Salic Law were less likely to go to the king and officials were less likely to be responsible to him.[118] Probably first promulgated in 507 by Clovis, leader of the Franks, the *Lex Salica* existed in six recensions. The most important change to property laws in the latter code occurred in the sixth century when daughters were allowed to inherit property in the absence of sons as a protection against dispersal across all kin. Eventually daughters and sons inherited. Such developments meant that property passed by inheritance only to the immediate family and direct descendants.[119]

Adelheid's transfer of title of her royal courts, including Melara, to San Salvatore in Pavia contained a number of complex elements. Adelheid states, 'I live according to my birth under Salic Law.'[120] However, in the transfer of title, right and possession to the courts she acted according to Lombard custom.[121] The *Cartularium Langobardorum* records the cartularies that specify the procedures under Lombard, Salic and other law codes to effect the transfer of land ownership and possession.[122] Adelheid transferred title to the recipient, delivered right of ownership (*traditio*) and transferred possession to the recipient ('investiture') under the procedures of Lombard Law.[123]

Evidence for title lay in the existence of an initial charter that allocated the gifts to Adelheid, and later charters that confirmed her in the possession of property at various times. That property, given to her by her second husband (Otto I) on their marriage (documents known only through later charters), was confirmed by her son, Otto II, and her grandson, Otto III.[124] The documents for her transfer of goods to San Salvatore at Pavia, issued from Erstein in April 999, can be used to illustrate the procedures performed. When Adelheid placed the *festuca notata* (small staff denoting power, marked to serve as a memorandum, or alternatively *nodata*, meaning knot, the symbol of the promise)[125] on the *bergamena* (parchment) together with the symbols of what was to be transferred (the clod of earth for land and the branches of trees for woods) and then lifted the parchment from the ground together with the inkpot, she fulfilled part of the requirement for the *traditio*. We do not have a record of either the question or the answer, also required to complete the *traditio* under the Lombard Law, or the third element of the transaction, the carrying out of the 'investiture', that is, the corporeal handling of documents.[126] Under Lombard Law the manner of carrying out the investiture was relatively simple: investiture was satisfied by 'the delivery of a stick, the giving of the document, the solemn entry upon the land'.[127] Confirmation of the valid transfer of the property to the monastery of San Salvatore is confirmed by Matilda's charter of 1106, dated more than a hundred years after Adelheid's of 999 that states that the lands of Melara belonged to the monastery.

However, Adelheid's detailed and assured description of the processes contains an unexpected significance. She had been disappointed previously in attempts to transfer her dotal lands in the German empire in

985. The careful description of the handing over at Erstein most likely reflects the lessons learned. However, before I discuss those lessons, it is important to note the significance of Erstein in Adelheid's life. Adelheid had an interest in and was more prominent in the development of Erstein (in Alsace) as a major center. Her involvement in the significant change in the royal route between the two prominent places in Adelheid's life, Burgundy and Alsace, discussed earlier in this chapter, corroborates this matter. The evidence for her foundation of and continuing support for Selz and its linkage with Alsace is more direct and equally significant. It is consequently of interest that Adelheid issued the important document about to be discussed from Erstein.

First some background is required in order to understand the matter. Adelheid wanted to transfer to her daughter, Abbess Mathilda of Quedlinburg, a part of her property, given to her by Otto I. She tried to assert her rights by producing her own notary's draft from 985 to the chancery of her young grandson, King Otto III. The document stresses explicitly that those lands from Otto I were given to her as *dotem* and were her own property.[128] Otto III's chancery did not approve the draft, and Adelheid had to give up her claim of free disposal of the royal lands in the face of the opposition that must have come from her daughter-in-law and regent, Theophanu, and Archchancellor Willigis. One week later the chancery issued the gift document by Otto III in which Adelheid is named as the petitioner, but there is no mention of any right of property she might possess. Rather, the sole right of the king is stressed. She still could not dispose of her widow's portion in the same way as she could in the Italian kingdom. The attitude of the chancery and the ruler is seen to be on the side of the empire but is in conflict with the wording of the documents of gift or reverse dowry.[129]

Similarly German queens could not gain access to their reverse dowry at a later date. Emperor Henry II's widow, Kunigunde, could not dispose of her widow's portion as she wished in 1025. The new emperor, Conrad II, considered the arrangements of the empress invalid; he held the opinion that her entire widow's portion must revert to the crown after her death, although she too had received in the deeds of gift all those rights to which Adelheid had appealed. The texts of the documents with their individual formulaic phrases were in conflict with the current legal practice and the attitude of the people in power. In Germany, in the case of a gift from the imperial possessions, the right of transfer could only be given to a restricted extent. The possessions given were tied to the person receiving them, and therefore not transferable and also not hereditary, except in a narrow sense. Formulae of Italian origin in particular did not correspond to the actual practice of law in Germany. Thus in documents issued as the gifts from the king, there were inconsistencies that were particularly noticeable when the recipients and givers were members of the ruling house. The differences in the legal position of Adelheid in the German and Italian kingdoms therefore may be attributed on the one hand to the way the law was interpreted and on the other to the dynastic interest in undiminished imperial possessions.[130] The above analysis therefore throws light on Agnes's problem in accessing her dotal lands in the next century. Adelheid had foreshadowed Agnes's failure to have her rights of ownership of such lands concomitant with her rights of disposal.

Countess Matilda did not encounter the same problems as Adelheid or Agnes in such matters. By birth, Matilda fell under the jurisdiction of Lombard Law, but by marriage to Godfrey the Hunchback, she legally transferred to the authority of Salic Law, as she frequently stated in her charters.[131] Although Salic Law generally forbade inheritance by women, Matilda could inherit because she had no living male relatives.[132]

In addition to making full use of the inheritance rights of Salic Law, Matilda inherited a valuable right from her mother. Beatrice and her sister were two of the first non-royal women to dispose of their property without getting agreement from a guardian, although there were a few rare precedents: Countess Willa in 977 in the foundation document of Santa Maria in Florence and Countesses Ermingarda and Adalaxia after the deaths of their fathers. While Countess Adelaide of Turin from the eleventh-century family of the Arduinids (not to be confused with Empress Adelheid) managed, like Beatrice, to control the disposal of her property, the trend for women in the social class below absolute rulers to claim the complete right of disposal over their possessions did not, in general, extend into the eleventh and twelfth centuries. Despite the restriction Beatrice managed to transfer this important right to her daughter—but that right died with her.[133]

***

Adelheid, as queen and empress, had gained lands through a royal protocol, valid under Lombard Law. She had inherited from, or been given royal lands by, her father, King Rudolf II of Burgundy; her father-in-law, King Hugh of Italy; her husband, King Lothar of Italy; and her mother. Her second husband, King and later Emperor Otto I, also donated lands to his wife. Adelheid as empress widow had disagreed ~~with her daughter-in-law, son and son-in-law about wh~~ lands belonged to the royal fisc (thus subject to the emper~~ her widow's right (dotal lands, thus under her direct contr~~ from those disputes, Adelheid ensured that she disposed of her from her Italian heritage as the laws and customs allowed. In ~~mentary documents of 999, the dowager empress Adelheid indep~~ ~~ently disposed of her property in the last year of her life.

No such restrictions applied to the two leading female members of the margravial Canossan family in the later eleventh and early twelfth centuries who eventually acted independently of male advice. The ability of Beatrice and Matilda, noble women below the status of royalty, to manage property autonomously, was historically significant for the legal status of women of nobility in Italy in the high Middle Ages, but not lasting. Nevertheless, there was more freedom in Italy than in Germany: the women in the German *imperium* continued to be restricted in their ability to control their dotal property if they were royal or imperial lands.

The comparison of the three landholdings has demonstrated a number of matters pertaining to the two women under study, one royal and one comital. In the one hundred years between them, opportunities had changed for the two groups. A member of a comital family, just starting its rise to power, took advantage of unsettled times, chose the winning side by sheltering Queen Adelheid at his landholding at Canossa and so hoisted himself up the ladder of success. Adelheid and her new husband, future empress and emperor, rewarded the perspicacious and ambitious Adalbert Atto. Countess Matilda took advantage of the shrewdness and luck of her great-grandfather and the deaths of male relatives to increase and improve her landholdings so that she, and she alone, controlled vast estates in the kingdom of Italy.

Notes

1. Moore, 'Review Article: Duby's Eleventh Century', 38–40.
2. Chris Wickham, 'Land Disputes and their Social Framework in Lombard-Carolingian Italy, 700–900', in *Land and Power: Studies in Italian and European Social History, 400–1200*, ed. Chris Wickham (London: British School at Rome, 1994), 248.
3. Nelson, 'Wary Widow', II.83–88; Herlihy, 'Land', 89–120.
4. Herlihy, 'Marriage Market', 5; McNamara and Wemple, 'Power of Women', 86; Suzanne F. Wemple, *Women in Frankish Society:*

Marriage and the Cloister, 500 to 900 (Philadelphia: University of Pennsylvania Press, 1981), 45, 48, 112, 119; Le Jan, *Famille*, 268–70.

5. Wendy Davies and Paul Fouracre, eds, *Property and Power in the Early Middle Ages* (Cambridge: Cambridge University Press, 1995), 281: 'Usufruct: In Late Roman law, a qualified type of possession of property, limited in time (usually a life interest) and scope (usually to consumable goods), and without power of alienation. In the early Middle Ages, generally clearly distinguished from *possessio* ("Which assumes that possession and ownership coincide")', 281; 'Often, life interest, as in property given to a church, or in a widow's *dos*', 284.
6. Nelson, 'Wary Widow', II.88–9, 88n29.
7. Penelope Nash, 'Shifting Terrain–Italy and Germany Dancing in their own Tapestry', *JAEMA* 6 (2010), 59–60.
8. Simon MacLean, 'Queenship, Nunneries and Royal Widowhood in Carolingian Europe', *P&P*, no. 178 (2003) 25–26; Pauline Stafford, *Queen Emma and Queen Edith: Queenship and Women's Power in Eleventh-Century England* (Oxford: Blackwell, 1997), 115.
9. Bougard, 'Power', 39.
10. Hrotsvitha, *Gesta*, lines 469–695; Beyreuther, 'Kaiserin Adelheid', 47.
11. Bougard, 'Power', 39–40; Leyser, *Rule*, 45–46.
12. *Leges Langobardorum, 643–866*, ed. Franz Beyerle, 2nd ed. (Witzenhausen: 1962), 1.1, p. 100; 65.1, p. 130.
13. Leyser, *Rule*, 49–73.
14. *VMA*, 5–6; *VMP*, 11–12; Gilsdorf, *Queenship*, 14. For Queen Mathilda, Adelheid and Theophanu, see Giovanni Isabella, 'Matilde, Edgith e Adelaide: scontri generazionali e dotari delle regine in Germania', *Il patrimonio delle regine: beni del fisco e politica regia tra IX e X secolo. Reti Medievali Rivista*, edited by Tiziana Lazzari 13, 2 (2012), 203-45. DOI 10.6092/1593-2214/368.
15. For the general location of the lands in northern Italy see Chris Wickham, *Early Medieval Italy: Central Power and Local Society 400–1000* (London: Macmillan, 1981), Map 4, between xi and 1.
16. Schiaparelli, *Diplomi di Ugo*, Nr. 47, 143–44; M. Uhlirz, 'Die rechtliche Stellung der Kaiserinwitwe Adelheid im deutschen und im italischen Reich', *ZSRGA* 74 (1957), 86; S. Weinfurter,

'Kaiserin Adelheid und das ottonische Kaisertum', *FMSt* 33 (1999), 6.
17. Schiaparelli, *Diplomi di Ugo*, Nr. 3, 255–56; Uhlirz, 'Rechtliche Stellung', 86n3.
18. Schiaparelli, *Diplomi di Ugo*, Nr. 14, 282–83; Uhlirz, 'Rechtliche Stellung', 86n4; Niermeyer *Lexicon*, s.v. 'curtis'.
19. Schiaparelli, *Diplomi di Ugo*, Nr. 46, 139–41.
20. Adalbert of Magdeburg, *Continuatio Reginonis*, eds Albert Bauer and R. Rau, *AQDG* 8 (Darmstadt: Wissenschaftliche Buchgesellschaft, 2002), s.a. 953; Uhlirz, 'Rechtliche Stellung', 88n10. Bertha's death has been variously recorded as occurring in 961, 962 or 966, but 966 is most likely: Hlawitschka, *Ahnen* 1.1, p. 101 (961, after 962), 1.2, Table VIII (961); Gilsdorf, *Queenship*, 23 (*c.* 961); Golinelli, *Adelaide. Regina*, 175 (966); Uhlirz, 'Rechtliche Stellung', 86 (966).
21. See later confirmations by her son and grandson: *DO* II, Nr. 123; Böhmer, *RI* 2.2, Nr. 690; *DO* III, Nr. 36.
22. Weinfurter, 'Kaiserin Adelheid', 6, 13; Uhlirz, 'Rechtliche Stellung', 92; Beyreuther, 'Kaiserin Adelheid', 53.
23. Lattin, *Letters*, 53n1.
24. *DO* III, Nr. 36; Böhmer, *RI* 2.3, Nr. 994. On doubts about the efficacy of the formulae see Stafford, '*La Mutation Familiale*', 120–25.
25. Gerd Althoff, *Otto III*, trans. P. G. Jestice (Pennsylvania: Pennsylvania State University Press, 2003), 52.
26. *DO III*, Nrs 150; 155; 159; 160; 182; 231.
27. Gilsdorf, *Queenship*, 14–15; Syrus of Cluny, *Vita sancti Maioli*, 3.9; Niermeyer, *Index*, s.v. 'Syrus'.
28. Odilo, *Epitaphium*, ch. 5–6.
29. 'protervorum consilio iuvenum depravatus', Thietmar, *Chronicon*, 4.15.
30. Reynolds, *Fiefs*, 417.
31. Uhlirz, 'Rechtliche Stellung', 94–97.
32. *DO III*, Nr. 157.
33. Althoff, *Otto III*, 53. Hadwig's brother, Henry the Wrangler, arrives at Alemannia too.
34. Nelson, 'Wary Widow', II.86n13.
35. *DO I*, Nr. 368.
36. Weinfurter, 'Kaiserin Adelheid', 13–14.

37. *DO II*, Nr. 121; Böhmer, *RI* 2.2, Nrs. 702c, 703; *DO III*, Nrs 159, 160; Böhmer, *RI* 2.3, Nr. 1128a.
38. Hans J. Hummer, *Politics and Power in Early Medieval Europe: Alsace and the Frankish Realm, 600–1000* (Cambridge: Cambridge University Press, 2005), 228.
39. 'totam provinciam a Basilea usque Moguntiam, ubi maxima vis regni esse noscitur' ('the entire stretch of country from Basel to Mainz, where the principle strength of the realm is known to be'), Otto von Freising, *Gesta Frederici I. imperatoris*, ed. Franz-Joseph Schmale, *AQDG* 17 (Darmstadt: Wissenschaftliche Buchgesellschaft, 1974), 1.12; Nash, 'Shifting Terrain', 69–72; Weinfurter, 'Kaiserin Adelheid', 14.
40. *DO* I, Nr. 338; Gilsdorf, *Queenship*, 190n52.
41. *DO III*, Nr. 79.
42. Ibid., Nr. 130; Warner, *Ottonian Germany*, 182n121.
43. Thietmar, *Chronicon*, 4.43.
44. 'prediis, edificiis, auro et gemmis, vestibus pretiosissimis, aliisque variis ornatum suppellectilibus', Odilo, *Epitaphium*, ch. 10.
45. *DO III*, Nrs 159, 160.
46. Odilo, *Epitaphium*, ch. 10; Gilsdorf, *Queenship*, 190nn52, 53.
47. *DO III*, Nrs 77–80, 86–88, 130; Gilsdorf, *Queenship*, 191n55.
48. Nash, 'Shifting Terrain', 69–72.
49. Moore, 'Review Article: Duby's Eleventh Century', 38–40.
50. Herlihy, 'Land', 18.
51. Georges Duby, 'Lineage, Nobility and Knighthood: The Mâconnais in the Twelfth Century–A Review', in *The Chivalrous Society* (London: Arnold, 1977), 59–80; John B. Freed, 'German Source Collections: The Archdiocese of Salzburg as a Case Study', in *Medieval Women and the Sources of Medieval History*, ed. Joel Thomas Rosenthal (Athens, GA: University of Georgia Press, 1990), 80; Georges Duby, *Medieval Marriage: Two Models from Twelfth-Century France*, trans. Elborg Forster (Baltimore and London: Johns Hopkins University Press, 1978), 9–12.
52. P. Bange, 'The Image of Women of the Nobility in the German Chronicles', in *The Empress Theophano: Byzantium and the West at the Turn of the First Millennium*, ed. Adelbert Davids (Cambridge: Cambridge University Press, 1995), 160–62.

53. Vito Fumagalli, *Le origini di una grande dinastia feudale Adalberto-Atto di Canossa* (Tübingen: Max Niemeyer, 1971), 35–46, 47–48, 62, 77.
54. Although the Apennines are commonly thought to lie north/south as the vertical spine of Italy, the northernmost mountains curve to the west effectively separating Tuscany from the northern Italian regions of Emilia–Romagna and the Po valley. Thus Siegfried, and afterwards his son Adalbert Atto, had to cross the Apennines to take up their new northern land possessions.
55. Giovanni Tabacco, *The Struggle for Power in Medieval Italy: Structures of Political Rule*, trans. Rosalind Jensen Brown (Cambridge: Cambridge University Press, 1989), 162. See also Vito Fumagalli, 'Da Sigifredo "De Comitatu Lucensi" a Adalberto-Atto di Canossa', in *SM II*, 62–63.
56. Adalbert Atto appears in the records for the first time in 958: Fumagalli, *Le origini*, 3. It is probable that Atto was known in earlier records, now lost, since Atto's support of Adelheid and Otto occurred in 951.
57. *DO I*, Nr. 340; Fumagalli, *Le Origini*, 1–29; Giuseppe Sergi, 'I poteri dei Canossa: poteri delegati, poteri feudali, poteri signorili', in *I poteri dei Canossa. Da Reggio Emilia all'Europa*, ed. Paolo Golinelli (Bologna: Pàtron, 1994), 32.
58. Chris Wickham, "European Forests in the Early Middle Ages," in *Land and Power: Studies in Italian and European Social History, 400–1200* (London: British School at Rome, 1994), 194–95; Paolo Squatriti, *Water and Society in Early Medieval Italy, AD 400–1000* (Cambridge: Cambridge University Press, 1998), 72–73.
59. 'From a Greek word meaning "many-leaved", a written inventory of an estate's resources, including people, generally organized according to *mansi* ... ('peasant holdings')', in Davies, *Property*, s.vv. 'polyptych', 'mansus', 279, 281.
60. Chris Wickham, "Italy and the Early Middle Ages," in *Land and Power: Studies in Italian and European Social History, 400–1200* (London: British School at Rome, 1994), 115.
61. Wickham, *Early Medieval Italy*, 183.
62. Arnaldo Tincani, 'Le corti dei Canossa in area Padana', in *I poteri dei Canossa, da Reggio Emilia all'Europa: atti del convegno internazionale di studi (Reggio Emilia-Carpineti, 29–31 ottobre 1992)*,

ed. Paolo Golinelli (Bologna: Pàtron, 1994) 255–59; Marinella Zanarini, 'I Canossa', in *Lanfranco e Wiligelmo. Il duomo di Modena*, ed. E. Castelnuovo et al. (Modena: Panini, 1984), 46–47.
63. Paolo Squatriti, *Water and Society in Early Medieval Italy, AD 400-1000* (Cambridge: Cambridge University Press, 1998), 4–6; Pierre Bonnassie, 'A Family of the Barcelona Countryside and Its Economic Activities Around the Year 1000', in *Early Medieval Society*, ed. Sylvia L. Thrupp (New York: Appleton-Century-Crofts, 1967), 104, 110.
64. Zanarini, 'I Canossa', 54.
65. Bougard, 'Power', 51.
66. Tincani, 'Corti', 257; Sergi, 'Poteri', 33; Glass, *Sculpture*, 12.
67. Donizo, *VM*, 1.10, lines 813–15.
68. Matilda's siblings, Frederick and Beatrice, probably died sometime in late 1053 or during 1054. On 17 December 1053 they are mentioned as alive in a donation to the monastery of St Mary in Felonica: Goez, *Beatrix*, 20–21. However, Robinson reports that Henry III took all three children over the Alps to Germany in 1055: Robinson, *Henry* IV, 24.
69. Goez, *Beatrix*, 21, 22, 23, 74; Robinson, *Henry IV*, 24.
70. Goez, *Beatrix*, 23, 141.
71. Robinson, *Henry IV*, 20, 37.
72. Goez, *Beatrix*, 24. Godfrey the Bearded had been defeated and imprisoned by Henry III on two previous occasions.
73. Goez, *Reg. Bea.*, Nr. 11c; Goez, *Beatrix*, 24, 29–30.
74. Conrad II had created Boniface margrave (marquis/marquess) in Tuscany in 1027. However, Godfrey did not have entitlement to take over Boniface's titles, even by marrying Beatrice. Tabacco, 'Northern and Central Italy', 72; Goez, *Beatrix*, 25, 31.
75. Overmann, *Reg. Mat.*, Reg. 27b.
76. Goez, *Beatrix*, 85; Vito Fumagalli, 'Canossa', *LMA* 2:1442–43.
77. For emphyteuse, see Carlo Calisse, *History of Italian Law*, trans. Layton B. Register (Boston: Little, Brown, and Company, 1928), 721–30; P. S. Leicht, *Il diritto italiano preirneriano* (Bologna: Zanichelli, 1933), 168–80.
78. Calisse, *Italian Law*, 726.
79. Goez, *Beatrix*, 85, 87; Hay, *Military Leadership*, 7–12.
80. Zanarini, 'I Canossa', 46.

81. For the term *dux* see Goez, *Reg. Bea.*, Nr. 52; for attendance at synods see Nr. 15c; for donations of property see Nr. 13.
82. Goez, *Beatrix*, 20.
83. See Thomas Groß, *Lothar III. und die Mathildischen Güter* (Frankfurt am Main: Peter Lang, 1990), 144, 148–282; for the Lotharingian estates see 281–82.
84. Ibid., 144; I. S. Robinson, *The Papacy, 1073–1198: Continuity and Innovation* (Cambridge: Cambridge University Press, 1990), 51, 246, 247–48; Paolo Golinelli, *L'ancella di san Pietro: Matilde di Canossa e la Chiesa* (Milan: Jaca Book, 2015), 135–55.
85. *DD MT*, Nr. 93; Overmann, *Reg. Mat.*, p. 212.
86. City Population Melara (Rovigo), http://www.citypopulation.de/php/italy-veneto.php?cityid=029032, date accessed 28 July 2016.
87. Melara is four kilometers from Ostiglia as the crow flies: Groß, *Lothar III*, 212, 145.
88. Schiaparelli, *Diplomi di Ugo*, Nr. 3, 255–56.
89. *DO II*, Nr. 281; Böhmer, *RI* 2.2, Nr. 881.
90. Böhmer, *RI* 2.3, 1307b; Alessandro Colombo, 'I diplomi ottoniani e adelaidini e la fondazione del monastero di S. Salvatore in Pavia', in *Miscellanea Pavese*, ed. Renato Soriga (Turin: 1932), Nr. 3, 31–33. For the tendency for women to donate their lands to monasteries, sometimes when their ownership was under dispute, see Stafford, '*Mutation*', 120–22. However, Althoff sees Adelheid's dealings with San Salvatore as freely undertaken: Gerd Althoff, 'Probleme um die dos der Koniginnen im 10. und 11. Jahrhundert', in *Veuves et veuvage dans le haut Moyen Âge*, ed. Michel Parisse (Paris: Picard, 1993), 126.
91. Böhmer, *RI* 2.3, Nrs 1309a; 1309b; 1309c.
92. Ibid., Nrs 1308–18.
93. Groß, *Lothar III*, 242.
94. Goez, *Beatrix*, 84. For Matilda's association with Revere in 1113, see Vito Fumagalli, *Terra e società nell'Italia padana, I secoli IX e X* (Turin: 1976), 10 and 21n29.
95. 'Cuius dignis precibus annuentes et rem diligentius relatione nostrorum fidelium cognoscentes, tandem invenimus multorum congruo testimonio, quod in illa silva ... violentia, qualiter supradiximus, iniuste fuerat predicatae curti Melariae a nostris illata', *DD MT*, Nr. 93.

96. 'Notum igitur fieri volumus omnibus nostris fidelibus tam presentibus quam futuris predictam violentiam ad curte Melariae removisse, et ne aliquis nostrorum intra predictae silvae suprascripta confinia absque consensu illius prioris, qui pro tempore aderit in curte Melariae, porcos suos audeat retinere, firmiter precepisse', ibid., Nr. 93.
97. 'Si quis autem contra hanc nostrae institutionis paginam venire temptaverit et de hoc, quod fecimus pro remedio animae nostrae, predictam curtem sive iuste sive iniuste molestare voluerit, sciat se nostram iram incurrere et banni nostri poenam quinquaginta libras argenti debere persolvere, medietatem prefatae ecclesiae sancti Saluatoris, medietatem vero camerae nostrae', ibid., Nr. 93.
98. 'hoc tamen scripto in suo semper robore permanente. Quod ut verius credatur et futuris temporibus firmius habeatur, propriae manus subscriptione firmavimus', ibid., Nr. 93.
99. Katherine Fischer Drew, *The Lombard Laws* (Philadelphia: University of Pennsylvania Press, 1973), 21–22, and for Rothair's Edict, see Laws 13, 279, 19, 249, 238, 240.
100. Ibid., Rothair's Edict: Laws 349, 350. A siliqua was a Roman silver coin of the fourth and fifth centuries AD, with the value of 1/24th of a solidus, a gold coin: *OED Online*, s.vv. 'siliqua', 'solidus'.
101. Drew, *Lombard Laws*, Rothair's Edict: Laws 186, 191, 208, 209, 189, 6, 7, 182, 204; Neil McLeod, '*Cáin Adomnáin* and the Lombards', in *Language and Power in the Celtic World*, ed. Anders Ahlqvist and Pamela O'Neill (Sydney: Celtic Studies Foundation, University of Sydney, 2011), 257–60.
102. Gerd Althoff, '*Ira Regis*: Prolegomena to a History of Royal Anger', in *Anger's Past: The Social Uses of an Emotion in the Middle Ages*, ed. Barbara H. Rosenwein (Ithaca, NY: Cornell University Press, 1998), 59. For Matilda's signature see Mario Nobili, 'L'ideologia politica in Donizone', in *SM III*, 263–70; for her chancery see Ferrara, 'Gli anni di Matilde', 89–98.
103. *DO I*, Nr. 368. In 975 Adelheid's son, Emperor Otto II, and in 987, her grandson, King Otto III, confirmed the gift. The two documents specify the lands to be in Alsace, without naming Hochfelden, and that they were dotal gifts: *DO II*, Nr. 109; *DO III*, Nr. 36.
104. *DH IV*, Nr. 149.
105. Ibid., Nr. 79.

106. Ibid., Nr. 152; Mechtild Black-Veldtrup, *Kaiserin Agnes (1043–1077): Quellenkritische Studien*, Münstersche Historische Forschungen 7 (Cologne: Böhlau, 1995), 258–59.
107. Lampert, *Annales*, s.a. 1062; Robinson, *Henry IV*, 44.
108. Sergi, 'Poteri', 32–33.
109. Donizo, *VM*, 1.1, lines 120–22.
110. 'Ditescens Atto, mea moenia duxit in altum', ibid., 1.2, line 397.
111. *Me renovat semper turres fabbricando recentes*, Donizo, *VM*, 2, line 56; p. 127n13; Aldo A. Settia, 'Castelli e villaggi nelle terre canossiane tra X e XIII secoli', in *SM III*, 286, 292.
112. Wickham, *Early Medieval Italy*, 186–87. For the trend for families to adopt surnames taken from their castle names, see Chris Wickham, *The Mountains and the City: The Tuscan Appennines in the Early Middle Ages* (Oxford: Oxford University Press, 1988), 130. For the Canossan's self-consciousness as a dynasty: Sergi, 'Poteri', 35. For dynastic history in the Middle Ages: Leah Shopkow, 'Dynastic History', in *Historiography in the Middle Ages*, ed. D. M. Deliyannis (Leiden and Boston: Brill, 2003), 217–48.
113. Golinelli, 'Donizone e il suo poema', xi.
114. Settia, 'Castelli', 282, 287.
115. Ibid., 293.
116. Robinson, *Henry IV*, 160–64; Hanna Vollrath, 'The Western Empire under the Salians', *NCMH* 4, Part 2 (2004), 58–60.
117. For the Lombard laws, see *Leges Langobardorum, 643–866*, ed. Franz Beyerle; trans. Drew, *Lombard Laws*.
118. For the Salian laws, see *Lex Salica*, ed. Karl August Eckhardt, *MGH Leges* 4:2 (Hanover: 1969); trans. Katherine Fischer Drew, *The Laws of the Salian Franks* (Philadelphia: University of Pennsylvania Press, 1991). See also Patrick Wormald, '*Lex Scripta* and *Verbum Regis*: Legislation and Germanic Kingship, from Euric to Cnut', in *Early Medieval Kingship*, eds P. H. Sawyer and I. N. Wood (Leeds: University of Leeds, 1977), 107, 138.
119. Theodore John Rivers, *Laws of the Salian and Ripuarian Franks* (New York: AMS Press, 1986), pp. 2–4, 27; Wormald, '*Lex*', 108; Patrick Wormald, *The Making of English Law: King Alfred to the Twelfth Century*, vol. I. *Legislation and its Limits* (Oxford: Blackwell Publishers, 1999), 32–53; Maurizio Lupoi, *The Origins of the European Legal Order*, trans. Adrian Belton (Cambridge:

Cambridge University Press, 2000), 98–101; J. M. Wallace-Hadrill, *The Long-Haired Kings* (Toronto: University of Toronto Press, 1962), 2–4, 8–9, 95–120.
120. Böhmer, *RI* 2.3, Nr. 1307b.
121. Ibid., Nr. 1309a; Uhlirz, 'Rechtliche Stellung', 90.
122. *Cartularium Langobardorum*, ed. G. H. Pertz, *MGH, Leges* 4:595–602 (1869), Nr. 1.595: Böhmer, *RI* 2.3, Nr. 1307b; Wickham, 'Land Disputes', 245n32. For the use of the *festuca* and the *wadium* see Le Goff, 'Symbolic Ritual', 257–59.
123. Calisse, *Italian Law*, 704–8. Edward Jenks, *The Early History of Negotiable Instruments*, vol. 3 (Boston: Little, Brown, 1909), 44–45.
124. Adelheid's dotal gifts from her first husband, Lothar, are recorded in Schiaparelli, *Diplomi di Ugo*, Nr. 3. Property given to her by her second husband, Otto I, were confirmed by her son and grandson: *DO II*, Nr. 109; Böhmer, *RI* 2.2, Nr. 690; *DO III*, Nr. 36. See also Uhlirz, 'Rechtliche Stellung', 86n3, 89, 92.
125. Giulia Petracco Sicardi, 'La formula salica di investitura nell'età matildica e i suoi antecedenti storici', in *SM III*, 259–60.
126. Böhmer, *RI* 2.3, Nr. 1307b; Uhlirz, 'Rechtliche Stellung', 90.
127. Calisse, *Italian Law*, 704–9.
128. Böhmer, *RI* 2.3, Nr. 963; *DO III*, Nr. 7a.
129. *DO III*, Nr. 7b; Böhmer, *RI* 2.3, Nr. 964; Uhlirz, 'Rechtliche Stellung', 94–5; Pauline Stafford, *Queens, Concubines and Dowagers: The King's Wife in the Early Middle Ages* (London: Batsford Academic and Educational, 1983), 103.
130. Uhlirz, 'Rechtliche Stellung', 96–97; Stafford, *Queens, Concubines*, 102–3.
131. *DD MT*, Nrs 1, 6, 9, 10, 11, 23, 26, 27, 28, 33, 36, 40, 76, 98, 100, 111, 122, 127, 133, 138, 139.
132. Rivers, *Laws*, 27 and Nr. 108 at 135.
133. Goez, *Beatrix*, 35, 75–77. Further information about Ermingarda not available to me.

CHAPTER 4

Rule: Models of Rulership and the Tools of Justice

The leading authority on kingship and Saxon history in the tenth century was Widukind, a monk of Corvey, who finished his *Res gestae Saxonicae* (*Deeds of the Saxons*) probably in 967/968, adding the final chapters about Emperor Otto I's death in 973.[1] Having entered the monastery in 940, he lived almost contemporaneously with Otto's active leadership and Adelheid's marriage to Otto I. Widukind had the following to say about Adelheid's and Otto's courtship:

> Since the *virtue* [in all the Roman and medieval senses of the word] of the above-named queen [Adelheid] was not unknown to him, he [Otto I] resolved to make a pretended visit to Rome. But when he arrived in Lombardy, he attempted moreover *to try the love of the queen for him with gifts of gold*. Having reliably made trial of which, he made her his wife, *and along with her he obtained the city of Pavia which was the royal seat....* The king celebrated his nuptials in Italy with *royal magnificence,* and *set out* from there intending to celebrate the next Easter in Saxony, with the *fame* of his recent marriage *conferring great happiness and favor upon the fatherland.*[2]

Widukind's work is the definitive source for the understanding of monarchy and politics in the tenth century. His three books narrate the distinguished origin of the Saxons, the transfer of authority from the Franks to them under Henry I and the *res gestae* (literally 'things having been done') of the contemporary ruler Otto I. Widukind gave the name *Res*

© The Author(s) 2017
P. Nash, *Empress Adelheid and Countess Matilda,*
DOI 10.1057/978-1-137-58514-1_4

gestae Saxonicae (*Deeds of the Saxons*) to his work.[3] His purpose in writing is clear: Widukind expounded on the right actions of the good ruler, having set up Otto I as the perfect example. As a contemporary writer, Widukind remains a significant chronicler of the events related directly to his own interests.

Accordingly Widukind's polemic about why the Saxons had the right to rule remains an apt model, although not the only one, for Ottonian rulership in the mid- to late tenth century. Hrotsvitha of Gandersheim's *Gesta Ottonis imperatoris* (*Deeds of Emperor Otto*), written at a similar time to Widukind's *Gesta* and which especially values female rulership, is just as important in its portrayal of Saxon rulership in the latter half of the tenth century.[4] Nevertheless Widukind does lay out in a systematic manner the ideal qualities of the male ruler and initially this is the model examined.

Early Medieval Ottonian Kingship

To examine Ottonian female rulership it is necessary first to understand Ottonian kingship since the queen was dependent for her status on her relationship with the male ruler. Ottonian kingship derived from Carolingian kingship with its basis in itinerant kings, supported by the court palace and the web of counts and dukes throughout the kingdom through which the king exerted his authority (the royal *bannum*).[5] Ottonian kings did not rule from one geographical center, although Aachen had particular significance.[6] The court owed its existence and authority to the presence of the king; he ruled by traveling around the kingdom, and his queen, as evidenced by her frequent mentions in the official diplomata (the legal written instruments of government), often traveled with him. The authority and sacral nature of the king were displayed in formal ceremonies which punctuated his travels.

The king showed his superiority by a variety of non-verbal actions. He kept his subordinates waiting and was the first to enter important buildings such as the cathedral. He hunted, ate and drank with his kin and friends. He gave them gifts; he punished and forgave miscreants. He was influenced by the petitions of intermediaries. Ottonian and early Salian rulership was distinguished by its collective sacrality. In apparent contradiction, individual rulers were guided by those around them.[7] Formulaic and individualistic methods of rulership were ritualized in actions, rulings and recordings in diplomata, chronicles, annals, histories and other written works, in decorated Gospel books and on ivories, seals and coins. The king exhibited his pleasure, sorrow or anger. An example of the importance of the performance of rituals is the Latin and Old High German poem *De Heinrico*, copied in England in the first half of the eleventh century. A certain King Otto and a certain Duke Henry (not specifically identified) undertake rituals of obeisance and forgiveness.[8] *De Heinrico* is a reminder that the combination of private negotiations and public ceremonies saved face for the parties and encouraged a public, unified resolution.[9]

Otto I's kingship was only the second in what was to become the Ottonian dynasty. His father, Duke Henry of Saxony, had been nominated by King Conrad I (d. 918) and acclaimed as sole king by the people, but Henry had proceeded cautiously in the early years with the leading men of the realm. Similarly Otto remained in a precarious position in his initial years. Tensions arose because of the abandonment of the division of the kingdom among all the sons. Otto needed to take account of the *dignitas* of all those involved: he could not use his kingly powers of punishment unfettered. Nevertheless he could practice *clementia*, which retained historical clout as a Christian and imperial virtue. In the early sixth century Ennodius had flattered Theodoric, king of the Ostrogoths, by addressing him in old Roman terms as 'most merciful lord', 'renowned lord' and 'venerable prince'.[10] Otto paraded *clementia* when necessary because his kin's and the magnates' sensitivities to their rights of relationship and friendship under King Henry I had continued into Otto I's reign.[11] However, Otto varied his much flaunted *clementia* to meet the exigencies created by angry and powerful opponents.[12]

Otto I's conception of his own kingship can be detected in his first diploma, which indicates a shift in the understanding of kingship.[13] Otto gave to the members of the congregation at Quedlinburg, a monastery for women, 'extensive properties and incomes, royal protection, the right to an advocate from the Liudolfing family or its collateral relatives, and the prerogative to elect their abbess without outside interference'. Otto's first charter, in delineating Quedlinburg's legal status, redefined the nature of kingship: the charter contained notions of the '"indivisibility of the realm", the creation of a royal dynasty and the elective element in German kingship'.[14] Otto appears to confirm the idea that his progeny might legitimately rule or that others not of his progeny might have the right to rule if elected. In either case he nominated a member from his family group, the Liudolfings, the right of advocacy (*advocatus*), that is, protection, for the members of the community at Quedlinburg.[15] Otto used the word *cognatio* not *generatio*, by which he may have been advocating that in the case of the failure of the male line, the descendants of daughters or of Queen Mathilda's sisters would retain the right of advocacy for the monastery.[16]

In practice Otto I could not have been more dynastic. In 961 just before he departed for Italy the king crowned his young son joint king when six years of age. The ceremony, summarized as follows, incorporated the ideas of Christian kingship already established by the later tenth century:

> The king's role was to be the most strenuous of kings, the vanquisher of enemies, the guardian and defender of churches and the clergy. God was requested to crown him with 'the crown of justice and piety', to grant him victory over his enemies visible and invisible, and to bestow on him abundant harvests, health, peace, and heirs of his body.... to keep subject peoples loyal and magnates peaceable.... Otto [I] ... [was] likened to the rulers of the ancient Israelites ... anointed kings fighting in the name of God and ruling with justice and wisdom as mediators between God and people.[17]

The gesture of crowning Otto II joint king together with the ceremony itself sent a strong message of dynastic command and the leading men were not slow to understand Otto I's wishes; they reconfirmed Otto II as king by acclamation on his father's death in 973. Otto II did the same for his own son, acclaiming him as joint king at Verona in June 983 when he was barely three and from Italy organized his further coronation in the German lands at Aachen later that same year.[18]

Early Medieval Queenship

While early medieval rulers acted autonomously, their wives mostly acted as adjuncts to their husbands, as regents for their sons or, on very rare occasions, in their own right. Because they were usually present at the rituals of rulership with their husbands, queens were also prominent on the royal *iter* and at the concomitant councils at which the king issued judgments. The *iter* involved not only the physical travel around the kingdom but also attendance at the accompanying religious ceremonies, the most important of which included the celebration of the great feasts of the church at locations whose prestige was enhanced by the presence of the royal party.

The active duties of the queen in the Carolingian court had been laid down by Charlemagne in the early ninth century[19] and also by Hincmar of Reims in his *De ordine palatii* shortly before his death in 882:

> The good management of the palace, and especially the royal dignity, as well as the gifts given annually to the officers ... pertained especially to the queen, and under her to the chamberlain.[20]

In those words Hincmar gave the authority for the treasury to the queen, since the chamberlain included oversight of the royal treasury among his duties. She was held responsible for a vast quantity of valuable treasure, consisting of jewels, gold, silver, ornaments, luxury textiles and, in certain instances, the crown and the royal insignia. The written mode operated as a practical way to rule the kingdom in the late ninth century at the time when Hincmar wrote.[21] Even if Hincmar were proposing an ideal in 882 to instruct the young King Carloman, the setting out of such supports the importance of the queen's role in the royal household, the center of power in the kingdom.

Such duties were given to the queen so that the king might be freed of all concern for the household or the palace and could concentrate on the rulership and preservation of the state of the entire realm. She was required particularly to anticipate events and to ensure that everything that might be needed would be available. With access to the treasury, this gave the queen wide authority and one would think encouragement to be mentally nimble. In practice such responsibility went beyond mere actions but included the entire spectrum of display of such actions, discussed further below. The queen's duties of supervision of the royal household were followed in the Ottonian court. From the early ninth to the early eleventh centuries, the queen had a closeness to the ruler, the final supervisory role over the royal household and involvement in domain administration.[22] Undeniably the queen had not only the right but also the duty to collaborate in the government.[23]

The queen had other duties not always clearly specified as to their execution. She was expected to maintain the king's presence, especially during his absence on military campaigns. As an extension of her role as wife, her place by his side, she often traveled with him to support his kingship. Her role encompassed counselor, gift-giver, facilitator of the hierarchy and responsibility for order in the household and smoother of relationships within the royal family and among the king's war band by word and gesture. In 588 Theudelinda, daughter of the Bavarian ruler, Garibald, undertook the role of cupbearer in offering the cup of wine to the chief men of the Lombards in strict order of rank. She brought the kingship of the Lombards eventually to Agilulf, who was the man she served first.[24] Likewise in highlighting the supervision of the (male) cupbearers by Hermann the Frank, duke of Swabia, at Otto I's coronation in 936, Widukind demonstrated Hermann's high status and the importance of cupbearing.[25] By the early eleventh century when King Henry II was preoccupied on the battlefield, his wife Queen Kunigunde sent her cupbearer to the king to convey the news of important events in the kingdom and, in her husband's absence, it was expected that 'she should see to the welfare of the realm'.[26] Those ceremonies confirmed the tradition that the one responsible for the king's cup was the trusted confidant of the king.

Above all the queen bore the king's prospective heir. While the Ottonians established succession through primogeniture, inheritance by the king's son remained uncertain before the idea's firm acceptance in the later Ottonian period. Even when King Henry I designated his first-born Otto as his sole successor, his nomination did not settle the matter. Of his two sons the younger brother, Duke Henry of Bavaria, was championed by his mother over Otto I on the grounds that he, unlike Otto, had been born after his father became king. On King Henry I's death the leading men of the kingdom bickered about which son, Otto or Henry, would be the new king.[27] Otto I and Otto II ensured that each of their corresponding sons was crowned as a young boy to strengthen his claim to the throne in the event of his father's unexpected death. Thus although the East-Frankish kings were the first to break successfully with partible inheritance, some lingering uncertainty arising from earlier customs augmented the importance of the queen's role as protector of the infant son and thus increased her consequence.

The above discussion relates to the role of the queen while the king was alive. On his death there were precedents for the queen to rule in the West. Queen Adelaide (not to be confused with Empress Adelheid, the main subject of this book), the widow of Hugh Capet, king of France (d. 996), continued to exercise considerable authority more than seven months after Hugh's death, as witnessed by Gerbert of Aurillac's action in professing obedience to her.[28] In addition in an age when the fiction was kept that the young child himself was ruling, in practice a strong queen could in effect rule. On the death of Empress Adelheid's son, Emperor Otto II, her three-year old grandson, Otto III, succeeded to the kingship. Yet the three *dominae imperiales* (Empress Adelheid, Empress Theophanu and Abbess Mathilda of Quedlinburg) ruled as regents at various times during the eleven years before he reached his majority.[29] Nevertheless Adam of Bremen, in discussing Otto III's life, calculated Otto's reign from the age of three: 'The third Otto, although still a boy, succeeded to the throne and for eighteen years distinguished the scepter by a strong and just rule.'[30] The success of the queen in the role of regent 'was predicated not simply on her traditional occupation of it, nor on some structural property of familial or royal succession'; she had to use to capacity the 'personal, material, and symbolic resources at her disposal'.[31] After Otto II's death Adelheid, Theophanu and Mathilda of Quedlinburg most fully demonstrated their scope and the ability to employ them.

The queen's actions were not sufficient in themselves; documentation in words and via concrete symbols confirmed her authority. The writing down of oral proclamations spread the ruler's words and acted as a later reference standard.[32] The queen's role as intermediary, adviser and confirmer of government was chronicled. The frequency with which she was mentioned in the king's diplomata, the terms used and her titles reflected her importance. For example the successful intercession by Otto I's first wife, Edith, on behalf of her mother-in-law to restore the latter to the king's favor was recorded in Queen Mathilda's *Life*.[33] In addition via the commissioning of both images and slogans on coins, the use of elaborate document seals, the carving of images on altar pieces, and their creation in Gospel books, kings and queens reinforced their sovereignty. The ivory image of Otto II and Theophanu at the feet of Christ lifting up the young Otto III is an example of a public display. The figures are dressed in northern Continental style to impress the local onlookers.[34] This proclamation of 'an ideal of "queenship"' was especially relevant to the Ottonian kingdom.[35] Royal display contained the idea of performance with all the paraphernalia of exhibition—impressive people, on occasions in exotic costumes, undertaking ritualized movement or taking dramatic poses, including the staging of events. The banquet became an ideal setting with crown-wearing and the demonstration of wealth to show the rich resources of the royal party where the queen performed a major role. Consequently Otto III's habit of dining by himself in the midst of his followers was unusual enough to elicit comments.[36] As well as secular activities liturgical ceremonies remained a way of implying power by the public appearance of royalty and their entourage as did the queen's collection of holy relics of the saints and the maintenance of memoria for the dead.[37] Not only the presence of the king but also his exhibitions of ritualized or real emotions were imitated by the queen.[38]

Two examples of many provide relevant instances of the important use of ritual and of display by the *dominae imperiales* to impress their audience with the sacrality and authenticity of their rule. First, in 984 when the carriage of the regency for Otto III was finally settled on the three women after the great struggle within the kingdom between them and Henry the Wrangler, the *Quedlinburg Annals* report in great detail and with much fanfare how the three women took the young Otto to Abbess Mathilda's convent at Quedlinburg where a crowd of clergy, people and virgins was 'joyful [just as one would wish] at the long-awaited arrival of their spiritual mother [Abbess Mathilda] and at the king's triumph'.[39] Second, shortly after Theophanu's death, Bishop Thietmar of Merseburg and the *Quedlinburg Annals* highlighted the ceremony to consecrate the new church at Halberstadt in which Adelheid, Abbess Mathilda and the still under-age king participated with a great flourish with archbishops and other colleagues.[40] We should not, however, take the meaning of ritual overly seriously and programmatically.[41] Nevertheless contemporary writers include rituals too often for them to be disregarded. Consequently Adelheid's appearance at those important Ottonian events and the evidence of the documents as witnesses to the events has significance.

***

Neither the original ceremonial diploma, issued without doubt on the wedding of Otto I and Adelheid as king and queen in late 951, nor copies remain to complement Widukind of Corvey's brief but significant portrayal of Otto's courting of Adelheid, their wedding and their formal progress around the kingdom. Nevertheless Widukind's narrative contains all the essential ingredients in order to understand the processes of rulership that Otto and Adelheid followed as king and queen in the second half of the tenth century throughout the Italian and German kingdoms.

Otto had carefully selected his new bride, since the quality of her *virtus* made or broke a queen's reputation. Ancient Romans assigned seven distinct meanings to *virtus*, four of which applied to people. Those included manly spirit, especially as displayed in war; excellence of character or mind; moral excellence; and potency or efficacy. Medieval usages stressed further meanings of 'strength, force, vigour'; 'authority, power', and 'competence, right'.[42] Outstanding early medieval royal wives in their character and virtues were generally allowed to be 'as fully "virile"' as their husbands.[43] Since Widukind attributed *virtus* to Adelheid, he was applauding her manly spirit, excellence of character, moral excellence, strength, authority and competence.[44]

Renowned lineage and connections could bestow *virtus*. Adelheid's impeccable pedigree, as the daughter of King Rudolf II of Burgundy and Bertha of Swabia (herself daughter of Reginlind of Zurich and Duke Burchard of Swabia) and widow of King Lothar of Italy (d. 950), was enhanced by retaining the queenship of the kingdom of Italy after Lothar's death. Over her lifetime her connections with royalty were extraordinary. '[S]he was the daughter, sister, and aunt of three kings of Burgundy, the wife, mother, and grandmother of three emperors of Germany, sister-in-law, mother-in-law, and grandmother of three French kings, not to say widow of a king of Lombard Italy.'[45] We can add that she was the mother, grandmother and aunt to many abbesses and bishops. In addition, her physical beauty added to her intrinsic virtue. Otto I had inquired as to Adelheid's reputation in all the matters related to *virtus*, since for the tricky amalgamation of the kingdom of Italy with his kingship over the Germans he had to be certain of the loyalty of the person he might woo. Otto could not test a woman in the same way he could a man, that is, on the battlefield, and so he chose another method: according to Widukind, he or his messengers tested her allegiance with gifts of the most important of material goods—gold.[46]

Hrotsvitha's judiciously worded *Gesta Ottonis* provides clues to Otto I's predicament and the names of those with whom Adelheid might be tempted to be disloyal. Hrotsvitha describes Otto's enquiries about Adelheid but avoids criticizing his younger brother Henry, duke of Bavaria, and Otto's son, Liudolf, by his first wife. Some background is necessary to understand Hrotsvitha's careful niceties. A number of points of tension among three people threatened the stability of the kingdom. First, primogeniture was only beginning to be established in the Ottonian kingdom. King Henry I had nominated his first-born son, Otto, as the sole inheritor of the kingdom but his queen, Mathilda, favored their second son Henry. On King Henry I's death in 936 Otto was acclaimed as sovereign by the magnates, according to his father's wishes. The chroniclers of the day reported the disharmony within the Ottonian house, especially between the two brothers, because Henry demanded the throne for himself. Henry rebelled against Otto I, initially conspiring with Eberhard of Franconia and Giselbert of Lotharingia and later with a group of east Saxon warriors. By 951 Henry had been reconciled with the new king and had consolidated his own position in the kingdom as duke of the important duchy of Bavaria with close physical and social ties to Italy.[47]

Second, Liudolf had every reason to expect to inherit the kingdom when Otto I died. As the only legitimate son and heir at that time, he had been given in marriage in 947 to Ida, daughter of the duke of the prestigious duchy of Swabia, and Otto had paraded with the newly married couple throughout the kingdom of Italy. However, in late 951 Otto's new young wife, who could produce another heir, threatened to usurp Liudolf. Since all his kingly ambitions were in danger of being thwarted, he had every reason to cherish his father's widowerhood. Shortly after the wedding he rebelled, accompanied by his brother-in-law, Conrad the Red, duke of Lotharingia.[48]

Third, Gerberga (II) of Gandersheim, to whom Hrotsvitha owed obedience because Gerberga was her abbess, had directed her to write the *Gesta Ottonis*. However, Gerberga had significant family ties to the formerly rebellious, now faithful, Duke Henry I of Bavaria as his daughter.[49] Consequently in her writing Hrotsvitha needed to be sensitive to the relationships between Duke Henry, Duke Liudolf and Abbess Gerberga as brother, son and niece to Otto I.

Aware of the history Hrotsvitha presents a long passage in which she notes Otto I's careful checking of Adelheid's credentials, consulting with his leading men who had been the recipients of Adelheid's very sweet tenderness ('praedulcem ... pietatem'). They frequently repeated to him her manifold loyalty ('multiplicem ... pietatem') and that none other was so worthy as she to be conducted to the royal marriage couch. Hrotsvitha further details the king's careful consideration of a marriage with Adelheid and his recall of so many benefices ('tantae pietatis') by Adelheid in a third usage of *pietas* in reference to her. By now he has become acquainted with Adelheid's integrity ('bonitatem'). Hrotsvitha's most decisive passage emphasizes very strongly the faithfulness exhibited by Adelheid in her progress through northern Italy to Otto, accompanied by his brother, Henry, and a troop of guards. Otto directs Henry to meet Adelheid with all due deference and to escort her to him at Pavia, which he did. She immediately found favor with Otto and was chosen to be the worthy helpmate of his empire.[50] The significance of the term *consors regni*, especially as applied to Adelheid, is discussed later in this chapter. Hrotsvitha notes that Liudolf (Otto's son by his former wife), who had every reason to dislike a new spouse, nevertheless attested to her loyalty: 'she [Adelheid] subjected herself [to Otto] with all eagerness of belief.'[51]

Otto's reasons for apprehension related to Henry's and Liudolf's loyalty and are resolved, at least for that short period. Hrotsvitha shows the complexity of the interrelations in the Ottonian household and presents Otto's and Adelheid's concerns and their resolution as directly as she can within the constraints of her situation. Hrotsvitha presents the reasons for Otto's eagerness and the methods he used to test the faithfulness of his potential new wife. Unlike Widukind of Corvey, Hrotsvitha avoids the word *virtus* in describing Adelheid but favors dutiful respect (*pietas*), goodness (*bonitas*), worthy of homage (*veneranda*) and faith (*fides*). In the medieval world, *fides* holds the additional meaning of loyalty to a lord and is particularly associated with oaths of fealty.[52] Given his sensitivity to plots past and plots to come, Otto wooed Adelheid after thoroughly testing her 'loyalty' to his cause.

Adelheid, having been proven loyal, with an excellent pedigree and conforming to the Italian tradition of conveying royalty through the female line, reinforced Otto I's claim to the kingdom of Italy, symbolized by its capital Pavia.[53] The strength of that tradition in Adelheid's case bears testing. It is uncertain whether the wedding or the entitlement occurred first. Otto marched into Italy, took the kingdom, married Adelheid and 'received the commendation of the northern Italian nobility at Pavia to complete his claim to Italy'.[54] Otto issued three diplomata in which he called himself *rex Langobardorum* and *rex Italicorum*.[55] His marriage to Adelheid extended his rule to include Burgundy and Italy as well as Germany.[56] Karl Leyser notes that after Adelheid joined Otto at Pavia the 'wealth and *honor* of the Italian kingdom could now become his by right'.[57] The Latin word *honor* has a sense of 'unassailable state of rights and property, well-established legal position'.[58] The intention and the sequence of events appear to be that Otto conquered the kingdom of Lombardy, and consequently the *regnum Italiae*, and then married Adelheid. Otto may have claimed the kingship of the Franks and Lombards before his wedding.[59] There is uncertainty about to what extent the custom, exercised at the time of Lombard rule, to have the widowed queen determine a new ruler by her remarriage still applied in Italy in the middle of the tenth century.[60] Nevertheless contemporaries endorsed Otto's right, by marriage to the king's widow and by conquest, to designate himself king of the Lombards at the royal city of Pavia, with homage paid but no election by the magnates.[61] Despite the uncertainty of the sequence of events, there is no doubt that because *that* dowager queen was the widow of the king of Italy, significant power was vested in her as bearer of the Italian kingdom.

From fragments of evidence the date and place of Adelheid's and Otto's wedding can be determined with plausible assurance, even though the date is not precisely determined in the sources. The *Annales Einsiedlenses* places the wedding at Pavia in 952; in the terse words of the Annalist: '952 King Otto with his son [Liudolf] in Italy, *and his royal wedding at Pavia*'.[62] Adalbert of Magdeburg and Widukind state that after the wedding Liudolf departed for Saalfeld and celebrated Christmas there; Flodoard of Reims begins the year 952 by recording that the ceremony and Christmas had been celebrated.[63] It can be dated to 9 October 951 with reasonable assurance. Otto issued diplomata from the old Lombard capital, Pavia, on 23 September and 9 October of that year. On 10 October and 15 October he added new titles: he called himself *rex Francorum et Langobardorum* and *rex Francorum et Italicorum*.[64] The feast of St Denis, the saint who brought Christianity to France, is celebrated on 9 October. Charlemagne chose 9 October for his own coronation in 768. Although Otto might have considered himself entitled to be king of the Franks *and* the Lombards by virtue of his military success, his choice of Pavia (the historical capital of Italy) and his activities on and about that date sent a strong public message of a new Charlemagne, who now viewed the Italian and German people as his subjects.[65] The evidence, presented together, is highly suggestive that the wedding was celebrated on 9 October and strengthens the idea of the ongoing and superior right of the Italian queen to bring the kingdom of Italy to her husband.

Otto fulfilled expectations of kingly display: 'with his nuptials having been celebrated [with] royal magnificence'.[66] With his new queen, he consolidated his expanded kingship via the royal *iter*, progressing quickly from Pavia north across the Alps to his duchy of Saxony, from where the majority of his kinspeople and followers came.[67] Consequently by visiting them first within weeks of the wedding, Otto formally demonstrated his view of the importance of the mutual *amicitia* among his Saxon magnates, himself and his new queen.

Rulership was effected by the direct interference of the king as mediator and dictator whose actions were recorded and propagated throughout the kingdom and by the binding of people to the ruler. Consequently decisions were made during the royal *iter* with its accompanying festivals and councils and all the rituals of royalty, legitimized by the diplomata and by the presentation of the ruler as representative of Christ on earth leading men (mainly) to Christian war for the conversion of the heathens.[68] In what follows the ruler's extensive expression of real and ritualized emotion is explored in detail. In summary, rulership was accomplished through deeds (enacted), legalized by words (encoded) and demonstrated in ritualized images (displayed).

While Adelheid had a significant heritage to draw on, especially from her Italian linkages, this chapter shows that she consciously developed a model of queenship beyond that which she had inherited from her Italian connections. She did not do this without a struggle. She used certain events as pivotal points that enabled her to stand out from previous models of queenship. The imperial crowning in 962 with Otto I, eleven years after their wedding, added further legitimacy.[69]

A Model for Queenship

The Italian queens had a unique longstanding role in legitimizing the kingdom. When Theudelinda's first Lombard husband, Authari, died in September 590, the Lombard leading men asked her to select a new husband and leader. She chose Agilulf, a kinsman of her deceased husband. After Agilulf died the Lombard leading men swore fealty to her. Similarly her daughter was attributed with the same power to place a new husband on the Lombard throne.[70] Empress Angelberga was a powerbroker in Italy up to the death of her husband Louis II in 875.[71] In the mid-tenth century Adelheid strengthened and legitimized Otto's right to the Italian kingdom.

According to Hrotsvitha, Adelheid's first husband, King Lothar, had acted 'rightly' in 'leaving the kingdom of Italy to be held fast by the merit of the eminent queen'.[72] In addition, 'She possessed such pre-eminent natural abilities that she could have ruled worthily the state bequeathed to her'.[73] Odilo of Cluny grants her the honor of bringing not just the queenship, through her marriage to Lothar, but also the empire to Otto I. Otto married Adelheid before he had fought and won the prestigious Battle of the Lech in 955. Otto's father, King Henry I, nominated Otto as successor to the East-Frankish lands over his younger brother, Henry, who may have had some entitlement because (unlike Otto) he had been born after his father became king. However, Henry's entitlement to the throne, asserted by Liudprand and by the unknown author of the *'Later Life' of Queen Mathilda*, was spurious since the kingdom had already become indivisible.[74] Nevertheless further legitimization was needed and Otto's marriage to Adelheid provided that.

Sometime after Otto I succeeded his father, he made his brother Henry duke of Bavaria. The anonymous writer of the *Vita Mathildis* and Odilo of Cluny in his *Epitaphium* used the same word 'prefecit', with the meaning of 'put in charge (of)' or 'ascribed to (a person) the charge (of)'. The contemporary use of this word is worth examining further. Adelheid played a key role in helping to secure Otto's claims to the Italian throne, paved the way for his imperial coronation and took a prominent position in imperial politics, with a particular influence on '"policies" in the *regnum Italiae*'.[75] Moreover she did not merely bolster Otto's power and her influence was more important than simply bringing the lands under his sway; she may have taken a more active part than is realized.[76] In more detail the word *praeficere* (*or preficere*) means to put in charge of or to set over military forces, units of civil administration, another person or places; to ascribe to a person the charge of something; or to cause to take precedence of or to prefer to.[77] The word has an interesting history in Ottonian times. In the *Vita Mathildis* Otto I put his brother, Henry, in charge ('prefecit') over the Bavarian people as *dux* in 947.[78] Adalbert of Magdeburg records that Otto gave precedence to ('prefecit') the venerable Geilo as abbot of the cloister of St Peter at Weißenburg in 957.[79] Odilo of Cluny notes in his *Epitaphium* that Adelheid set ('prefecit') noble king Otto over Rome as its Caesar or, according to the translation by David Warner, 'installed' Otto as emperor.[80] There is no doubt that Otto I had the power and right to give Henry the dukedom and Geilo the abbacy. Consequently it is of interest that Odilo chose to associate the same word 'prefecit' with Adelheid's actions in relation to Otto. Did Odilo mean to imply that Adelheid might have had the power and right to give Otto the emperorship or that she opened previously unimagined new dimensions in a deeper background sense, as Stefan Weinfurter suggests?[81] We cannot tell. Odilo's choice of 'prefecit', nevertheless, is intriguing and deserves attention, but his reason for that choice remains unknowable.

Adelheid's Queenship

Immediately after her wedding to Otto, Adelheid took on the actions of rulership, traveling extensively with him on the kingly *iter*. The places from which the diplomata were issued reflect her direct involvement in the workings of government. Even though the extant diplomata may not show every location she visited, sufficient remain for a reasonable grasp of the probable routes. The diplomata recorded the names of the influential persons, called interveners, who successfully interceded with the ruler for favors on behalf of others. Maps developed for this book illustrate Adelheid's travels, demonstrating in graphic form the number of times she stayed in a location as queen or empress consort, as registered by her interventions in the diplomata of Otto I and her sole interventions in Otto III's diplomata when she acted as regent for him after his mother's death and before he attained his majority. The maps may have some inaccuracies: not all charters contain a place of issue; the locations of some named places are uncertain; and whether the name of a queen/empress in a charter means that she has intervened is subject to interpretation because the terms used are varied and inconsistent. Despite these reservations tentative conclusions can be drawn about the involvement of the queen/empress in the rulership of the empire by the variety and scope of her physical travels.

Otto I and Adelheid traveled extensively in Germany and Italy during their marriage. That period lasted from their wedding on 9 October 951 until Otto I's death on 7 May 973. The number of Otto's extant diplomata during that time are shown by the size of the darker circles on a map, the larger the circle the greater the number of diplomata issued at the location (see Map 4.1).

The number of Adelheid's interventions compared with Otto's are shown in a lighter color superimposed over Otto's circles. The larger the lighter circle the higher the proportion of Adelheid's interventions at that location. The number of Adelheid's interventions at the locations are a measure of her influence and involvement in the government. The higher the number the greater her influence at that location. Caution needs to be exercised in analysis of all the maps, however, because data is only shown from extant diplomata, which may not be totally representative of all issued. Of the royal monasteries, Adelheid and Otto favored celebrating the major feasts of Easter and Christmas at Quedlinburg.[82] Not surprisingly Pavia as the Lombard capital appears frequently as a place of issue with many interventions by Adelheid. The maps also show clearly the clusters of places where Adelheid with Otto issued their diplomata: they centered around Nijmegen in the northwest, Quedlinburg in the northeast, two locations along the Rhine around Wiesbaden and Erstein, and around Rohr. As well her influence on policies in the *regnum Italiae* remained strong during her marriage to Otto, especially in Ravenna and in Venice.[83] Her decisions there in her husband's absence were not recorded as her interventions in his diplomata. Her activities in Italy remain difficult to evaluate in detail; therefore her influence in Italy is underrepresented but nevertheless important.

After Otto I's death in May 973 Adelheid's son, Otto II, and daughter-in-law, Theophanu, traveled widely, ruling the empire, albeit with

144 P. NASH

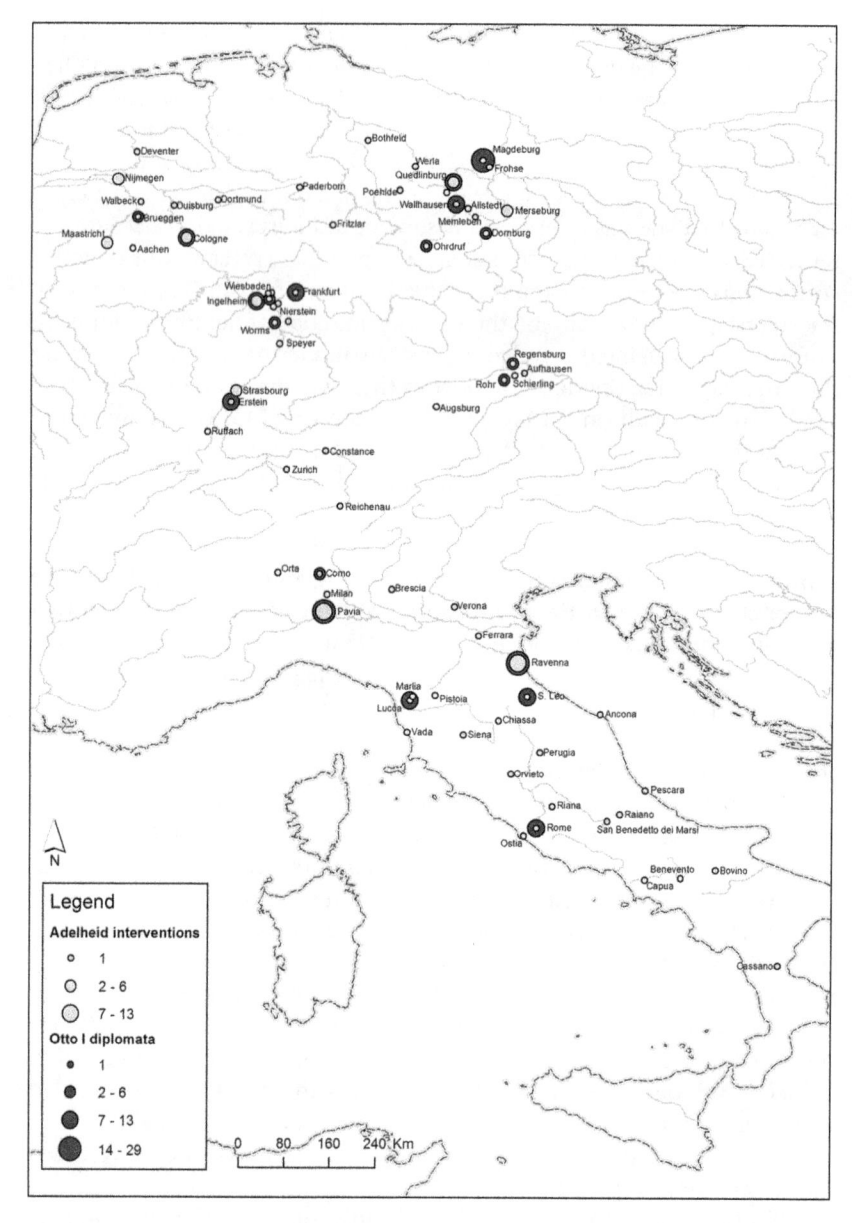

Map 4.1 Adelheid's interventions with Otto I (Map specified by Penelope Nash. Map prepared by Koolena Mapping)

Adelheid's guiding hand for the first year.[84] At the time of Otto II's death unexpectedly on 7 December 983, Adelheid had been dowager empress for ten years while her daughter-in-law had been *consors regni*. Adelheid's infant grandson, the future Otto III, inherited the kingdom. Empresses Adelheid and Theophanu and Abbess Mathilda took on the rulership on his behalf with Theophanu accepting most of the responsibility until her death in 991. Adelheid 'took his mother's place', maintaining the regency until Otto III came of age and retaining significant influence in the empire afterwards.[85] In 991 there was no debate about a smooth transition of the rulership to Adelheid. However, this had been by no means a foregone conclusion on her son's death when the chroniclers record a struggle for power among Henry the Wrangler, Lothair West Frankish king (both uncles of Otto III) and the three *dominae imperiales*, and their various supporters.

It was not merely because the leading men were displeased with Henry the Wrangler that they had turned to support the three women at the crisis of Otto II's unexpected death in 983. Although the men had sworn an oath to the child-king, Otto II's son, the women needed to present a credible alternative rulership. A number of circumstances were in favor of the women. Since Frankish, English and Byzantine queens had ruled in their husband's absence or as regents and as rulers in practice for their young sons, precedents existed for Theophanu as the mother of a young king to act as regent until his coming of age.[86] From the Ottonian household Abbess Mathilda of Quedlinburg had ruled from 968 to 971 during the absence of her father, Otto I, in Italy.[87] Adelheid had ruled as King Lothar of Italy's widow. On her second widowhood she had acted for her son and his young wife from 7 May 973 until June 974.[88] Otto II had reached his majority (he was born in 955) but perhaps the *puella* Theophanu, of unknown age (but perhaps as young as nine) when she came to the Ottonian court, needed support.[89] Of the fifty-eight diplomata that Otto II and Theophanu issued during their first year of marriage, when Adelheid was undertaking the regency for the young couple, Theophanu intervened in four with Adelheid—once each for Worms, Aachen, Frankfurt and Allstedt—and only two on her own.[90] All were in northern Germany.

By December 983 when Otto II died Adelheid had demonstrated that she had successfully ruled as independent queen/empress twice. Although a female regent was not unknown, three women appointed together as regent remained unprecedented. In the ensuing conflict, the magnates of the kingdom supported the two empresses, Adelheid and Theophanu, and Abbess Mathilda of Quedlinburg; Henry the Wrangler was required to exhibit penitence. From 984 the women brought stability to the empire. However, the abbess had religious duties to attend to with her community and two empresses were unlikely to be able to rule together in harmony. After Adelheid and Theophanu quarreled (see Chap. 2) the older woman moved to Pavia in July 985. There she steadied the region of northern Italy by undertaking some administrative functions (the details of which are not clear) and presided over the law court.[91] She had maintained her ties to ecclesiastical and lay magnates in the Italian kingdom and Venice.[92] After Theophanu made John Philagathos chancellor in Italy in May 990, Adelheid withdrew to Burgundy to the kingdom of her brother Conrad.[93] Theophanu traveled around the empire with her son, Otto III, intervening in the documents issued in his name more frequently than that of her mother-in-law during this time; the mother of the putative king took precedence over the grandmother, eminent although the latter was. As wife of the most recent former emperor Theophanu's status in Germany superseded that of her mother-in-law, although both now were dowager empresses. Particulars about Adelheid's travels are sparse and do not provide enough information for detailed analysis for that period.

On Theophanu's death in 991 Adelheid was invited to take on the regency for a third time for the empire, this time with sole authority, when she was about sixty. Because there was a smooth transition, her right, and presumably her competency, had been established.[94] Adelheid undertook the role until Otto III attained his majority at about the age of fourteen: either on 6 July 994, when he gave Eschwege to his sister Sophie; or on September 994, when he received his arms; or in early 995, when Adelheid and Abbess Mathilda ceased rulership.[95] Adelheid intervened at twenty locations, all in northern Germany, nearly half the forty-two diplomata issued under Otto III's name during the period from 15 July 991 until December 994 (see Map 4.2).

During this period she had the most freedom as an individual in controlling the empire since there was no longer a husband, a son or a daughter-in-law who might have a say in its running. For example, in 992 with the support of Archbishop Willigis of Mainz she was able to re-grant property that had been alienated from the abbey of St Maximin in the time of Otto I.[96] Most of her multiple interventions occurred in a single stopover, except at Allstedt, where she intervened on separate visits in 992 and early 994,[97] and at Pöhlde, where she intervened in two separate

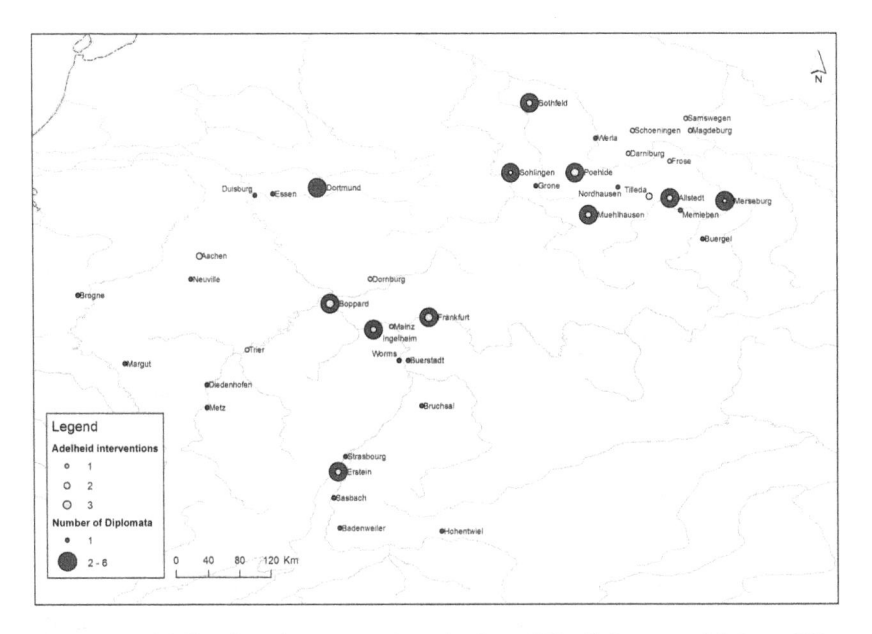

RULE: MODELS OF RULERSHIP AND THE TOOLS OF JUSTICE 147

Map 4.2 Adelheid's sole interventions in Otto III's diplomata—15 June 991–December 994 (Map specified by Penelope Nash. Map prepared by Koolena Mapping)

visits, one in late 991/early 992 and another in late 992.[98] Her stopovers occurred mainly around the Rhine in the west or the two main court cities of Quedlinburg and Magdeburg in the northeast.

After Otto III came of age Adelheid's political activities changed, although she was present at important ceremonies. In 997 when he departed for Italy, Otto III appointed Abbess Mathilda, at about forty-two years of age, as regent in Saxony, rather than his grandmother.[99] In 999 Adelheid traveled to Burgundy where she achieved a formal reconciliation between her nephew Rudolf III of Burgundy and his unruly magnates. Many of her other travels at that time related to worship and almsgiving at Payerne, St Maurice d'Agaune on the Rhine, St Victor in modern-day Geneva, Notre Dame at Lausanne and finally Selz.[100] Adelheid's activities show a determined woman, taking advantage of the situations that she could control and adapting to those more challenging.

Two other ways to evaluate the status of the queen as ruler are to examine the number of times she intervened and the titles used for her with their frequency in official documents.[101] Adelheid is named in diplomata issued by her two husbands. The first of the extant royal diplomata which mentions her details the property that King Hugh of Italy jointly with his son, Lothar, gave to her on her engagement to Lothar in December 937 when she was about seven years old. Ten years later a second diploma, addressing her as queen, was issued by her husband, now of age and king. In the third Lothar gives her property from his deceased father's estate.[102] Because the first donation rightly belongs to King Hugh's diplomata, the realistic proportion of mentions in Lothar's diplomata is two out of sixteen or 12.5 percent.

In Germany, until Otto I married Adelheid, interventions, few and mostly private, pertained almost exclusively to recipients from the Saxon duchy.[103] Otto's first wife, Edith, is mentioned sixteen times in the diplomata after their wedding in 936. Six (and probably seven) of these are interventions and all are joint, the majority with their son Liudolf.[104] In another Otto I reports, in a rather delightful phrase, that Edith and Liudolf 'nostras pulsaverunt aures' ('have beaten our ears'), that is, they have argued very strongly in pleading a case for Folcmar and Richbert, sons of the royal *fidelis* ('vassal') Frederick.[105] Since no other Ottonian or Salian royal documents use that phrase, we can presume that it was not a chancery formula and that Otto used it here with a mixture of amusement, affection for and frustration with his wife and son: Folcmar and Richbert perhaps did not deserve their gifts of several hundred *mansi* ('peasant holdings' or working farms).[106] The remaining eight diplomata that refer to Edith were issued in remembrance after her death.[107]

After Adelheid married Otto I, the number of interventions by the queen in the Ottonian court increased dramatically. Between 951 and Otto's death in 973, assuming the wedding took place on 9 October, Adelheid intervened ninety-two times out of a total of 289 extant diplomata, a proportion of just under one-third, and, of those, interventions by her alone numbered forty and interventions jointly with others fifty-two. Of the ninety-two, Adelheid intervened in Italy twenty-nine times (of these sole interventions numbered twenty-one) and in Germany sixty-three times (of these sole interventions numbered nineteen).[108]

Otto II's wife, Theophanu, intervened approximately sixty-eight times during his life—thirty-four times by herself, eight times jointly with Adelheid and twenty-six times with other notables, with one of those including Adelheid also.[109] (Otto II ruled from 8 May 973 until 7 December 983.) It is impossible to obtain the exact number and meaning of the interventions since *petitio, votum, rogatus* and *interventus* are some of the many terms used, with at times *petitio* distinguished from *interventus*.[110] Nevertheless the count errs on the side of generosity, rather than taking a narrow interpretation. Even allowing for the slight discrepancy in the numbers recorded by various authors, Theophanu's proportion of interventions, at just under one quarter, remains significantly fewer than those of Adelheid when she also reigned as the monarch's spouse.[111] By that measure Adelheid's influence in the kingdom during the lifetime of her emperor-husband was demonstrably greater than that of her daughter-in-law.

When the young king Otto III ascended the throne the kingdom was ruled in reality by the three regents, his mother (Theophanu), grandmother (Adelheid) and aunt (Abbess Mathilda). The number of interventions by Adelheid decreased at that time and disagreements appear between the reigning empress Theophanu (now in the most powerful position as mother of the young king) and her. Such disputes were not uncommon when two dowager empresses or a dowager empress and an empress, a wife of the reigning emperor, remained in the same kingdom. Similar frictions had occurred when the new queen Edith, after the death of her father-in-law King Henry I, confronted the dowager queen Mathilda, who remained in the palace.[112] Adelheid and Theophanu had interests in different localities of Italy—Adelheid with the lay and ecclesiastical leading men in the kingdom of Italy and in Venice and Theophanu in southern Italy because of landholdings there and alliances with Greek-speaking people.[113] Although the information is sparse, we know that Adelheid spent much of her time in Italy or Burgundy when Theophanu ruled for Otto III.[114] After 15 June 991 Adelheid's name quickly reappeared in the diplomata; she evidently filled the breach left by her daughter-in-law's death.

The large number of interventions by Adelheid and Theophanu shows their influence within the German court compared with the queens of the English court. The presence of the English queen Edith (wife of King Edward the Confessor of England and not to be confused with Otto I's first wife) in the English charter lists of the kings in the eleventh century fluctuates. As she continues to fail to produce an heir, her presence dwindles but later, because the sources are scarce, it is difficult to assess her influence. After 1046 she disappears from the charter witness lists.[115] Nevertheless she is the only early eleventh-century woman even to be in the lists.[116] In comparison Adelheid's and Theophanu's status and impact on the Continent remain all the more remarkable.

Not only did the number of times that the queen interceded in her husband's documents indicate her influence but the diplomata, in recording her designated title, demonstrate the esteem in which the queen was held. In 950 King Lothar had addressed his queen, Adelheid, as 'amantissimae coniugi nostrae et consorti regni nostri' ('to our most beloved wife and consort in the realm').[117] From the early 960s, Adelheid brought the phrase 'consors regni' ('sharer, consort or co-regent in the kingdom') from Italy to the empire.[118] After the crowning of Otto I as emperor on 2 February 962, the term entered the language of the German chancery in a donation to the bishops' church of Lucca on 13 March 962.[119] Subsequently a series of seventeen diplomata until 973 name Adelheid alternatively 'consors regni nostri', 'imperii nostri', 'regnorum nostrorum', 'particeps imperii nostri' and 'comes imperii nostri'.[120] Fifteen uses of 'consors' are documented during her marriage to Otto I as 'consors regni' or 'consors regnorum' or 'imperii consors' and one each for 'imperii particeps' and 'comes imperii'. While by itself the concept *consors* could be understood also in the sense of wife, the additions (*regni, imperii*) and synonyms (*particeps, comes*) do, however, make finally clear that *consors* designates above all 'comrade in rule'.[121] The last diploma for her with the term 'consors imperii' is dated from Quedlinburg on 28 March 973 (within two months of Otto I's death on 7 May 973).[122] With the start of her son's rule, Adelheid's titles as joint intervener with Theophanu in the diplomata, though less frequent, encompassed 'karissimae', 'carae nostrae', 'delictissimae', 'imperatricis augustae dilectae', 'amabillimae matris nostrae imperatricis', 'nostre serenissime domine matris auguste', 'venerande matris', and 'dilecte genitricis nostrae'.[123] Now in the role of dowager empress Adelheid's influence in the palace waned as that of the new king's wife increased.

During Otto II's rulership, especially early in the marriage, Theophanu's titles had included the following affectionate terms 'dilectae coniugis nostrae', 'dilectissima coniunx nostra', 'uxoris amantissime Theufanu auguste', 'imperatrix augusta', 'carissima'.[124] Theophanu first bore the title 'coimperatrix augusta' when she and Otto II were childless and it was used a further three times. According to Byzantine custom 'this title designated to Theophanu the right of succession in the case that the pair remained childless'[125]—a very powerful right! Initially, praise was plentiful. After bearing four daughters (only three survived infancy) the longed-for male heir (the future Otto III) arrived in 980. However, by that time terms of endearment were few. She hardly ever now appeared as intervener in her husband's diplomata.

In comparison with Theophanu, Otto I's terms of endearment directed toward his wife, Adelheid, in his diplomata remain strikingly affectionate and increased in number and significance during their marriage. Other queens, such as Queen Emma of England, were not so respected, being designated merely 'conlaterana regis' ('she who is at the king's side' / 'wife') or 'coniunx' ('wife').[126] While the secondary sources record minor differences in the number of uses of particular terms, their basic premise is consistent: Adelheid's titles were distinctive and exceptional.

Adelheid did not appropriate one title that her daughter-in-law applied to herself in fine imperial style. During the latter's reign the term 'imperatrix augusta', until then infrequently used, became common: both empresses used it.[127] However, Theophanu's boldest imperial moment came in 990 in the signing of the two diplomata issued under her own name: the first was dated by her son's regnal years but the second implied eighteen years of her full emperorship.[128] In the second diploma Theophanu in an unprecedented action called herself 'imperator augustus', the masculine form of emperor. She also states that anyone acting against her *mundeburdium* or investiture would have to pay with hundred pounds in weight of best gold. Authentication was with her ring. Previously Otto II, under the guidance of his half-brother, Archbishop William of Mainz, had confirmed in 963 his father's diploma for Hilwartshausen and taken the convent into his *defensio* and *mundeburdium*.[129] By doing this he was taking the convent specifically under his protection as a vassal by his lord and a man's guardianship.[130] Otto II's purpose was to banish the claims of kinsmen.[131] Extraordinarily, by the use of the masculine terms 'imperator augustus' and *mundeburdium* in her diploma of 991 Theophanu was asserting the male right of emperorship and guardianship.

Adelheid never took on the masculine forms of rule. Nevertheless, although subject to the perspectives of their various authors, the narrative histories, hagiographies and annals, in addition to the diplomata, confirm the high regard in which Adelheid was held by her contemporaries or near contemporaries. The imperial term *imperatrix* with variations and *imperatrix augusta* appear frequently in the *Annals of Quedlinburg*, *Annals of Weissenburg*, Lampert of Hersfeld's *Annals*, Odilo of Cluny's *Epitaph of the August Lady Adelheid* and Thietmar's *Chronicon*.[132] Outside the diplomata the words of imperial authority accorded to Adelheid persist. For the year 999 the *Annals of Quedlinburg* use the phrase 'imperatorum tamen consulto patrum' when referring to Abbess Mathilda's consultation of the imperial couple, Adelheid and her grandson Otto III.[133] The *Annals* use the masculine plural forms of 'imperator' and of 'pater', consequently allocating equal weight to both rulers as equivalent heads of the household. Any use of the word 'inclita' is even more suggestive. In medieval Latin 'inclita' holds two meanings—one having the classical sense of 'famous', 'renowned' or 'celebrated', used in describing eminent people, and the other of later origin having the sense of 'entire' or 'complete', often used for describing land.[134] The meaning, holding imperial overtones (see the example, 'inclyte domine' ['renowned lord'] with which Ennodius hailed Theodoric, king of the Ostrogoths, that was discussed above), was applied to Adelheid. The *Annals of Quedlinburg* refer to her not only as 'Romanorum imperatrix augusta' but also as 'inclita Romanorum imperatrix augusta'; Thietmar names her 'inclita mater Ethelheidis' and 'inclita inperatrix Athelheidis'; and Hrotsvitha refers to Adelheid as 'inclita ... regina'.[135] Hrotsvitha not only links 'inclita' to Adelheid as queen but also to the title 'imperatrix augusta' adding 'Romanorum', therefore strongly endorsing Adelheid's entitlement as imperial ruler of the Romans. Accordingly Adelheid's imperial power is endorsed in both the formulaic diplomata and in other influential contemporary or near-contemporary writings.

In addition it is important to compare the terms used to or about Adelheid with those used by Widukind of Corvey about kingly power. Widukind's epithet of *pius* (also a praiseworthy Roman imperial description),[136] applied to Otto I, was also used with reference to Adelheid. She directed Otto II's growth to manhood, according to Thietmar, as that of a '[p]iae genitricis' ('pious mother') while Hrotsvitha calls her 'regina piissima' ('most virtuous queen').[137] Hrotsvitha reports that Otto I's supporters remembered Adelheid's 'praedulcem ... pietatem' ('beneficent kindness') and her 'multiplicem ... pietatem' ('manifold benefices').[138] Otto I also recalled Adelheid's previous support when once he had been expelled from his own country (about which Widukind does not elaborate); consequently, 'donis tantae pietatis' ('in return for her benefices'),[139] he entered Italy. Both Thietmar's and Hrotsvitha's uses of the term 'pius' are placed within the broader context of Adelheid's rulership. In calling Adelheid 'pius' Hrotsvitha was building the case for Adelheid's suitability as Otto's wife and queen, and even future empress when she called Otto 'augustus'. In summary, Hrotsvitha's arguments in favor of Adelheid include the endorsement of Otto I's supporters, the favorable comparison of Adelheid with Otto's first queen, Edith (albeit that Adelheid had the advantage of being the living queen), and a carefully fashioned explanation of Otto's obligation to support her in return for her earlier aid to him. Hrotsvitha's *Gesta* is a subtly crafted reflection of Widukind's *Gesta*, supporting a model queen rather than a model king.

The display of the queen was as important as were the words written to and about her. Her crowning and anointing helped to create her queen persona via public performance and confirmed her legitimacy.[140] Although anointing of a king in the West was first recorded in 672, it was not until 751 or 754 that Bertrada was possibly consecrated queen at her wedding.[141] In 856 at the palace of Verberie when Æthelwulf, king of the West Anglians, married Judith, daughter of Charles the Bald, king of West Francia, Bishop Hincmar of Reims placed a crown on the bride's head as part of a new ritual that came to be known as the Judith *ordo*.[142] Otto I's first wife, Edith, was probably crowned and anointed, although at a later ceremony after their wedding at Aachen in 936.[143] The assembly of the Mainz *ordo* between 950 and 963, containing *formulae* for the coronation of a queen, supports the idea that Adelheid was crowned and anointed at her wedding to Otto in 951.[144]

The new tradition of crowning the empress began with Adelheid. The particular *ordines* that were used in 951 for her wedding to Otto or in 962 for her coronation and anointing as empress are unknown.[145] The rite most probably included a formula spoken at the entrance to the church, then a prayer of blessing before the altar, a prayer while anointing the queen and a prayer while setting the crown. Although the *ordo* used at the imperial coronation of Otto and Adelheid may have been the Mainz *ordo*, created specially, it is plausible that the imperial couple had used the Judith *ordo*, which clearly contains words for the action of anointing.[146]

Even before Adelheid married her first husband, Lothar, a history of display with Byzantine elements existed in early medieval wedding documents and ceremony in the West. In the early eighth century the Lombard King Aripert II confirmed the return of the patrimony of the Cottian Alps to the papacy in a royal charter written in gold letters.[147] In Francia in the late ninth century Charles the Bald had instituted Byzantine liturgy, court ritual ceremonies and even court dress.[148] Byzantine influences at ceremonies for the Frankish kings had pervaded court life extensively by the middle of the tenth century.[149] Consequently in the tradition of elaborately worked documents for important occasions, there can be no doubt that the wedding of Adelheid and Otto in 951 produced an elaborate Marriage Charter (or Wedding Certificate). Although that document is no longer extant, later references in the diplomata produced by each of the three Ottos broadly reveal its contents.[150]

Two later documents pertaining to Adelheid's missing Marriage Charter survive: the *Ottonianum* of Otto I and the Marriage Charter of Otto II and Theophanu.[151] In creating the first document in 962, Otto

I confirmed the old Carolingian arrangements with the papacy, including consultation by the Romans with the emperor before election of a pope. Otto I demonstrated in the ceremonial form of the document that the kingdom had a notion of decoration and of display that, although influenced by Byzantine elements, presented its own concepts and identity. The second document was created for the wedding of Adelheid's son and daughter-in-law in 972. Their Marriage Charter is a magnificent document written in calligraphic gold ink on purple parchment, enhanced by religious images of Christ, the Virgin Mary, and the Apostles, and secular images of animals and vegetation. The document demonstrates the power of a queen in the early Middle Ages, particularly the queens of early medieval Germany. Theophanu's Marriage Charter also records the details of the reverse dowry that she received from Otto II.[152] While the Charter includes strong Byzantine images, many probably brought by Theophanu and her retinue from the East in 972, the form and content can be presumed to be influenced by Adelheid's proposed Marriage Charter and the *Ottonianum* of Otto I.

Since image was an important marker of rulership, it is inconceivable that Otto II, with the two models of rulership (Adelheid's Marriage Charter and the *Ottonianum*) and under the tutelage of his imperial mother and father, would not use them as prototypes for his own Marriage Charter. They demonstrated the sophistication of the German court and documented the agreements. Many of the contemporary sources note the wedding; the display as much as the words exhibited majesty. The role given immediately to the new bride is noteworthy because Otto II decided to take her 'in the bond of legitimate matrimony and as empress-consort'.[153] The extant examples of display in the *Ottonianum* and Theophanu's Marriage Charter show the importance of public ratification of power. I have argued that those two documents had a foundation in a missing Marriage Charter of Adelheid. If that document did exist, conclusions about Adelheid's rulership can be drawn: Adelheid's proposed Marriage Charter must also have formed a significant part of the public ritual of her queenship.

The display of the queen was very important in the creation of the queen persona through religious and secular images. Images of Adelheid exist in two different milieu: on a ciborium over an altar and in a Gospel book. The relief carving dated to about 972 on a pediment of the large ciborium over the altar at the church of Sant'Ambrogio in Milan confirms the secular power of the female ruler under God.[154] At the northern end relief carvings of presumably Adelheid on the left, already crowned, and Theophanu on the right, not yet crowned, bow in front of a figure, possibly Mary, the mother of God, with their hands stretched out in supplication to her.[155] At the southern end two figures, thought to be Otto I and his son Otto II, are depicted kneeling in front of a cleric, probably St Ambrose.[156] Thus two royal scenes flank the ciborium, supporting the obeisance of the earthly rulers to the majesty of Christ and his mother, yet, in so doing, reinforcing the earthly majesty of the rulers.

Folio 22r of the Saint-Gereon Gospels (Cod. W 312), produced in the Cologne school between 990 and 1000 and attributed to Otto III's patronage, appears to depict Adelheid in a square-shaped medallion on the left in the *Incipit* of St Matthew with Theophanu in the bottom roundel and Otto III in a square-shaped medallion on the right. In the top roundel Christ, the Lamb of God, stands. Adelheid and Otto III halfface each other, positioned equidistant between Christ, whereas the image of Theophanu is placed below the image of the Lamb in a matching circular frame. It is possible that Otto III ordered the Gospel book on the occasion of his coronation on 21 May 996. If so that would imply Theophanu's image is posthumous.[157] The depiction of the two women, rather than Otto III's male ancestors, argues for Adelheid's involvement in the creation of the image and possibly an earlier date when she was ruling as regent. In either case the image in the *Incipit* recognizes her effective power in the kingdom.

Contemporaries perceived the extent of political power exercised by a woman to be measured by the number of times that she was depicted or named on coins and whether she possessed a personal seal.[158] Consequently the frequency of Adelheid's name on coins should provide a measure of her political power displayed to the people at all levels of society. I have not found coins that show her image, although there are many that contain her name and Otto's name and depict a church, possibly an image of Aachen, the traditional seat for Carolingian royal coronations from Charlemagne's time and where Adelheid and Otto I arranged for both their son and grandson to be crowned as kings. Letters around the outside of the church image can be read as Adelheid in various spellings. On the other side the wording OTTO or (O-D-D-O) often appears in a square format in the middle of the coin surrounded by letters that may include REX.[159] It is not always certain whether the 'Otto' referred to is her husband or her grandson. Consequently the coins can only be dated to between 951 and 1000. (The dates correspond to Adelheid's wedding to Otto I in 951 and to just after her death in 999.) The visual representation of a church coupled with the rulers' names link Christianity directly with rulership. The inclusion of Adelheid shows an acknowledgment of her importance in the realm and to the king/emperor, true whether her husband or grandson is depicted. While there exist a number of seals for the three Ottos and a decorative medallion for Otto III, no seals depicting Adelheid, or including her name, remain.[160] Evidence for the early use of seals by queens exists but the seal of Empress Kunigunde, dated from 1002, is the first evidence in Germany for a female user.[161] The absence of personal seals by the queens in Germany is not a reflection of the women's lack of prominence but rather a question of later adoption of that mark of rulership. In any case, it is unlikely that Adelheid had seals struck in her own name, even when she acted alone for her young grandson. The narrative of the child-king ruling could not be overthrown by such a dramatic contradiction as a seal used in the name of the regent: any seals struck during that period for public acts would have been under his name.

The contemporary or near-contemporary written documents (diplomata, hagiography, chronicles) and images (Gospel book, altar ciborium and coins), that either refer to, or present, an image of Adelheid, emphasize her relationship with God in the heavenly sphere and her position under God in the secular sphere. Legitimization under both categories was needed to confirm—not once, but again and again—the ruler's right to the kingdom and empire.

By the beginning of 999 Adelheid could at last believe that she had secured the kingdom for Otto III. The revolts of Otto I's first son, Liudolf, and his own brother, Duke Henry I of Bavaria; Otto I's death; Otto II's battle loss in 982; his death shortly afterwards with the disruption over the transfer of power to Otto III; and the conflicts with her daughter-in-law, Theophanu, and with her grandson, Otto III, had all passed for Adelheid. Even the death of her daughter, Abbess Mathilda of Quedlinburg, in February of 999 did not destroy the pre-eminence of the Ottonian family. With the concurrence of her grandson, Adelheid appointed her granddaughter, Adelheid, as the new abbess of Quedlinburg. Otto III had been ruling successfully for six years. The papacy appeared safe with the appointment of Pope Gregory V, the first German pope, and grandson of Liudgard, Otto I's daughter with his first wife, Edith. After Gregory's unexpected death in early 999, Adelheid saw the papacy bestowed satisfactorily on the new pope, Sylvester II, previously Gerbert of Aurillac, the trusted former tutor of Otto III and a strong supporter of the Ottonian house. In the same way that she had endeavored to ensure that the power and wealth invested in her lands were passed on through the Ottonian line, so Adelheid endeavored to ensure that the power developed through her rulership was passed on to her grandson.

Adelheid could not know that just over two years after her death in December 999, her grandson would die without heirs and Pope Sylvester would be dead a year later. Although Henry II, grandson of Otto I's brother Henry of Bavaria, became the next Ottonian king and emperor, the Ottonian line ultimately continued only directly through a woman, Liudgard, Otto I's daughter with his first wife, Edith, and hence not through Adelheid. Adelheid's rulership legacy would be taken up by another woman, not a queen nor an empress but a countess, Matilda of Tuscany, in quite a different way.

Countess Matilda as Victor

The year was 1092: the place the mountains of Giumegna and Lintergnano in northern Italy. Countess Matilda, hearing that Emperor Henry IV had unexpectedly left San Polo and set out for Canossa, hurriedly left her fortress there and traveled north toward nearby Bianello with her troops. In the cool autumn air the breaths of the soldiers from each army floated in front of them. The feet of the men and the shoes of the horses scraped and slipped on stony and muddy paths. Armor clinked and trumpets signaled. Walking on tracks on different mountains, each army passed in opposite directions; loud sounds echoed back and forth between them. Although each army could hear the noises of the other as they marched neither could see each other and each shrank from the presence of the other. Countess Matilda, having reached Bianello and conferred there with her leading men from both Canossa and Bianello, gathered her most important people and, together with a selection of her soldiers, quickly turned back to defend the rock of Canossa. Inside the chapel at fortress Canossa Abbot John and his monks sang the psalms and silently invoked all the saints to defend them against the enemy. Suddenly a fog came down around the castle. Although Henry IV's men let the javelins fly the defenders captured the emperor's standard bearer. Henry descended from his vantage point on a nearby hill and advanced toward Canossa, but soon neither he nor anyone else could see the castle through the thickening enveloping mist. The emperor, perceiving the day lost, turned the reins of his horse and retreated north toward Bibbiano:

> Having a heart dejected beyond measure, because he saw that the moment had turned against him.
> He did not want to ride that road, nor even to know ... it,
> Not for four thousand pounds!
> The loss of the banner marked his defeat,
> So that henceforth his reputation for losing soldiers grew.[162]

Those events, reported by Matilda's biographer, Donizo, marked the waning of Emperor Henry IV's power, not only in Italy but also in the German duchies.[163] In being labeled *Officiperdi*, the literal translation meaning 'for losing soldiers', Henry and his reputation had now been ruined.[164] Sometime in the first half of 1093 Henry IV's son, Conrad, and his forces defected to Matilda's side. Henry, effectively cut off in Italy, was unable to return to Germany until spring 1097, having spent seven years south of the Alps. The troops he left behind, charged with the elimination of Matilda and her army, failed to do so.

The army of Emperor Henry IV had been fighting the army of Countess Matilda of Tuscany for nearly three years. At first the emperor's conquest seemed assured. In 1090 Ripalta and Gubernola surrendered, as did Mantua and the castle of Minervia in 1091 when Matilda's defeat at Tricontai also occurred. By the end of the year Henry held the region north of the Po except for the towns of Piadena and Nogara. In early 1092 Henry's triumphs continued with the surrender of Monte Morello, his taking of Monte Alfredo and the promising siege of Monteveglio. However, at Carpineti in September Henry's fortunes began to change. Matilda and her council rejected his offer of terms while Henry was forced to abandon Monteveglio.[165] It is at this point that the events described in the opening to this chapter transpired. From that time onwards Henry became a spent force in Italy.

Not only victors write history. For important events, 'multiple narratives' are told. David Warner, in introducing Otto I's second and third expeditions to Italy (961 to 964/966 to 972) just over 100 years before Henry's travels there, highlights the time when Otto himself began to rule the realm directly as a turning point in Ottonian monarchy and an event modern German and Italian historians approach from different viewpoints.[166] Not dissimilarly, Countess Matilda of Tuscany's stories were told by writers mostly roughly contemporaneous with her life but from different perspectives; papal and allied chroniclers presented views that at different times agreed and disagreed with those on the imperial side. Compared to those, the narrative told by Matilda's chronicler, Donizo, is unusual because it contains the only accounts of many incidents that occurred in the conflict, it evokes a strong sense of place and it gives prominence to the active leader of the troops, a woman with titles in her own right of countess (*comitissa*, and *comes* on one occasion), marchioness (*marchionissa*) and duke or duchess (*dux* or *ducatrix*).[167]

One hundred years earlier Empress Adelheid's expression of rulership was less concerned with direct conflict than Matilda's. Nevertheless both were engrossed by their own standing as rulers and its concomitant expression. Family background, geography, the exercise of justice, the control of violence and its attendant reconciliations contributed to our knowledge of how the two women exercised their rulership. Both women came from, or were associated with, families who had struggled to become eminent. Adelheid came from fraught and fractured Burgundian and Italian royal families to the Ottonian court where her husband Otto I needed to assert his authority again and again over petulant family members and disaffected magnates. Matilda's aggressive and acquisitive ancestors ascended into the comital class via a great-grandfather, first heard about as a minor vassal. Both women were subject to the vagaries of the geography over which they ruled and through which they traveled to effect that rule. The physical scale of Adelheid's geographical reach, encompassing as it did Germany and Italy and forays to her brother Conrad's kingdom of Burgundy, her original homeland, exceeded Matilda's localities of predominantly Tuscany and the lands around the River Po, although northern Italy and Rome acted as a stage in common for them both. The locations of the lands and their ability to travel through them affected how they ruled. Each woman recorded her commands and wishes in documents in pursuit of the public paths of power.

Nothing illustrates the similarities between them more than how they managed the strife inherent in their times. The various comments made by their contemporaries or near contemporaries elucidate these startlingly. On many occasions Adelheid and Matilda negotiated for peace more successfully than their male contemporaries. As discussed in Chap. 2, Adelheid, her daughter-in-law, Theophanu, and daughter, Abbess Mathilda of Quedlinburg, had reconciled with Henry the Wrangler when he claimed the throne in 984 and after that they successfully negotiated with the northeastern tribal groups. After Theophanu's death Adelheid maintained the peace until her grandson, Otto III, reached his majority in 994. There is no doubt that not only did Matilda negotiate amicable settlements but she also emulated the Christian male warrior model against a tyrant-ruler.[168] Piety and interest in church reform among the laity were not unusual in the Middle Ages. Examples abound. In the early ninth century Dhuoda wrote a manual for her son about how to live a pious life. In the late ninth century King Alfred combined a warrior kingship with a pious life. William of Aquitaine founded Cluny in the early tenth century and presumably defended it. Gerald of Aurillac, a contemporary of William and a layman, emulated the life of a monk as far as he could. Those are a few of the notables who acted in one or both fields. Consequently while lay piety and interest in church reform did not remain Matilda's prerogative by any means, no man or woman fought literally so directly and passionately for church reform in an age of idealism. Her battles against Henry IV remained less about rulership per se than the transformation of the church, illustrated by the support she gave to seven popes whose power and status she bolstered during her active life.

Ruling in Italy

In France, Carolingian ways had collapsed by the beginning of the eleventh century; kings were notably absent from the action and power was held by individual noble families through the possession of land and the exercise of military might.[169] In Germany, the victories and imperial glory of the king and emperor were more or less recognized, although claimants to the throne, in itself an acknowledgment of the importance of kingship, caused disturbances throughout the tenth and eleventh centuries.[170] In Tuscany, albeit fragmented, the Carolingian manifestation of government in public assemblies and rituals prevailed in the tenth century and into the eleventh century in ways it did not in other areas of Europe, giving way in the late eleventh century directly to the age of the communes.[171] Consequently both Adelheid and Matilda operated in worlds still structured on Carolingian principles.

In the course of the breakup of the Carolingian empire, Italy experienced disruption and disorder until Otto I intervened. After his first incursion there in 951 to 952, Otto left the kingdom in the control of a 'client king', Berengar II. Ten years later Otto seized the opportunity presented by Pope John XII's invitation to enter Italy against the now rebellious Berengar, who claimed the papal states of Italy. The tit-for-tat with the pope netted Otto the emperorship in 962.[172] The relevance of kings had not been a focus for the Italian upper classes either before 962 or for the following 150 years, as evidenced in the memories of chroniclers from the seventh until the twelfth centuries. Many contemporary writers were remiss in largely ignoring royalty in Italy before the imperial coronations of Otto I and Adelheid at Rome.[173] Despite the insouciance of the chroniclers in this regard, the Italian state in 950, just before Adelheid married Otto and brought the Italian kingdom to him, remained 'the most sophisticated in Western Christendom, with a complex legal–administrative system that ran courts and collected dues across the Po plain and Tuscany in a more systematic manner than any other part of the Carolingian empire, and certainly far more systematically than in England'.[174] The evidence for the use of and interest in the legal system is the extensive glossing and cross-referencing of the legal codes from between 800 to 1100.[175] The literacy of the Lombards contributed to such a comprehensive and complex system and also to its documentation.[176] Before the mantle of wealth had shifted from Italy to England (in the 1180s John, son of Nigel, reported on the 'untold riches of this kingdom' of England),[177] Italy's kings were 'the richest in the West'.[178] Yet despite the importance of Adelheid's strong royal credentials, derived from her family background and her two marriages, which linked the kingdoms of Burgundy, Italy and the *regnum* of East Francia, one hundred years later the royal house in Italy had become irrelevant.

The effective rulers in Italy in the late eleventh century were not called 'kings' any more nor did they aspire to kingship. That title, borne by the kings of Germany for more than one hundred years, since Otto I had become king of the Lombards, had no resonance in Italy where diverse and fractured rulership now resided in the many male counts, dukes and margraves, often quarrelling with each other from their petty territories. At that time Matilda, lacking direct descent from the reigning family, female, and without the support of reliable male family members, could not even call upon any lingering traditions of Italian sovereignty to support a strong female rulership. However, an orientation away from centralized kingship did not necessarily mean that the state could not run a 'complex legal-administrative system'.[179] Although Matilda's father, Boniface, had set up a robust power base, even establishing a ducal palace at Mantua, and her mother, Beatrice, had continued the rulership tradition after both her husbands' deaths, issuing diplomata under her own name, subsequent to Beatrice's death in 1076 Matilda needed to establish and to maintain her own credentials. There existed no contemporary man on whom to model herself: her father, Boniface, was dead and in any case a generation too early; her two husbands became short-lived millstones; and the Normans were considered upstarts.[180] Countess Matilda, perhaps with initial help from her mother, defying the norm, collecting dues and dispensing justice, fashioned herself into a great lord of the late eleventh to early twelfth centuries.[181] How she did this and how this differed from Adelheid's self-fashioning is now examined in this chapter.

A Strong Center

Any ruler who attempted to function in Italy did not inherit a well-founded court culture based in an historical center as did the Ottonians in Germany, the English kings or the early Capetians in France. Even though Charlemagne's invasion of 774 remained in historical memory, the inaccuracy of recall by the limited number of chroniclers subverted a united kingdom and contributed to the rise of a unique town culture.[182] The Ottonians acquiesced to Pavia continuing as a center of authority over the Italian kingdom but set their royal seat more firmly in the north at Aachen. Later the Salians shifted their kingship to Speyer with forays to retain the Italian kingdom. Matilda turned an apparent weakness into an advantage when she began to rule in northern Italy. Strategically Pavia, the former royal capital, proved unsuitable as a delegated center of power for lordship. Matilda retained interests there as one of many important cities, but her power bases were situated in Tuscany and in fortresses along the Po, east of Pavia. Besides, the city had a history of violence; in 1004 the inhabitants entrapped Henry II, newly crowned king of the Lombards, in the royal palace and in 1024 they burnt the same palace with the excuse that the interregnum between the death of Emperor Henry II and the election of King, and later, Emperor, Conrad II, justified their action.[183] Nevertheless the ideology of kingship in Italy remained a potent force.[184] Meanwhile the fortress Canossa, while retaining a strong historical link to the royal family because of its former role in sheltering the Italian queen, could be considered a legitimate center of power, retaining the kudos of royalty without claiming the title. Donizo confirmed this idea by entitling his work *De principibus canusinis* (*About the Princes of Canossa*) while dedicating it to the last in the Canossan line.

Both the Ottonian and Canossan dynasties maintained their states in Italy by using 'military forces from over the mountains': the Ottonians for more than a century maintained Italy with soldiers from north of the Alps; the Canossans maintained their territories that were located northeast of the Apennines from Tuscany.[185] Similarly Fulk Nerra, count of Anjou, began state-building by enhancing his ancestors' landed acquisitions, starting with building up the fortifications between population centers. With strategic marriages and by increasing their influence around their local area, the Angevin counts followed a similar path to the Canossans. By these means they cemented their lordship over a corresponding period from the mid-tenth to the early twelfth centuries. In a violent age and in a land where kingship had even less influence, the counts of Anjou achieved their suzerainty with more viciousness than the Canossans, although Matilda's father, Boniface, was noted for his ferocity.[186] Like the German royal house, the lords in Italy were subjected to outbursts of violence from time to time. The inhabitants of Pavia pugnaciously stood against the new Salian King Conrad II until defeated in 1027 and those of Lucca expelled marchesal overlordship from their city in 1081. Starting in 1091 the residents of Mantua betrayed Matilda and had to be brought to heel more than once.[187] Nevertheless Countess Matilda's own peripatetic court sessions continued to operate and Matilda deliberately chose more strategic ways to assert her lordship in the cities than had her father. 'When Matilda died in 1115, the march coexisted not only with counts and other substantial aristocrats with their own power bases, but with the newly established city communes.'[188] Despite the transfer of real hegemony from the royal house to the new lords, in 'Tuscany there was, in effect, no break between the Carolingian world and the age of the communes; one gave way directly to the other'.[189]

In managing these two ages, one passing and the other in formation, Matilda's practice was to employ a string of impregnable forts around her lands to which she could withdraw or from which she could exit to attack a vulnerable opponent. The Apennine defense of castles and towers built along intimidating ridges was bolstered with effective methods of communication so that Matilda always possessed very good information about the whereabouts of Henry IV. Canossa, though defensible because it was built on a steep high rock and with various added ramparts, walls and other barricades to withstand sieges, could not last long without other supporting fortifications. Matilda used Canossa as a capital in the sense of a strong base and her leading fortified structure. In addition she maintained a number of other fortresses and castles as a connected thread of defenses acting as a block. These encompassed Monteveglio, marking the most easterly extremity of the Apennine defense system; the *Quattro Castelli* (that is, the closely set hills of Montevetero, Bianello, Montelucio and Montezane); Rossena and Rossenella, west of and visible from Canossa; and Carpineti to the southeast—all locations discernible today.[190] Furthermore the identifiable locations from which she issued all her diplomata show the extremely wide geographical extent of her power (see Map 4.3).

While the physical presence of Canossa and the string of communicating locations remained important, the ability to hold the networks linking the fortifications became just as critical in the exercise of military power and court justice. Consequently Matilda's fortresses in the mountains and around the River Po, connected by the roads and the Po itself, became points of strength in a ribbon of control.

Holding the Roads

Success in battle could not follow without control of the roads since the one who controlled the roads held the rulership. A striking example of the connection between the kingdom and the roads is shown in Adelheid's letter dated about 994 to 995 that commanded 'G' (a Würzburg clerk, possibly the *vicedominus*,[191] or perhaps even Gozpert, the Abbot of Tegernsee) to prepare for the arrival of her royal party at the bishopric of Würzburg on a specified date. Tegernsee had been re-established by Otto II in 979 after the ancient abbey, having been stripped of extensive property, had fallen into ruin in the early tenth century. In the absence of the bishop Adelheid sought out the abbot to see to her needs. Her letter confirms her royal authority to command the occupants of the abbey to service her and her entourage with accommodation, funds and victuals, and food for the traveling animals.[192] In her obvious ability to use safely the roads to reach Würzburg and in expecting the monks to organize food and shelter for her and her retinue, Adelheid confirmed her right not only to control the roads but also to the goods of the monastery.

Safe passage had always been and remained an important element of rulership. In the fifth century the Roman roads of the empire still functioned as a reliable public way. In 467 Gaius Sollius Apollinaris Sidonius described his journey from Lyons to Rome to his friend Heronius in a letter wherein he attested to finding the 'state-post' at his disposal and

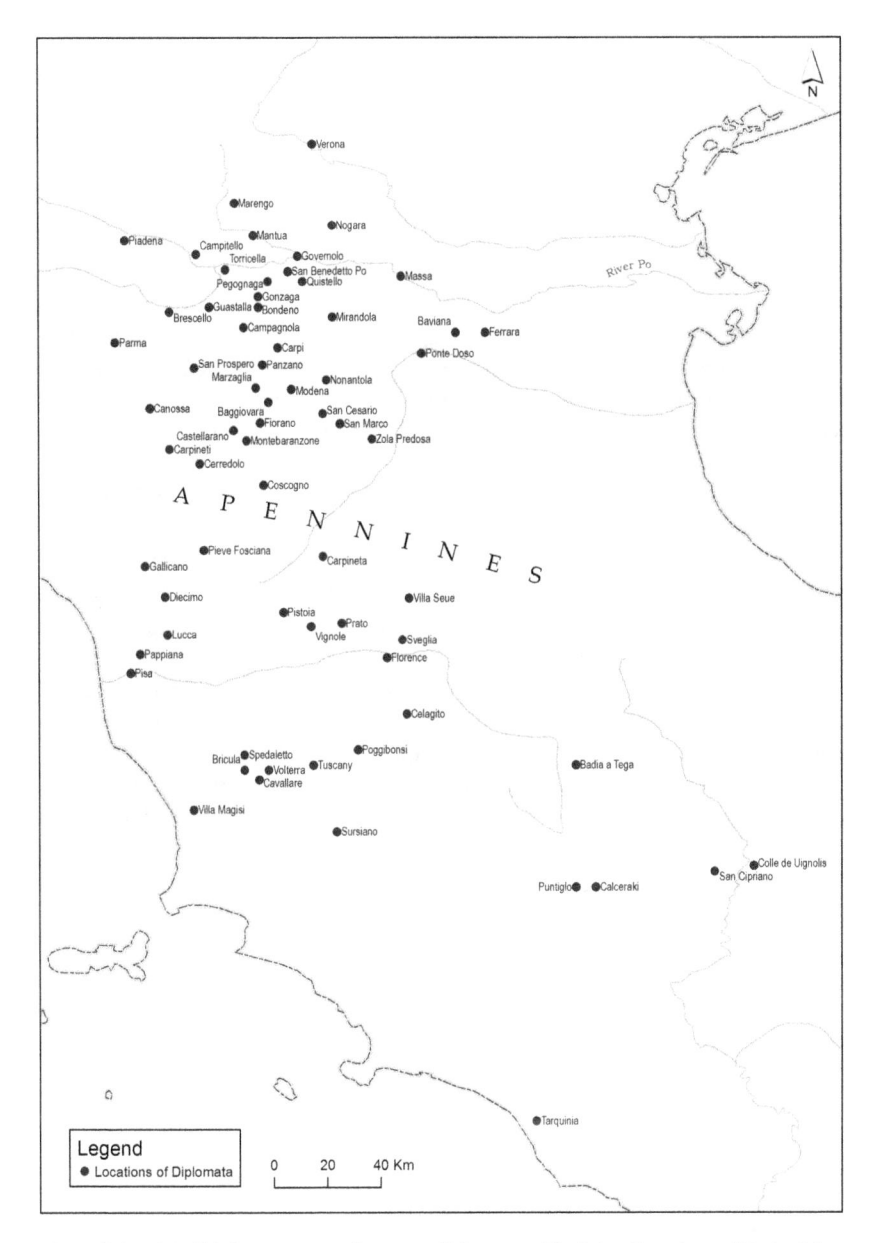

RULE: MODELS OF RULERSHIP AND THE TOOLS OF JUSTICE 165

Map 4.3 Matilda's centers of power (Map specified by Penelope Nash. Map prepared by Koolena Mapping)

the availability 'of post-horses' plentiful, since he was on the emperor's business. At Pavia he was able to board 'a packet boat (so they called the vessel)' that traveled down a tributary of the River Po, into the Po itself.[193] Two striking incidents that occurred before and after Adelheid's and Matilda's exploits illustrate the dramatic change in control of and access to the roads. By the middle of the eighth century Pope Stephen II was indebted to the Lombard king Aistulf, for permission to travel north to meet Pippin, king of the Franks. The Frankish envoys had to negotiate with King Aistulf to allow the pope to travel on to France. Eventually Aistulf gave him leave to go, although he delayed him still and tried to persuade him to deviate from his journey, so much so that Pope Stephen had to hurry over the Great Saint Bernard Pass through the 'mountain fortifications of the Franks' in case Aistulf stopped him.[194]

A second incident occurred in the late twelfth century when, for access to the city of Verona, Emperor Frederick Barbarossa and his men depended on local inhabitants who, to limit possible looting by the soldiers, separated them from the populace by only allowing access via a temporary bridge of logs upstream of the city. In 1155 the residents sought to hinder the approach of the emperor by building a flimsy bridge on which he and his army had no option but to cross.[195] Although the soldiers successfully negotiated the hazard on this occasion, it was evident that the emperor depended on his subjects for entrée to the city. Between these two illustrative events the Ottonians and their following alone had free and easy access to all parts of their empire. Two examples should suffice: in 971 Emperor Otto I and his queen Adelheid provided safe passage for St Ulrich to return from Ravenna to his bishopric of Augsburg and in February 1001 Otto III similarly provided safe passage for Bishop Bernward on his return from near Rome to Hildesheim. By 1076 the importance of the control of the roads had not changed when King Henry IV too exercised his power to refuse safe passage for Pope Gregory VII after the latter had accepted an invitation from the German princes to cross the Alps from Italy. King Henry IV, in controlling the roads across the Alps, held the upper hand but, as Karl Leyser so rightly points out, lost the advantage when he appeared as a penitent outside Countess Matilda's castle of Canossa. Pope Gregory VII had hurried there on her invitation after Henry thwarted Gregory's proposed journey to Germany. Gregory had thus failed in his original mission to summon the northern bishops to his own cause. In the same way as Otto I had controlled the roads one hundred years before, Gregory could not progress through Lombardy and further north from Italy without Henry to guarantee his way. The right of passage of the roads operated at the caprice of the owner.[196]

Control of the roads was consequently a critical factor in cases of conflict. In the early 1060s Beatrice thwarted Bishop Cadalus of Parma's attempt at the papacy by hindering his progress over the Apennines 'by means of ambushes and other tricks.'[197] A few decades later, in contrast with the command exercised by the Ottonians a century before and Henry IV's control in 1076, the situation was reversed for Henry from 1093 until 1096 when he had no access to Germany across the Alpine passes because they were held by either his vassal Matilda or his estranged wife's family. In 1091 Adelaide, margravine of Turin, Henry IV's mother-in-law from his first wife, Bertha, had shared power with Frederick, count of Mömpelgard, husband of her granddaughter and cousin of Matilda of Tuscany. In so doing Adelaide and Frederick ruled the March of Turin and thus controlled the Alpine passes and the corresponding roads through Turin, Susa and Ivrea and between Asti and Genoa'.[198] In 1091 both Adelaide and Frederick died and Henry designated his son Conrad to regain the march for him. However, in early 1093 Conrad with his troops defected to Matilda.[199] Matilda's husband, Welf V, and her father-in-law, Welf IV, also blocked Henry's access to the remaining Alpine passes until 1096. Then Welf IV, realizing that Matilda would not release control of the March of Tuscany and other property to her husband and himself, reconciled with Henry who, having been confined to the northeast of Italy, was then able to access the Alpine passes and return to Germany in early 1097.[200]

The roads made of earth were not the only strategic thoroughfares. 'Ipsa Padi stratam tenet' ('She [Matilda] held the road of the Po').[201] Donizo used the word 'strata', often employed with the meaning of a stone road but here used to indicate the strength of Matilda's hold on the River Po itself. Just as Boniface issued orders from his boat on the Po, so the Po especially, together with the Rivers Adige and Tartaro, remained extremely important parts of the connecting infrastructure in Matilda's territories.[202] Towns were defined by their relation to the Po and positions south or north of the rivers were significant in battle strategy, since whether the rivers were fordable or not affected battle outcomes. Donizo records that in 1091 '[t]he king [Henry IV] held almost all the lands beyond the Po, / Except for Piadena and Nogara, which were the illustrious towns'.[203] In the winter of that year Donizo reports that Henry IV managed to cross the River Adige but shortly afterwards both the Po and

Adige rivers thwarted the attempts by Matilda's troops to follow him.[204] In October of the following year, the Po had a decisive role in Henry's defeat after his failure to capture Canossa, since it was across that river that Henry and his men fled swiftly with Matilda's forces (and probably Matilda) in hot pursuit.[205] The apparent similarity in how Adelheid and Matilda held the roads hides a fundamental difference between their exercise of rulership: Adelheid's power originated in and continued in prerogatives derived from royal privileges whereas Matilda, acting as an independent ruler, used comital rights to control the roads on land and water.

The Tools of Justice: Comital Courts and Their Records

A ruling woman exercising comital rights, although unusual, was not unknown. About the time when Matilda started to become active in northern Italy, Gercendis played a leading role in the revolt at Le Mans, first heard of as a commune in 1070. There, documentation in two charters shows Gercendis acting as a count in her own and her family's interest. She came from illustrious comital ancestors, the Counts of Maine, herself being the daughter of Count Herbert (called 'Wake the Dog'): she had originally been married to a duke; she afterwards married a margrave; she became the ward and then the mistress of another noble man, Geoffrey of Mayenne. She remained during the uprising in Le Mans, although Geoffrey withdrew to a castle, and had the power to decide how she might hand the city over to Geoffrey. Her son, Hugh, eventually became count at Le Mans but was deposed by William the Conqueror.[206]

Matilda's exercise of comital rights had its basis in the authority of a far more powerful comital family than that of Gercendis, although the counts of Anjou would rival it. One of the more significant demonstrations of her powers can be seen in Matilda's application of justice through her *diplomata* and her letters. Elke and Werner Goez's fine presentation and extensive examination of the extant documents provides a firm basis for analysis, supporting 139 as genuine (of which seventy-four are preserved in the original, sixty-three are copies and two are from early printed documents), 115 as fragments of probable lost items, 14 as *spuria* or false and 13 as issued by others (that refer to Matilda in various ways such as an agreement with her, a reference to her or to her presence, or requests of her).[207] Of the 115 fragments all have a probable or certain date but only seventeen indicate the location from which they were issued and the editors construe fifty-three as uncertain, doubtful or false.[208] The fourteen *spuria* are of interest because of the apparent value to the forgers in creating them. Twelve, concerning allocation of rights and privileges relating to land, named receivers of the benefit.[209] The remaining two shored up Matilda's political support: in the first she reputedly asked Welf V to marry her (in a diploma possibly dated to 1089), and in the second, she exhorted Henry IV's son, Conrad, to rise up against his father in support of the liberation of Italy (1100).[210] Only two of those fourteen are dated before 1100, by which time the name of Matilda, now well-established in her power base, added legitimacy to claims.[211] Twelve of the fourteen forgeries can be allocated locations of issue, many corresponding to those from where Matilda's genuine documents were written.[212]

The total number of diplomata that Matilda issued remains unknown for a number of reasons. The authenticity of certain charters that the editors have listed as genuine can be questioned.[213] Other references to Matilda occur in the diplomata of Henry IV, where he gives away her property.[214] The reasons certain diplomata and not others survive to the present time include some elements of chance. Consequently the conclusions from the analysis of the remaining charters must be tentative. Nevertheless cautious examination of the extant diplomata indicates where she considered her power bases to lie since, all in all, the archival legacy of work by and about Matilda is the most comprehensive for any female ruler of the late eleventh and early twelfth centuries.[215]

The Centers of Justice

Matilda issued her diplomata from the places where she exercised authority. Naturally only the extant charters can be displayed and the following discussion refers to the implications of the dates and places of issue for the authenticated diplomata. As many as 131 of the 139 of these can be located. A map created especially displays all the locatable places from which Matilda issued her diplomata during the period in which she remained active, from Verona in the north to Tarquinia in the south.[216] A map shows the number of diplomata issued at each location for all locations: the greater the size of the circle, the greater the number of diplomata issued at that place (see Map 4.4).

Matilda issued her diplomata from a wide range of locations, many from north of the Apennines—for example, she issued five or more from each of Mantua, Piadena, Bondeno, Panzano and San Cesario. However, she also

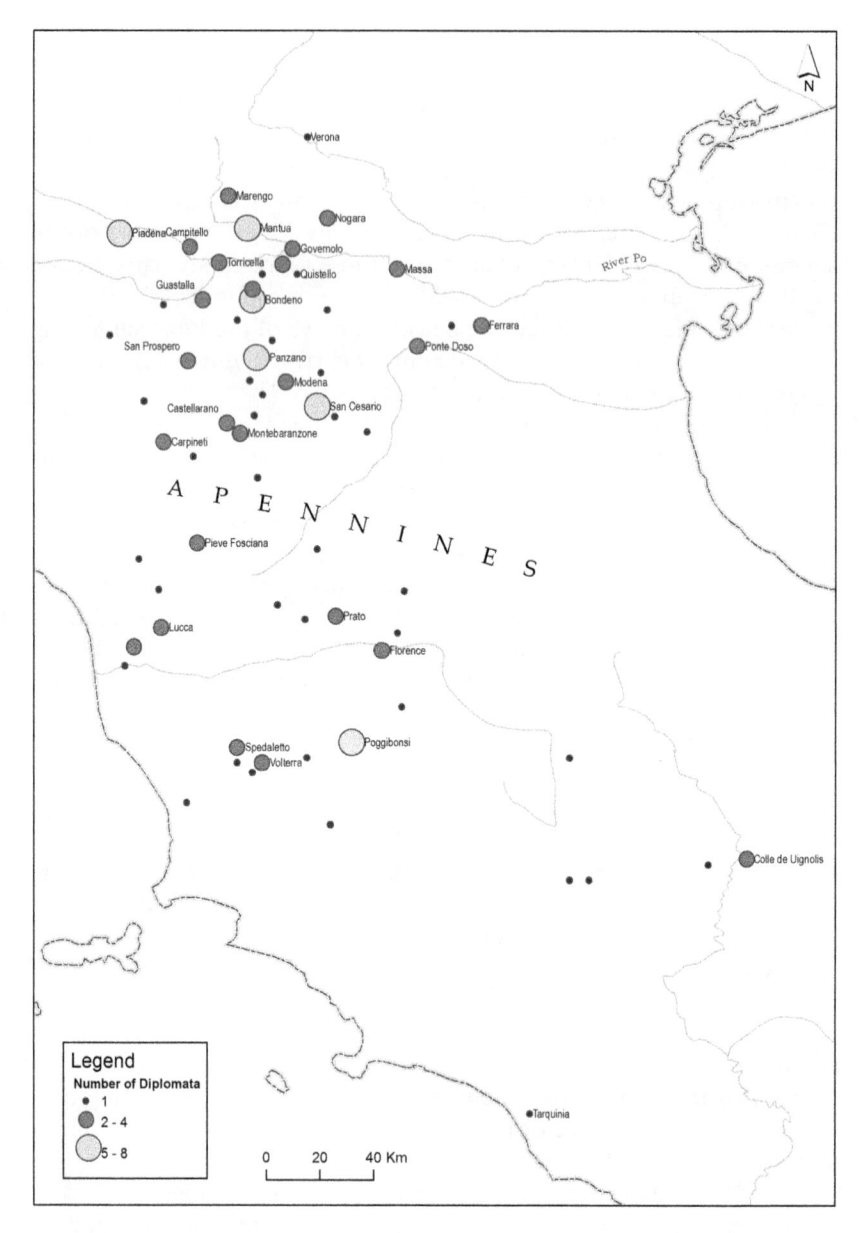

Map 4.4 Matilda's diplomata (Map specified by Penelope Nash. Map prepared by Koolena Mapping)

favored power bases south of the Apennines such as Lucca, Florence and even as far south as Poggibonsi.[217] It should be noted that the River Po has changed its course between the Bronze Age and the Late Middle Ages when it flowed in a belt about twenty kilometers wide and shifted from south to north.[218] Consequently the placement of the river according to modern maps is now further north than it was in the tenth and eleventh centuries and the maps do not exactly reflect its medieval course relative to the medieval towns, especially around Bondeno.

Further analysis of four significant periods primarily related to Matilda's great struggles with Henry IV reveals her establishment of comital authority, setbacks under Henry and finally the zenith of powerful lordship. The first of the four periods covers the time of Matilda's acting in concert with her mother from when she issued her first diploma up to Beatrice's death on 18 April 1076. Surrounded by judges, advocates, notaries and witnesses, Matilda started to exercise justice from 1072 when she was probably twenty-five. The first extant diploma issued with her mother, dated 19 January 1072 and disseminated from Mantua, probably corresponds to her first actual diploma, since the elaborate *arenga* names Beatrice as the daughter of Frederick and Matilda as the daughter of Boniface. It confirms their relationship as mother and daughter, their titles as *comitissae* and *ducatrices*, and that they operate under Salic Law.[219] Since statements about the two women's relationships to their fathers were not repeated until 18 August 1073 (for Matilda) and 10 September 1073 (for Beatrice), it is highly unlikely that all these matters would be listed in as much detail if this were not the first diploma.[220] Subsequently, Matilda and her mother issued five more diplomata jointly, after which Matilda issued her first diploma without Beatrice on 8 February 1073 from Lucca (Borgo San Frediano), donating holdings in Lucca and Villanova to Eritha, Abbess of San Salvatore and Santa Giustina in Lucca, and establishing the protection of the lord emperor ('bannum do(mi)ni imperatoris').[221] Of the eighteen extant diplomata, the place of issue of number 18 cannot be reliably established.[222] Matilda issued eleven of the seventeen locatable diplomata jointly with her mother from a wide range of localities: from Verona north of the Apennines, southwest across the Apennines to Lucca and Pisa, and southeast to the Colle de Uignolis, located eight kilometers east southeast of Perugia.[223] The decisions made and the locations chosen for this first period of more than four years show choices most likely made by Beatrice in a guiding role rather than Matilda.

The second period of Matilda's early independence from April 1076 up to March 1081 contains fifteen extant diplomata. After Beatrice's death Matilda took her first opportunity to flex her muscles without her mother and almost certainly independently from any other single dominant person. That period of five years covers Matilda's early years of comparative political stability. Until March 1081 Italy remained relatively peaceful. King Henry IV's direct intervention there was minimal, apart from his brief humble visit to Matilda's castle of Canossa to beg Pope Gregory VII's forgiveness in Matilda's presence after the pope's first excommunication of him. The hiatus allowed Matilda the opportunity to develop her power bases relatively independently of influence from Germany. The map shows a wider spread of places for the derivation of the diplomata than during her first period of rule with Beatrice. Matilda's travels ranged from north of the Apennines, this time from Marengo (not quite as north as Verona), to Pappiano in the southwest (seven kilometers northeast of Pisa), to San Cipriano in the southeast (further east of Colle de Uignolis) and to the south at Tarquinia (well south of Calceraki and Colle de Uignolis). Matilda issued diplomata from Marengo, Mantua, San Prospero and Florence, as she did with her mother in the previous period, but the later time frame included the new locations of Ferrara, Bricula, Tuscany (no more closely specified than the region) and Tarquinia. The wider geographical range of locations from which Matilda issued diplomata during that relatively brief period hints at her increased confidence and power. The period ended abruptly when in 1080 Gregory excommunicated Henry IV for a second time and Henry re-entered Italy in March 1081.

The third period lasting from March 1081 until spring 1097, one of trouble and strife for Matilda, covered Henry IV's renewed campaigns in Italy, his final defeat at Canossa and his peripatetic travels around northeastern Italy until his return to Germany. During the first three dire years Henry ravaged northern Italy until his own antipope, Clement III, crowned him emperor at Rome, but on 27 May 1084 Henry was forced to abandon the city. From March 1081 until sometime after 27 May 1084 five of Matilda's diplomata remain but of those only three locations of issue are certain—Zola Predosa, Carpineta and Mantua.[224] The remaining two are letters. Number 38 was addressed to the faithful dwelling in the kingdom of the Germans ('omnibus fidelibus in Theuthonicorum regno commorantibus') and disseminated the important information that Henry had stolen the pope's seal.[225] Although Henry had departed, temporarily satisfied with his coronation as emperor by the pope he had placed on the papal throne, change and turbulence still affected events in northern Italy. Pope Gregory VII and Matilda's great spiritual supporter, Bishop Anselm II of Lucca, died; Pope Urban II was elected; and Matilda married her second husband, Welf V. These events occurred between 28 May 1084 and spring 1090. Five diplomata remain from that period, one from Nogara and four from Mantua.[226] In March 1090 Henry descended again into Italy. His power peaked toward the end of 1092 when Matilda's troops were almost defeated, but she gained the victory at Canossa in October of that year, the scene that opened the section on Countess Matilda as victor above in this chapter. Matilda's extant diplomata, issued during Henry's last campaign in Italy when she battled and skirmished with him and his followers in Italy for seven years, number only four, one each issued from Mantua and her fortress castle of Carpineti and three from Piadena, probably in a single visit. Those last four diplomata of that anxious period, from March 1090 until the last diploma extant, probably dated 21 May 1095, show the geographic and temporal ranges of Matilda's travels, but not much information can be gleaned from their origins, spread as they were from summer 1090 in Mantua, autumn 1092 in Carpineti and spring 1095 in Piadena.[227] Since the early years of that period were a time of intense fighting, irregular engagements, feints and bluffs carried out throughout Matilda's territory, it is hardly surprising that a scant fourteen diplomata remain for the period of sixteen years, two of which have unidentified locations of issue.[228] Yet despite the tumultuous events, her diplomata after about 1085 were 'of judgment and privilege' establishing a 'lord-princess attentive to the needs of local order'.[229]

It is in the fourth period, one of stable success, from after spring 1097 when Henry IV left Italy until her death on 16 July 1115, that the number of Matilda's extant diplomata increases dramatically. Matilda's consolidation of her lordship lasted seventeen years. Her diplomata then show the real power that she could exercise directly and personally. Matilda's confidence and range of influence flowered far more than in any of the earlier three periods. A map of the locations she visited shows her confidence in her own lordship. Of the ninety-two diplomata available eighty-seven can be associated with a place of issue (see Map 4.5).[230]

A few examples show the range of Matilda's activities and the attention to detail that she exhibited in undertaking her powerful and effective role and in acting with justice and lordship. In 1101, Matilda ordered that her followers should no longer harass the people of the bishop's church of Reggio in the region of the Correggio and Mandrio and the people of the

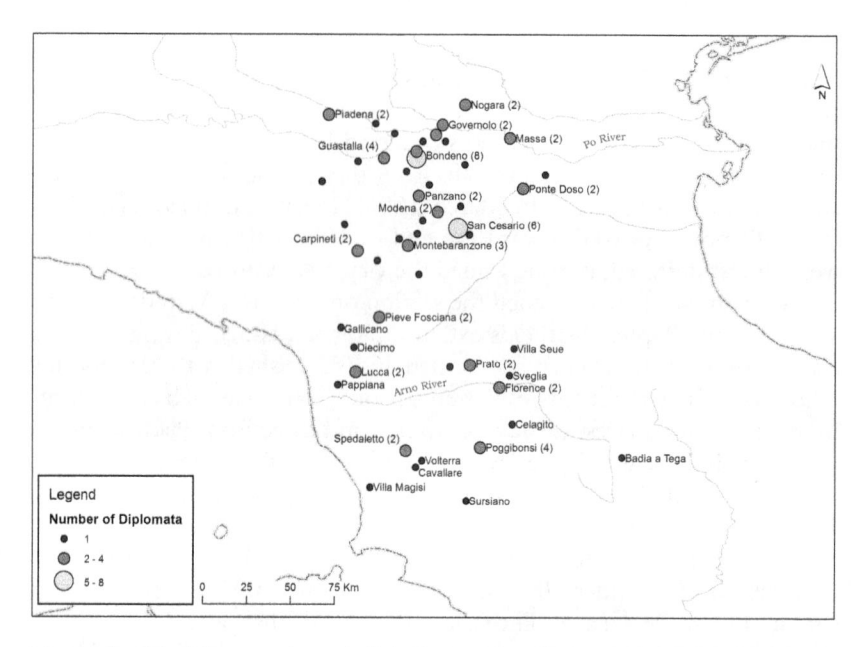

Map 4.5 Matilda—number of diplomata—after Spring 1097–July 1115 (Map specified by Penelope Nash. Map prepared by Koolena Mapping)

monastery of San Prospero in the ambit of Guastalla.[231] Late in 1109 at Poggibonsi Matilda was involved in the details of the position of a storage building. She gave permission to Abbot Henry of San Salvatore dell'Isola, to modify or to relocate the building, currently situated alongside the monastery.[232] Her actions in 1106 in chastising her men from Revere for allowing their pigs to run on the lands of Melara, already examined in Chap. 2, provide another example.[233] The judgments recorded in her diplomata reveal her careful scrutiny of the facts, her inclusion of monetary punishment of the wrongdoers, the importance of the documentation of an event with its resulting decisions and a distinct awareness of the strength of her own authority.

While Adelheid always needed the authority or at least the nominal authority of the king/emperor in the issued diplomata, even when she acted as sole regent between the period after Theophanu's death in 991 and Otto III's coming of age in 994, Matilda acted alone. Matilda's extant diplomata provide evidence for her strong personal presence; no formulaic words of intervention tempered her authority. The locations from which the diplomata were dispensed provide valuable evidence for Matilda's sense of her strong centers of government and power. While some locations may have been opportunistic, particularly in the cases when she was being harried by Henry IV, nevertheless analysis of her visits to those places demonstrates her view of these centers as adding *gravitas* to her statements of rule. In addition, the fact that a decision was considered important enough to be documented during a period when priority might have been given to addressing the conflict, gives further weight to the idea that Matilda considered that her rulings should not only be heard but also exist as a tangible and lasting witness.

Violence and Reconciliation

The periods when Matilda's diplomata are sparse correspond with periods of warfare and disruption. Both Adelheid and Matilda lived during violent periods of history when two main strategies were deployed in combat. Either large numbers of men fought directly or fortifications were used. In 955, King Otto I's well-disciplined foot soldiers of between 8000 and 10,000 in number won victory at the Battle of the Lech over the archers of the Magyars. In the next century, Matilda employed her network of fortifications to decoy and to bluff as well as to fight outright, in the tradition of Alfred the Great in the late ninth century, Henry the Fowler in Germany in the early tenth century and Fulk Nerra in Anjou in the early eleventh century but without their superior resources.[234] To undertake warfare a tremendous amount of support by means of people and technology was required. Men, and it was mainly men, used the tools of horses, armor and weapons to form a coherent force that might be called collectively the military apparatus. However, during the time between Adelheid and that of Matilda important changes had occurred in how men and their technology became involved in warfare and negotiation.

Developing the Military Apparatus

The missive from Empress Adelheid to the monks of Tegernsee, discussed above in this chapter, illustrates an important component of Ottonian rulership: in the late tenth century, rulership was exercised to a great extent through the bishops. Dated to about 994, either just before or just after

Otto III attained his majority, the letter illustrates the fact that Adelheid would normally expect the bishop, acting as second-in-command to her, to organize the support for the royal tour:

> Therefore, since we remember that our great friend the bishop will not be at home, our people advised that it would be circumspect to send a messenger so that you could order a place to be prepared for us to stay, food provided for the carts and horses, and stipends/tribute for us and our companions.[235]

Nevertheless a bishop's jurisdiction might not be uncontested. For example, the complex interactions between the bishop and the *cives* are shown at Cremona. In 996 Otto III gave a privilege to the city allowing concessions for the transport of goods and income along the River Po from the mouth of the Adda to the port of Vulpariolo. Later the same year Otto chose to withdraw the concession but reasserted the episcopal privileges imposed on certain citizens to avert the formation of, in effect, a port around which the citizens could organize and gain a collective power, separate from both the bishop and ultimately the kingdom.[236]

By 1098 the citizens of the northern Italian towns had a stronger hold on their rights. Two examples illustrate this shift in power. In the first example Matilda had gained the ability to source troops from two different origins. In Cremona the bishop formally retained the responsibility for the military, centered in both the *capitanei* ('prominent citizens')[237] and the *ceteri homines* in the city. However, the *capitanei* now operated independently of the bishop, if they so chose, and consequently could paralyze his military 'apparatus' and the military 'structures' of the city. Meanwhile the *ceteri homines* of the city, struggling to work together, could also offer a military service separate from the bishop, despite the responsibility of such a service formally residing with him. Thus Matilda had two potential sources for military support. By that time the control of military power had shifted from the bishops. Countess Matilda now held that power since she acted directly in concert with the people of Cremona who, with her permission, committed the bishop as a third party.[238] Even if that document is false (because of the unusual and early use of *capitanei* and *commune*)[239] it in no way diminishes the power vested in Matilda as described in the document. Consequently we find that one hundred years after Adelheid's rulership the bishop was subordinated to both the people of his town and the lord who ruled the territory. The second example provides even stronger evidence for the shift from royal control exercised through the bishops to comital control. Florence remained loyal to Matilda for various reasons and in 1115 went straight to a commune, bypassing episcopal regulation.[240] In one hundred years power had shifted from royal to comital control, from bishops to town citizens.

Choosing Negotiation or Warfare

Kingly power had been firmly based on military superiority. Otto I quickly asserted his authority. His reign had begun and continued violent since he contended with threats to his rulership from the time of his (probable) acclamation as king on the battlefield in 936 until his death in 973. After her escape from his imprisonment and until Otto's troops could support her, Adelheid had to hide in the fields from the vengeance of Berengar II. When Adelheid married Otto I she became linked to the violence associated with him by default. While at different times she accompanied both her husbands, Lothar and Otto, to various battlefields, there is no record of her on the field of combat. Similarly her daughter-in-law, Theophanu, as far as we know, was associated with, but not actively engaged in, warfare. In the conflict between Otto II and King Lothair of West Francia in summer 978, Theophanu remained nearby at Aachen but did not join her husband on the battlefield.[241] Again at the encounters in 982 with the Greeks at Taranto and with the Saracens at Capo Colonne (or Crotone) in southern Italy, the former a victory and the latter a dismal failure, Theophanu remained nearby at Rossano.[242]

After that catastrophic defeat of Otto II, the Slavs, perceiving a weakness in the empire, revolted in their homeland in the northeast of Germany during the summer of the following year. The opportunity to exploit the empire's vulnerability remained too tempting for those whose recent conversion to Christianity remained tentative at best. Otto died shortly afterwards, leaving the disputes unresolved, his death no doubt hastened by anxiety about the restlessness in the north of the empire. Before, however, those problems could be addressed, the three *dominae imperiales* (Adelheid; her daughter-in-law, Theophanu; and her daughter, Abbess Mathilda) had to deal with the claims to leadership of the now vacant realm, centered in Saxony, by Henry the Wrangler and, to a lesser extent, by Lothair of West Francia, each having some entitlement to the throne as uncles and accordingly guardians of the under-age Otto III.[243] While both bids for control of the kingdom remained threatening, no fighting ensued. During the above struggle for the empire Gerbert of Aurillac supported the two dowager empresses (Adelheid and Theophanu) with letters to them and other followers while they waited at Rome during the first half of 984 until Archbishop Willigis of Mainz declared the north safe for their return and reunion with Abbess Mathilda.[244]

To consider Adelheid's effect in military matters it is necessary to understand the state of the kingdom following Otto II's premature death during the time of Otto III's minority from 984 until mid-994 to early 995. After the three women had been accepted as the legitimate regents for the new king, they had to attend rapidly to the disturbances by the Slavs in the northeast with whom the Ottonians had a long history of difficult relations.[245] The three *dominae imperiales* used a combination of negotiation and fighting to manage the East, although detailed information remains sparse. The accounts of Flodoard of Reims, Hrotsvitha of Gandersheim and Widukind of Corvey stop short of the relevant period, and Odilo of Cluny, who comments on Adelheid's role as ruler, omits any direct mention of involvement in the affairs of war. Bishop Thietmar of Merseburg and the *Annals of Quedlinburg* provide most of the scanty information. In 986, 987 and 988 the king (although in reality his men) undertook many fierce campaigns against the Slavs who 'were made subordinate to the king' in 988.[246] During that period Otto III was still a young child of between six and eight years of age and so Theophanu, if not Adelheid also, remained in charge of the fighting men of the empire. When Adelheid took over the regency alone after Theophanu's death, Count Siegfried, Bishop Thietmar's father, served her faithfully in 'both military and domestic matters' ('domi miliciaque'),[247] presumably one of many leading men to do so. Thietmar did not elaborate on this statement about Adelheid's control of military matters; however, he contributed a small but significant piece of evidence about Adelheid's role as leader in military affairs.

Modern historians continue to have difficulty in gauging Adelheid's involvement in military matters. Diplomata and other documents issued under Otto III's name while Theophanu was alive and most active as regent and, after her death, through Adelheid give limited information about the military activity of the kingdom under the women. Johannes Fried proposes that Theophanu consciously pursued an energetic and planned policy in the northeast but he does not discuss Adelheid's involvement.[248] Even if the negotiations with the eastern tribes were not so much part of a wider policy, the actions of the three women can be assessed as remarkably effective for either male or female rulers, although not well-documented. The peace that pervaded the empire during the joint reign of the three powerful women remained unusual even for strong kings.[249] Although scanty, the evidence indicates that conciliation remained the tool that the women employed most effectively. A whole world of planning was involved that can only be seen in the successful results.

One hundred years later there is no doubt that Countess Matilda actively participated as a military leader of men. In such actions she followed the example of her mother, Beatrice of Lotharingia, for whom evidence exists that not only did she hinder Bishop Cadalus of Parma's progress over the Alps but she also had the influence and means to bring troops to guard a synod.[250] The abundant evidence of the success of Beatrice's daughter as a strong war leader, testified to by Matilda's contemporaries or near contemporaries, remains one of the most striking differences between Matilda and Adelheid. Even the quite abbreviated accounts of Matilda's war experiences in comparison with those of Adelheid note the active involvement of Matilda in the strategies of war. As an adult Matilda never ventured north of the Alps nor would it have been within her sphere of control to do so. She was concerned with papal reform and her view of Henry IV was colored by her perception of his wrongs in relation to church reform. Matilda's tactics of warfare were executed when Henry IV came to Italy to do battle or when his troops remained in his name.

While the primary sources do not state directly how or even if Matilda participated on the battlefield, evidence of her extensive involvement in warfare exists firstly in the words used to describe her and her followers. The most significant of these are *dux*, *miles* and *virago*. Matilda was called the first of these significant words, *dux*, in various forms both masculine and feminine: 'prudentissimae ducis Mathildae' and 'prudentissimam ducem'[251] (both refer to the 'most prudent leader', the former in a masculine form and the latter a mixed gender), 'ducatrix'[252] ('[female] leader') and, in Italy, 'nobilissima dux Mathildis' ('most celebrated leader Matilda', mixed gender).[253] Matilda was frequently addressed as 'domina', 'comitissa' and 'ducatrix'.[254] There is no doubt she took on the mantle of leader, inherited from her father and then her mother. Although the masculine form 'dux', rather than the feminine form 'ducatrix', is used inconsistently, no reliable conclusions can be drawn from the different uses, except that strong leadership is meant by the use of either form.[255]

The men Matilda led, her *milites*, appear prominently in contemporary writing. According to Bernold of Constance, at the Battle of Sorbara in 1084 'milites prudentissimae ducis Mathildae in Longobardia contra fautores Heinrici et inimicos sancti Petri viriliter pugnaverunt'.[256] The early use of *miles* was a term of rising status, especially in West Francia and Italy, but still the lowest rung of the aristocracy, best translated as 'soldier' before the first millennium.[257] Across the eleventh century the term transformed into the 'heroic defender, the champion of Christendom', and eventually to *miles sancti Petri,* for those 'who lent their sword to the cause of the papacy' in Pope Gregory VII's military clashes with Emperor Henry IV.[258] Matilda's great-grandfather Adalbert Atto, in being named a *miles* of Bishop Adelard of Reggio, may well have been providing service to the bishop based on personal rather than military links.[259] Later a more nuanced translation of *miles* during the period of Matilda's rule is 'warrior', that captures more closely the valiant aura that surrounded the polemics of Matilda's contemporary sources. Consequently the following translation of Bernold of Constance for the Battle of Sorbara presents the right balance: 'the warriors of the most prudent leader Matilda fought manfully against the supporters of Henry and the enemies of St Peter in Lombardy'.[260]

As well as referring to Matilda's men as warriors, on numerous occasions contemporary writers referred to Matilda herself as 'miles' or 'miles catholica'.[261] In Lombardy in 1085 'Matilda' was 'the most prudent leader and most faithful *warrior* of St Peter'.[262] In 1093, again in Lombardy, Matilda and her husband Welf V were both denoted as 'prudentissimi milites sancti Petri'. The full sentence, 'the *most prudent warriors of St Peter,* duke Welf and his wife Matilda, by now *fighting manfully* for three years against the schismatics, were finally greatly strengthened against them, with God bringing aid', remains a strong statement of military and spiritual struggle.[263] Here Bernold of Constance placed Matilda's name as wife second to Welf, *dux,* although he added that they both fought 'viriliter'. Bernold recorded that Matilda ('nobilissima dux', 'tanto virilius') with her husband labored greatly against the excommunicates and the schismatics in 1089 and in 1092.[264] Even though Bernold admired Matilda, during the time that she and Welf remained together as wife and husband, he always referred to her as an adjunct to Welf. Only after she had separated from Welf in 1097 does Bernold mention her alone again, and with great praise.[265]

Other contemporary writers noted Matilda's robust military intervention when about twenty. Bonizo of Sutri implies that she participated directly in mid-1067 with her stepfather and mother at the campaign that drove the Normans back over the River Garigliano. The reference is subtle:

For that duke [Godfrey the Bearded, Matilda's stepfather] had chanced to come to Italy at this time [1067], bringing with him the most excellent Countess Matilda, daughter of the famous Duke Boniface. He gathered the whole multitude of his army and came to Rome with his wife [Beatrice] and the most noble Matilda; he expelled the Normans from the Campagna without a battle and restored it to Roman jurisdiction. This was the first service that the most excellent daughter of Boniface [that is, Matilda] offered to the blessed prince of the apostles [Pope Urban II]. Not long afterwards, *as a result of her many services pleasing to God, she deserved to be called the daughter of St Peter*.[266]

The references to 'first service' and her 'many services' imply much more than Matilda's mere attendance at the expulsion of the Normans. Even though Matilda's services are only mentioned in Bonizo's version and in no other eleventh-century account, it is credible that Matilda actively helped the duke to drive the Normans out and that it is for this reason she was first called 'daughter of St Peter'.[267] After the above campaign other contemporary writers began to apply the epithet 'daughter of St Peter' to Matilda. The papacy gave the title 'son' or 'daughter of St Peter' to those 'who lent their swords to the cause of the papacy', that is, those who fought physically for the church.[268] Although the evidence is not conclusive, the association of the phrase with Matilda suggests her active involvement in battle.[269]

Three intriguing pieces of evidence exist for Matilda's presence on the battlefield. Bishop Anselm II of Lucca reports that Matilda was 'prepared not only to sacrifice all earthly considerations for the sake of defending righteousness but also to struggle *even to the shedding of her own blood* to bring about your confusion and for the sake of reverence for the glory and exaltation of holy Church, until the Lord delivers His enemy into the hands of a woman'. Anselm's phrase 'usque ad sanguine ... certare' remains inconclusive but could imply that Matilda was either wounded or might have been wounded, because she had put herself in harm's way.[270] The second is the sale in the marketplace at Reggio in 1622 of two suits of armor, originating in one of the Quattro Castelli and coyly noted to be of a different shape from men's armor.[271] The armor reputedly belonged to Matilda, but the source is seventeenth century and is not mentioned elsewhere. In any case even if the suits belonged to Matilda the wearing of defensive covering is merely indicative of attention to self-protection, not evidence of direct participation on the battlefield.[272] The third piece of evidence relates to Bonizo of Sutri's description of the Battle of Volta, south of Lake Garda, which took place in mid-October 1080. 'A few days after these events occurred, his son [Henry IV's heir, Conrad, or else Henry's illegitimate son] *contended in battle against the army of the most excellent Matilda* and obtained the victory.'[273] Whether Matilda fought directly or not, the overwhelming evidence for her intense involvement in battle strategy and tactics entitles her to be called 'commander' and 'warrior'.

While the meaning of *miles* has been the subject of some debate, there is no doubt about the meaning of *virago*: 'A woman having the qualities of a man'; 'a physically strong woman' or 'a warlike or heroic woman'.[274] It was a frequently used term of commendation for women in the Middle Ages: 'to praise lordly women who wielded authoritative powers that were generally conceived as male'.[275] Æthelflæd, Lady of the Mercians, a 'virgo virago', reigned as queen in her own right from 911 until 918, built defensive *burhs*, acted as a military commander in her territory, sent armies into Wales and resisted the Danish forces.[276] St Liutberga (died about 870), referred to as 'felix ... virago' ('happy virago') and 'virago ... aptis' ('virago capable of everything'), exhibited noteworthy holiness in her actions.[277] In the early eleventh century, Empress Kunigunde, the wife of Emperor Henry II, in bending her knee to God as king, was called a *virago* for her holiness.[278] In contrast there exists only one rather oblique reference to Empress Adelheid as *virago* by the cleric Garin, who addressed a copy of Odilo of Cluny's *Epitaphium Adalheidae* to Adela of Flanders (1009–1079). In his accompanying letter Garin refers to Adelheid as a *virago*, 'always to be praised'.[279] Odilo never terms Adelheid *virago* in his extensive *Epitaphium* that otherwise comprehends full approbation of her holy life as a ruler.

While use of the term *virago* in the early eleventh and in the thirteenth centuries on occasion acquired the derogatory meaning of 'shrew' or 'scold',[280] no such disparaging connotation ever attached to John of Mantua's and Hugh of Flavigny's uses of the term in referring to Matilda of Tuscany. Both contemporary writers provide ample evidence for Matilda being a strong war leader of men by their extensive use of *virago*. John of Mantua's polemic on a commentary on the *Song of Songs*, written at Matilda's request, has only admiration in addressing her as 'o virago catholica' ('o Catholic warrior woman') and 'virago prudentissima' ('most foresighted [perhaps sagacious] warrior woman').[281] He urges her to imitate David who is sanctioned in bearing arms.[282] Similarly, Hugh of Flavigny admiringly refers to Matilda as *virago* in a comprehensive passage:

But indeed Countess Matilda, daughter of the Roman church, holding the steadfastness *of a manly mind ['virilis animi'],* the more boldly she used to resist him [Henry IV], so much to a greater extent she had learnt cleverness and the honesty of the pope. For alone then among women is her discovery of the right season, she having scorned the power of the king, now certainly matched his shrewdness and military force, *so that she merited being named virago ['ut merito nominetur virago'],* [since] *she now led men by the virtue of her mind ['quae virtute animi etiam viros praeibat'.*][283]

Bernold of Constance's chronicle finishes in 1100. In the last few years he evaluated the good and bad ends of several of his contemporaries. In 1097 he wrote a glowing assessment of Matilda:

Lady Matilda exceptional duke and marchioness, most devoted daughter of St Peter, gained everywhere at this time a great name for herself. *For she nearly alone with her own (troops) fought [Nam ipsa pene sola cum suis ... pugnavit]* against Henry and the heretical Wibert and their confederates by now for seven years most wisely, and at last *she drove* Henry quite out of Lombardy *with manly vigor ['viriliter']* and she did not cease to give thanks to God and St Peter for having been restored to her own goods.[284]

Many chroniclers besides Bernold endorsed her by calling her *milites, virago* and *viriliter,* and compared her with the Old Testament warrior Deborah—'that like another Deborah ... she should practice warfare'.[285] Such praise provides the most cogent evidence for Matilda's real leadership in battle, although not necessarily direct participation. She led her troops as *ducatrix* and *dux.* It was her competence that drove Henry definitively out of Italy.

Domina Matilda comitissa atque ducatrix

For Matilda action was not sufficient; to broadcast her persona she needed an effective administrative arm. Matilda followed similar practices to Otto I who operated with a small chancery containing a clerical elite that ministered to the royal need to document the commands and decisions of the kingdom.[286] Those processes did not change in the main when the Ottonian women took the central role in running the kingdom. The charters that followed the formulaic outline of *arenga,* body and conclusions upheld traditional public power. Likewise, Matilda supported a chancery of sorts, although its members, probably less concerned with the concept of a physical center of government than the royal court north of the Alps one hundred years before, changed more frequently in response to the locations where she issued her judgments.[287] Although many of the people who witnessed her charters appeared frequently, none was indispensable as she moved around her areas of influence. Her chancery continued to operate in the Carolingian milieu and in imitation of the empire's practices, which markedly affected her way of ruling. She held great courts that issued *placita* and charters to resolve disputes, to redistribute goods and to reprimand miscreants in the tradition of great lordship and in imitation of the kings of yore.[288] Consequently in the administration of their respective realms Matilda carried on a tradition not much changed from Adelheid's royal procedures.

Both Matilda and Adelheid were addressed or referred to in terms that accorded with their roles. So Adelheid, *regina*, vied in function with Matilda, *dux* or *ducatrix* (*duchess*), *marchionissa* (marchioness) and *comitissa* (countess). Accordingly Petrus *notarius* wrote from Florence on 2 March 1100: 'And I Peter notary write by the order of the Lady (*domina*) Matilda by the grace of God Duke (*dux*) and Marchioness (*marchionissa*) and on the advice of the judge.'[289] Although the use of either the masculine or feminine forms for *dux* was probably not significant, *domina* was another matter. While Rather of Verona used *domina* for Adelheid as a courtesy, the phrase *dominae imperiales*, in the *Annals of Quedlinburg* and in the letters of Gerbert of Aurillac to refer to Adelheid, Theophanu and Mathilda of Quedlinburg, carried the sense of veneration and power. Since *dominus* denoted the possessor of a *castrum* or *castra*,[290] the use of the term *domina* (as the feminine of *dominus*) for Countess Matilda of Tuscany had special significance since she was the lord of many *castra*, and as a consequence, she had numerous *domini* reporting to her. When commanding servants in her role within the household corresponding to the manly actions outside, the *domina* held lordly status: the English term 'lady' does not convey the lordly power she held. As the responsibility of a woman expanded beyond the realm of the household, the term *domina*, already meant as the equivalent of *dominus*, expanded too.[291]

Certain nomenclature carried imperial overtones. Not only was Adelheid called *inclita* in the *Annals of Quedlinburg*,[292] by Hrotsvitha,[293] and by Bishop Thietmar of Merseburg,[294] but Matilda also received that designation on more than one occasion. When in 1067 Matilda's stepfather, Godfrey the Bearded, brought Matilda with him to Italy, the young Matilda was praised as 'the most excellent countess Matilda, daughter of the renowned Duke Boniface' ('excellentissimam cometissam Matildam, incliti ducis Bonifacii filiam'). Her father was remembered with those same imperial overtones, even though by this time he had been dead for fifteen years.[295] The designation *inclita* was appropriated later by Donizo for Matilda. In noting Matilda's attendance at the translation of relics of St Geminianus at the cathedral in Modena in 1106 Donizo referred to her as '[i]nclita Mathildis'.[296] Shortly afterwards, in 1107, Matilda entitled herself *inclita* in her own diplomata together with the female form of *dux*, 'do(mi)na inclita comitissa Matilda duccatris'.[297] The use by Matilda and others of 'inclita', with its overtones of an old Roman imperial title, remains highly significant: not only did she aspire to imperial honors but others also perceived her in that way.

Although Adelheid's status remained high, as demonstrated by her enduring regal titles, in comparison with Matilda she retained relatively restricted ability to craft her image directly through the royal diplomata because of the protocols involved which hid her real authority. As wife of the king/emperor to a great extent she complied with his wishes, and, although in an extremely powerful position as chief intercessor, she depended on him while he lived. The published and propagated diplomata included only those of whom the ruler approved and whose petition was successful. The suggestions and pleadings which did not succeed did not generate actions and consequent records and so do not survive. As sole regent for the years between 991 and 994 Adelheid could operate more freely although, since she acted always through the king's name, her actions appeared subject to influential advisers in the court such as the powerful Archbishop Willigis of Mainz, pre-eminent bishop by canonical right.[298] In addition Adelheid's hagiographical persona was bounded, at least to some extent, by earlier models of sanctity. However, we must not forget her daughter-in-law, Theophanu, who issued at least two diplomata in her own name from Italy, and that Adelheid and Theophanu operated as effective rulers when regents. To their contemporaries the image which was presented by the requisite conventions of the diplomata did not disguise the powers of the spouse and regent.

Matilda's lines of authority at first consideration appear clear and direct as she remained a vassal of King (and from 1084, Emperor) Henry IV. Nevertheless, the great Countess Matilda determined the agenda of each of her diplomata with far more independence within her territory than Adelheid. Some extant letters written by Matilda to the recipients of various diplomata complement the diplomata and reveal her motives.

The diplomata formally set out the decisions that she made on particular occasions and provide unique insight into her thoughts. In particular they show her ability to persuade and to negotiate, coupled with her strong sense of justice since at times she rebuked her own men.

The letters from popes, bishops and monks to Matilda also reveal her as a great lord. The seven popes whom Matilda championed held her in high esteem. Most of the extant letters to popes relate to correspondence between Matilda and Pope Gregory VII. One dated 3 March 1079, a reply to one of hers and intimate in tone, informed her of his personal views on a number of matters—the proposed marriage of Duke Theoderic of Upper Lotharingia, his preference for the formal sending of legates to King Henry IV, rather than using her suggestion of employing the negotiating skills of an unnamed duke, and his excommunication of another unnamed duke. Gregory's intentions, we may reasonably presume, were to convey information and to inform her of his decisions after discussing the various events with her.[299] So too the example of the church of St Florian acts as a useful guide to understanding Matilda and the papacy's complex relationship. According to Pope Urban II's letter to Matilda, exact date unknown but necessarily during his reign from 1088 to 1099, Matilda had confirmed her father's donation of the church of St Florian to the monastery of St Benedict, which gift had also been confirmed by the church. However, in a dispute between the abbey and the bishop of Mantua, the bishop had claimed the church. In the letter Pope Urban reasserted the right of the monastery to possess the church and informed Matilda of his decision to support the abbot against the bishop of Mantua. But the letter was not written merely to convey information; Pope Urban II authorized Matilda to chastise the bishop in front of witnesses and to regulate the dispute in favor of the abbot:

> We want, therefore, and order that our monastery, which was yours, receive whatever it held by right completely; that it suffer no diminution of the things it held in any way. It is fitting therefore that in the presence of the bishop of Reggio and other prudent men, you [Matilda] summon the bishop of Mantua and order him to restore what belonged to the monastery and permit it to possess other things in peace.[300]

There are further matters to note about the letter. Pope Urban used several significant phrases: 'we order' ('praecipimus') that the monastery receive its rights undiminished; that Matilda in summoning the bishop of Mantua 'order him' ('ei praecipias') to attend a public forum; that this forum should include the bishop of Reggio in the presence 'of other prudent men' ('aliorum prudentium virorum'). Later Pope Paschal ordered Matilda ('we entrust to your love') to ensure that the abbot of Frassinoro restored plunder taken from the church of Carpi.[301] In such words and phrases Matilda was authorized, as delegate of popes, to carry out restitution and to dictate to bishops.

Matilda deliberately created a self-image most effectively through her own diplomata, issued with the assistance of a team of varying associates, notaries and witnesses. From the first diploma in 1072 Matilda, possibly coached by her mother, Beatrice, already exhibited an understanding of the power of title. The twenty-five-year-old and her mother styled themselves 'comitisse' (countesses) and 'ducatrice' (duchesses).[302] Until 8 December Beatrice's name appeared first and then Matilda's, the latter also acknowledged as Beatrice's daughter in most of the charters. The diploma is carefully crafted: 'Beatrice, *daughter* of a certain Frederick, and Matilda, *daughter* of a certain Boniface, *mother and daughter, countesses and duchesses*, who *declared we are to live by Salian Law*.'[303] Issued on 19 January 1072, this first diploma lays out what is of importance to create the identity of each of the two women: lineage, familial relationships, titles and legal distinction. The diploma, in stating their relationship to their ancestors as daughters of their deceased fathers rather than their mothers, confirms their lineage in the agnatic line: Beatrice as the daughter of Frederick, duke of Lotharingia, and Matilda as the daughter of Boniface, margrave of Tuscany. The familial relationship between Beatrice and Matilda is defined as mother and daughter and their status through their titles as countess and duchess, using the feminine form of the Latin. Since Beatrice's first husband, Boniface, had died in 1052, her second husband, Godfrey the Bearded, in 1069, and by 1071 Matilda had separated from her husband, Godfrey the Hunchback, the women acted together under their own initiative in this first diploma. Issued from Mantua, the location where Matilda's father had established his palace, it established a framework founded on lineal and legal relationships and incorporated principles on which Matilda based her later diplomata. From Lucca just over a year later, Matilda, then about twenty-six, issued her first diploma without her mother.[304] Here Matilda is styled 'marchionissa' and 'ducatrix', using the feminine forms of the Latin for both words. Since Beatrice died in 1076, at about age fifty-nine, we might confidently speculate that Beatrice had possibly formally handed over the inheritance, including the title, to Matilda for that first independent diploma.

Matilda's father, Boniface, the great margrave of Tuscany, reputedly courted Matilda's mother, Beatrice, in an impressive fashion in 1038. He went to meet her after having ordered that his own horses and those of his retinue should not be shod with iron shoes and nails but with silver. This was not an end to the spectacle. The nails were left deliberately loose so that, as the shoes fell off, the people in the fields could pick them up to keep.[305] Thus Boniface exhibited himself and emphasized his wealth, in such style that the spectacular display would be remembered. As indeed it was. That Donizo recorded the story more than eighty years after the event is witness to the importance that pageants of wealth and power were accorded in the early twelfth century.[306] The recording of the event at that time on behalf of a margrave rather than a king provides further evidence for the shifting in power from regal to comital families.

Not just in elaborate spectacle did a dominant authority exhibit her or his power and wealth. Thietmar and other contemporaries could not restrain their surprise at Otto III's assumption of foreign, in his case Byzantine, ways of eating: Otto ate alone at a semi-circular table that was raised above everyone else, contrary to the norm of eating communally with his *fideles*. Although Thietmar attributed his unusual dining habits to a wish 'to renew the ancient custom of the Romans', according to the norms of the tenth and eleventh centuries, Otto's actions illustrated his peculiar attitude of mind.'[307] The aristocracy differed from the poor in the way they displayed themselves in a social setting. Not surprisingly the aristocracies had a greater quantity of and more varied clothing and demonstrated their power with gifts from their hoard. Nevertheless it was not in that area that the greater distinction appeared but rather in the type and quantity of food: the northern aristocrats ate meat almost exclusively while the poor ate mostly vegetables and grain. 'The rich ate vegetables, too, indeed. But in general, and above all in their *self-image*, they were restricted to a single diet.'[308] The subtleties of their meat diet contributed to their 'self-definition'. The examples of what the aristocrats ate and their manner of eating illustrate the real importance of orchestrated display in every action of public life. Henry IV's manner of drumming his fingernails on the table at the conclusion of the negotiations at Canossa in 1077, discussed in Chap. 1 of this book, sent a public message of his extreme displeasure with the outcome of negotiations.

Rulers showed their power in ways other than by stylized actions. Male rulers had a whole iconography attached to their appearance. Sidonius Apollinaris, in writing about Theodoric II, king of the Visigoths (reigned 453–466), described his physical characteristics in detail, focusing on his well-proportioned figure and the shape of his face and body.[309] Writing a short time later, Ennodius distinguished the Ostrogothic King Theodoric (reigned 474–526) by his gaze: 'the eyes of our king'.[310] In the early ninth century Einhard listed Charlemagne's physical characteristics after the manner of Sidonius Apollinaris and Ennodius.[311] The eyes of Charlemagne were 'piercing and unusually large' although his 'expression was gay and good-humored'.[312] In the tenth century Widukind of Corvey lauded Otto I's physical appearance, including the fire and power of his gaze: 'his eyes glowing ('rutilantes') with a bright reddish color and emitting a certain brilliance like flashing shafts of lightning'.[313]

Notwithstanding a certain lack of historical iconographic prototypes for the physical description of female rulers,[314] contemporary writers did applaud the beauty of worthy Ottonian royal women. In praising them Hrotsvitha ignored the tradition of lauding the physical appearance of ruling men, who nevertheless remain important in her *Gesta*. Instead she commented in detail on the demeanor, manner and expression of Otto I's first wife, Edith, his brother Henry's wife, Judith, and his second wife, Adelheid, as to how they contributed to good Christian rulership. Edith 'was glowing with the remarkable grace of queenly beauty'.[315] In that case Hrotsvitha and Widukind use the same word, *rutilare*, in describing Otto and Edith. Judith was both beautiful and good.[316] Hrotsvitha linked the reigning Queen Adelheid's admirable physical appearance to her lineage and couched it within an acceptable Christian context. The queen generally delighted as 'a woman illustrious in the comeliness of her queenly beauty and solicitous in affairs worthy of her character, and by her actions she corresponded to her regal lineage'.[317] Hrotsvitha too recorded Otto's evaluation of Adelheid: 'with frequent ponderings of heart ... [he] remembered the distinguished Queen Adelaide, and longed to behold the queenly countenance of her whose excellence of character he already knew'.[318] In positioning Otto to appraise Adelheid's worth and in so couching Otto I's worthiness to rule in terms of his correct evaluation of Adelheid, Hrotsvitha proposed a different standard to evaluate the king's right to rule, that based on his worthiness in comparison with his queen.

The contemporary chronicler Liudprand seldom had a good word for any woman—Ermengard, widow of Margrave Adalbert of Ivrea, used her beauty to gain power in Italy by practicing 'carnal trafficking with everyone' ('carnale cum omnibus ... commercium') and ensuring that all 'were aroused by jealousy' ('zelo ... trahebantur'); Wido's unnamed wife remained a temptress and a murderer with 'snakish cunning' ('vipperina'); and Willa 'because of her boundless tyranny is rightly called a second Jezebel, and because of her insatiate greed for plunder a Lamia vampire'.[319] However, about the reigning queen Adelheid he wrote that she was 'charming both by the beauty of her person and the excellence of her character'.[320] Liudprand passed no judgment about Otto I's first wife, Edith, restricting his comments to facts ('Before he came to the throne King Otto had married an English lady of high rank, Otwith [Edith] niece of King Æthelstan, and by her had a son named Liutolf [Liudolf]'.[321]) Liudprand's glowing panegyric of Adelheid, written shortly after she and Otto I were crowned empress and emperor of the Romans, appeared with ceremonial solemnity in the Preface to *Relatio de legatione Constantinopolitana*:

> That the Ottos, the invincible august emperors of the Romans and the most noble Adelaide the august empress, may always flourish, prosper and triumph, is the earnest wish, desire and prayer of Liudprand bishop of the holy church of Cremona.[322]

While Edith's status had fallen since she now remained only in memory, albeit revered, Adelheid's had correspondingly risen as the queen currently pre-eminent and, concurrently with her husband Otto I, Liudprand's patron. Liudprand's agenda included legitimacy of his benefactors and corresponding denigration of anyone who might be a threat to them.[323] Although Liudprand no doubt wrote with an eye to promotion, his positive attitude toward Adelheid seems striking, beyond mere flattery.

In the late tenth century both Hrotsvitha and Liudprand were aware of the medieval models of kingship in their presentation of the physical characteristics of Queen/Empress Adelheid, although modifying the male iconography in presenting female iconography in their works. A century later the contemporary chroniclers of Countess Matilda differed markedly in their treatment of her physical features. Donizo noted the beauty of Matilda's mother. He called her 'Magna Beatrix' ('Great Beatrix) and, like the contemporary commentators on Adelheid a century before, celebrated her royal ancestors: 'Beautiful Beatrix was begot by a royal lineage'.[324] In contrast physical descriptions of Matilda remain strikingly few. Donizo gloried in her as 'eloquent, clever, politically astute and skilled in rulership' because he believed that the overriding matter of importance was the character and role of Matilda.[325] The anonymous eulogist who wrote about her after her death concurred: 'she was most eloquent in conversation and most astute in deliberations, sympathetic to all.'[326] Donizo's portrait of Matilda may have prefigured the age of renewed intellectualism of the twelfth century: the superiority of Matilda's character and her role in presaging the new era made her appearance unimportant to her hagiographer,[327] or perhaps she was not good-looking.

For Adelheid and Matilda the kind and manner of physical descriptions differed from typical accounts of ruling men. The emphasis for Adelheid remained on virtue, beauty deriving from virtue, and eminent ancestors. Although Donizo's work lacks descriptions of Matilda's physical appearance, he did incorporate pictures of her in the manuscript at the time of his writing.[328] The two images of Matilda are stylized, portraying a young woman of about thirty years. The image of Matilda with Abbot Hugh of Cluny and King Henry IV at their meeting at Canossa in 1077 corresponds to a woman of about Matilda's age at that meeting.[329] The portrait is captioned with the partial sentence 'Rex rogat abbatem! Mathildim supplicat atq[ue];' ('The king asks the abbot! And pleads with Matilda;'). The picture summarizes a series of events from Donizo's *Vita*.[330] This is the scene probably in front of Matilda's castle of Canossa just before King Henry IV sought reconciliation with Pope Gregory VII. Henry needed Gregory to lift his excommunication of him so that Henry's men would obey him once more and he could continue to rule. Henry initially asked his godfather, Abbot Hugh of Cluny, to intercede on his behalf. In the picture Hugh is speaking or pointing to Matilda, indicating that Henry should ask her, his kinswoman and the most powerful count in the land, rather than himself. Matilda is seated under a canopy (perhaps the entrance to her castle), wrapped closely in a decorated cloak with an elaborate border, perhaps made of fur, and wearing a simple headdress. Turned toward the larger figure of the abbot and the kneeling Henry, her pose appears conciliatory. She and others did intercede successfully for Henry with the pope. A second image shows Matilda when she was about sixty-three years of age, although she is depicted as just as youthful as in the former portrait.[331] While she, depicted in a larger image, stands or is perhaps half-seated in a higher and consequently superior position, the two smaller figures stand on either side. The man to her left, holding a sword, probably represents her chief military man, Arduinus de Palude.[332] To her right a tonsured man, probably the monk Donizo, holds up his book to her. The iconography of the latter depiction matches two important images from the early eleventh centuries. The first comes from the Hitda Codex, which shows Abbess Hitda of Meschede presenting her Gospel book to St Walburga, the patron saint of the abbey.[333] The second depicts the presentation of another book, the *Encomium Emmae Reginae*, commissioned by the English Queen Emma, consort first of King Æthelread the Unready and then of King Canute I, and written between 1041 and 1042.[334] While the abbess and the saint stand in the Hitda Codex, in the *Encomium* Emma is seated and the kneeling writer, the Encomiast, presents her with his book, while her two sons, Harthacnut and Edward, look on. Matilda, like Emma, is seated, enthroned or just in front of an elaborate seat with a red drape behind her and framed by a canopy or 'timpano' (a triangular recess on a pediment or below an arch), an allusion to a regal room.[335] Her knees are wide apart and her feet are planted firmly on the ground, toes pointed downwards, to receive the book dedicated to her.[336] The iconography is very similar to that in two Ottonian Gospel books, originating in Reichenau, which show Adelheid's son and grandson as emperors in majesty.[337] In Donizo's book Matilda holds a *ramus arboris*, a flowering twig, that symbolizes justice and adjudication as ruler in northern Italy.[338] The Carolingians and the Ottonians used the sign of the fleur-de-lis as part of their regalia from time to time.[339] Matilda wears on her head a pointed hat rather like a cone. That headgear was worn by the enthroned Charlemagne in an image from a tenth-century manuscript.[340] Matilda's mother and father, Beatrice and Boniface, wear prominent caps in Donizo's manuscript, as does her ancestor, Countess Giulia.[341] Matilda's author stands (although in the image recording the 1077 events, Matilda's supplicant, Henry, kneels like the Encomiast). The portrait illustrates the partial sentence 'Mathildis lucens precor hoc cape cara volumen' ('O resplendent Matilda, I entreat [you] beloved take this [volume]'.) No such images exist for Adelheid.

Two images from a thirteenth-century manuscript, displayed in the Cathedral Museum at Modena, show Matilda overseeing the translation of the relics of St Geminianus at two sacred events. The drawings are briefly examined here to demonstrate how they promulgate Matilda's image as ruler, rather than for her interest in spirituality. Matilda is again portrayed as a young woman, although at that time she was about sixty. The two images, executed as colored line drawings in the manuscript of the *Relatio translationis corporis sancti Geminiani*, differ in style and in intent from the depictions of Adelheid.[342] Here the woman is depicted as performing as ruler at the very height of the reformist zeal of the early twelfth century. Some allowance has to be made for the fact that the thirteenth-century manuscript must be influenced by the issues prominent at the period when the manuscript was created and illustrated. Nevertheless the drawings, albeit from a later time, emphasize the central role that Matilda took. There is no image of Christ in pictures of Matilda. However, she is known to have sponsored at least one Gospel book, created at San Benedetto Polirone around 1099 and known as the Gospels of Matilda of Tuscany from Polirone. The most striking of the nineteen color and twelve black-and-white images is that of Christ cleansing the Temple, an example of a direct challenge to those who might be considering defying church authority.[343]

While both Adelheid and Matilda appear in Gospel or books otherwise of a religious nature, their images therein illustrate quite different iconography. The two images of Adelheid, discussed earlier in this chapter, show a powerful woman in subjection to God, personified in Jesus Christ (on the Initial Page of the Matthew Evangelistary in the Gospel of St Gereon) and an empress, powerful in this world but submissively kneeling at the feet of the Virgin Mary (on the altar canopy at the church of Sant'Ambrogio in Milan). The difference in portrayal between the two rulers, Adelheid and Matilda, is the difference between passivity and activity. Both present grandly and with a strong religious focus. However, Adelheid's images show a woman subservient to God; Matilda's images show a woman active in God's service.

The difference in both the portrayal and the reality of direct as opposed to passive activity continues into Matilda's use of signatures and seals. Extant coins show Adelheid and Otto (it is not certain whether the Otto is her husband or her grandson); no coins were minted by Matilda because to strike coins remained a royal prerogative. Both Adelheid and Matilda employed scribes, but Adelheid did not sign nor affix a seal in her name to any of the charters with which she was associated, although evidence for seals exists for the three Ottos.[344] In contrast Matilda took great interest in her personal signature and the affixing of her seal to her documents, very unusual for lay rulers in Italy at the time. Although her father signed his own documents personally, the reading and writing ability of her mother is in doubt, as Beatrice only signed symbolically with a Latin cross. After Beatrice died, Matilda developed her own distinct signature that was much more stylized than her father's. Her famous statement, 'Matilda dei gratia si quid est' ('Matilda by the grace of God is who she is') within a cross, has been interpreted with two contradictory meanings: she had doubts about, and she was certain about, her own authority.[345] I think her meaning falls between these two views: she had placed herself in the service of God and whatever she had been able to achieve in this world she owed to him, not to herself.

Matilda closed her diplomata with her signature and with her own distinctive seal, an option only open to a queen or an empress in Germany in 1002, when Queen Kunigunde became the first queen there known to have affixed her seal.[346] The seal of the under-age King Otto III would always have confirmed the legitimacy of a document, even though Adelheid was ruling. Consequently no seal is known in Adelheid's name. Within a century of Adelheid's death Countess Matilda authenticated at least eighteen of her documents with a seal. In the imprint of a seal, purported to be Matilda's, the undoubtedly female image may sport loose flowing hair (most unusual in any iconography of female rulers whose hair was always tightly bound) and is reminiscent of virgin saints, especially virgin martyrs.[347] Matilda's seal image should be compared with that used for the *Liber Censuum*, the register of the church's jurisdiction and properties compiled in 1192 by Cardinal Cencio Savelli under the papacy of Celestine III (1191–1198) and the most authoritative attempt to keep a record of money owing to the Roman church.[348] If the seal of the *Liber Censuum* took its model from that of Matilda then the authority of Matilda's seal is reinforced. Later designers of the seal of the *Liber Censuum* must have wished to replicate the earlier authority of the noteworthy Matilda. As well as the above seal image, an actual seal with a different image belonging to Matilda currently exists. It shows a standing female figure holding a flower in her left hand and a book in her right. Surrounding the image are the words 'uxor Gotfridi Mathildi(s)' ('Matilda wife of Godfrey'), which undoubtedly dates the seal to the period of her marriage to Godfrey between 1069 and 1074.[349] Further confirmation, if it is needed, about the authority of Matilda appears in her letter to her own and Pope Gregory VII's followers about the theft of his seal.[350] Matilda informed them about the loss and charged them to believe only words received from her legates directly: none other than she had the authority of the pope's command.

On Bended Knee

When the writer of the twelfth-century *Annales Sancti Disibodi*, in the monastery at Disibodenberg in the diocese of Mainz, addressed Matilda in the following way: 'to the most powerful woman of her time Matilda by name',[351] she may have been aware of the work of another anonymous author who wrote a very evocative eulogy very soon after Matilda's death. Of all the images, verbal and pictorial, the most redolent of Matilda's power and mystique comes from this second writer, when no direct heirs or competing *comites* might need flattering.

> She [Matilda] *respected* greatly altogether pious clerics, she *protected* plunderers not at all, she *governed* the peasants, she *governed* all leading men, margraves, counts, all other nobles and warriors with so much diligence that *they used to prostrate themselves most eagerly on bended knee in deliberations before her*.[352]

This is a powerful statement about the authority Matilda wielded, a very valuable indication of the visible expression of her jurisdiction. The author has carefully listed the range of people with whom Matilda dealt, covering the clerical and the lay, the wealthy and the poor, the rulers and the followers. He emphasized her role as a wise ruler, repudiating thieves and dispensing justice across the territories she governed—a person honored and respected by all members of the community; in fact, a king in all but name.

Notes

1. For the argument that Widukind's original draft should be dated to 961, before Adelheid's and Otto I's imperial coronations, see Steven Robbie, 'Can silence speak volumes? Widukind's *Res Gestae Saxonicae* and the coronation of Otto I reconsidered', *EME* 20, no. 3 (2012), 338.
2. 'Cumque eum *virtus* prefatae reginae non lateret, simulato itinere Romam proficisci statuit. Cumque in Longobardiam ventum esset, *aureis muneribus amorem reginae* super *se probare* temptavit. *Quo fideliter experto*, in coniugium sibi eam sociavit *cumque ea urbem Papiam, quae est sedes regia, obtinuit.* ... Rex vero in Italia celebratis iuxta *magnificentiam regalem* nuptiis *proficiscitur* inde cum novi matrimonii *claritate* acturus proximum pascha in Saxonia, *laetitiam patriae magnamque gratiam conferens* [my italics]', Widukind, *Res*, 3.9–3.10.

3. Sverre Bagge, *Kings, Politics, and the Right Order of the World in German Historiography c. 950–1150* (Leiden: Brill, 2002), 25–26.
4. John O. Ward, 'After Rome: Medieval Epic', in *Roman Epic*, ed. A. J. Boyle (London: Routledge, 1993), 285–89; Carl Erdmann, 'The Ottonian Empire as *Imperium Romanum*', in *The Rise of the First Reich: Germany in the Tenth Century*, ed. Boyd H. Hill (New York: Wiley, 1969), 97–99.
5. Olson, *Early Middle Ages*, 210; Niermeyer, *Lexicon*, s.v. 'bannus'.
6. Janet Nelson, 'Aachen as a Place of Power', in *Courts, Elites, and Gendered Power in the Early Middle Ages: Charlemagne and Others*, ed. Janet Nelson (Aldershot: Ashgate, 2007), XIV.1–19.
7. Leyser, *Rule*, 74–107; Sarah Hamilton, 'Review article: Early Medieval Rulers and their Modern Biographers', *EME* 9, no. 2 (2000) 260; Janet Nelson, 'Rulers and Government', *NCMH* 3 (1999), 103.
8. *De Heinrico*, ed. K. Strecker, *Die Cambridger Lieder. MGH SSrG* [40] (Hanover: 1926), 57–60; Marion E. Gibbs and Sidney M. Johnson, *Medieval German Literature* (New York: Routledge, 2000), 53.
9. David A. Warner, 'Thietmar of Merseburg on Rituals of Kingship', *Viator* 26 (1995), 53–76, especially 74–75; Karl Leyser, 'Ritual, Ceremony, and Gesture: Ottonian Germany', in *Communications and Power in Medieval Europe: The Carolingian and Ottonian Centuries*, ed. Timothy Reuter (London: Hambledon Press, 1994), 192–202; Matthew Innes, *State and Society in the Early Middle Ages: The Middle Rhine Valley, 400–1000* (Cambridge: Cambridge University Press, 2000), 233–39.
10. 'clementissime domine', 'inclyte domine' and 'princeps venerabilis': Ennodius, *Panegyricus dictus clementissimo regi Theoderico*, ed. F. Vogel, *Magni Felicis Ennodi Opera, MGH SS AA* 7:203–214 (1885), 1.203, 3.205, 7.206.
11. Althoff, 'Königsherrschaft, 290. Leyser, *Rule*, 9–47.
12. Penelope Nash, 'Reality and Ritual in the Medieval King's Emotions of *Ira* and *Clementia*', in *Understanding Emotions in Medieval and Early Modern Europe*, ed. Michael Champion and Andrew Lynch (Turnhout: Brepols, 2015), 258–61.
13. *DO* I, Nr. 1.

14. John William Bernhardt, *Itinerant Kingship and Royal Monasteries in Early Medieval Germany, c. 936–1075* (Cambridge: Cambridge University Press, 1993), 6–7.
15. 'Advocacy' could apply to the abbesses who were appointed to Quedlinburg from the Liudolfing family for several generations. Two early abbesses were direct descendants of Empress Adelheid. Her daughter, Mathilda, became abbess in 966 and then Adelheid, her granddaughter through her son, Otto II, became abbess on the death of Abbess Mathilda in 999. Abbess Adelheid ruled until her death in 1043.
16. Leyser, 'Maternal Kin', 182–83. See the discussion of *cognatio* in Chap. 2 in this book.
17. Julia M. H. Smith, *Europe after Rome: A New Cultural History 500–1000* (Oxford: Oxford University Press, 2005), 239–40.
18. Thietmar, *Chronicon*, 3.24, 3.26.
19. *Capitulare de villis*, ed. A. Boretius, *MGH Capitularia regum Francorum, Legum sectio* I:32:82–91 (Hanover: 1883).
20. Hincmar of Reims, *Hincmarus de ordine palatii*, ed. Thomas Gross and Rudolf Schieffer, *MGH Fontes* 3 (Hanover, 1980), ch. 22, lines 360–63.
21. Rosamond McKitterick, *The Carolingians and the Written Word* (Cambridge: Cambridge University Press, 1989), 25–37; Janet Nelson, 'Legislation and Consensus in the Reign of Charles the Bald', in *Ideal and Reality in Frankish and Anglo-Saxon Society: Studies Presented to J.M. Wallace-Hadrill*, ed. Patrick Wormald (Oxford: Blackwell, 1983), 202–27; Stafford, *Queens, Concubines*, 104–6; Edouard Perroy, 'Carolingian Administration', in *Early Medieval Society*, ed. Sylvia L. Thrupp (New York: Appleton-Century-Crofts, 1967), 134.
22. Franz-Reiner Erkens, 'Die Frau als Herrscherin in ottonisch-frühsalischer Zeit', in von Euw, *Kaiserin Theophanu: Begegnung des Ostens und Westens um die Wende des ersten Jahrtausands*, ed. Anton von Euw and Peter Schreiner (Cologne: Schnütgen-Museum, 1991), 246; Julia M. H. Smith, 'Introduction: Gendering the Early Medieval World', in Brubaker, *Gender in the Early Medieval World*, 242–43; Michael J. Enright, *Lady with a Mead Cup: Ritual, Prophecy, and Lordship in the European Warband from La Tène to the Viking Age* (Dublin: Four Courts, 1996), 28–29.

23. For further discussion of the queen's role in the household, see Nash, 'Maintaining Elite Households', in *Elite and Royal Households in Later Medieval and Early Modern Europe*, ed. Theresa Earenfight (Leiden: Brill, forthcoming 2017).
24. Paul the Deacon, *Historia Langobardorum*, ed. G. Waitz, *MGH SSrG* [48] (Hanover: 1878), 3.30, 3.35; Enright, *Lady*, 12.
25. Widukind, *Res*, 2.2.
26. 'regnum prout curaretur ab ea', Thietmar, *Chronicon*, 6.74.
27. *VMP*, chs 6, 9.
28. Gerbert, *Epistolae*, Letter 181, trans. Lattin, *Letters*, Letter 221.
29. Adelheid, Theophanu and Abbess Mathilda are referred to as *dominae imperiales* in the *AQ*, s.aa. 984, 985. At a later period the expression *dominae imperiales* was also applied to the two abbesses Sophie and Adelheid, daughters of Theophanu and granddaughters of Adelheid: *AQ*, s.aa. 1000, 1002.
30. 'Illi tercius Otto, cum adhuc puer esset, in regnum substitutus annos XVIII forti et iusto sceptrum ornavit imperio', Adam of Bremen, *Gesta Hammaburgensis ecclesiae pontificum*, ed. Werner Trillmich and Rudolf Buchner, 2nd ed., *AQDG* 11:137–499 (Darmstadt: Wissenschaftliche Buchgesellschaft, 1968), 2.24.
31. Gilsdorf, *Queenship*, 11.
32. Everett, *Literacy*, 180, 186–96; Rosamond McKitterick, 'The Written Word and Oral Communication: Rome's Legacy to the Franks', in *The Frankish Kings and Culture in the Early Middle Ages* (Aldershot: Variorum, 1995) X.89–112; Rosamond McKitterick, 'Latin and Romance: An Historian's Perspective', in *The Frankish Kings and Culture in the Early Middle Ages*, IX.130–145; Janet Nelson, 'Literacy in Carolingian Government', in *The Uses of Literacy in Early Mediaeval Europe*, ed. Rosamond McKitterick (Cambridge: Cambridge University Press, 1990), 265–96; Franz H. Bäuml, 'Varieties and Consequences of Medieval Literacy and Illiteracy', *Speculum* 55, no. 2 (Apr., 1980), 237–65.
33. *VMP*, chs 12–13.
34. Ottonian Ivory Relief, Otto II, Theophanu and Otto III at the Feet of Christ, Mary and St. Maurice, c. 980, Milan: Civiche Raccolte d'Arte Applicata, Museo del Castello Sforzesco; Erkens, 'Frau', 255.
35. McKitterick, 'Women', XI.87–95.

36. Thietmar, *Chronicon*, 4.47; Brun of Querfurt, *Passio sancti Adalberti episcopi et martyris (Leidensgeschichte des heiligen Bischofs und Märtyrers Adalbert)*, ed. Jerzy Strzelczyk and Lorenz Weinrich, *AQDG* 23:70–117 (Darmstadt: Wissenschaftliche Buchgesellschaft, 2005), 18–20.
37. Gilsdorf, *Queenship*, 27–30.
38. Nash, 'Reality and Ritual', 264–65.
39. *AQ*, s.a. 984, trans. adapted from Warner, *Ottonian Germany*, 155n23; Bernhardt, *Kingship*, 143n46.
40. Thietmar, *Chronicon*, 4.18; *AQ*, s.a. 992.
41. David A. Warner, 'The Representation of Empire: Otto I at Ravenna', in *Representations of Power in Medieval Germany, 800–1500*, ed. Björn Weiler and Simon MacLean (Turnhout: Brepols, 2006), 124–8.
42. Niermeyer, *Lexicon*, s.v. 'virtus'.
43. Enright, *Lady*, 1.
44. Widukind, *Res*, 3.7.
45. Ferrante, *To the Glory*, 233n27. See also Stafford, *Queens, Concubines*, 116.
46. Widukind, *Res*, 3.9; Thietmar, *Chronicon*, 2.5; Adalbert of Magdeburg, *Continuatio Reginonis*, s.a. 951.
47. Liudprand, *Antapodosis*, 4.18, 4.29; Hrotsvitha, *Gesta*, lines 202–36; *VMP*, chs 6, 9; Leyser, 'Ottonians and Wessex', 85–86.
48. Flodoard of Reims, *Annales*, s.a. 953; Timothy Reuter, '*Regemque, quem in Francia pene perdidit, in patria magnifice recepit*: Ottonian Ruler-Representation in Synchronic and Diachronic Comparison', in *Medieval Polities and Modern Mentalities*, ed. Janet Nelson (Cambridge: Cambridge University Press, 2006), 128.
49. Katharina M. Wilson, 'The Saxon Canoness: Hrotsvit of Gandersheim', in *Medieval Women Writers* (Manchester: Manchester University Press, 1984), 31 and 43n9; Odilo Engels, 'Theophano, the Western Empress from the East', in Davids, *The Empress Theophano*, 33–35.
50. Hrotsvitha, *Gesta*, lines 656–665.
51. 'suae fidei studio se subdidit omni', ibid., line 739.
52. Charlton Thomas Lewis and Charles Short, *A Latin Dictionary. Founded on Andrews' Edition of Freund's Latin Dictionary*, 1st ed. (Oxford: Clarendon Press, 1879), s.vv. 'pietas', 'bonitas',

'veneror', 'fides'. Niermeyer, *Lexicon*, s.vv. 'pietas', 'fides'. *Pietas* can also be translated as 'goodness', 'charity', 'beneficence', 'alms', 'pity' and 'compassion'.

53. Cristina La Rocca, *Italy in the Early Middle Ages: 476–1000* (Oxford: Oxford University Press, 2002), 39–40.
54. Bernhardt, *Kingship*, 24; Müller-Mertens, 'Ottonians', 247.
55. *DO I*, Nrs. 138–140.
56. Giuseppe Sergi, 'The Kingdom of Italy', *NCMH* 3 (1999), 356.
57. Leyser, *Rule*, 20.
58. Niermeyer, *Lexicon*, s.v. 'honor'.
59. For the idea that Otto was already 'totius italiae possessor', see Bougard, 'Power', 40.
60. Erkens, 'Frau', 258.
61. Adalbert of Magdeburg, *Continuatio*, s.aa., 951, 952; Widukind, *Res*, 3.9; Fleckenstein, *Early Medieval Germany*, 145–46.
62. '952 Otto rex una [sic] cum filio in Italiam, *ac nuptię regales Papię* [my italics]', *Annales Einsiedlenses (Die Annalen des Klosters Einsiedeln Edition und Kommentar)*, ed. C. von Planta, *MGH SSrG* [78] (Hanover: 2007), s.a. 952.
63. Adalbert of Magdeburg, *Continuatio*, s.aa. 951, 952; Widukind, *Res*, 3.9; Flodoard of Reims, *Annales*, s.aa. 951, 952.
64. *DO I*, Nrs. 138, 139.
65. Diana Webb, *Pilgrimage in Medieval England* (London: Hambledon and London, 2000), 77; Joanna Story, *Carolingian Connections: Anglo-Saxon England and Carolingian Francia, c. 750–870* (Aldershot: Ashgate, 2003), 65.
66. Widukind, *Res*, 3.10; Böhmer, *RI* 2.1, 201a.
67. Hrotsvitha, *Gesta*, lines 690–695.
68. Bernhardt, *Kingship*, 57–64; Levi Roach, 'Hosting the King: Hospitality and the Royal *iter* in Tenth-Century England', *JMH* 37, no. 1 (2011), 34–46.
69. Robert Folz, *The Concept of Empire in Western Europe from the Fifth to the Fourteenth Century* (London: Edward Arnold, 1969), 61–74.
70. Paul the Deacon, *Historia*, 3.35; Enright, *Lady*, 25–26; Skinner, *Women*, 55–59; Walter Pohl, 'Gender and Ethnicity', in Brubaker, *Gender in the Early Medieval World*, 38; Valerie L. Garver, *Women and Aristocratic Culture in the Carolingian World* (Ithaca, NY: Cornell University Press, 2009), 195.

71. Charles E. Odegaard, 'The Empress Engelberge', *Speculum* 26, no. 1 (Jan, 1951), 84–86.
72. 'Italiae regnum linquens merito retinendum / Summae reginae', Hrotsvitha, *Gesta*, lines 735–39.
73. 'Scilicet ingenio fuerat praelucida tanto, / Ut posset regnum digne rexisse relictum', ibid., lines 478–79.
74. Leyser, *Rule*, 16; Liudprand, *Antapodosis*, 4.18; *VMP*, ch. 9.
75. Warner, 'Representation', 140; Fleckenstein, *Germany*, 146–49.
76. Ludger Körntgen, 'Starke Frauen: Edgith-Adelheid-Theophanu', in Puhle, *Otto der Große*, vol. I, 122–26.
77. *OLD*, s.v. 'praeficio'.
78. 'rex Otto *prefecit* fratrem suum Heinricum ducem super Baiowariorum gentem [my italics]', *VMP*, ch. 9.
79. 'virum venerabilem Geilonem eidem coenobio abbatem *prefecit* [my italics]', Adalbert of Magdeburg, *Continuatio*, s.a. 957.
80. 'Ottonem regem nobilem / Rome *prefecit* cesarem [my italics]', Odilo, *Epitaphium*, ch. 3; Warner, 'Representation', 140.
81. Nelson, 'Tenth-Century Kingship Comparatively', 302; Warner, 'Representation', 139; La Rocca, *Italy*, 39–40. See also Adelheid's immense influence in Weinfurter, 'Kaiserin Adelheid', 1–19, esp. 9–10.
82. Eckhard Müller-Mertens, *Die Reichsstruktur im Spiegel der Herrschaftspraxis Otto des Großen*, Forschungen zur mittelalterlichen Geschichte 25 (Berlin: 1980), Table 2, 267–68.
83. Warner argues for Ravenna and Fößel for Venice; Warner, 'Representation', 140; Amalie Fößel, *Die Königin im mittelalterlichen Reich. Herrschaftsausübung, Herrschaftsrechte, Handlungsspielräume*, Mittelalter-Forschungen 4 (Stuttgart: Jan Thorbecke, 2000), 283–85.
84. Thietmar, *Chronicon*, 3.1; Odilo, *Epitaphium*, ch. 5.
85. 'vice matris secum', Thietmar, *Chronicon*, 4.15.
86. Rosamond McKitterick, 'Ottonian Intellectual Culture in the Tenth Century', in Davids, *The Empress Theophano*, 188. For the practice continuing into the early modern period, see, for example, Charles Beem, ed., *The Royal Minorities of Medieval and Early Modern England* (New York: Palgrave Macmillan, 2008).
87. Althoff, 'Saxony and the Elbe Slavs', 290.
88. Odilo, *Epitaphium*, chs 1–3, 5; Thietmar, *Chronicon*, 3.1; Lattin, *Letters*, Letter 30, p. 68n4.

89. Gunther Wolf, 'Das Itinerar der Prinzessin Theophano/Kaiserin Theophanu 972–991', in *Kaiserin Theophanu: Prinzessin aus der Fremde—des Westreichs Grosse Kaiserin* (Cologne: Böhlau, 1991), 5; Penelope Nash, 'Adelheid's Travels During the Regencies', (Paper presented at the International Medieval Congress, University of Leeds, 7–10 July 2014).
90. For the diplomata from Frankfurt (Nr. 57) and Allstedt (Nr. 82) as false, see Sean Gilsdorf, *Favor of Friends: Intercession and Aristocratic Politics in Carolingian and Ottonian Europe* (Leiden: Brill, 2014), 179.
91. Böhmer, *RI* 2.3, Nr. 972a; Gerd Althoff, *Otto III*, trans. Phyllis G. Jestice (Pennsylvania: Pennsylvania State University Press, 2003), 50; Gerd Althoff, 'Vormundschaft, Erzieher, Lehrer—Einflusse auf Otto III', in von Euw, *Kaiserin Theophanu*, 281.
92. Odilo, *Epitaphium*, ch. 13.
93. Böhmer, *RI* 2.3, Nr. 1020c.
94. Odilo, *Epitaphium*, ch. 7; Thietmar, *Chronicon*, 4.15.
95. Herwig Wolfram, *Conrad II 990–1039: Emperor of Three Kingdoms*, trans. Denise A. Kaiser (University Park: Pennsylvania State University Press, 2006), 24; Althoff, *Otto III*, 52; Müller-Mertens, 'Ottonians', 257; John M. Jeep, *Medieval Germany: An Encyclopedia* (New York: Garland, 2001), 961; Böhmer, *RI 2.3*, Nr. 1134b.
96. *DO III*, Nr. 95; Gilsdorf, *Favor*, 33.
97. *DO III*, Nrs. 97 and 142.
98. Ibid., Nrs. 77–79 and 110.
99. *AQ*, s.a. 997; *Annales Hildesheimenses*, ed. G. Waitz, *MGH SSrG* [8] (Hanover: 1878, repr. 1947), s.a. 997; Thietmar, *Chronicon*, 4.41–4.42.
100. Odilo, *Epitaphium*, chs 12, 14, 16, 18; Bouchard, 'Burgundy and Provence', 342.
101. Warner, 'Ideals', 15; Leyser, *'Theophanu'*, 1–27.
102. Schiaparelli, *Diplomi di Ugo*, Nrs. 47, 3, 14.
103. Erkens, 'Frau', 247.
104. *DO I*, Nrs. 3, 6, 7, 13, 24, 50, 306.
105. Ibid., Nr. 69; David S. Bachrach, *Warfare in Tenth-Century Germany* (Woodbridge: Boydell Press, 2012), 89.
106. Davies and Fouracre, *Property and Power*, s.v. 'mansus', 281.
107. *DO I*, Nrs. 74, 75, 88, 91, 107, 112, 121, 159.

108. Adelheid's number of interventions as a proportion of the total number of diplomata issued by Otto I during her marriage to him was 31.8 percent. Fößel's count differs because she dates the wedding from February 952: Fößel, *Königin*, 125. See also Rudolf Schetter, 'Die Intervenienz der weltlichen und geistlichen Fürsten in den deutschen Königsurkunden von 911–1056' (PhD diss., Friedrich-Wilhelms-Universität, 1935), 6. Gilsdorf's otherwise valuable analysis does not distinguish between Otto I's two wives nor divide Otto III's regency period into two (before and after Theophanu's death in June 991) and consequently understates Adelheid's contribution in the latter half of Otto III's regency when she acted alone: Sean Gilsdorf, *Favor*, 173–76.
109. Schetter counts sixty-six, Fößel sixty-seven. Reuter in the footnotes to Leyser's paper highlights the discrepancy between the number of interventions in Leyser's text (seventy-six), the number he listed (sixty-seven) and the number of interventions identified by Schetter. Reuter appears to have omitted the joint intervention of Adelheid and Theophanu in June 983, bringing the total to sixty-eight. *DO I*, Nr. 298. Leyser, '*Theophanu*', 21; Schetter, 'Intervenienz', 6; Fößel, *Königin*, 125. See also K. Codea, 'Intervenienten und Petenten vornehmlich für lothringische Empfänger in den Diplomen der liudolfingischen Herrscher (919–1024). Eine prosopographische Darstellung' (PhD diss., Rheinischen Friedrich-Wilhelms-Universität, 2008), 273–77.
110. Leyser, '*Theophanu*', 21n88.
111. Schetter's, Fößel's and Reuter's numbers and percentages are sixty-six, sixty-seven and sixty-eight out of 284, that is, 23.2, 23.6, and 23.9 percent.
112. Kurt-Ulriche Jäschke, Anne Duggan and Janet Nelson, 'From Famous Empresses to Unspectacular Queens: The Romano-German Empire to Margaret of Brabant, Countess of Luxemburg and Queen of the Romans (d. 1311)', in Duggan, *Queens and Queenship in Medieval Europe*, 92; Leyser, 'Ottonians and Wessex', 86–90; Stafford, *Queens, Concubines*, 104.
113. Gilsdorf, *Queenship*, 13–14; Schetter, 'Intervenienz', 6–7; Uhlirz, 'Rechtliche Stellung', 85–97, esp. 90, for Adelheid's donation of all her Italian property at a private court sitting at Erstein.

114. For Adelheid's presence in Burgundy in 988 and 990 see Lattin, *Letters*, Letter 137, Laon, 30 August 988, 167–68, 168n4; Böhmer, *RI 2.3*, Nr. 1020c.
115. Stafford, *Queen Emma*, 265–66.
116. Pauline Stafford, 'Emma: The Powers of the Queen in the Eleventh Century', in Duggan, *Queens and Queenship in Medieval Europe*, 8.
117. Schiaparelli, *Diplomi di Ugo*, Nr. 14.
118. Niermeyer, *Lexicon*, s.v. 'consors'.
119. *DO I*, Nr. 238.
120. Ibid., Nrs. 238, 240, 247, 248, 251, 260, 265, 339, 343, 368, 369, 381, 395, 403, 407, 412, 429; Thilo Vogelsang, *Die Frau als Herrscherin im hohen Mittelalter: Studien zur 'consors regni' Formel* (Göttingen, Frankfurt, Berlin: 1954), 22.
121. The relevant diplomata for each term are: *DO* I, Nrs. 238; Nrs. 251, 260, 403; Nr. 240; Nrs. 247, 368, 369, 395; Nrs. 248, 265, 343, 381, 412, 429; Nr. 339; Nr. 407. Erkens, 'Frau', 248.
122. *DO* I, Nr. 429.
123. *DO* II, Nrs. 42, 53, 57, 82, 131, 299, 306, 307.
124. Wolf, 'Das Itinerar', 6–12.
125. *DO* II, Nrs. 76; John William Bernhardt, 'Concepts and Practice of Empire in Ottonian Germany (950–1024)', in Weiler, *Representations of Power*, 149–50.
126. Stafford, *Queen Emma*, 59.
127. Leyser, '*Theophanu*', 21–22; Josef Fleckenstein, 'Hofkapelle und Kanzlei unter der Kaiserin Theophanu', in von Euw, *Kaiserin Theophanu*, vol. 2, 307. The term 'imperatrix augusta' appeared fifteen times for Theophanu between 974 and 983: Gunther Wolf, 'Wer war Theophanu?', in von Euw, *Kaiserin Theophanu*, vol. 2, 389n65.
128. *DO* III, Theophanu, Nrs. 1, 2,. See also Böhmer, *RI 2.3* 1017, 1019k; Leyser, '*Theophanu*', 26–7; Stafford, 'Emma: Powers', 9n28; Fleckenstein, 'Hofkapelle und Kanzlei', 309–10.
129. *DO* II, Nr. 6; J. F. Böhmer, *RI 2.2*, Nr. 580; Leyser, *Rule*, 68.
130. Olson, *Early Middle Ages*, 220; Lynette Olson, 'Women and Gender in Europe at the End of the *First* Millennium', (unpublished paper: University of Sydney, Australia, 2000), 4; Niermeyer, *Lexicon*, s.vv. 'defensio', ' mundiburdis', 'mundiburdus'.
131. Bernhardt, *Kingship*, 217.

132. For *imperatrix* and variations, see *AQ*, s.aa. 996, 999; *AW*, s.a. 1000; Lampert, *Annales*, s.a. 999; Odilo, *Epitaphium*, ch. 1; Thietmar, *Chronicon*, 2.44, 4.1, 4.15, 4.18, 4.43. For Adelheid as 'imperatrix augusta' see *AQ*, s.aa., 964, 991, 999, 1000.
133. *AQ*, s.a. 999.
134. Du Cange, s.v. 'inclitus'.
135. *AQ*, s.a. 999; Thietmar, *Chronicon*, 2.15; 4.15; Hrotsvitha, *Gesta*, line 525.
136. *OLD*, s.v. 'pius'.
137. Thietmar, *Chronicon*, 3.1; Hrotsvitha, *Gesta*, line 546.
138. Hrotsvitha, *Gesta*, lines 590, 592.
139. Ibid., line 605.
140. Janet Nelson, 'Queens as Jezebels: The Careers of Brunhild and Balthild in Merovingian History', in *Debating the Middle Ages: Issues and Readings*, ed. Lester K. Little and Barbara H. Rosenwein (Malden, MA: Blackwell, 1998), 219–53; Janet Nelson, 'Medieval Queenship', in *Women in Medieval Western European Culture*, ed. Linda Elizabeth Mitchell (New York: Garland, 1999), 179–207.
141. The first people to anoint were the Visigoths, and the Franks employed the ritual in the mid-eighth century: Olson, *Early Middle Ages*, 70; Janet Nelson, 'Symbols in Context: Rulers' Inauguration Rituals in Byzantium and the West in the Early Middle Ages', in *Politics and Ritual in Early Medieval Europe* (London: Hambledon Press, 1986), 270–75.
142. *Annales Bertiniani*, ed. G. Waitz, *MGH SSrG* [5] (Hanover: 1883), s.a. 856; *Coronatio Iudithae Karoli II Filiae*, ed. A. Boretius, *MGH Capitularia regum Francorum, Legum sectio* 2.II:425–427 (Hanover: 1883, 1893, repr. 1960), 426.
143. Thietmar, *Chronicon*, 2.1; *Annalista Saxo*, s.a. 936; Leyser, 'Ottonians and Wessex', 87.
144. Cyrille Vogel et al., *Medieval Liturgy: An Introduction to the Sources* (Washington, DC: Pastoral Press, 1986), 2, 235. *Contra* Vogel, see Simon MacLean, *History and Politics in Late Carolingian and Ottonian Europe: The Chronicle of Regino of Prüm and Adalbert of Magdeburg* (Manchester: Manchester University Press, 2009), 252n112.
145. Böhmer, *RI* 2.1, Nrs. 201a, 309c; *VMP*, ch. 21; *VMA*, ch. 11; Fleckenstein, *Germany*, 147.

146. Jonathan Shepard, 'Marriages towards the Millennium', in *Byzantium in the Year 1000*, ed. Paul Magdalino (Brill, 2003), 17; Janet Nelson, 'Early Medieval Rites of Queen-Making and the Shaping of Medieval Queenship', in Duggan, *Queens and Queenship in Medieval Europe*, 301–15, esp. 313–15; Nikolaus Gussone, 'Trauung und Krönung. Zur Hochzeit der byzantinischen Prinzessin Theophanu mit Kaiser Otto II', in von Euw, *Kaiserin Theophanu*, vol. 2, 167–68, 170–72. For the splendid jewelry that Adelheid may have worn at her coronations, see Wolfram, *Conrad II*, 156–57.

147. Everett, *Literacy*, 196, 288.

148. Julie Ann Smith, 'The Earliest Queen-Making Rites', *Church History* 66, no. 1 (March, 1997), 18–19, 32–33.

149. Ernst Hartwig Kantorowicz, *Laudes regiae: A Study in Liturgical Acclamations and Mediaeval Rules Worship* (Berkeley and Los Angeles: University of California Press, 1946), 28, 48–49, 69–70, 72, 75, 85, 95.

150. Gussone, 'Trauung', 162. See Chap. 3 above, which details the history of Adelheid's lands.

151. Ottonianum, 962 (Rome: Archivio Segreto Vaticano); Marriage Charter of Theophanu, 972 (Wolfenbüttel, Niedersächsisches Staatsarchiv), 6, fol. 11.

152. Wolfgang Georgi, 'Ottonianum und Heiratsurkunde 962/972', in von Euw, *Kaiserin Theophanu*, vol. 2, 135–60; Jacqueline Lafontaine-Dosogne, 'The Art of Byzantium and its Relation to Germany in the Time of the Empress Theophano', in Davids, *The Empress Theophano*, 211–12; Gussone, 'Trauung', 162; Fleckenstein, *Germany*, 148–49.

153. 'in copulam legitimi matrimonii consortiumque imperii', *DO II*, Nr. 21, trans. Boyd H. Hill, *Medieval Monarchy in Action: The German Empire from Henry I to Henry IV* (London: Allen & Unwin, 1972), 164.

154. For the dating of the image to 972 see Fößel, *Königin*, Abb. 1, between 176 and 177 and Patrick Corbet, 'Les impératrices ottoniennes et le modèle marial. Autour de l'ivoire du château Sforza de Milan', in *Marie: Le culte de la Vierge dans la société médiévale*, ed. D. Iogna-Prat et al. (Paris: Beauchesne, 1996), 116.

155. Corbet, 'Impératrices', 115–17.

156. The identification of these images has been the subject of debate. See especially Grzegorz Pac, 'Crowned Mary, Crowning Mary. Queen of Heavens and Queenship Ideology in Art from 10th and 11th c. England and Empire' (Paper presented at the International Medieval Congress, University of Leeds, July 2013); Adriano Peroni, 'La plastica in stucco nel S. Ambrogio di Milano: arte ottoniana e romanica in Lombardia', in *Kolloquium über spätantike und frühmittelalterliche Skulptur*, ed. V. Milojcic (Mainz, 1972), 59–119, esp. 88–94, and Tables 43 and 44; C. Nordenfalk, 'Milano e l'arte ottoniana: problemi di fondo sinora poco osservati', in *Il millennio ambrosiano. La città del vescovo dai carolingi al Barbarossa*, ed. C. Bertelli (Milano: Electa, 1988), 102–3.

157. Initial Page of the Matthew Evangelistary, Adelheid, Theophanu, Otto III and Lamb of God, Gospel of St. Gereon, 990-1000 (Cologne: Historisches Archiv der Stadt, Cod. W 312), fol. 22r; Rainer Kahsnitz, 'Ein Bildnis der Theophanu? Zur Tradition der Münz- und Medaillon- Bildnisse in der karolingischen und ottonischen Buchmalerei', in von Euw, *Kaiserin Theophanu*, vol. 2, 132, 134.

158. Alan M. Stahl, 'Coinage in the Name of Medieval Women', in *Medieval Women and the Sources of Medieval History*, ed. Joel Thomas Rosenthal (Athens, GA: University of Georgia Press, 1990), 321–23.

159. See Erika Uitz, Barbara Pätzold, and Gerald Beyreuther, eds, *Herrscherinnen und Nonnen: Frauengestalten von der Ottonenzeit bis zu den Staufern* (Berlin: Wissenschaften, 1990), fig. 28, between 192 and 193. For other examples see Hermann Dannenberg, *Die deutschen Münzen der sächsischen und fränkischen Kaiserzeit*, 4 vols (Berlin: Weidmann, 1876–1905), 1:450, 2:701–17, 3:830–58, 4:958–66, as referenced in Stahl, 'Coinage', 331.

160. Percy Ernst Schramm, and Florentine Mütherich, *Die deutschen Kaiser und Könige in Bildern ihrer Zeit 751–1190* (Munich: 1983), 333, 340, 341, 347, 348, 349, 352.

161. Genevra Kornbluth, 'Richildis and her Seal. Carolingian Self-Reference and the Imagery of Power', in *Saints, Sinners, and Sisters: Gender and Northern Art in Medieval and Early Modern Europe*, ed. Alison G. Stewart and Jane Louise Carroll (Aldershot: Ashgate, 2003), 161–79; Brigitte Bedos-Rezak, 'Women, Seals,

and Power in Medieval France, 1150–1350', in *Form and Order in Medieval France* (Aldershot, Hampshire: Variorum, 1993), IX.63.
162. 'habebat / Cor nimium mestum, videt erga se quia tempus / Mutatum; libras per milia quatturo istam / Nollet habere viam calcatam, scire nec ipsam. / Perditio signi defectum signat, abhinc quin / Nomen ei crescit quod dicitur "Officiperdi"', Donizo, *VM*, 2.7, lines 714–19, trans. Hay, *Military Leadership*, 140.
163. Donizo, *VM*, 2.7, lines 680–719.
164. For the origin and uses of *officiperdi*, see W. Martin Bloomer, *The School of Rome: Latin Studies and the Origins of Liberal Education* (Berkeley: University of California Press, 2011), example 4.42, p. 141 and pp. 139–41; Hay, *Military Leadership*, 156n145; Odo of Cluny, *Collationum libri tres*, PL 133:517–638, col. 612D; Peter of Blois, *Epistolae*, PL 207:1–560, Epistles 25, col. 0089; 102, col. 0319A, 109, col. 0490C; Auctor incertus (Isidorus Hispalensis?), *Appendix XXIV. 443 Liber glossarum. Ex variis Glossariis quae sub Isidori nomine circumferuntur collectus*, PL 83:1331–1378, col. 1363, 1159, s.v. 'officiperdi'.
165. Valerie Eads, 'The Last Italian Expedition of Henry IV: Re-reading the *Vita Mathildis* of Donizone of Canossa', *JoMMH* 8, no. 2 (2010) 66–67, 43–45, 52.
166. Warner, 'Representation', 121–23.
167. For *comes*, see *DD MT*, Nr. 4; Robert Helmerichs, '*Princeps, Comes, Dux Normannorum*: Early Rollonid Designators and their Significance', *HSJ* 9 (1997), 55–77.
168. Roland Herbert Bainton, *Christian Attitudes toward War and Peace: A Historical Survey and Critical Re-evaluation* (London: Hodder and Stoughton, 1961), 108–9.
169. Scott Ashley, 'The Lay Intellectual in Anglo-Saxon England', in *Lay Intellectuals in the Carolingian World*, ed. Patrick Wormald and Janet Nelson (Cambridge: Cambridge University Press, 2007), 235. For a history of the connection between military service and land ownership, see Bernard S. Bachrach, 'Military Lands in Historical Perspective', *HSJ* 9 (1997), 95–122. For the collapse of Carolingian ways in France: Georges Duby, *The Early Growth of the European Economy: Warriors and Peasants from the Seventh to the Twelfth Century* (London: Weidenfeld & Nicolson, 1974), 162–63; and *contra* Duby, Dominique Barthélemy, *La*

Société dans le comté de Vendôme de l'an mil au XIVe siècle (Paris: Fayard, 1993); Dominique Barthélemy, *The Serf, the Knight, and the Historian* (Ithaca: Cornell University Press, 2009).
170. Reynolds, *Fiefs*, 403–15; Wickham, *Inheritance*, 451–52.
171. Chris Wickham, *Sleepwalking into a New World: The Emergence of Italian City Communes in the Twelfth Century*, The Lawrence Stone Lectures (Princeton, NJ: Princeton University Press, 2015); Warren Brown, *Unjust Seizure: Conflict, Interest and Authority in an Early Medieval Society* (Ithaca, NY: Cornell University Press, 2001), 10–11.
172. For an overview of Otto I's rule in Italy, see Warner, 'Representation', 123, with his footnotes following: Helmut Beumann, *Die Ottonen*, 2nd ed. (Stuttgart: W. Kohlhammer, 1991), 68–71, 83–4, 88–98, 100–4, 108–10; Ovidio Capitani, *Storia dell'Italia medievale*, 3rd ed. (Rome: Laterza, 1992), 160–78; Rudolf Schieffer, 'Das 'Italienerlebnis' Ottos des Großen', in Puhle, *Otto der Große, Magdeburg und Europa*, vol. I, 446–60; Johannes Laudage, *Otto der Grosse (912–973): Eine Biographie* (Regensburg: Friedrich Pustet, 2001), 158–207.
173. For example, Paul the Deacon, Agnellus, Andreas of Bergamo, the Continuator of Paul the Deacon (880s), Liudprand of Cremona, the anonymous author of the *Chronicon Novaliciense*, Landulf Senior and the anonymous authors of the law codes and commentaries: Chris Wickham, 'Lawyers' Time: History and Memory in Tenth- and Eleventh-Century Italy', in *Land and Power: Studies in Italian and European Social History, 400–1200*, ed. C. Wickham (London: British School at Rome, 1994), 278–84.
174. Ibid., 276.
175. Wickham, 'Land Disputes', 237.
176. Everett, *Literacy*, 195.
177. Richard FitzNigel (or Fitzneale), *Dialogus de Scaccario (The Course of the Exchequer)*, trans. C. Johnson, F. E. L. Carter and D. E. Greenway (Oxford: Oxford University Press, 1983), 2.7.
178. Wickham, 'Lawyers' Time', 276.
179. Ibid., 276.
180. Tabacco, 'Northern and Central Italy', 80, 84–86.
181. Bisson, *Crisis*, 122–25.
182. Wickham, 'Lawyers' Time', 278–85.

183. Wipo, *Gesta Chuonradi II. imperatoris*, ed. Werner Trillmich and Rudolf Buchner, 2nd ed., *AQDG* 11:507–613 (Darmstadt: Wissenschaftliche Buchgesellschaft, 1968), 7, 12; Wolfram, *Conrad II*, 43; C. Ehlers, 'Having the King—Losing the King', *Viator* 33 (2002), 9.
184. Wickham, 'Lawyers' Time', 275–76.
185. Wickham, *Mountains*, xxxi; Wickham, *Early Medieval Italy*, 185.
186. For the strategic and tactical characteristics of the Angevin fortifications, the accumulation of *castra* as the basis of the rise of the family Angevin and as a demonstration of power see Bernard S. Bachrach, 'The Angevin Strategy of Castle Building in the Reign of Fulk Nerra, 987–1040', *AHA* 88, no. 3 (1983) 533–60; Bernard S. Bachrach, 'Fulk Nerra and his Accession as Count of Anjou', in *State-Building in Medieval France: Studies in Early Angevin History*, ed. Bernard S. Bachrach (Aldershot: Variorum, 1994), VI.331–342; Bernard S. Bachrach, *Fulk Nerra, the Neo-Roman Consul, 987–1040: A Political Biography of the Angevin Count* (Berkeley: University of California Press, 1993). For the relationship of ownership of castles to lordship, especially in the tenth and eleventh centuries, see R. W. Southern, *The Making of the Middle Ages* (London: Cresset Library, 1987), 79–90.
187. Donizo, *VM*, 2.4–2.5, lines 489–549; Wickham, *Mountains*, xvii, xxxi, 110.
188. For the linkage of castle building to military and political ends and the correspondence between southern Tuscany and the Po valley in their focus on *castra* as centers of lordship see Valerie Ramseyer, 'Territorial Lordships in the Principality of Salerno, 1050–1150', *HSJ* 9 (1997) 81. For a detailed analysis of the similarity between northern Tuscany and the Po valley, two places where Matilda operated, see Chris Wickham, 'La signoria rurale in toscana', in *Strutture e trasformazioni della signoria rurale nei secoli X–XIII*, ed. Gerhard Dilcher and Cinzio Violente (Bologna: 1996), 343–409.
189. Wickham, *Mountains*, xxxi.
190. Ibid., 31–2, 41, 43–5, 47, 50–1, 55–7, 61, and also from the author's personal observations.
191. Leyser, 'Ottonian Government', 747.
192. Froumond, *Die Tegernseer Briefsammlung*, ed. K. Strecker, *MGH Epp. sel.* 3:1–96 (Berlin: Weidmann, 1925, repr. 1964), Letter 16,

trans. Joan Ferrante, 'Letter from Adelaide of Burgundy, Ottonian empress (995) to abbot Gozpert', in *MWLL*, http://epistolae.ccnmtl.columbia.edu/letter/53.html, date accessed 15 May 2016; *DO II*, Nr. 192; Wolfram, *Conrad II*, 127, 299–300.
193. 'veredorum ... cursoriam (sic navigio nomen)', Sidonius Apollinaris, *Poems and Letters*, ed. W. B. Anderson, 2 vols, The Loeb Classical Library (London: W. Heinemann, 1936, repr. 1965), vol. 1, Introduction, xl; Letters, 5.2, 5.3.
194. L. Duchesne, *Le Liber pontificalis*, 2nd ed., 3 vols (Paris: E. de Boccard, 1955), vol. 1, 94, Stephanus II (752–757), 22–24.
195. Otto of Freising, *Gesta Frederici*, 2.39.
196. Leyser, 'Ottonian Government', 746–47.
197. Valerie Eads, 'Means, Motive, Opportunity: Medieval Women and the Recourse to Arms', *Paper Presented at The Twentieth Barnard Medieval & Renaissance Conference 'War and Peace in the Middle Ages & Renaissance'* (2 December 2006), http://www.deremilitari.org/wp-content/uploads/2012/09/Eads-MeansMotivesOpp.pdf, date accessed 20 August 2016; Goez, *Beatrix*, 158–59; *Bea. Reg.*, 15a, p. 206.
198. Robinson, *Henry IV*, 287.
199. Bernold, *Chronicon*, s.a. 1093.
200. *DH IV*, Nrs. 442–52; Bernold, *Chronicon*, s.a. 1093–95; Robinson, *Henry IV*, 287, 289, 293–95; Hay, *Military Leadership*, 146; Eads, 'Last Expedition', 67; Tabacco, 'Northern and Central Italy', 87.
201. Donizo, *VM*, 2.3, line 335; Du Cange, s.v. 'strata'.
202. Eads, 'Last Expedition', 41–42.
203. 'Rex terras ultra tenuitque Padum fere cunctas, / Plathena, Nogara nisi, quae sunt oppida clara', Donizo, *VM*, 2.6, lines 554–55.
204. Ibid., 2.6, line 575; Eads, 'Last Expedition', 33–35, 66.
205. Donizo, *VM*, 2.7, lines 724–28, trans. Hay, *Military Leadership*, 140.
206. *Act. Pont. Cenom*, 33, pp. 376–81; Olson, *Early Middle Ages*, 186–88.
207. *DD MT*, 1; Pierre Chaplais, 'XV The Authenticity of the Royal Anglo-Saxon Diplomas of Exeter', in *Essays in Medieval Diplomacy and Administration*, ed. P. Chaplais (London: Hambledon Press, 1981), XV.1–XV.3.

208. For the seventeen whose locations of issue have been identified, see *DD MT*, Dep. Nrs. 5, 7, 8, 31, 37, 50, 56, 59, 67, 71, 72, 79, 80, 83, 84, 86, 89. For those which are false or doubtful see ibid., Dep. Nrs. 1–3, 5–7, 12, 14, 15, 22–25, 36, 38, 40–47, 50, 55, 59, 60, 62, 67–69, 74, 80–82, 84–88, 93, 94, 98, 99, 101, 103–106, 109, 110, 113, 115.
209. Ibid., Nrs. 141, 143–53. For Italian charters and their proper notarization, see Wickham, 'Land Disputes', 229–56.
210. *DD MT*, Nrs. 140, 142.
211. Ibid., Nrs. 140, 141.
212. Ibid., Nrs. 141, 142, 143, 144, 146, 147, 148, 149, 150, 151, 152 and 153 were issued from the following locations: Casadei, Mantua, Notale, Guastalla, Pratovecchio, San Cesario, Pegognaga, San Cesario, Pontremoli, Bondeno, Canneto sull'Oglio, Bondeno.
213. Ibid., Nrs. 19, 41, 48, 68; Golinelli, 'Review of *Die Urkunden und Briefe*', 87–88.
214. *DH IV*, Nrs. 373, 379, 385.
215. *DD MT*, 1; Zanarini, 'I Canossa', 47–65; see also the two maps in Groß, *Lothar III.* and the backpocket. Gianluca Bottazzi, 'Viabilità medievale nella collina e montagna parmense tra i torrenti Parma ed Enza', in *SM IV*, 202–5; Sonia Moroni, 'Il Medioevo nel territorio di Traversetolo e la presenza della famiglia Baratti', in *SM IV*, 136–37.
216. Ghirardini, *Storia critica*, 21–52. For Matilda's jurisdictional activity, especially concerning Tuscany, see Margherita Giuliana Bertolini, 'I Canossiani e la loro attività giurisdizionale con particolare riguardo alla Toscana', in Capitani, *Margherita Giuliana Bertolini*, 41–84.
217. The extant diplomata issued from Mantua number 7; from Piadena, 5; from Bondeno, 8; from Panzano, 5; from San Cesario, 6; from Lucca, 4; from Florence, 4; and from Poggibonsi, 6.
218. D. Castaldini, M. Marchetti, and A. Cardarelli, 'Some Notes on Geomorphological and Archaeological Aspects in the Central Po Plain', in *Ol' Man River: Geo-Archaeological Aspects of Rivers and River Plains*, ed. M. De Dapper et al. (Ghent: Academia Press, 2009), 208; Gianfranco Gasperi, and Maurizio Pellegrini, 'Strutture geologiche è idrografia della bassa Pianura Modenes', in *Mirandola e le terre del basso corso del Secchia dal Medioevo all'età contemporanea*, ed. Giordano Bertuzzi (Modena: 1984), 107–10.

219. *DD MT*, Nr. 1.
220. Ibid., Nrs. 9, 10.
221. Ibid., Nr. 7.
222. Ibid., Nr. 18.
223. Ibid., Nrs. 1–6, 8–11, 14.
224. Ibid., Nrs. 34–38. Nrs 34–36 were issued from Zola Predosa, Carpineta and Mantua.
225. Ibid., Nrs. 37, 38.
226. Ibid., Nrs. 39–43.
227. Ibid., Nrs. 44–47.
228. Ibid., Nrs. 34–47.
229. Bisson, *Crisis*, 123.
230. The five diplomata not able to be associated with any locations are Nrs. 62, 63, 68, 84 and 117.
231. *DD MT*, Nr. 65.
232. Ibid., Nr. 121.
233. Ibid., Nr. 93; Bisson, *Crisis*, 125.
234. Bernard S. Bachrach, 'On Roman Ramparts 300–1300', in *The Cambridge Illustrated History of Warfare: The Triumph of the West*, ed. Geoffrey Parker (Cambridge: Cambridge University Press, 2008), 83, 85; David S. Bachrach, 'The Military Organization of Ottonian Germany, c. 900–1018: The Views of Bishop Thietmar of Merseburg', *JMH* 72, no. 4 (2008) 1061–88; Karl Leyser, 'The Battle at the Lech, 955. A Study in Tenth-Century Warfare', *History* 50, no. 168 (1965) 1–25.
235. Froumond, *Tegernseer Briefsammlung*, Letter 16, trans. Ferrante, 'Letter from Adelaide (995) to Gozpert'.
236. For the original concession, see *DO III*, Nr. 198; for its withdrawal, see Nr. 222.
237. Niermeyer, *Lexicon*, s.v. 'capitaneus'.
238. Tabacco, *Struggle*, 327–29.
239. *DD MT*, Nr. 48; Golinelli, 'Review of *Die Urkunden und Briefe*', 88. For *commune*, see O. Banti, '"Civitas" e "commune" nelle fonti italiane dei secoli xi e xii', *Critica storica* 9 (1972), 572–74.
240. Dameron, *Episcopal Power*, 67.
241. Richer, *Histories*, vol. 2, 3.68; Wolf, 'Itinerar', 9.
242. Thietmar, *Chronicon*, 3.20, 3.21, Leyser, *Rule*, p. 58; Althoff, *Otto III*, 29, 92.
243. Lattin, *Letters*, 68n4.

244. Gerbert, *Epistolae*, Letters 39, 17, 20, 22, 26, 27, 33, trans. Lattin, *Letters*, 24, 25, 28, 30, 34, 35, 41.
245. Widukind, *Res*, 1.35; 2.14; 2.20–21; 3.42; 3.44–3.45; 3.53–3.55; 3.67–3.68; 3.75; Adalbert of Magdeburg, *Continuatio*,. s.a. 955; s.a. 958; s.a. 963; s.a. 965; Liudprand, *Relatio*, 2.28.
246. 'subduntur regi', Thietmar, *Chronicon*, 4.18, and 4.9; *AQ*, s.a. 987.
247. Thietmar, *Chronicon*, 4.16.
248. Fried, 'Theophanu und die Slawen', 367–69.
249. Leyser, *Rule*, 49–51; Althoff, *Otto III*, 40–51; Fleckenstein, *Germany*, 165–66.
250. Eads, 'Means', 9.
251. Bernold, *Chronicon*, s.aa. 1084, 1085.
252. Donizo, *VM*, 2.6, line 596.
253. Bernold, *Chronicon*, s.a.1089, 477–78.
254. Matilda was frequently addressed as 'domina', 'comitissa' and 'ducatrix': see *DD MT*, Nrs. 16, 17, 21, 22, 25, 30, 55, 60, 95, 98, 102, 113.
255. Rosalind Jaeger Reynolds, 'Reading Matilda: The Self-Fashioning of a Duchess', *Essays in Medieval Studies* 19 (2002), 1–7; Stafford, 'Emma: Powers', 9–10.
256. Bernold, *Chronicon*, s.a. 1084. See the use of 'militibus' and 'viriliter' in the contemporary Bayeux Tapestry, where William exhorts his men to prepare themselves with manliness: 'Hic Willelm dux alloquitur suis militibus ut prepararentse viriliter', David M. Wilson, *The Bayeux Tapestry: The Complete Tapestry in Colour* (London: Thames and Hudson, 1985), 57–58.
257. Wickham, *Inheritance*, 519–22.
258. R. I. Moore, *The First European Revolution, c. 970–1215* (Oxford: Blackwell, 2000), 97.
259. Tony Hunt, 'The Emergence of the Knight in France and England 1000–1200', *Forum for Modern Language Studies* 17, no. 2 (1981), 95; Timothy Reuter, '*Filii matris nostrae pugnant adversum nos*: Bonds and Tensions between German Prelates and their *milites* in the High Middle Ages', in *Chiesa e mondo feudale nei secoli X–XII: atti della dodicesima Settimana internazionale di studio, Mendola, 24–28 agosto 1992* (Milan: Vita e pensiero, 1995), 247–76; Paolo Golinelli, *Matilde e i Canossa*, 2nd ed. (Milan: Mursia, 2004), 30.

260. Bernold, *Chronicon*, s.a. 1084.
261. John of Mantua, *Iohannis Mantuani in Cantica canticorum*, 2.15.
262. 'Mathildam, prudentissimam ducem et fidelissimam sancti Petri *militem* [my italics]', Bernold, *Chronicon*, s.a. 1085.
263. 'In Longobardia *prudentissimi milites sancti Petri*, Welfo dux et *uxor eius Mathilda*, iam triennio contra scismaticos *viriliter dimicantes*, tandem multum contra ipsos, Deo opitulante, confortati sunt [my italics]', ibid., s.a. 1093.
264. Bernold, *Chronicon*, s.aa. 1089; 1092.
265. 'Domna Mathildis egregia dux et marchionissa, devotissima sancti Petri filia, magnum sibi nomen ubique eo tempore acquisivit', ibid., s.a. 1097.
266. 'Forte enim his diebus prefatus dux venerat Italiam, ducens secum excellentissimam cometissam Matildam, incliti ducis Bonifacii filiam. Is congregans universam exercitus sui multitudinem, cum uxore et nobilissima Matilda Romam veniens, Normannos a Campania absque bello expulit et eam Romanę reddidit dicioni. Et hoc primum servicium excellentissima Bonifacii filia beato apostolorum principi obtulit; que non multo post *per multa et Deo amabilia servicia beati Petri meruit dici filia* [my italics]', Bonizo of Sutri, *Liber ad amicum*, 6.599, trans. I. S. Robinson, *Book to a Friend*, 6, pp. 215–16. The duke to whom Bonizo referred was more likely to be Matilda's stepfather, Godfrey the Bearded, rather than her husband, Godfrey the Hunchback, since she did not marry him until 1069.
267. Robinson, *Papal Reform*, 49n296; 216n141; Megan McLaughlin, *Sex, Gender, and Episcopal Authority in an Age of Reform, 1000–1122* (Cambridge: Cambridge University Press, 2010), 204.
268. Moore, *First Revolution*, 97.
269. For a general discussion about Matilda and her role as commander, see Hay, *Military Leadership*, 4–16.
270. 'parata pro defensione iusticiae non solum terrena omnia distribuere, sed *usque ad sanguinem* pro vestra confusione et reverentia ad sanctae ecclesiae gloriam et exaltationem certare, donec tradat Dominus inimicum suum in manu feminae [my italics]', Anselm of Lucca, *Liber contra Wibertum*, I:527, trans. Robinson, *Papal Reform*, 47; Eads, 'Means', 12.

271. 'Due armature di lei di forma assai differente da quelle, che portano gl'huomini', Lodovico Vedriani, *Historia del'antichissima città di Modena*, 2 vols (Modena: 1666, 1667), 2.11, pp. 19–20.
272. In the Bayeux Tapestry Bishop Odo appears to be attired in protective clothing, unlike the fighting men who are wearing chainmail: Wilson, *Bayeux*, 67.
273. 'Post paucos vero dies, postquam hęc gesta sunt, eius filius *cum exercitu excellentissimę M[atildę] pugnavit*
    et victoriam obtinuit [my italics]', Bonizo of Sutri, *Liber ad amicum*, 9, p. 613, trans. adapted from Robinson, *To a Friend*, p. 248.
274. *OLD*, s.v. 'virago'.
275. Kimberley A. LoPrete, 'Gendering Viragos: Medieval Perceptions of Powerful Women', in *Studies on Medieval and Early Modern Women 4: Victims or Viragos?*, ed. Christine Meek and Catherine Lawless (Dublin: Four Courts Press, 2005), 21.
276. Henry of Huntingdon, *The Chronicle of Henry of Huntingdon*, trans. Thomas Forester (London: 1853), 168n3; the Mercian Chronicle in *The Anglo-Saxon Chronicle: A Collaborative Edition*, ed. Simon Keynes et al. (Cambridge: D.S. Brewer, 1983); Pauline Stafford, '"The Annals of Æthelflæd": Annals, History and Politics in Early Tenth-Century England', in *Myth, Rulership, Church and Charters: Essays in Honour of Nicholas Brooks*, ed. Julia Barrow and Andrew Wareham (Aldershot: Ashgate, 2008), 101–16.
277. *Vita Liutbirgae virginis (Das Leben der Liutbirg)*, ed. Ottokar Menzel, *Deutsches Mittelalter: Kritische Studientexte des Reichsinstitut für ältere deutsche Geschichtskunde (MGH)* 3 (Leipzig: Karl W. Hiersemann, 1937), chs 4, 5, p. 13; J. M. Catling, *A History of Women's Writing in Germany, Austria and Switzerland* (Cambridge: Cambridge University Press, 1999).
278. *Vitae S. Heinrici additamentum*, ed. G. H. Pertz, *MGH SS* 4:816–820 (1841), 820.
279. 'semper laudanda virago'. Garin's letter is included in Pertz's edition: Odilo of Cluny, *Epitaphium Adalheidae imperatricis*, ed. G. H. Pertz, *MGH SS* 4:633–45 (1841), 635, line 33.
280. R. E. Latham, *Revised Medieval Latin Word-List from British and Irish Sources* (London: Oxford University Press, 1965), s.v. 'virago', *OED Online*. s.v. 'virago'.

281. John of Mantua, *Cantica*, 1.5, 1.16; Ernst-Dieter Hehl, 'War, Peace and the Christian Order', *NCMH* 4, Part I (2004), 204.
282. John of Mantua, *Cantica*, 1.16.
283. 'At vero Mathildis comitissa, Romanae aecclesiae filia, *virilis animi* constantiam tenens, tanto ei fortius resistebat, quanto magis huius astutias et papae innocentiam noverat. Sola enim tunc temporis inventa est inter feminas, quae regis potentiam aspernata sit, quae calliditatibus eius et potentiae etiam bellico certamine obviaverit, *ut merito nominetur virago, quae virtute animi etiam viros praeibat* [my translation and my italics]', Hugh of Flavigny, *Chronicon Hugonis*, 2.462, s.a. 1084; Healy, '*Merito nominetur virago*', 55.
284. [my translation and my italics] Bernold, *Chronicon*, s.a. 1097.
285. 'ut quasi altera Delbora ... militiam peragat', Pseudo-Bardo, *Vita Anselmi*, ch. 11, p. 16.
286. Leyser, 'Ottonian Government', 725–32.
287. *DD MT*, pp. 18, 21; Ferrara, 'Gli anni di Matilde', 89–98.
288. Wickham, *Mountains*, xxx–xxxi; Wickham, *Inheritance*, 513.
289. 'Et ego Petrus notarius ex iussione do(mi)ne Mattilde dei gratia ducis et marchionisse et iudicum amonitione scripsi', *DD MT*, Nr. 56.
290. W. Scott Jessee, *Robert the Burgundian and the Counts of Anjou, ca. 1025–1098* (Washington: Catholic University of America Press, 2000), 1–2; Bisson, *Crisis*, 49–50.
291. LoPrete, 'Viragos', 37; Gilsdorf, *Queenship*, 66.
292. *AQ*, s.a. 999.
293. Hrotsvitha, *Gesta*, line 525.
294. Thietmar, *Chronicon*, 2.15.
295. Bonizo of Sutri, *Liber ad amicum*, 6.
296. Donizo, *VM*, 2.19, line 1272.
297. *DD MT*, Nr. 102.
298. Gerd Althoff, Johannes Fried, and Patrick J. Geary, *Medieval Concepts of the Past: Ritual, Memory, Historiography* (Washington, DC: Cambridge University Press, 2002), 29.
299. Gregory VII, *Registrum*, Letter 6.22.
300. *PL*, 151, c.527–28, Letter 267, trans. in Urban II, 'Letter sent by Urban II, pope', *Epistolae: Medieval Women Latin Letters.* (*PL* 151:527–28, ep.267), in *MWLL*, http://epistolae.ccnmtl.columbia.edu/letter/233.html, date accessed 12 August 2016.

301. 'Mandamus ... dilectioni tuae'. The text is now only available in the Decretals of Gregory IX of 1234: *PL*, 163, c.366, Letter. 408, trans. in Paschal II, 'Letter sent by Pascal II, pope', *Epistolae: Medieval Women Latin Letters*. (*PL* 163 c.366, ep.408), in *MWLL*, http://epistolae.ccnmtl.columbia.edu/letter/234.html, date accessed 16 May 2016.
302. *DD MT*, Nrs. 1–4, 32; 36, 38, 39; 40, 41; and 43.
303. 'Beatrix, *filia* quondam Federici, atque Matilda, *filia* quondam Bonifacii, *mater et filia, comitisse ac ducatrices*, que *professe sumus lege vivere Salica* [my italics]', ibid., Nr. 1.
304. Ibid., Nr. 7.
305. Donizo, *VM*, 1.10, lines 801–9.
306. János M. Bak, 'Medieval Symbology of the State: Percy E. Schramm's Contribution', in *Studying Medieval Rulers and Their Subjects: Central Europe and Beyond*, ed. B. Nagy and G. Klaniczay (Farnham: Ashgate Variorum, 2010), I.33–I.63.
307. Thietmar, *Chronicon*, 4.47.
308. Chris Wickham, "Pastorialism and Underdevelopment in the Early Middle Ages", in *Land and Power: Studies in Italian and European Social History, 400–1200*, ed. C. Wickham (London: British School at Rome, 1994), 139. For the Eastern emperor's diet, see Liudprand, *Relatio*, 11, 20, 32.
309. Sidonius Apollinaris, *Poems*, vol. 1, Letter, 1.2.
310. 'regis nostri oculos', Ennodius, *Panegyricus Theoderico*, 12.211.
311. David Ganz, 'Einhard's Charlemagne: The Characterisation of Greatness', in *Charlemagne: Empire and Society*, ed. Joanna Story (Manchester: Manchester University Press, 2005), 40, 44–47.
312. 'oculis praegrandibus ac vegetis' and 'facie laeta et hilari': Einhard, *Vita Karoli*, ed. G. Waitz, *MGH SSrG* [25] (Hanover: 1911), 3.22.
313. 'oculi rutilantes et in modum fulguris cita repercussione splendorem quendam emittentes', Widukind, *Res*, 2.36.
314. Deslee Campbell, 'The Iconography of Women: A Study of the Art of Byzantium and the Byzantine-Influenced Western Mediterranean, AD 395–1204' (PhD diss., University of Sydney, 2008).
315. 'Regalis formae miro rutilabat honore': Hrotsvitha, *Gesta*, line 88.
316. 'vultus splendore coruscam / Ac fulgore magis cunctae nitidam bonitatis', ibid., lines 158–59.

317. 'Haec quoque regalis formae praeclara decore, / Atque suae causis personae sedula dignis / Factis regali respondit nobilitati', ibid., lines 475–78.
318. 'Reginae satis egregiae memor est Aedelheithae, / Regalem certe cupiens quandoque videre / Ipsius faciem, cuius didicit bonitatem', ibid., lines 638–640.
319. 'quae ob inmensitatem tyrannidis secunda Iezabel et ob rapinarum insacietatem Lamia proprio apellatur vocabulo', Liudprand, *Antapodosis*, 3.1, 3.7–3.8, 1.32. In Greek mythology Lamia was a child-eating monster, a kind of vampire.
320. 'cum forma honestissima tum morum probitate gratiosam', ibid., 4.13.
321. Ibid., 4.17.
322. 'Ottones Romanorum invictissimos imperatores augustos gloriosissimamque Adelheidem imperatricem augustam Liudprandus sanctae Cremonensis ecclesiae episcopus semper valere, prosperari, triumphare anhelat, desiderat, optat', Liudprand, *Relatio*, Preface to Book I.
323. Philippe Buc, 'Italian Hussies and German Matrons. Liutprand of Cremona on Dynastic Legitimacy', *FMSt* 29 (1995), 217–25.
324. 'Stirpe fuit genita regali pulchra Beatrix', Donizo, *VM*, 1.9, lines 782–83.
325. Skinner, *Women*, 140.
326. 'sermone erat facundissima et in consiliis astutissima, affabilis ad omnes', *Notae de Mathilda comitissa*, ed. P. E. Schramm, *MGH SS* 30/2:973–75 (1929), 975.
327. Skinner, *Women*, 140.
328. Golinelli, 'Donizone e il suo poema', 11.
329. Donizo, Vita Mathildis, (Vatican: Biblioteca Apostolica Vaticana, Cod. Vat. Lat. 4922), f. 49r.
330. Donizo, *VM*, 2.1, lines 87–97.
331. Donizo, Vita Mathildis, (Cod. Vat. Lat. 4922), f. 7v.
332. For the participation of Arduinus de Palude in Matilda's diplomata, see Nash, *Maintaining Elite Households*.
333. Abbess Hitda Presents her Book to St Walburga, Hitda Codex, c. 1000–20 (Darmstadt: Landesbibliotek, Cod. 1640), fol. 6; Henry Mayr-Harting, *Ottonian Book Illumination: An Historical Study*, 2 vols (London: Oxford University Press, 1991), Part Two, Books, 99–117.

334. Frontispiece. Queen Emma, King Harthacnut, and Prince Edward, with the Author of the *Encomium Emmae* Kneeling in Front. Mid-eleventh century (London: BL, Add. 33241), fol. 1v; *Encomium Emmae Reginae*, ed. A. Campbell and Simon Keynes (Cambridge: Cambridge University Press, 1949, repr. 1998), xiii–xiv; Frank Barlow, *Edward the Confessor* (London: Eyre & Spottiswoode, 1970), illus. 2, betw. 40 and 41.

335. See, for example, the canopy under which King Edward the Confessor sits, enthroned in state and consequently displaying his regal authority, in the contemporary Bayeux Tapestry: Wilson, *Bayeux*, 1.

336. Golinelli, 'Donizone', 13.

337. Registrum Gregorii, c. 983 (Chantilly, Musée Conde, MS 14), single sheet; Gospel Book of Otto III, c. 998 (Munich: Bayerische Staatsbibliothek, Col. 4453), fol. 24; Rosamond McKitterick, 'Ottonische Kultur und Bildung', in Puhle, *Otto der Große*, vol. I, Abb. 7, 217; D. A. Bullough, 'After Charlemagne: The Empire under the Ottonians', in *The Dawn of European Civilization: The Dark Ages*, ed. Talbot David Rice (New York: McGraw-Hill, 1965), 305.

338. Verzar, 'Picturing Matilda', 77.

339. Bedos-Rezak, 'Suger and the Symbolism of Royal Power: The Seal of Louis VII', in *Form and Order in Medieval France*, V.10.

340. Charlemagne and Pippin (Modena: Archivio Capitolare, Cod. O.I.2), fol. 154v.

341. Donizo, Vita Mathildis, (Cod. Vat. Lat. 4922), f. 30v; f. 28v; f. 21v. See also Donizo, *VM*, tables 4–6, betw. xvi and xvii; Verzar, 'Picturing Matilda', 77.

342. Relatio translationis corporis sancti Geminiani (Modena: Archivio capitolare, Cod. O.II), fol. 10r; *Relatio translationis corporis sancti Geminiani*, ed. Giulio Bertoni, *RIS2* VI/1 (Bologna: 1907).

343. Christ Cleansing the Temple, Gospels of Mathilda of Tuscany from Polirone (New York: Pierpont Morgan Library, M 492), fol. 84r; G. Warner, *Gospels of Matilda, Countess of Tuscany, 1055–1115. Nineteen Plates in Gold and Colour, and 12 in Monochrome from the Manuscript in the Library of John Pierpont Morgan*, vol. 172 ([Oxford]: Privately printed for presentation to the Roxburghe Club, 1917), Introduction, 9–37; Rough, *Reformist Illuminations*, especially 60–65.

344. Bedos-Rezak, 'The King Enthroned, a New Theme in Anglo-Saxon Royal Iconography: The Seal of Edward the Confessor and its Political Implications'. In *Form and Order in Medieval France*, IV.53-IV.88. See especially the seal of Otto III, dated to when he was ruling in his own right at IV.83, Fig. 2.
345. Reynolds, 'Reading Matilda', 8–9; Nobili, 'Ideologia politica', 263–79.
346. Bedos-Rezak, 'Seals', IX.63.
347. *DD MT*, 7–8, 12–13; Reynolds, 'Reading Matilda', 7–8.
348. Robinson, *Papacy*, 260–62; *DD MT*, 14; *ODP*, s.v. 'Celestine III'.
349. Paolo Golinelli, *I mille volti di Matilde di Canossa: Immagini di un mito nei secoli* (Milan: Frederico Motta Editore, 2003), 65–66.
350. *DD MT*, Nr. 38, trans. Joan Ferrante, 'Matilda of Tuscany, countess of Tuscany, duchess of Lorraine, to the Germans', in *MWLL*, http://epistolae.ccnmtl.columbia.edu/letter/209.html, date accessed 20 August 2016.
351. 'ad praepotentissimam tunc temporis feminam Mathildam nomine', *Annales S. Disibodi*, ed. G. Waitz, *MGH SS* 17:4–30 (1861), s.a. 1093.
352. 'Clericos religiosos oppido valde *honorabat*, latrones minime *servabat*, rusticos *gubernabat*, omnes principes, marchiones, comites, proceres ceteros omnesque milites tanta diligentia *gubernabat*, quod genu flexo in consiliis ante illam avidissime se prosternebant [my italics]', *Notae de Mathilda comitissa*, 975.

Epilogue

R. W. Southern's statement about the changes in society which occurred between the end of the tenth and the beginning of the twelfth centuries, quoted in the Introduction to this book, encapsulates the dilemma of the period: a more organized male-oriented lay and clerical society, emphasizing less flexible government structures, curtailed the opportunities of those who did not fit. This reorientation mostly affected women. Much historical analysis has been carried out elsewhere on elite men—the kings and magnates who ruled Germany and northern Italy—and how the changes affected them during that period. Relatively little coordinated, in-depth and systematic work has been undertaken on the comparative effect of the changes on ruling women. This examination of the lives of two women, the one active before and the other active toward the end of the period of change, exposes their relative ability to accumulate and retain their wealth and power. The comparison has been made by focusing on three categories: kin and kith, land and rule.

Adelheid and Matilda lived in societies that prized close interactions between kin and kith. At a relatively young age the two women were separated from many of their near kin because of either the deaths of their relatives or other changes in circumstances which caused their removal to different locations. They learned independence and how to forge new alliances. Neither seems to have been especially intimate with many women. Adelheid's relationship with her brother Conrad, king of

Burgundy, appears to have been close. Gerbert, monk of Aurillac and later Pope Sylvester II, admired her, and Archbishop Willigis of Mainz supported her in the main. Adelheid and her daughter-in-law, Theophanu, empress after Otto I died, worked well together mostly and unquestionably so when it was critical. Information about Adelheid's interactions with her two daughters, Queen Emma of Francia and Abbess Mathilda of Quedlinburg, is sparse. However, Emma wrote to her mother requesting that she use her power to free her from captivity. Adelheid and Abbess Mathilda met regularly at the royal councils and to celebrate the great feasts of the church. Adelheid's spiritual family included her confessor, Ekkeman; Abbot Maiolus of Cluny; and Abbot Odilo of Cluny (Maiolus's successor), who wrote her *Epitaphium*.

After Countess Matilda's mother died, Matilda was left with few intimate female acquaintances. Many of the men who witnessed her charters continued to do so for many years, unless the event under scrutiny was of only local interest. Her two marriages were politically arranged and not lasting. The power of this effective ruling countess could be circumscribed by a count, and in the longer term, Matilda was not willing to be restricted. Toward the end of her life, with no living children, she was preoccupied with who would inherit her property and tried a number of solutions including adoption, but the men she chose either proved unsuitable or did not survive her. She gathered around her a court of like-minded intellectuals who backed her support of church reform. Her spiritual advisors included seven popes, beginning with Pope Gregory VII, whom she supported unstintingly against the twice-excommunicated King and then Emperor Henry IV. She associated with other leading clerical men of the day and they sought her advice. Her confessor was Bishop Anselm II of Lucca. Her enemies attacked her as a woman, as Adelheid never was.

'[L]and was a crucial resource':[1] Chris Wickham's statement has proved pertinent to how the fortunes of Empress Adelheid and Countess Matilda were obtained and held. Adelheid's father-in-law, King Hugh, and first husband, King Lothar, had given her lands as a reverse dowry on her engagement and marriage. Her second husband, King and then Emperor Otto I, gave her dotal property in Alsace on the edge of his kingdom. She inherited further estates located there at Erstein from her mother, so much so that she owned more than her son, Otto II. This book has shown how she built up Erstein as a major center and, because of her interest there and in Burgundy, changed the imperial route for the emperors' journeys to and from Italy so that it ran through Alsace and the Burgundian Gate rather than through Lotharingia down the Moselle River. Consequently she significantly increased the status and wealth of Alsace while enhancing Burgundy's prospects through imperial association and trade.

One hundred years later Countess Matilda of Tuscany inherited property from her father, *dux* Boniface, and mother, *dux/ducatrix* Beatrice. Matilda is most associated with her castle fortress of Canossa, built on a rock on the northern side of the Apennine mountains, bordering on the Po River valley. There her great-grandfather, Adalbert Atto, kept Adelheid safe after her escape from Berengar II following the death of King Lothar. Since Adelheid would bring the Italian kingdom by right of Lombard law to a second husband, Berengar wanted her to marry his son. Adelheid's rescue by Atto set the Canossan family on the road to success: Adelheid married Otto I, who rewarded Atto for his help and loyalty. Canossa was not the only property link between Adelheid and Matilda. In 982 Adelheid donated her great royal estates around Melara, situated on the River Po, to San Salvatore at Pavia. The priory located at Melara was an outpost of the mother house. Although Matilda had no direct association with the monastery's lands, her property adjoined the priory. In 1106 she severely reprimanded her men for allowing the trespass of their pigs on the lands at Melara. Property and its use needed careful and just management. A third estate at Hochfelden, given to Adelheid as dotal property by Otto I, appeared in 1065 as dotal property of Empress Agnes, wife of Emperor Henry III. Agnes's dotal property was given away among other imperial redistributions to a count, without acknowledgement of its origins. Agnes's situation was related to but not the same as Adelheid's, when she found herself in 985 not free to give other dotal property to her daughter. These situations qualify the real power that imperial women maintained over their dotal property. Countess Matilda suffered also from insecurity regarding her estates: Matilda's control of her lands was threatened when Henry IV punished her with their forfeiture. After her death, disputes between the papacy and the empire about the ownership of the Matildine lands lasted over two hundred years.

Adelheid and Matilda governed by traveling through their dominions in the tradition of the kings and emperors. Adelheid was restrained by the convention that the man ruled, even when under-age. She appears in charters, the main records of government, as intervener, never as issuer, since the fiction in public documents of a ruling male figure remained, although in practical actions she overrode that restriction. An indirect measure of the strength of her actual rule is the distinctiveness of the titles that were conferred on her in the charters, the number in which she intervened and her presence at many locations across the kingdom and empire. She acted as regent on four distinct occasions, three of them on behalf of the empire which experienced relative peace during those periods. Her imperial portrait appears in a stylized form in a Gospel book. I argue that image was an important aspect of rulership and that it is likely that her marriage charter was created as an elaborately designed certificate to confirm both the queen's and the king's importance. Despite her name appearing on coins with Otto (either her husband or her grandson) she did not have her own seal. Although Otto I issued coins with his own stylized image, he did not order a Gospel image of the emperor in majesty like those that his son and grandson favored for themselves, possibly influenced by the Byzantine Theophanu's arrival at the Western court in 972. In this way Adelheid kept a lower profile in the decorative arts, matching that of her husband. Nevertheless Adelheid was the first crowned empress. This book has brought together evidence for three matters not previously determined: the date of her wedding to Otto I (9 October 951), her decisive role as bearer of the Italian kingdom to Otto and her daughter-in-law's age (possibly as young as nine) at her wedding to Otto II. Many of the contemporary chroniclers praised Adelheid, and she was never accused of sexual sinfulness, an allegation commonly made about women by their enemies. Details about her activities in Italy are scanty, but she apparently ruled there very effectively.

Matilda had no such restrictions: in her own name she issued at least 139 diplomata, in which she recorded the lordly justice which she dispensed. She signed her charters herself and had them stamped with her own seal. No coins appear to have been minted in her name, since such options were usually a royal prerogative. She led her troops into battle against Henry IV on several occasions in support of church reform and eventually drove him out of Italy. As countess, marchioness and *dux/ducatrix*, she acted like a king, albeit ruling over territories of lesser size than those over which Adelheid presided as queen and empress. Maps developed for this book illustrate for the two women the range of their travels and their centers of power.

***

This book set out to compare two women: first, for their relative ability to accumulate and to retain their wealth and power and, second, for their exemplification or otherwise of the paradigm: that women in the Early Middle Ages, at a time of fewer restrictions and less oversight, could do better than women in the later eleventh century and indeed the later Middle Ages. The comparison is of particular interest because the two women lived at either end of a most tumultuous period of social change. In the latter half of the tenth century Adelheid conformed to a great extent to the expectations of her times, albeit taking advantage of her available opportunities and succeeding well beyond the norm. One hundred years later, Matilda, in the more structured environment that was potentially less conducive to female achievement, should not have garnered so much success—if the paradigm is correct.

The answer as to whether the lives of those two women support that paradigm is nuanced and complex: sometimes they do and at other times they do not. During the period of upheaval from the end of the tenth century until the early twelfth century, the structure of the family undoubtedly changed. The extreme concern about celibacy and purity affected the church and the laity profoundly. Nevertheless women did not become ciphers. Adelheid's life in the earlier time was not unconstrained nor was Matilda's life of effective action in the later period available to her alone. With landholdings, albeit hedged about with covenants and restrictions, women could always exercise power.

Both Adelheid and Matilda succeeded admirably in their societies. At first examination Adelheid appears to have followed the tradition of early medieval queens in obtaining at least some of her status from her husbands, in producing the heir and in leading a devout life. In transcending the stereotype by, for example, taking an active ruling role, she could be considered to be conforming to the paradigm, that is, using the freedom of a less structured society to explore opportunities. However, she was not able to do this unfettered. Control of property remained an issue for her as for Matilda, who, in adapting herself to the more organized male-oriented society by making herself a power-broker in that milieu, flourished. To a great extent she took on a masculine model, eschewing male partners, except briefly for political ends. Although other female comital lords at about the same time did exercise power and prospered, Matilda's achievements were great because of her persistence and her uncompromising stance, and like Adelheid, she could call on her great wealth. Matilda did not allow restrictions to defeat her. Her success was more individual.

Karl Leyser's perceptive and subtle analysis about the tenth century in contrast with the changes afterward is worth quoting in detail:

> It is often said that the twelfth century saw the first emancipation of women in our civilization and that they participated in its spiritual movements, whether orthodox or heretical, as never before. This view could be questioned. The piety of the tenth-century Saxon noble women fulfilled itself in action, in offices performed, alms given and works done. It was at once lordly and circumscribed but the foundresses, abbesses, nuns and women in general played a more essential role in the early Christian neighbourhoods and family foyers of their recently converted stemland than did their successors in the twelfth century. Nor must we underrate their share in the literary, artistic and architectural creativeness of their – the Ottonian – renaissance.[2]

That a woman could succeed in that way in the late eleventh century is most interesting. Not many men or women have been followed with such devotion by their dependents nor been celebrated for such wide-ranging influence as have Adelheid and Matilda. Odilo of Cluny, writing within a few years of her death, called Adelheid 'the most august of all empresses'[3] and wrote verses in praise:

> No one before her
> So helped the republic;
> Obstinate Germany
> And fruitful Italy—
> These and their princes
> She put under Rome's power.
> She set noble King Otto
> Over Rome as its Caesar;
> And bore him a son
> Fit for Rule supreme.[4]

Similarly modern historians can only note with approval the overwhelming admiration of the anonymous author of the *Notae de Mathilda comitissa*, also written shortly after the subject's death: 'she had the friendship of the emperor of Constantinople and of the princes of Apulia, of both the Franks and the Teutons, of the king of Hungary, and of the judges of Sardinia, and of the princes of other islands, and also of others whose names it seems impossible to record'.[5]

May *those* epitaphs be remembered.

Notes

1. Wickham, 'Land Disputes', 248.
2. Leyser, *Rule*, 73.
3. 'augustarum omnium augustissima', Odilo, *Epitaphium*, 3.
4. 'Nemo ante illam/Ita auxit rem publicam/Cervicosam Germaniam/ Ac fecundam Italiam/Has cum suis principibus/Romanis subdidit arcibus./Ottonem regem nobilem/Rome prefecit cesarem,/Ex quo genuit filium/Imperio dignissimum', ibid., 3.
5. 'Amicitiam habebat Constantinopolitani imperatoris et Apulie principum et Francigenarum et Theotonicorum, Ungarici regis et Sardinie iudicum et aliarum insularum principum et ceterorum, quorum nomina impossibile esse videtur perscribere', *Notae de Mathilda comitissa*, 975. I am indebted to Professor Thomas Bisson for drawing these words in the *Notae* to my attention.

List of Abbreviations

Act. Pont. Cenom.	Actus pontificum Cenomannis in urbe degentium. Edited by Georges Busson, Ambroise Ledru and Eugène Vallée. Archives Historiques du Maine, Paris: La Société des Archives Historiques, 1901
AQ	Annales Quedlinburgenses. Edited by M. Giese, MGH SSrG [72]. Hanover, 2004
AQDG	Ausgewählte Quellen zur deutschen Geschichte des Mittelalters (Freiherr-von-Stein-Gedächtnis-Ausgabe)
AW	Annales Weissenburgenses, ed. O. Holder-Egger, Lamperti monachi Hersfeldensis Opera, MGH SSrG [38]:9–57 (Hanover: 1894)
Bernard, Chartes	Bernard, Auguste and Alexander Bruel, eds. Recueil des chartes de l'abbaye de Cluny. 6 vols (Paris, 1876–1903)
Bernold, Chronicon	Bernold of Constance, Chronicon: Die Chroniken Bertholds von Reichenau und Bernolds von Konstanz, 1054–1100, ed. I. S. Robinson, MGH SSrG n.s. 14:383–540 (Hanover: 2003)

LIST OF ABBREVIATIONS

Böhmer, *RI* 2.1   Böhmer, J. F., *Regesta imperii 2.1 (Sächsisches Haus 919–1024): Die Regesten des Kaiserreiches unter Heinrich I. und Otto I. 919–973*, new edn by E. Ottenthal, with additions by H. H. Kaminsky. Hildesheim, 1967

Böhmer, *RI* 2.2   Böhmer, J. F., *Regesta Imperii 2. 2: (Sächsisches Haus 919–1024): Die Regesten des Kaiserreiches unter Otto II*, ed. H. L. Mikoletzky (Graz: Böhlau, 1950)

Böhmer, *RI* 2.3   Böhmer, J. F., *Regesta imperii 2.3 (Sächsisches Haus 919–1024): Die Regesten des Kaiserreiches unter Otto III 980 (983)–1002*, new edn by M. Uhlirz. Cologne and Graz, 1956

Du Cange   du Cange et al., *Glossarium mediæ et infirmæ latinitatis*. Nova ed. Niort: L. Favr, 1678, 1883–1887, http://ducange.enc.sorbonne.fr/

CCM   *Cahiers de Civilisation Médiévale*

DD MT   *Die Urkunden und Briefe der Markgräfin Mathilde von Tuszien*, eds E. Goez and W. Goez, *MGH Laienfürsten- und Dynastenurkunden der Kaiserzeit II*, Hanover (1998)

DH IV   Henry IV, *Diplomata*. eds D. von Gladiss and A. Gawlik, *Die Urkunden Heinrichs IV.* (*MGH* Dip. regum VI.1-3) Weimer (1941–78)

DO I   Otto I. *Diplomata*. Edited by T. Sickel, *Die Urkunden Konrad I., Heinrich I., und Otto I.* (*MGH* Dip. *regum Is*). Hanover (1879–1884), repr. Berlin, 1956

DO II   Otto II, *Diplomata*, ed. T. Sickel, *Die Urkunden Otto des II.* (*MGH* Dip. regum II.I), Hanover (1888), repr. Berlin, 1956

DO III   Otto III, *Diplomata*, ed. T. Sickel, *Die Urkunden Otto des III.* (*MGH* Dip. regum II.2), Hanover (1893), repr. Berlin, 1957

Donizo, *VM*	Donizo. *Vita Mathildis (Vita di Matilde di Canossa)*. Edited by P. Golinelli and V. Fumagalli. Milan: Jaca Book, 2008
FMSt	*Frühmittelalterliche Studien*
FS	*Feminist Studies*
Goez, *Reg. Bea.*	Goez, E. *Beatrix von Canossa und Tuszien: Eine Untersuching zur Geschichte des 11. Jahrhunderts.* Sigmaringen: Jan Thorbecke, 1995: Register, 192–235
Gregory VII, *Registrum*	Gregory VII. *Gregorii VII registrum (Das Register Gregors VII.).* Edited by E. Caspar. 2nd ed. 2 vols, *MGH Epp. sel.* 2. Berlin: Weidmann, 1955
Hrotsvitha, *Gesta*	Hrotsvitha of Gandersheim. *Gesta Ottonis.* In *Hrotsvit Opera omnia.* Edited by Walter Berschin, 273–305. Munich: K. G. Sur, 2001
HSJ	*The Haskins Society Journal*
JAEMA	*Journal of the Australian Medieval Association*
JEH	*Journal of Ecclesiastical History*
JMH	*Journal of Medieval History*
JoMMH	*Journal of Medieval Military History*
JTS	*Journal of Theological Studies*
Lampert, *Annales*	Lampert of Hersfeld, *Lamperti Hersfeldensis Annales.* Edited by O. Holder-Egger, *Lamperti monachi Hersfeldensis Opera, MGH SSrG* [38]: 3–304. Hanover, 1894
Liudprand, *Antapodosis*	Liudprand of Cremona. *Antapodosis.* Edited by A. Bauer and R. Rau. 5th ed, *AQDG* 8:244–495. Darmstadt: Wissenschaftliche Buchgesellschaft, 2002
Liudprand, *Liber*	Liudprand of Cremona. *Liber de ottone rege.* Edited by A. Bauer and R. Rau. 5th ed, *AQDG* 8. Darmstadt: Wissenschaftliche Buchgesellschaft, 2002.
Liudprand, *Relatio*	Liudprand of Cremona. *Relatio de legatione Constantinopolitana.* Edited by A. Bauer and R. Rau. 5th ed, *AQDG*

LMA	8:524–89. Darmstadt: Wissenschaftliche Buchgesellschaft, 2002 *Lexikon des Mittelalters*, ed. Robert Auty, 9 vols. (München & Zürich: Artemis-Verlag, 1977–1998)
MGH	*Monumenta Germaniae Historica, inde ab anno Christi quintesimo usque ad annum millesimum et quingentesimum* (Hanover/Berlin, 1824–) with subseries: http://www.dmgh.de/
Dip. regum	*Diplomata regum et imperatorum Germaniae: Die Urkunden der Deutschen Könige und Kaiser* I, ed. T. Sickel, Hanover (1879–84); II.I, ed. T. Sickel, Hanover (1888); II.2, ed. T. Sickel, Hanover (1893); III, eds H. Bresslau, H. Bloch and R. Holtzmann, Hanover (1900–3); IV, ed. H. Bresslau, Berlin (1909); VI, eds D. Von Gladiss, A. Gawlick, Weimer (1941, 1959, 1978)
Epp. sel.	*Epistolae selectae in usum scholarum*, 5 volumes, Hanover (1887–91)
Ldl	*Libelli de lite imperatorum et pontificum*
Lib. Mem.	*Libri Memoriales* and *Libri Memoriales et Necrologia nova series*, Hanover (1979–)
SRL	*Scriptores rerum Langobardicarum et Italicarum saec.* VI–IX
SSrG	*Scriptores rerum Germanicarum in usum scholarum separatim editi*, 63 vols., Hanover (1871–1987)
SS	*Scriptores* (in Folio), 39 volumes, Hanover (1824–1924), reprint 1963
MIöG	*Mitteilungen des Instituts für österreichische Geschichtsforschung* (1880–1922); *Mitteilungen des österreichischen Instituts für Geschichtsforschung*, 1923ff
MWLL	*Medieval Women Latin Letters* at website edited by J. Ferrante: http://epistolae.ccnmtl.columbia.edu/letters

NCMH	*The New Cambridge Medieval History*, 7 Volumes, Cambridge University Press, Cambridge (1995–2005)
Niermeyer, *Index*	Niermeyer, J., C. van de Kieft, G. S. M. M. Lake-Schoonebeek. *Mediae Latinitatis lexicon minus: abbreviationes et index fontium*. In Niermeyer. *Mediae latinitatis lexicon minus*, vol 2, 1–83
Niermeyer, *Lexicon*	Niermeyer, J. F., C. van de Kieft, and J. W. J. Burgers. *Mediae latinitatis lexicon minus*. 2nd ed. 2 vols. Leiden: Brill, 2002
n. s.	nova series, new series
ODP	*Oxford Dictionary of Popes*. Edited by J. N. D. Kelly. Oxford: Oxford University Press, 1986
OED Online	*Oxford English Dictionary Online*. Oxford: Oxford University Press, 2000. http://www.oed.com.ezproxy1.library.usyd.edu.au/
OLD	*Oxford Latin Dictionary*, ed. P. G. W. Glare. Oxford, Clarendon Press, 1968–82
Overmann, *Reg. Mat.*	Overmann, *Regesten* in *Gräfin Mathilde von Tuscien. Ihre Besitzungen, Geschichte ihres Gutes von 1115–1230 und ihre Regesten*, 123–90. Innsbruck: 1895; repr. Frankfurt am Main: Minerva, 1965
PL	*Patrologie cursus completus... Series Latina*, ed. Jacques-Paul Migne, 221 vols., Paris (1841–64) http://setis.library.usyd.edu.au/pld/index.html
P&P	*Past and Present*
Schiaparelli, *Diplomi di Ugo*	Schiaparelli, L., ed., *I diplomi di Ugo e di Lotario, di Berengario II e di Adalberto*, vol. 1: *Diplomi secolo X*, Fonti per la storia d'Italia 38 (Rome: 1924)
SG	*Studi Gregoriani*
SM I	*Studi matildici: atti e memorie del I Convegno di studi matildici (Modena e*

	Reggio Emilia 19, 20, 21 ottobre 1963) (Modena: Aedes Muratoriana, 1964)
SM II	*Studi matildici: atti e memorie del II Convegno di studi matildici (Modena e Reggio Emilia 1, 2, 3 maggio 1970)* (Modena: Aedes Muratoriana, 1971)
SM III	*Studi matildici: atti e memorie del III Convegno di studi matildici (Reggio Emilia 7 – 8 – 9 ottobre 1977)* Deputazione di storia patria per le antiche provincie modenesi. Biblioteca Nuova Serie N. 44 (Modena: Aedes Muratoriana, 1978)
SM IV	Bonacini, Pierpaolo, ed. *Studi matildici IV: atti e memorie del Convegno 'Il territorio parmense da Carlo Magno ai Canossa', Neviano degli Arduini, 17 settembre 1995.* (Modena: Aedes Muratoriana, 1997)
SMGB	*Studien und Mitteilungen zur Geschichte des Benediktinerordens*
Thietmar, *Chronicon*	Thietmar of Merseburg. *Chronicon*. Edited by W. Trillmich. 8th ed, *AQDG* 9. Darmstadt: Wissenschaftliche Buchgesellschaft, 2002
VMA	*Vita Mathildis reginae antiquior.* Edited by Bernd Schütte, *Die Lebensbeschreibungen der Königin Mathilde*, MGH SSrG [66:107–42]. Hanover: Hahn, 1994 [= The 'Older Life' of Queen Mathilda]
VMP	*Vita Mathildis reginae posterior.* Edited by Bernd Schütte, *Die Lebensbeschreibungen der Königin Mathilde*, MGH SSrG [66:143–202]. Hanover: Hahn, 1994 [= The 'Later Life' of Queen Mathilda]
Widukind, *Res*	Widukind of Corvey. *Res gestae Saxonicae.* Edited by A. Bauer and R. Rau. 5th ed, *AQDG* 8. Darmstadt: Wissenschaftliche Buchgesellschaft, 2002
ZSRGA	*Zeitschrift der Savigny-Stiftung für Rechtsgeschichte*, Germanistische Abteilung

Notes on Sources and Translations

To simplify most notes include only the reference to the original source in Latin by book number, chapter number and line number, where appropriate. If a printed English translation exists, but book and chapter numbers or letter numbers do not correspond to the Latin source, that reference is also included. If the translation is my own or the printed English translation corresponds in book and chapter numbers or letter numbers, no reference is included.

The most important sources which have printed English translations are Gerbert, *Epistolae*; Hrotsvitha, *Gesta Ottonis*; Odilo, *Epitaphium*; Thietmar, *Chronicon*; *Vita Mathildis reginae antiquior*; *Vita Mathildis reginae posterior*; and Widukind, *Res gestae Saxonicae*.

The following lists printed Latin sources and corresponding printed English translations. These translations have been used and adapted where necessary throughout. If there is no corresponding translation listed here or in the footnotes, translations are my own.

Original Text
Adalbert of Magdeburg, *Continuatio*
Adam of Bremen, *Gesta*
Annales Quedlinburgenses
Anselm of Canterbury, *Sancti Anselmi Cantuariensis*

English Translation
MacLean, *History and Politics*
Tschan, *History*
Warner, *Ottonian Germany*, for some passages
Fröhlich, *Letters*

238 NOTES ON SOURCES AND TRANSLATIONS

Anselm of Canterbury, *Sancti Anselmi opera*	Ferrante, 'Medieval Women's Latin Letters'
Anselm of Lucca, *Liber contra Wibertum*	Robinson, *Papal Reform*, for one passage
Bernold of Constance (St Blasien), *Chronicon*	Robinson, *Bernold of St Blasien*
Bonizo, *Liber ad amicum*	Robinson, *Book to a Friend*
Busson, *Actus pontificum Cenomannis*	Barton, *Deeds of Bishop Arnald*
Capitulare missorum generale	King, *Charlemagne*
Donizo, *Vita Mathildis*	Hay, *Military Leadership*, for some passages
Duchesne, *Liber pontificalis*	Davis, *Lives*
Einhard, *Vita Karoli*	Thorpe, *Life of Charlemagne*
Ennodius, *Panegyricus*	Cook, *Life of Saint Epiphanius*
Froumond, *Tegernseer Briefsammlung*	Ferrante, 'Medieval Women's Latin Letters'
Gerbert, *Epistolae*	Lattin, *Letters*. Since Lattin's numbering system differs from Weigle's and Havet's, her letter numbers have been identified in the notes.
Goez, *Die Urkunden und Briefe der Markgräfin Mathilde* (*DD MT*)	Fröhlich, *Letters*, for Letter 84; Ferrante, 'Medieval Women Latin Letters', for Nr. 38
Gregory VII, *Registrum*	Cowdrey, *Register*
Hincmar, *Hincmarus*	Herlihy, *On Governance*
Hrotsvitha, *Gesta Ottonis*	Bergman, 'Achievements of Otto'; Wilson, 'A Florilegium'
Hugh of Flavigny, *Chronicon*	Ferrante, 'Medieval Women's Latin Letters'
Leges Langobardorum	Drew, *Lombard Laws*
Liudprand, *Liudprandi Opera*	Squatriti, *Complete Works*; Wright, *Works*
Odilo, *Epitaphium*	Gilsdorf, *Epitaph of Adelheid*; Warner, *Epitaph of the August Lady, Adelheid*
Otto II, *Diplomata* (*DO II*)	Hill, *Medieval Monarchy*, for Diploma number 21.
Otto of Freising, *Gesta Friderici I*	Mierow, *Deeds of Frederick Barbarossa*
Patrologie cursus completus	Urban II, *Medieval Women Latin Letters*; Paschal II, *Medieval Women Latin Letters*
Paul the Deacon, *Historia Langobardorum*	Foulke, *History of the Lombards*
Peter Damian, *Epistolae*	Blum, *Letters*
Rahewin, *Gesta Friderici*	Mierow, *Deeds of Frederick Barbarossa*
Salvian, *Salviani*	O'Sullivan, *Writings*
Thietmar, *Chronicon*	Warner, *Ottonian Germany*
Vita Heinrici IV	Mommsen, *Imperial Lives*
Vita Mathildis reginae antiquior	Gilsdorf, 'Older Life'
Vita Mathildis reginae posterior	Gilsdorf, 'Later Life'
Widukind, *Res gestae Saxonicae*	Bachrach, *Widukind*; Dolan, *Widukind*; Wood, 'Three Books'
Wipo, *Gesta Chuonradi II*	Mommsen, *Imperial Lives*

BIBLIOGRAPHY

MANUSCRIPT SOURCES

Abbess Hitda Presents her Book to St Walburga, Hitda Codex, c. 1000–20. Darmstadt: Landesbibliotek, Cod. 1640, fol. 6.

Charlemagne and Pippin. Caroli Magni o Liber legum (IX–X sec.). Modena: Archivio Capitolare, Cod. O.I.2, fol. 154v.

Christ Cleansing the Temple. Gospels of Mathilda of Tuscany from Polirone. New York: Pierpont Morgan Library, M 492, fol 84r.

Donizo. Vita Mathildis. Vatican: Biblioteca Apostolica Vaticana, Cod. Vat. Lat. 4922.

Frontispiece. Queen Emma, King Harthacnut, and Prince Edward, with the Author of the *Encomium Emmae* Kneeling in Front. Mid-eleventh century. London: BL, Add. 33241, fol. 1v.

Gospel Book of Otto III, c. 998. Munich, Bayerische Staatsbibliothek, Col. 4453, fol. 24.

Gospels of Mathilda of Tuscany from Polirone. New York: Pierpont Morgan Library, M 492.

Initial Page of the Matthew Evangelistary, Adelheid, Theophanu, Otto III and Lamb of God. Gospel of St. Gereon, 990–1000. Cologne: Historisches Archiv der Stadt, Cod. W 312, fol. 22r.

Marriage Charter of Theophanu, 972. Wolfenbüttel: Niedersächsisches Staatsarchiv, 6, fol. 11.

Orationes sive meditationes. Admont: Stiftsbibliothek, MS 289.

Ottonian Ivory Relief, Otto II, Theophanu and Otto III at the Feet of Christ, Mary and St. Maurice, c. 980. Milan: Civiche Raccolte d'Arte Applicata, Museo del Castello Sforzesco.

Ottonianum, 962. Rome: Archivio Segreto Vaticano.
Registrum Gregorii. c. 983, Chantilly: Musée Conde, MS 14, single sheet.
Relatio translationis corporis sancti Geminiani. Modena: Archivio capitolare, Cod. O.II, fol. 10r.

Primary and Early Sources

D'Achery. *Spicilegium sive collectio veterum aliquot scriptorum qui in Galliae bibliothecis delituerant.* Vol. III. Paris, 1723.
Actus pontificum Cenomannis in urbe degentium. Edited by Georges Busson, Ambroise Ledru and Eugène Vallée. Archives Historiques du Maine, Paris: La Société des Archives Historiques, 1901.
Adalbert of Magdeburg. *Continuatio Reginonis.* Edited by A. Bauer and R. Rau, *AQDG* 8. Darmstadt: Wissenschaftliche Buchgesellschaft, 2002.
Adam of Bremen. *Gesta Hammaburgensis ecclesiae pontificum.* Edited by Werner Trillmich and Rudolf Buchner. 2nd ed, *AQDG* 11:137–499. Darmstadt: Wissenschaftliche Buchgesellschaft, 1968.
Adelaide of Turin and Susa. 'Women's Biography: Adelaide of Turin and Susa'. In *MWLL,* http://epistolae.ccnmtl.columbia.edu/woman/105.html, date accessed 4 April 2016.
The Anglo-Saxon Chronicle: A Collaborative Edition. Edited by Simon Keynes, D. N. Dumville, Simon Taylor, Patrick W. Conner, Janet Bately, Michael Lapidge and G. P. Cubbin. Cambridge: D.S. Brewer, 1983.
Annales Bertiniani. Edited by G. Waitz, *MGH SSrG* [5]. Hanover, 1883.
Annales Einsiedlenses (Die Annalen des Klosters Einsiedeln Edition und Kommentar). Edited by C. von Planta, *MGH SSrG* [78]. Hanover, 2007.
Annales Hildesheimenses. Edited by G. Waitz, *MGH SSrG* [8]. Hanover, 1878, repr. 1947.
Annales Magdeburgenses. Edited by G. H. Pertz, *MGH SS* 16:105–96, 1859.
Annales Quedlinburgenses. Edited by M. Giese, *MGH SSrG* [72]. Hanover, 2004.
Annales Regni Francorum. Edited by F. Kurze, *MGH SSrG* [6]. Hanover, 1895.
Annales S. Disibodi. Edited by G. Waitz, *MGH SS* 17:4–30, 1861.
Annalista Saxo. Edited by K. Nass, *MGH SS* 37, 2006.
Annales Weissenburgenses. Edited by O. Holder-Egger, *Lamperti monachi Hersfeldensis Opera, MGH SSrG* [38]:9–57. Hanover, 1894.
Anselm of Canterbury. *Sancti Anselmi Cantuariensis archiepiscopi opera omnia.* Edited by F. S. Schmitt. 6 vols. Edinburgh: Thomas Nelson, 1946–63.
Anselm of Lucca. *Collectio canonum una cum collectione minore.* Edited by F. Thaner. Aalen: Scientia, 1915, rev. 1965.
Anselm of Lucca. *Liber contra Wibertum.* Edited by E. Bernheim, *MGH Ldl* I:517–28.

Auctor incertus (Isidorus Hispalensis?). *Appendix XXIV. 443 Liber glossarum. Ex variis Glossariis quae sub Isidori nomine circumferuntur collectus*, PL 83:1331–1378.
Bachrach, David S., and Bernard S. Bachrach. *Widukind of Corvey. Deeds of the Saxons*, Medieval Texts in Translation. Washington, DC: Catholic University of America Press, 2014.
Barton, Richard E. *The Deeds of Bishop Arnald of Le Mans and the Le Mans Commune, 1065–1081*, Internet Medieval Sourcebook, http://www.fordham.edu/halsall/source/1081gestaarnaldi.asp, 1998.
Bergman, Mary Bernardine. 'The Achievements of Otto (*Gesta Ottonis*), Ph. D. dissertation, St Louis University, 1942, 39–85'. In *Medieval Monarchy in Action: The German Empire from Henry I to Henry IV*, edited by Boyd H. Hill, 118–37. London: George Allen & Unwin, 1972.
Bernard, Auguste and Alexander Bruel, eds. *Recueil des chartes de l'abbaye de Cluny*. 6 vols. (Paris, 1876-1903).
Bernold of Constance. *Chronicon: Die Chroniken Bertholds von Reichenau und Bernolds von Konstanz, 1054–1100*. Edited by I. S. Robinson, *MGH SSrG* n.s. 14:383–540. Hanover, 2003.
Berthold of Reichenau. *Chronicon: Die Chroniken Bertholds von Reichenau und Bernolds von Konstanz, 1054–1100*. Edited by I. S. Robinson, *MGH SSrG* n.s. 14:161–381. Hanover, 2003.
Blum, Owen. J. *Letters of Peter Damian*. 6 vols. Washington, DC: Catholic University of America Press, 1989.
Böhmer, Johann Friedrich. *Regesta Imperii 2.1: (Sächsisches Haus 919–1024): Die Regesten des Kaiserreiches unter Heinrich I. und Otto I. 919-973*. Edited by E. Ottenthal and H. K. Kaminsky. Hildesheim: Böhlau, 1967.
Böhmer, Johann Friedrich. *Regesta Imperii 2.2: (Sächsisches Haus 919–1024): Die Regesten des Kaiserreiches unter Otto II*. Edited by H. L. Mikoletzky. Graz: Böhlau, 1950.
Böhmer, Johann Friedrich. *Regesta Imperii 2.3: (Sächsisches Haus 919–1024): Die Regesten des Kaiserreiches unter Otto III (980 (983)–1002)*. Edited by M. Uhlirz. Cologne: Böhlau, 1956.
Bonizo of Sutri. *Liber ad amicum*. Edited by E. Dümmler, *MGH Ldl* I:568–620.
Bonizo of Sutri. *Liber de vita Christiana*. Edited by E. Perels. Berlin: Weidman, 1930.
Brun of Querfurt. *Passio sancti Adalberti episcopi et martyris (Leidensgeschichte des heiligen Bischofs und Märtyrers Adalbert)*. Edited by Jerzy Strzelczyk and Lorenz Weinrich, *AQDG* 23:70–117. Darmstadt: Wissenschaftliche Buchgesellschaft, 2005.
Capitulare de villis. Edited by A. Boretius, *MGH Capitularia regum Francorum, Legum sectio* I:32:82–91. Hanover, 1883.
Capitulare missorum generale. Edited by A. Boretius, *MGH Capitularia regum Francorum, Legum sectio* I:33:91–99. Hanover, 1883.

Cartularium Langobardorum. Edited by G. H. Pertz, *MGH, Leges* 4:595–602, 1869.
Chronica monasterii Casinensis: (Die Chronik von Montecassino). Edited by H. Hoffmann, *MGH SS* 34, 1980.
Colombo, Alessandro. 'I diplomi ottoniani e adelaidini e la fondazione del monastero di S. Salvatore in Pavia'. In *Miscellanea Pavese*, edited by Renato Soriga, 1–39. Turin, 1932.
Cook, G. M. *The Life of Saint Epiphanius.* Washington, DC: Catholic Univ. of America, 1942.
Coronatio Iudithae Karoli II Filiae. Edited by A. Boretius, *MGH Capitularia regum Francorum, Legum sectio* 2.II:425–427. Hanover, 1883, 1893, repr. 1960.
Cowdrey, H. E. J. *The Register of Pope Gregory VII, 1073–1085: An English Translation.* Oxford: Oxford University Press, 2002.
Davis, R. *The Lives of the Eighth-Century Popes (Liber pontificalis): The Ancient Biographies of Nine Popes from AD 715 to AD 817.* Liverpool: Liverpool University Press, 1992.
De Heinrico. Edited by Karl Strecker, *Die Cambridger Lieder. MGH SSrG* [40]. Hanover, 1926.
Deusdedit. *Collectio canonum. Die Kanonessammlung des Kardinals Deusdedit.* Edited by Victor Wolf von Glanvell. Vol. 1. Aalen: Scientia, 1967.
Deusdedit. *Libellus contra invasores et symoniacos et reliquos schismaticos.* Edited by E. Sackur, *MGH Ldl* II: 292–365, 1892.
Dolan, C. J. *Widukind, the Monk of Corvey: Relating the Deeds of the Saxons. Historical Survey and Translation of Book III*, 1957.
Donizo. *Vita Mathildis (Vita di Matilde di Canossa).* Edited by Paolo Golinelli and V. Fumagalli. Milan: Jaca Book, 2008.
Drew, Katherine Fischer. *The Laws of the Salian Franks.* Philadelphia: University of Pennsylvania Press, 1991.
Drew, Katherine Fischer. *The Lombard Laws.* Philadelphia: University of Pennsylvania Press, 1973.
Duchesne, L. Le *Liber pontificalis.* 2nd ed. 3 vols. Paris: E. de Boccard, 1955.
Einhard. *Vita Karoli.* Edited by G. Waitz, *MGH SSrG* [25]. Hanover, 1911.
Encomium Emmae Reginae. Edited by A. Campbell and Simon Keynes. Cambridge: Cambridge University Press, 1949, repr. 1998.
Ennodius. *Panegyricus dictus clementissimo regi Theoderico.* Edited by Friederich Vogel, *Magni Felicis Ennodi Opera, MGH SS AA* 7:203–214, 1885.
Epistolae diversorum ad S. Hugonem, PL 159:931–946.
Ferrante, Joan. 'Anselm of Canterbury to Matilda of Tuscany, Prologue to the Prayers'. In *MWLL,* http://epistolae.ccnmtl.columbia.edu/letter/236.html, date accessed 16 May 2016.
Ferrante, Joan. 'Hugh, bishop of Die, archbishop of Lyon, to Matilda of Tuscany'. In *MWLL,* http://epistolae.ccnmtl.columbia.edu/letter/231.html, date accessed 15 May 2016.

Ferrante, Joan. 'Letter from Adelaide of Burgundy, Ottonian empress (995) to abbot Gozpert'. In *MWLL*, http://epistolae.ccnmtl.columbia.edu/letter/53.html, date accessed 15 May 2016.

Ferrante, Joan. 'Matilda of Tuscany, countess of Tuscany, duchess of Lorraine, to the Germans'. In *MWLL*, http://epistolae.ccnmtl.columbia.edu/letter/209.html, date accessed 20 August 2016.

FitzNigel (or Fitzneale), Richard. *Dialogus de Scaccario (The Course of the Exchequer)*. Translated by Charles Johnson, F. E. L. Carter and Diana E. Greenway. Oxford: Oxford University Press, 1983.

Flodoard of Reims. *Les Annales de Flodoard de Reims*. Edited by Philippe Lauer. Paris: Picard, 1905.

Foulke, W. D. *History of the Lombards*. Philadelphia: University of Pennsylvania Press, 1907, repr. 1974.

Fröhlich, Walter. *The Letters of Saint Anselm of Canterbury*. 3 vols. Kalamazoo: Cistercian Publications, 1990, 1993, 1994.

Froumond. *Die Tegernseer Briefsammlung*. Edited by Karl Strecker, *MGH Epp. sel.* 3:1–96. Berlin: Weidmann, 1925, repr. 1964.

Gerbert. *Epistolae (Die Briefsammlung Gerberts von Reims)*. Edited by F. Weigle, *MGH Briefe* 2. Berlin: Weidmann, 1966.

Gilsdorf, Sean. *The Epitaph of Adelheid*. In Gilsdorf, *Queenship and Sanctity*, 128–43.

Gilsdorf, Sean. *The 'Later Life' of Queen Mathilda*. In Gilsdorf, *Queenship and Sanctity*, 88–127.

Gilsdorf, Sean. *The 'Older Life' of Queen Mathilda*. In Gilsdorf, *Queenship and Sanctity*, 71–87.

Goez, E., and W. Goez, eds. *Die Urkunden und Briefe der Markgräfin Mathilde von Tuszien, MGH Laienfürsten- und Dynastenurkunden der Kaiserzeit* II. Hanover, 1998.

Gregory of Tours. *Miracles of the Bishop St. Martin*. In *Saints and their Miracles in Late Antique Gaul*, edited by Raymond Van Dam, 199–303. Princeton, NJ: Princeton University Press, 1993.

Gregory VII. *Registrum*. Edited by E. Caspar. 2nd ed. 2 vols, *MGH Epp. sel.* 2. Berlin: Weidmann, 1955.

Henry IV, *Diplomata*. eds D. von Gladiss and A. Gawlik, *Die Urkunden Heinrichs IV.* (*MGH* Dip. regum VI.1–3) Weimer (1941–78).

Henry of Huntingdon. *The Chronicle of Henry of Huntingdon*. Translated by Thomas Forester. London, 1853.

Herlihy, D. *On the Governance of the Palace*. In *The History of Feudalism*, 208–27. London: Macmillan, 1971.

Hincmar of Reims. *Hincmarus de ordine palatii*. Edited by Thomas Gross and Rudolf Schieffer, *MGH Fontes* 3. Hanover, 1980.

Hill, Boyd H. *Medieval Monarchy in Action: The German Empire from Henry I to Henry IV*. London: Allen & Unwin, 1972.

Hrotsvitha of Gandersheim. *Gesta Ottonis*. In *Hrotsvit: Opera omnia*. Edited by Walter Berschin, 273–305. Munich: K. G. Sur, 2001.
Hugh of Flavigny. *Chronicon Hugonis monachi Virdunensis et Divionensis Abbatis Flaviniacensis*. Edited by G. H. Pertz, *MGH SS* 8:280–502, 1848.
John of Mantua. *Iohannis Mantuani in Cantica canticorum et de sancta Maria Tractatus ad Comitissam Matildam*. Edited by B. Bischoff and B. Taeger, Spicilegium Friburgense 19. Freiburg: Universitätsverlag, 1973.
Jotsaldus. *Vita Odilonis abb. Cluniacensis*. Edited by G. Waitz, *MGH SS* 15/1:812–820.
Jotsaldus. *Vita Odilonis de Cluny*, PL 142:879–940.
King, P. D. *Charlemagne: Translated Sources*. Kendal: P. D. King, 1987.
Lampert of Hersfeld. *Lamperti Hersfeldensis Annales*. Edited by O. Holder-Egger, *Lamperti monachi Hersfeldensis Opera*, MGH SSrG [38]:3–304. Hanover, 1894.
Landulf Senior. *Historia Mediolanensis*. Edited by L. C. Bethmann and W. Wattenbach, *MGH SS* 8:32–100, 1848.
Lattin, Harriet Pratt. *The Letters of Gerbert, with His Papal Privileges as Sylvester II*. New York: Columbia University Press, 1961.
Leges Langobardorum, 643–866. Edited by Franz Beyerle. 2nd ed. Witzenhausen, 1962.
Lex Salica. Edited by Karl August Eckhardt, *MGH Leges* 4:2. Hanover: 1969.
Liber de unitate ecclesiae conservanda. Edited by W. Schwenkenbecher, *MGH Ldl* II: 173–291, 1892.
Liber miraculorum sancte Adelaide or 'Der Wunderbericht'. Edited by H. Paulhart, in *Die Lebensbeschreibung der Kaiserin Adelheid von Abt Odilo von Cluny*, 45–54. Graz and Cologne: Böhlau, 1962.
Liudprand of Cremona. *Antapodosis*. Edited by A. Bauer and R. Rau. 5th ed, *AQDG* 8:244–495. Darmstadt: Wissenschaftliche Buchgesellschaft, 2002.
Liudprand of Cremona. *Liber de ottone rege*. Edited by A. Bauer and R. Rau. 5th ed, *AQDG* 8:496–523. Darmstadt: Wissenschaftliche Buchgesellschaft, 2002.
Liudprand of Cremona. *Relatio de legatione Constantinopolitana*. Edited by A. Bauer and R. Rau. 5th ed, *AQDG* 8:524–89. Darmstadt: Wissenschaftliche Buchgesellschaft, 2002.
MacLean, Simon. *History and Politics in Late Carolingian and Ottonian Europe: The Chronicle of Regino of Prüm and Adalbert of Magdeburg*. Manchester: Manchester University Press, 2009.
Manegold of Lautenbach. *Liber ad Gebehardum*. Edited by K. Francke, *MGH Ldl* I: 308–430.
Mierow, Charles Christopher. *The Deeds of Frederick Barbarossa*. New York: Norton, 1966.
Mommsen, T. E., and K. F. Morrison. *Imperial Lives and Letters of the Eleventh Century*. New York: Columbia University Press, 1962.

Muratori, L. A. *Delle antichità estensi ed italiane*. Vol. 1. Modena, 1717.
Notae de Mathilda comitissa. Edited by P. E. Schramm, *MGH SS* 30/2:973–5, 1929.
Odilo of Cluny. *Epitaphium domine Adalheide auguste (Die Lebensbeschreibung der Kaiserin Adelheid von Abt Odilo von Cluny)*. Edited by H. Paulhart, (= *Festschrift zur Jahrtausendfeier der Kaiserkrönung Ottos des Großen*, vol. 2. [MIöG, Ergänzungsband 20/2]). Graz and Cologne: Böhlau, 1962.
Odilo of Cluny, *Epitaphium Adalheidae imperatricis*, ed. G. H. Pertz, *MGH SS* 4:633–45, 1841.
Odo of Cluny. *Collationum libri tres*, *PL* 133:517–638.
O'Sullivan, J. F. *The Writings of Salvian, the Presbyter*. In *The Fathers of the Church: A New Translation*. Washington, DC: Catholic University of America Press, 1947.
Otto I. *Diplomata*. Edited by T. Sickel, *Die Urkunden Konrad I., Heinrich I., und Otto I. (MGH Dip. regum I)*. Hanover (1879–1884), repr. Berlin, 1956.
Otto II. *Diplomata*. Edited by T. Sickel, *Die Urkunden Otto des II. (MGH Dip. regum* II.I). Hanover (1888), repr. Berlin, 1956.
Otto III. *Diplomata*. Edited by T. Sickel, *Die Urkunden Otto des III. (MGH Dip. regum* II.2). Hanover (1893), repr. Berlin, 1957.
Otto of Freising. *Gesta Frederici I. imperatoris*. Edited by Franz-Josef Schmale, *AQDG* 17. Darmstadt: Wissenschaftliche Buchgesellschaft, 1974.
Paschal II. 'Letter Sent by Paschal II, Pope'. *Epistolae: Medieval Women Latin Letters*. (*PL* 163 c.366, ep.408). In *MWLL*, http://epistolae.ccnmtl.columbia.edu/letter/234.html, date accessed 16 May 2016.
Paul of Bernried. *Vita Gregorii VII papae*. Edited by J. B. M. Watterich, in *Pontificum Romanorum vitae* 1:474–545. Aalen: Scientia Verlag, 1966.
Paul the Deacon. *Historia Langobardorum*. Edited by G. Waitz, *MGH SSrG* [48]. Hanover, 1878.
Peter Damian. *Epistolae*. Edited by K. Reindel. 4 vols, *Die Briefe des Petrus Damiani, MGH Briefe*. Munich, 1983–93.
Peter of Blois. *Epistolae, PL* 207:1–560.
Pseudo-Bardo. *Anselmi episcopi Lucensis vitae primariae fragmenta*. Edited by W. Arndt, *MGH SS* 20:692–6, 1868.
Pseudo-Bardo. *Vita Anselmi episcopi Lucensis*. Edited by R. Wilmans, *MGH SS* 12:13–35, 1856.
Quellen zur geschichte Kaiser Heinrichs IV. Edited by Franz-Josef Schmale and Irene Schmale-Ott. 2nd ed, *AQDG* 12. Darmstadt: Wissenschaftliche Buchgesellschaft, 1968.
Rahewin. *Gesta Friderici imperatoris, libri III et IV*. Edited by G. Waitz and B. von Simpson, *MGH SSrG* [46]:162–346, 1912.
Rangerius of Lucca. *Vita metrica sancti Anselmi Lucensis episcopi*. Edited by E. Sackur, G. Schwartz and B. Schmeidler, *MGH SS* 30/2:1152–1307, 1929.

Relatio translationis corporis sancti Geminiani. Edited by Giulio Bertoni, *RIS2* VI/1. Bologna, 1907.

Richer. *Histories. Richer of Saint-Rémi.* Translated by Justin Lake. 2 vols, Dumbarton Oaks Medieval Library. Cambridge, MA: Harvard University Press, 2011.

Rivers, T. J. *Laws of the Salian and Ripuarian Franks.* New York: AMS Press, 1986.

Robinson, I. S. *Book to a Friend.* In *The Papal Reform of the Eleventh Century*, 158–261.

Robinson, I. S. *Bernold of St Blasien, Chronicle.* In *Eleventh-Century Germany: The Swabian Chronicles*, 245–337. Manchester: Manchester University Press, 2008.

Robinson, I. S. *The Papal Reform of the Eleventh Century: Lives of Pope Leo IX and Pope Gregory VII.* Manchester: Manchester University Press, 2004.

Sala, Giuliano, and Giorgio Vedovelli. *Vita e miracoli di Adelaide di Borgogna. Epitaphium Adalheidae imp. Liber miraculorum.* Torri del Benaco, 1990.

Salvian of Marseille. *Salviani presbyteri Massiliensis libri qui supersunt.* Edited by C. Halm, *MGH AA* 1.1. Berlin: Weidmann, 1877.

Schiaparelli, L., ed. *I diplomi di Ugo e di Lotario, di Berengario II e di Adalberto.* Vol. 1: *Diplomi secolo X.* Fonti per la storia d'Italia 38. Rome, 1924.

Sidonius Apollinaris. *Poems and Letters.* Edited by W. B. Anderson. 2 vols. London: W. Heinemann, 1936, repr. 1965.

Syrus of Cluny. *Vita sancti Maioli.* Edited by Dominique Iogna-Prat. In *Agni Immaculati*, 163–285. Paris: Éditions du Cerf, 1988.

Thietmar of Merseburg. *Chronicon.* Edited by Werner Trillmich. 8th ed, *AQDG* 9. Darmstadt: Wissenschaftliche Buchgesellschaft, 2002.

Thorpe, L. G. M. *Life of Charlemagne.* In *Two Lives of Charlemagne.* Harmondsworth: Penguin, 1969.

Tschan, Francis J. *History of the Archbishops of Hamburg-Bremen.* New York: Columbia University Press, 1959.

Urban II. 'Letter Sent by Urban II, Pope'. *Epistolae: Medieval Women Latin Letters.* (*PL* 151:527–28, ep.267). In *MWLL*, http://epistolae.ccnmtl.columbia.edu/letter/233.html, date accessed 12 August 2016.

Die Urkunden der burgundischen Rudolfinger. Edited by T. Schieffer and H. E. Mayer, *MGH, Regum Burgundiae e stirpe Rudolfina Diplomata.* Munich, 1977.

Die Urkunden und Briefe der Markgräfin Mathilde von Tuszien, eds E. Goez and W. Goez, *MGH Laienfürsten- und Dynastenurkunden der Kaiserzeit II*, Hanover (1998).

Vedriani, Lodovico. *Historia dell'antichissima città di Modena.* 2 vols. Modena, 1666, 1667.

Vita Heinrici IV. Imperatoris. Edited by W. Eberhard, *MGH SSrG* [58]. Hanover and Leipzig, 1899.

Vita Liutbirgae virginis (Das Leben der Liutbirg). Edited by O. Menzel, *Deutsches Mittelalter: Kritische Studientexte des Reichsinstitut für ältere deutsche Geschichtskunde (MGH)* 3. Leipzig: Karl W. Hiersemann, 1937.

Vita Mathildis reginae antiquior (Die Lebensbeschreibungen der Königin Mathilde). Edited by B. Schütte, *MGH SSrG* [66:107–42]. Hanover, 1994.

Vita Mathildis reginae posterior (Die Lebensbeschreibungen der Königin Mathilde). Edited by B. Schütte, *MGH SSrG* [66:143–202]. Hanover, 1994.

Vitae S. Heinrici additamentum. Edited by G. H. Pertz, *MGH SS* 4:816–820, 1841.

Warner, David A. *Epitaph of the August Lady, Adelheid.* Edited by T. Head, *Medieval Hagiography: An Anthology.* New York: Routledge, 2001.

Warner, David A. *Ottonian Germany: The Chronicon of Thietmar of Merseburg.* Manchester: Manchester University Press, 2001.

Widukind of Corvey. *Res gestae Saxonicae.* Edited by A. Bauer and R. Rau. 5th ed, *AQDG* 8. Darmstadt: Wissenschaftliche Buchgesellschaft, 2002.

Wilmart, André. 'Cinque textes de prière composés par Anselme de Lucques pour la comtesse Mathilde'. *Revue d'ascétique et de mystique* 19 (1938, reedited 1964): 23–72 (text, 49–72).

Wilson, Katharina M. *Hrotsvit of Gandersheim: A Florilegium of her Works*, Library of Medieval Women. Woodbridge, Suffolk: D.S. Brewer, 1998.

Wipo. *Gesta Chuonradi II. imperatoris.* Edited by Werner Trillmich and Rudolf Buchner. 2nd ed, *AQDG* 11:507–613. Darmstadt: Wissenschaftliche Buchgesellschaft, 1968.

Wood, R. F. 'The Three Books of the Deeds of the Saxons, by Widukind of Corvey'. PhD diss., University of California, Berkeley, 1949.

Secondary Sources

Aird, William M. *Robert Curthose: Duke of Normandy (c.1050–1134).* Woodbridge: Boydell Press, 2008.

Althoff, Gerd. *Family, Friends and Followers: The Political Importance of Group Bonds in the Early Middle Ages.* New York: Cambridge University Press, 2004.

Althoff, Gerd. '*Ira Regis*: Prolegomena to a History of Royal Anger'. In *Anger's Past: The Social Uses of an Emotion in the Middle Ages*, edited by Barbara H. Rosenwein, 59–74. Ithaca, NY: Cornell University Press, 1998.

Althoff, Gerd. 'Königsherrschaft und Konfliktbewältigung im 10. und 11. Jahrhundert'. *FMSt* 23 (1989): 265–90.

Althoff, Gerd. *Otto III.* Translated by Phyllis G. Jestice. Pennsylvania: Pennsylvania State University Press, 2003.

Althoff, Gerd. 'Probleme um die dos der Koniginnen im 10. und 11. Jahrhundert'. In *Veuves et veuvage dans le haut Moyen Âge*, edited by M. Parisse, 123–33. Paris: Picard, 1993.

Althoff, Gerd. 'Saxony and the Elbe Slavs in the Tenth Century'. *NCMH* 3 (1999): 267–92.
Althoff, Gerd. 'Vormundschaft, Erzieher, Lehrer—Einflusse auf Otto III'. In von Euw, *Kaiserin Theophanu*, vol. 2, 277–89.
Althoff, Gerd, Johannes Fried, and Patrick J. Geary. *Medieval Concepts of the Past: Ritual, Memory, Historiography*. Washington, DC: Cambridge University Press, 2002.
Amargier, Paul. 'Saint Maïeul et sainte Adélaïde, une amitié'. In *Saint Maïeul et son temps. Millénaire de la mort de Saint Maïeul, 4ᵉ abbé de Cluny, 994–1994*, 185–89. Digne-les-Bains, 1997.
Ashley, Scott. 'The Lay Intellectual in Anglo-Saxon England'. In *Lay Intellectuals in the Carolingian World*, edited by Patrick Wormald and Janet Nelson, 218–45. Cambridge: Cambridge University Press, 2007.
Austin-Broos, Diane J. *Arrernte Present, Arrernte Past: Invasion, Violence, and Imagination in Indigenous Central Australia*. Chicago: University of Chicago Press, 2009.
Bachrach, Bernard S. 'The Angevin Strategy of Castle Building in the Reign of Fulk Nerra, 987–1040'. *AHA* 88, no. 3 (1983): 533–60.
Bachrach, Bernard S. 'Fulk Nerra and His Accession as Count of Anjou'. In *State-Building in Medieval France*, VI.331–42.
Bachrach, Bernard S. *Fulk Nerra, the Neo-Roman Consul, 987–1040: A Political Biography of the Angevin Count*. Berkeley: University of California Press, 1993.
Bachrach, Bernard S. 'Military Lands in Historical Perspective'. *HSJ* 9 (1997): 95–122.
Bachrach, Bernard S. 'On Roman Ramparts 300–1300'. In *The Cambridge Illustrated History of Warfare: The Triumph of the West*, edited by G. Parker, 64–91. Cambridge: Cambridge University Press, 2008.
Bachrach, Bernard S. *State-Building in Medieval France: Studies in Early Angevin History*. Aldershot: Variorum, 1994.
Bachrach, David S. 'The Military Organization of Ottonian Germany, c. 900–1018: The Views of Bishop Thietmar of Merseburg'. *JMH* 72, no. 4 (2008): 1061–88.
Bachrach, David S. *Warfare in Tenth-Century Germany*. Woodbridge: Boydell Press, 2012.
Bagge, Sverre. *Kings, Politics, and the Right Order of the World in German Historiography c. 950–1150*. Leiden: Brill, 2002.
Bainton, Roland Herbert. *Christian Attitudes toward War and Peace: A Historical Survey and Critical Re-evaluation*. London: Hodder and Stoughton, 1961.
Bak, János M. 'Medieval Symbology of the State: Percy E. Schramm's Contribution'. In *Studying Medieval Rulers and Their Subjects: Central Europe and Beyond*, edited by B. Nagy and G. Klaniczay, I.33–I.63. Farnham: Ashgate Variorum, 2010.

Bange, P. 'The Image of Women of the Nobility in the German Chronicles'. In Davids, *The Empress Theophano*, 150–68.
Banti, O. '"Civitas" e "commune" nelle fonti italiane dei seconli xi e xii'. *Critica storica* 9 (1972): 568–84.
Barlow, Frank. *Edward the Confessor*. London: Eyre & Spottiswoode, 1970.
Barthélemy, Dominique. *The Serf, the Knight, and the Historian*. Ithaca: Cornell University Press, 2009.
Barthélemy, Dominique. *La Société dans le comté de Vendôme de l'an mil au XIVe siècle*. Paris: Fayard, 1993.
Barton, Richard E. *Lordship in the County of Maine, c.890–1160*. Woodbridge: Boydell, 2004.
Bäuml, Franz H. 'Varieties and Consequences of Medieval Literacy and Illiteracy'. *Speculum* 55, no. 2 (Apr., 1980): 237–65.
Beach, Alison I. *Women as Scribes: Book Production and Monastic Reform in Twelfth-Century Bavaria*. Cambridge: Cambridge University Press, 2004.
Bedos-Rezak, Brigitte, ed. *Form and Order in Medieval France: Studies in Social and Quantitative Sigillography*. Aldershot: Variorum, 1993.
Bedos-Rezak, Brigitte. 'The King Enthroned, a New Theme in Anglo-Saxon Royal Iconography: The Seal of Edward the Confessor and its Political Implications'. In *Form and Order in Medieval France*, IV.53–IV.88.
Bedos-Rezak, Brigitte. 'Suger and the Symbolism of Royal Power: The Seal of Louis VII'. In *Form and Order in Medieval France*, V.1–V.18.
Bedos-Rezak, Brigitte. 'Women, Seals, and Power in Medieval France, 1150–1350'. In *Form and Order in Medieval France*, IX.61–IX.82.
Beem, Charles, ed. *The Royal Minorities of Medieval and Early Modern England*. New York: Palgrave Macmillan, 2008.
Bernhardt, John William. 'Concepts and Practice of Empire in Ottonian Germany (950–1024)'. In Weiler, *Representations of Power*, 141–64.
Bernhardt, John William. *Itinerant Kingship and Royal Monasteries in Early Medieval Germany, c. 936–1075*. Cambridge: Cambridge University Press, 1993.
Berman, Constance Hoffman, ed. *Medieval Religion: New Approaches*. New York and London: Routledge, 2005.
Bertolini, Margherita Giuliana. 'I Canossiani e la loro attività giurisdizionale con particolare riguardo alla Toscana'. In Capitani, *Margherita Giuliana Bertolini*, 41–84.
Bertolini, Margherita Giuliana. 'Note di genealogia e di storia canossiana'. In Capitani, *Margherita Giuliana Bertolini*, 1–30.
Beumann, Helmut. *Die Ottonen*. 2nd ed. Stuttgart: W. Kohlhammer, 1991.
Beumann, Helmut. *Widukind von Korvei*. Weimar, 1950.
Beyreuther, Gerald. 'Kaiserin Adelheid: "Mutter der Königreiche"'. In Uitz, *Herrscherinnen und Nonnen*, 43–79.

Bisson, Thomas N. *The Crisis of the Twelfth Century: Power, Lordship, and the Origins of European Government*. Princeton, NJ: Princeton University Press, 2009.
Bisson, Thomas N. 'Review of *Die Urkunden und Briefe der Markgräfin Mathilde von Tuszien*, by E. Goez, W. Goez'. *Speculum* 76, no. 2 (April 2001): 456–58.
Black-Veldtrup, Mechtild. *Kaiserin Agnes (1043–1077): Quellenkritische Studien*, Münstersche Historische Forschungen 7. Cologne: Böhlau, 1995.
Bloch, Marc. *Feudal Society*. Translated by L. A. Manyon. 2nd ed. London: Routledge & Kegan, 1962.
Bloomer, W. Martin. *The School of Rome: Latin Studies and the Origins of Liberal Education*. Berkeley: University of California Press, 2011.
Blumenthal, Uta-Renate. *The Early Councils of Pope Paschal II, 1100–1110*. Toronto: Pontifical Institute of Mediaeval Studies, 1978.
Bolton, Brenda. '*Totius christianitatis caput*. The Pope and the Princes'. In *Adrian IV The English Pope (1154–1159): Studies and Texts*, edited by Brenda Bolton and Anne J. Duggan, 105–56. Aldershot: Ashgate, 2003.
Bonnassie, Pierre. 'A Family of the Barcelona Countryside and Its Economic Activities Around the Year 1000'. In *Early Medieval Society*, edited by Sylvia L. Thrupp, 103–23. New York: Appleton-Century-Crofts, 1967.
Bottazzi, Gianluca. 'Viabilità medievale nella collina e montagna parmense tra i torrenti Parma ed Enza'. In *SM IV*, 153–206.
Bouchard, Constance Brittain. 'The Bosonids or Rising to Power in the Late Carolingian Age'. *French Historical Studies* 15, no. 3 (1988): 407–31.
Bouchard, Constance Brittain. 'Burgundy and Provence, 879–1032'. *NCMH* 3 (1999): 328–45.
Bouchard, Constance Brittain. *Sword, Miter, and Cloister: Nobility and the Church in Burgundy, 980–1198*. Ithaca, NY, and London: Cornell University Press, 1987.
Bouchard, Constance Brittain. *'Those of My Blood': Constructing Noble Families in Medieval Francia*. Philadelphia: University of Pennsylvania Press, 2001.
Bougard, François. 'Public Power and Authority'. In La Rocca, *Italy in the Early Middle Ages*, 34–58.
Bourgard, François. 'Public Power and Authority'. In La Rocca, *Italy in the Early Middle Ages*, 34–58.
Brown, Warren. *Unjust Seizure: Conflict, Interest and Authority in an Early Medieval Society*. Ithaca, NY: Cornell University Press, 2001.
Brubaker, Leslie and Julia M. H. Smith, eds. *Gender in the Early Medieval World: East and West, 300–900*. Cambridge: Cambridge University Press, 2004.
Bruce, Scott G. 'Local Sanctity and Civic Typology in Early Medieval Pavia: The Example of the Cult of Abbot Maiolus of Cluny'. In *Cities, Texts, and Social Networks, 400–1500: Experiences and Perceptions of Medieval Urban Space*, edited by Caroline Goodson, Anne Elisabeth Lester and Carol Symes, 177–92. Farnham, Surrey: Ashgate, 2010.

Buc, Philippe. 'Italian Hussies and German Matrons. Liutprand of Cremona on Dynastic Legitimacy'. *FMSt* 29 (1995): 207–25.
Bull, Marcus Graham, Norman Housley, P. W. Edbury, and Jonathan Phillips. *The Experience of Crusading, Volume 1: Western Approaches*. 2 vols. Cambridge: Cambridge University Press, 2003.
Bullough, D. A. 'After Charlemagne: The Empire under the Ottonians'. In *The Dawn of European Civilization: The Dark Ages*, edited by T. D. Rice, 299–326. New York: McGraw-Hill, 1965.
Bullough, D. A. 'Early Medieval Social Groupings: The Terminology of Kinship'. *P&P*, no. 45 (1969): 3–18.
Calisse, Carlo. *History of Italian Law*. Translated by Layton B. Register. Boston: Little, Brown, and Company, 1928.
Campbell, Deslee. 'The Iconography of Women: A Study of the Art of Byzantium and the Byzantine-Influenced Western Mediterranean, AD 395-1204'. PhD diss., University of Sydney, 2008.
Cantelli, Silvia. 'Le preghiere a Maria di Anselmo da Lucca'. In *Sant'Anselmo, Mantova e la lotta per le Investiture*, edited by Paolo Golinelli, 291–9. Bologna: Pàtron, 1987.
Capitani, Ovidio and Paolo Golinelli, Bertolini (eds). *Margherita Giuliana Bertolini: studi canossiani*. Bologna: Pàtron, 2004.
Capitani, Ovidio. *Storia dell'Italia medievale*. 3rd ed. Rome: Laterza, 1992.
Castaldini, D., M. Marchetti, and A. Cardarelli. 'Some Notes on Geomorphological and Archaeological Aspects in the Central Po Plain'. In *Ol' Man River: Geo-Archaeological Aspects of Rivers and River Plains*, edited by M. De Dapper, F. Vermeulen, S. Deprez and D. Taelman, 193–212. Ghent: Academia Press, 2009.
Castelnuovo, Guido. 'L'aristocrazia del Vaud sino alla conquista Sabauda (inizio XI–metà XIII secolo)'. *Bolletino Storico-Bibliografico Subalpino* 86 (1988): 469–522.
Catling, J. M. *A History of Women's Writing in Germany, Austria and Switzerland*. Cambridge: Cambridge University Press, 1999.
Chaplais, Pierre. 'XV The Authenticity of the Royal Anglo-Saxon Diplomas of Exeter'. In *Essays in Medieval Diplomacy and Administration*, XV.1–XV.34. London: Hambledon Press, 1981.
Cimino, Roberta. 'Angelberga: il monastero di San Sisto di Piacenza e il corso del piume Po'. In *Il patrimonio delle regine: beni del fisco e politica regia fra IX e X secolo*, edited by Tiziana Lazzari. *Reti Medievali Rivista* 13, no. 2 (2012): 141–62. doi:10.6092/1593-2214/365.
City Population Melara (Rovigo), http://www.citypopulation.de/php/italy-veneto.php?cityid=029032, date accessed 28 July 2016.
Clayton, Mary. *The Cult of the Virgin Mary in Anglo-Saxon England*. Cambridge: Cambridge University Press, 1990.

Codea, Krista. 'Intervenienten und Petenten vornehmlich für lothringische Empfänger in den Diplomen der liudolfingischen Herrscher (919–1024). Eine prosopographische Darstellung'. PhD diss., Rheinischen Friedrich-Wilhelms-Universität, 2008.

Cohen, Adam. S. *The Uta Codex: Art, Philosophy, and Reform in Eleventh-Century Germany*. University Park: Pennnsylvania State University Press, 2000.

Constable, Giles, ed. *The Abbey of Cluny: A Collection of Essays to Mark the Eleventh-Hundredth Anniversary of Its Foundation*. Berlin: LIT, 2010.

Constable, Giles. 'Cluniac Reform in the Eleventh Century'. In *The Abbey of Cluny*, 81–111.

Constable, Giles. 'Cluny and the Investiture Controversy'. In *The Abbey of Cluny*, 179–86.

Constable, Giles. 'Liturgical Commemoration'. In Constable, *The Abbey of Cluny*, 121–30.

Constable, Giles. *Three Studies in Medieval Religious and Social Thought*. Cambridge: Cambridge University Press, 1995.

Corbet, Patrick, Monique Gouillet and Dominique Iogna-Prat, eds. *Adélaïde de Bourgogne: Genèse et représentations d'une sainteté impériale*. Dijon: Université de Dijon, 2002.

Corbet, Patrick. 'Les impératrices ottoniennes et le modèle marial. Autour de l'ivorie du château Sforza de Milan'. In *Marie: Le culte de la Vierge dans la société médiévale*, edited by Dominique Iogna-Prat, E. Palazzo and D. Russo, 109–35. Paris: Beauchesne, 1996.

Corbet, Patrick. *Les saints ottoniens: sainteté dynastique, sainteté royale et sainteté féminine autour de l'an Mil*. Sigmaringen: Thorbecke, 1986.

Costambeys, Marios, Matthew Innes, and Simon MacLean. *The Carolingian World*. Cambridge: Cambridge University Press, 2011.

Cowan, Mairi. 'The Spiritual Ties of Kinship in Pre-Reformation Scotland'. In *Finding the Family in Medieval and Early Modern Scotland*, edited by E. Ewan and J. Nugent, 115–25. Aldershot: Ashgate, 2008.

Cowdrey, H. E. J. *The Age of Abbot Desiderius: Montecassino, the Papacy, and the Normans in the Eleventh and Early Twelfth Centuries*. Oxford: Clarendon Press, 1983.

Cowdrey, H. E. J. 'Christianity and the Morality of Warfare during the First Century of Crusading'. In *The Experience of Crusading, Volume 1: Western Approaches*, edited by Marcus Graham Bull and Norman Housley, 175–92. Cambridge: Cambridge University Press, 2003.

Cowdrey, H. E. J. *The Cluniacs and the Gregorian Reform*. Oxford: Clarendon Press, 1970.

Cowdrey, H. E. J. *Pope Gregory VII, 1073–1085*. Oxford: Clarendon Press, 1998.

Cowdrey, H. E. J. 'Review of *Die Urkunden und Briefe der Markgräfin Mathilde von Tuszien*, by E. Goez and W. Goez'. *JEH* 51, no. 3 (2000): 604–5.

Cushing, Kathleen G. 'Events that Led to Sainthood: Sanctity and the Reformers in the Eleventh Century'. In *Belief and Culture in the Middle Ages: Studies Presented to Henry Mayr-Harting*, edited by Richard Gameson and Henrietta Leyser, 186–96. Oxford: Oxford University Press, 2001.

Cushing, Kathleen G. *Papacy and Law in the Gregorian Revolution: The Canonistic Work of Anselm of Lucca.* Oxford: Clarendon Press, 1998.

Dameron, George W. *Episcopal Power and Florentine Society, 1000–1320.* Cambridge, MA: Harvard University Press, 1991.

Dannenberg, Hermann. *Die deutschen Münzen der sächsischen und fränkischen Kaiserzeit.* 4 vols. Berlin: Weidmann, 1876–1905.

Dark, K. R. *Civitas to Kingdom: British Political Continuity 300–800.* London: Leicester University Press, 1999.

Davids, Adelbert, ed. *The Empress Theophano: Byzantium and the West at the Turn of the First Millennium.* Cambridge: Cambridge University Press, 1995.

Davies, Wendy, and Paul Fouracre, eds. *Property and Power in the Early Middle Ages.* Cambridge: Cambridge University Press, 1995.

Dempsey, John A. 'From Holy War to Patient Endurance: Henry IV, Matilda of Tuscany, and the Evolution of Bonizo of Sutri's Response to Heretical Princes'. In *War and Peace: Critical Issues in European Societies and Literature 800–1800*, edited by Albrecht Classen and N. Margolis, 217–52. Berlin: De Gruyter, 2011.

Deutsch-Englisch-Wörtenburh. http//www.dict.cc/.

Du Cange et al., *Glossarium mediæ et infirmæ latinitatis.* Nova ed. Niort: L. Favr, 1678, 1883–1887, http://ducange.enc.sorbonne.fr/.

Duby, Georges. *The Early Growth of the European Economy: Warriors and Peasants from the Seventh to the Twelfth Century.* London: Weidenfeld & Nicolson, 1974.

Duby, Georges. *The Knight, the Lady and the Priest: The Making of Modern Marriage in Medieval France.* Harmondsworth, UK: Penguin, 1985.

Duby, Georges. 'Lineage, Nobility and Knighthood: The Mâconnais in the Twelfth Century–A Review'. In *The Chivalrous Society*, 59–80. London: Arnold, 1977.

Duby, Georges. *Medieval Marriage: Two Models from Twelfth-Century France.* Translated by Elborg Forster. Baltimore and London: Johns Hopkins University Press, 1978.

Duggan, Anne, ed. *Queens and Queenship in Medieval Europe, Proceedings of a Conference held at King's College London, April 1995.* Woodbridge: Boydell, 1997.

Eads, Valerie. 'The Geography of Power: Matilda of Tuscany and the Strategy of Active Defense'. In *Crusaders, Condottieri and Cannon: Medieval Warfare in Societies around the Mediterranean*, edited by L. J. Andrew Villalon and Donald J. Kagay, 355–87. Leiden: Brill, 2002.

Eads, Valerie. 'The Last Italian Expedition of Henry IV: Re-reading the *Vita Mathildis* of Donizone of Canossa'. *JoMMH* 8, no. 2 (2010): 23–68.
Eads, Valerie. 'Means, Motive, Opportunity: Medieval Women and the Recourse to Arms'. *Paper Presented at The Twentieth Barnard Medieval & Renaissance Conference 'War and Peace in the Middle Ages & Renaissance'* (2 December 2006), http://www.deremilitari.org/wp-content/uploads/2012/09/Eads-MeansMotivesOpp.pdf, date accessed 20 August 2016.
Edsall, Mary Agnes. 'Learning from the Exemplar: Anselm's *Prayers and Meditations* and the Charismatic Text'. *Mediaeval Studies* 72 (2010): 161–96.
Ehlers, Caspar. 'Having the King—Losing the King'. *Viator* 33 (2002): 1–42.
Elliott, Dyan. 'The Priest's Wife: Female Erasure and the Gregorian Reform'. In Berman, *Medieval Religion*, 123–55.
Engels, Odilo. 'Theophano, the Western Empress from the East'. In Davids, *The Empress Theophano*, 28–48.
Enright, Michael J. *Lady with a Mead Cup: Ritual, Prophecy, and Lordship in the European Warband from La Tène to the Viking Age*. Dublin: Four Courts, 1996.
Erdmann, Carl. 'The Ottonian Empire as *Imperium Romanum*'. In *The Rise of the First Reich: Germany in the Tenth Century*, edited by Boyd H. Hill, 96–101. New York: Wiley, 1969.
Erkens, Franz-Reiner. 'Die Frau als Herrscherin in ottonisch-frühsalischer Zeit'. In von Euw, *Kaiserin Theophanu*, vol. 2, 245–60.
Everett, Nicholas. *Literacy in Lombard Italy, c. 568–774*. Cambridge: Cambridge University Press, 2003.
Everett, Nicholas. 'Paulinus of Aquileia's *Sponsio episcoporum*: Written Oaths and Ecclesiastical Discipline in Carolingian Italy'. In *Textual Cultures of Medieval Italy*, edited by William Robins, 167–216. Toronto: University of Toronto, 2011.
Von Euw, Anton and Peter Schreiner, *Kaiserin Theophanu: Begegnung des Ostens und Westens um die Wende des ersten Jahrtausands. Gedegnung des Kölner Schnütgen-Museums zum 1000. Todesjahr der Kaiserin*. 2 Vols. Cologne: Schnütgen-Museum, 1991.
Ferrante, Joan. *To the Glory of Her Sex: Women's Roles in the Composition of Medieval Texts*. Bloomington: Indiana University Press, 1997.
Ferrara, Roberto. 'Gli anni di Matilde (1072–1115). Osservazioni sulla "cancelleria" canossiana'. In *I poteri dei Canossa*, edited by Paolo Golinelli, 89–98.
Fleckenstein, Josef. *Early Medieval Germany*. Translated by Bernard S. Smith. Amsterdam: North-Holland, 1978.
Fleckenstein, Josef. *Die Hofkapelle der deutschen Konige: Die Hofkapelle im Rahmen der ottonisch-salischen Reichskirche*. 2 vols. Vol. 2. Stuttgart: Hiersemann, 1966.
Fleckenstein, Josef. 'Hofkapelle und Kanzlei unter der Kaiserin Theophanu'. In von Euw, *Kaiserin Theophanu*, vol. 2, 305–10.

Folz, Robert. *The Concept of Empire in Western Europe from the Fifth to the Fourteenth Century*. London: Edward Arnold, 1969.
Fößel, Amalie. *Die Königin im mittelalterlichen Reich. Herrschaftsausübung, Herrschaftsrechte, Handlungsspielräume*. Mittelalter-Forschungen 4. Stuttgart: Jan Thorbecke, 2000.
France, John. 'Holy War and Holy Men: Erdmann and the Lives of the Saints'. In *The Experience of Crusading, Volume 1: Western Approaches*, edited by Marcus Graham Bull and Norman Housley, 193–208. Cambridge: Cambridge University Press, 2003.
Freed, John B. 'German Source Collections: The Archdiocese of Salzburg as a Case Study'. In *Medieval Women and the Sources of Medieval History*, edited by Joel Thomas Rosenthal, 80–121. Athens, GA: University of Georgia Press, 1990.
Freed, John B. *Noble Bondsmen: Ministerial Marriages in the Archdiocese of Salzburg, 1100–1343*. Ithaca, NY: Cornell University Press, 1995.
Fried, Johannes. 'Theophanu und die Slawen. Bemerkungen zur Ostpolitik der Kaiserin'. In von Euw, *Kaiserin Theophanu*, vol. 2, 361–70.
Fulton, Rachel. *From Judgment to Passion: Devotion to Christ and the Virgin Mary, 800–1200*. New York: Columbia University Press, 2002.
Fulton, Rachel. 'Praying with Anselm at Admont: A Meditation on Practice'. *Speculum* 81, no. 3 (2006): 700–33.
Fumagalli, Vito. 'Canossa', *LMA* 2: 1442–43.
Fumagalli, Vito. 'Da Sigifredo "De Comitatu Lucensi" a Adalberto-Atto di Canossa'. In *SM II*, 59–65.
Fumagalli, Vito. *Le origini di una grande dinastia feudale Adalberto-Atto di Canossa*. Tübingen: Max Niemeyer, 1971.
Fumagalli, Vito. *Terra e società nell'Italia padana, I secoli IX e X*. Turin, 1976.
Ganz, David. 'Einhard's Charlemagne: The Characterisation of Greatness'. In *Charlemagne: Empire and Society*, edited by Joanna Story, 38–51. Manchester: Manchester University Press, 2005.
Garver, Valerie L. *Women and Aristocratic Culture in the Carolingian World*. Ithaca, NY: Cornell University Press, 2009.
Gasperi, Gianfranco, and Maurizio Pellegrini. 'Strutture geologiche è idrografia della bassa Pianura Modenes'. In *Mirandola e le terre del basso corso del Secchia dal Medioevo all'età contemporanea*, edited by Giordano Bertuzzi, 97–114. Modena, 1984.
Geary, Patrick J. *Phantoms of Remembrance: Memory and Oblivion at the End of the First Millennium*. Princeton, NJ: Princeton University Press, 1994.
Georgi, Wolfgang. 'Ottonianum und Heiratsurkunde 962/972'. In von Euw, *Kaiserin Theophanu*, vol. 2, 135–60.
Ghirardini, Lino Lionello. *Storia critica di Matilde di Canossa: problemi (e misteri) della più grande Donna della storia d'Italia*. Modena: Aedes Muratoriana, 1989.

Gibbs, Marion E., and Sidney M. Johnson. *Medieval German Literature*. New York: Routledge, 2000.
Gilsdorf, Sean. *Queenship and Sanctity: The Lives of Mathilda and the Epitaph of Adelheid*. Washington, DC: Catholic University of America Press, 2004.
Gilsdorf, Sean. *The Favor of Friends: Intercession and Aristocratic Politics in Carolingian and Ottonian Europe*. Leiden: Brill, 2014.
Glass, Dorothy F. 'The Bishops of Piacenza'. In *The Bishop Reformed: Studies of Episcopal Power and Culture in the Central Middle Ages*, edited by J. S. Ott and A. T. Jones, 219–36. Aldershot: Ashgate, 2007.
Glass, Dorothy F. *The Sculpture of Reform in North Italy, ca. 1095–1130: History and Patronage of Romanesque Façades*. Farnham, England: Ashgate, 2010.
Glocker, Winfrid. *Die Verwandten der Ottonen und ihre Bedeutung in der Politik. Studien zur Familienpolitik und zur Genealogie des sächsischen Kaiserhauses*. Cologne and Vienna: Böhlau, 1989.
Goez, Elke. *Beatrix von Canossa und Tuszien: Eine Untersuching zur Geschichte des 11. Jahrhunderts*. Sigmaringen: Jan Thorbecke, 1995.
Goez, Elke. *Beatrix von Canossa und Tuszien: Eine Untersuching zur Geschichte des 11. Jahrhunderts*. Sigmaringen: Jan Thorbecke, 1995: Register, 192–235.
Le Goff, Jacques. 'The Symbolic Ritual of Vassalage'. In *Time, Work and Culture in the Middle Ages*, edited by J. Le Goff, 237–87. Chicago: University of Chicago Press, 1980.
Golinelli, Paolo, ed. *I poteri dei Canossa. Da Reggio Emilia all'Europa. Atti del convegno internazionale di studi (Reggio Emilia-Carpineti, 29–31 ottobre 1992)*. Bologna: Pàtron, 1994.
Golinelli, Paolo. *Adelaide. Regina Santa d'Europa*, Donna d'Oriente e d'Occidente. Milan: Jaca Book, 2001.
Golinelli, Paolo. *L'ancella di san Pietro: Matilde di Canossa e la Chiesa*. Milan: Jaca Book, 2015.
Golinelli, Paolo. 'Donizone e il suo poema per Matilde'. In *Vita di Matilde di Canossa*, edited by Paolo Golinelli, ix–xvi. Milan: Jaca Book, 2008.
Golinelli, Paolo. *I mille volti di Matilde di Canossa: Immagini di un mito nei secoli*. Milan: Frederico Motta Editore, 2003.
Golinelli, Paolo. *Matilde e i Canossa*. 2nd ed. Milan: Mursia, 2004.
Golinelli, Paolo. 'Modena 1106: istantanee dal Medioevo'. In *Romanica, Arte e liturgia nelle terre di San Geminiano e Matilde di Canossa*, edited by Adriano Peroni and Francesca Piccinini, 1–20. Modena: Franco Cosimo Panini, 2006.
Golinelli, Paolo. 'Non semel tantum sed pluribus vicibus': The Relations between Anselm of Canterbury and Mathilda of Tuscany'. (paper read at the International Congress on 'Saint Anselm and His Legacy', Canterbursy, 22–25 April, 2009), http://www.paologolinelli.it/1/saint_anselm_725953.html, date accessed 22 August 2016.
Golinelli, Paolo. 'Review of *Die Urkunden und Briefe der Markgräfin Mathilde von Tuszien*, by Elke Goez et W. Goez'. *CCM* 45, no. 177 (2002): 85–89.

Golinelli, Paolo. 'Sul preteso 'figlio adottivo' di Matilde di Canossa, Guido V Guerra'. In *Medioevo Reggiano. Studi in ricordo di Odoardo Rombaldi*, edited by Gino Badini and Andrea Gamberini, 123–32. Milan: Franco Angeli, 2007.

Goody, Jack. *The Development of the Family and Marriage in Europe*. Cambridge: Cambridge University Press, 1983.

Groß, Thomas. *Lothar III. und die Mathildischen Güter*. Frankfurt am Main: Peter Lang, 1990.

Gude, Monika. 'Die *fideles sancti Petri* im Streit um die Nachfolge Papst Gregors VII'. *FMSt* 27 (1993): 290–316.

Gussone, Nikolaus. 'Trauung und Krönung. Zur Hochzeit der byzantinischen Prinzessin Theophanu mit Kaiser Otto II'. In von Euw, *Kaiserin Theophanu*, vol. 2, 161–73.

Haluska-Rausch, Elizabeth. 'Transformations in the Powers of Wives and Widows Near Montpellier, 985–1213'. In *The Experience of Power in Medieval Europe: 950–1350*, edited by Robert F. Berkhofer, Alan Cooper and Adam J. Kosto, 153–68. Aldershot: Ashgate, 2005.

Hamilton, Sarah. 'Review Article: Early Medieval Rulers and Their Modern Biographers'. *EME* 9, no. 2 (2000): 247–60.

Hay, David J. 'The Campaigns of Countess Matilda of Canossa (1046–1115): An Analysis of the History and Social Significance of a Woman's Military Leadership'. PhD diss., University of Toronto, 2000.

Hay, David J. *The Military Leadership of Matilda of Canossa 1046–1115*. Manchester: Manchester University Press, 2008.

Healy, Patrick. *The Chronicle of Hugh of Flavigny: Reform and the Investiture Contest in the Late Eleventh Century*. Aldershot: Ashgate, 2006.

Healy, Patrick. '*Merito nominetur virago*: Matilda of Tuscany in the Polemics of the Investiture Contest'. In *Studies on Medieval and Early Modern Women 4: Victims or Viragos?*, edited by Christine Meek and Catherine Lawless, 49–56. Dublin: Four Courts, 2005.

Hehl, Ernst-Dieter. 'War, Peace and the Christian Order'. *NCMH* 4, Part I (2004): 185–228.

Helmerichs, Robert. '*Princeps, Comes, Dux Normannorum*: Early Rollonid Designators and their Significance'. *HSJ* 9 (1997): 57–77.

Herlihy, David. *The History of Feudalism*. London: Macmillan, 1971.

Herlihy, David. 'Land, Family and Women in Continental Europe, 701–1200'. In *Women in Medieval Society*, edited by Susan Mosher Stuard, 13–45. Philadelphia: University of Pennsylvania Press, 1976, repr. 1977.

Herlihy, David. *Medieval Households*. Cambridge, MA: Harvard University Press, 1985.

Herlihy, David. 'The Medieval Marriage Market'. In *Medieval and Renaissance Studies*, 3–27. Durham, NC: Duke University Press, 1976.

Heywood, William. *A History of Pisa: Eleventh and Twelfth Centuries*. Cambridge: Cambridge University Press, 1921, repr. 2010.

Hlawitschka, Eduard. *Die Ahnen der hochmittelalterlichen deutschen Könige, Kaiser und ihrer Gemahlinnen: Ein kommentiertes Tafelwerk.* 2 vols, *MGH*, Hilfsmittel, 25. Hanover, 2006.

Holdenried, Anke. *The Sibyl and Her Scribes: Manuscripts and Interpretation of the Latin Sibylla Tiburtina c. 1050–1500.* Aldershot: Ashgate, 2006.

Hummer, Hans J. *Politics and Power in Early Medieval Europe: Alsace and the Frankish Realm, 600–1000.* Cambridge: Cambridge University Press, 2005.

Hunt, Tony. 'The Emergence of the Knight in France and England 1000–1200'. *Forum for Modern Language Studies* 17, no. 2 (1981): 93–114.

Innes, Matthew. 'On the Material Culture of Legal Documents: Charters and Their Preservation in the Cluny Archive (9th–11th Centuries)'. In *Documentary Culture and the Laity in the Early Middle Ages*, edited by Warren Brown, Marios Costambeys, Matthew Innes and Adam J. Kosto, 283–320. Cambridge: Cambridge University Press, 2013.

Innes, Matthew. *State and Society in the Early Middle Ages: The Middle Rhine Valley, 400–1000.* Cambridge: Cambridge University Press, 2000.

Isabella, Giovanni. "Matilde, Edgith e Adelaide: scontri generazionali e dotari delle regine in Germania." *Il patrimonio delle regine: beni del fisco e politica regia tra IX e X secolo. Reti Medievali Rivista,* 13, 2 (2012), 203–245. DOI 10.6092/1593-2214/368: 203-45.

Jäschke, Kurt-Ulriche, Anne Duggan, and Janet Nelson. 'From Famous Empresses to Unspectacular Queens: The Romano-German Empire to Margaret of Brabant, Countess of Luxemburg and Queen of the Romans (d. 1311)'. In Duggan, *Queens and Queenship in Medieval Europe*, 75–108.

Jeep, John M. *Medieval Germany: An Encyclopedia.* New York: Garland, 2001.

Jenks, Edward. *The Early History of Negotiable Instruments.* Vol. 3. Boston: Little, Brown, 1909.

Jessee, W. Scott. *Robert the Burgundian and the Counts of Anjou, ca. 1025–1098.* Washington: Catholic University of America Press, 2000.

Jewell, Helen M. *Women in Dark Age and Early Medieval Europe c. 500–1200.* Basingstoke: Palgrave Macmillan, 2007.

Jones, A. H. M., J. R. Martindale and J. Morris. *The Prosopography of the Later Roman Empire.* 3 vols. Cambridge: Cambridge University Press, 1971.

Kahsnitz, Rainer. 'Ein Bildnis der Theophanu? Zur Tradition der Münz- und Medaillon- Bildnisse in der karolingischen und ottonischen Buchmalerei'. In von Euw, *Kaiserin Theophanu*, vol. 2, 101–34.

Kantorowicz, Ernst Hartwig. *Laudes regiae: A Study in Liturgical Acclamations and Mediaeval Rules Worship.* Berkeley and Los Angeles: University of California Press, 1946.

Kemp, Eric Waldram. *Canonization and Authority in the Western Church.* London: Oxford University Press, 1948.

Körntgen, Ludger. 'Starke Frauen: Edgith-Adelheid-Theophanu'. In Puhle, *Otto der Große*, Vol. I, 119–32.

Kornbluth, Genevra. 'Richildis and her Seal. Carolingian Self-Reference and the Imagery of Power'. In *Saints, Sinners, and Sisters: Gender and Northern Art in Medieval and Early Modern Europe*, edited by Alison G. Stewart and Jane Louise Carroll, 161–79. Aldershot: Ashgate, 2003.

Lafontaine-Dosogne, Jacqueline. 'The Art of Byzantium and its Relation to Germany in the Time of the Empress Theophano'. In Davids, *The Empress Theophano*, 211–30.

La Rocca, Cristina. *Italy in the Early Middle Ages: 476–1000*. Oxford: Oxford University Press, 2002.

Latham, R. E. *Revised Medieval Latin Word-List from British and Irish Sources*. London: Oxford University Press, 1965.

Laudage, Johannes. *Otto der Grosse (912–973): Eine Biographie*. Regensburg: Friedrich Pustet, 2001.

Lazzari, Tiziana. 'Before Matilde: Beatrice of Lorena "Dux et Marchio Tusciae"'. Paper presented at the International Medieval Congress, Leeds, England, July, 2012.

Lazzari, Tiziana. 'Goffredo di Lorena e Beatrice di Toscana'. Paper presented at the La reliquia del Sangue di Cristo. l'Italia e l'Europa al tempo di Leone IX, Convegno Internazionale di Studi Mantova (I), Mantua, 23–26 novembre 2011.

Lazzari, Tiziana. 'Miniature e versi: mimesi della regalità in Donizone'. In *Forme di potere nel pieno medioevo (secc. VIII–XII). Dinamiche e rappresentazioni*, edited by Giovanni Isabella, 57–92. Bologna, 2006 (Dpm quaderni-dottorato 6).

Leicht, P. S. *Il diritto italiano preirneriano*. Bologna: Zanichelli, 1933.

Le Jan, Régine. 'Adelheidis: le nom au premier millénaire. Formation, origine, dynamique'. In Corbet, *Adélaïde de Bourgogne*, 29–42.

Le Jan, Régine. *Famille et Pouvoir dans le Monde Franc (VIIe–Xe siècle): Essai d'Anthropologie Sociale*. Paris: Publications de la Sorbonne, 1995.

Lewis, Charlton Thomas, and Charles Short. *A Latin Dictionary. Founded on Andrews' Edition of Freund's Latin Dictionary*. Oxford: Clarendon Press, 1879.

Leyser, Henrietta. *Medieval Women: A Social History of Women in England, 450–1500*. London: Weidenfeld and Nicolson, 1995.

Leyser, Karl. 'The Battle at the Lech, 955. A Study in Tenth-Century Warfare'. *History* 50, no. 168 (1965): 1–25.

Leyser, Karl. 'The German Aristocracy from the Ninth to the Early Twelfth Century: A Historical and Cultural Sketch'. *P&P*, no. 41 (Dec., 1968): 25–53.

Leyser, Karl. 'Liudprand as Homilist'. In *Communications and Power in Medieval Europe: The Carolingian and Ottonian Centuries*, edited by Timothy Reuter, 111–24. London: Hambledon Press, 1994.

Leyser, Karl. 'Maternal Kin in Early Medieval Germany'. In *Communications and Power in Medieval Europe: The Carolingian and Ottonian Centuries*, edited by Timothy Reuter, 181–88. London: Hambledon Press, 1994.

Leyser, Karl. 'Maternal Kin in Early Medieval Germany. A Reply'. *P&P*, no. 49 (1970): 126–34.
Leyser, Karl. 'Ottonian Government'. *EHR* 96, no. 381 (1981): 721–53.
Leyser, Karl. 'The Ottonians and Wessex'. In *Communications and Power in Medieval Europe: The Carolingian and Ottonian Centuries*, edited by Timothy Reuter, 73–104. London: Hambledon Press, 1994.
Leyser, Karl. 'Ritual, Ceremony, and Gesture: Ottonian Germany'. In *Communications and Power in Medieval Europe: The Carolingian and Ottonian Centuries*, edited by Timothy Reuter, 189–213. London: Hambledon Press, 1994.
Leyser, Karl J. *Rule and Conflict in an Early Medieval Society: Ottonian Saxony*. London: Edward Arnold, 1979.
Leyser, Karl. '*Theophanu divina gratia imperatrix augusta*: Western and Eastern Emperorship in the Later Tenth Century'. In Davids, *The Empress Theophano*, 1–27.
Livingstone, Amy. *Out of Love for my Kin: Aristocratic Family Life in the Lands of the Loire, 1000–1200*. Ithaca, NY: Cornell University Press, 2010.
Lexikon des Mittelalters, ed. Robert Auty, 9 vols. (München & Zürich: Artemis-Verlag, 1977–1998).
LoPrete, Kimberly A. 'Gendering Viragos: Medieval Perceptions of Powerful Women'. In *Studies on Medieval and Early Modern Women 4: Victims or Viragos?*, edited by Christine Meek and Catherine Lawless, 17–38. Dublin: Four Courts, 2005.
Lupoi, Maurizio. *The Origins of the European Legal Order*. Translated by Adrian Belton. Cambridge: Cambridge University Press, 2000.
Lynch, Joseph H. 'Hugh I of Cluny's Sponsorship of Henry IV: Its Context and Consequences'. *Speculum* 60, no. 4 (1985): 800–26.
MacLean, Simon. 'Making a Difference in Tenth-Century Politics: King Athelstan's Sisters and Frankish Queenship'. In *Frankland: The Franks and the World of the Early Middle Ages. Essays in Honour of Dame Jinty Nelson*, edited by Paul Fouracre and D. Ganz, 167–90. Manchester: Manchester University Press, 2008.
MacLean, Simon. 'Queenship, Nunneries and Royal Widowhood in Carolingian Europe'. *P&P*, no. 178 (2003): 3–38.
Mayr-Harting, Henry. *Ottonian Book Illumination: An Historical Study*. 2 vols. London: Oxford University Press, 1991.
McKitterick, Rosamond. *The Carolingians and the Written Word*. Cambridge: Cambridge University Press, 1989.
McKitterick, Rosamond, ed. *The Frankish Kings and Culture in the Early Middle Ages*. Aldershot: Variorum, 1995.
McKitterick, Rosamond. 'Latin and Romance: An Historian's Perspective'. In *The Frankish Kings*, IX.130–45.

McKitterick, Rosamond. 'Ottonian Intellectual Culture in the Tenth Century'. In Davids, *The Empress Theophano*, 169–93.

McKitterick, Rosamond. 'Ottonische Kultur und Bildung'. In Puhle, *Otto der Große*, Vol. I, 209–25.

McKitterick, Rosamond. 'Women in the Ottonian Church: An Iconographic Perspective'. In *The Frankish Kings*, XI.79–100.

McKitterick, Rosamund. 'The Written Word and Oral Communication: Rome's Legacy to the Franks'. In *The Frankish Kings*, X.89–112.

McLaughlin, Megan. *Sex, Gender, and Episcopal Authority in an Age of Reform, 1000–1122*. Cambridge: Cambridge University Press, 2010.

McLeod, Neil. '*Cáin Adomnáin* and the Lombards'. In *Language and Power in the Celtic World*, edited by Anders Ahlqvist and Pamela O'Neill, 241–65. Sydney: Celtic Studies Foundation, University of Sydney, 2011.

McNamara, Jo Ann. 'Canossa and the Ungendering of the Public Man'. In Berman, *Medieval Religion*, 102–22.

McNamara, Jo Ann. 'Women and Power through the Family Revisited'. In *Gendering the Master Narrative: Women and Power in the Middle Ages*, edited by M. C. Erler and M. Kowaleski, 17–30. Ithaca, NY: Cornell University Press, 2003.

McNamara, Jo Ann, and Suzanne Wemple. 'The Power of Women through the Family in Medieval Europe, 500–1100'. In *Women and Power in the Middle Ages*, edited by M. C. Erler and M. Kowaleski, 83–101. Athens, GA: University of Georgia Press, 1988.

Mickel, Emmanuel J., ed. *Les Enfances de Godefroi and Le retour de Cornumarant*. Vol. 3, The Old French Crusade Cycle. Tuscaloosa, Alabama: University of Alabama Press, 1999.

Moore, R. I. *The First European Revolution, c. 970–1215*. Oxford: Blackwell, 2000.

Moore, R. I. *The Origins of European Dissent*. Oxford: Blackwell, 1977.

Moore, R. I. 'Review article: Duby's Eleventh Century'. *History* 69 (225) (1984): 36–49.

Moroni, Sonia. 'Il Medioevo nel territorio di Traversetolo e la presenza della famiglia Baratti'. In *SM IV*, 125–52.

Müller-Mertens, Eckhard. 'The Ottonians as Kings and Emperors'. *NCMH* 3 (1999): 233–66.

Müller-Mertens, Eckhard. *Die Reichsstruktur im Spiegel der Herrschaftspraxis Otto des Großen*, Forschungen zur mittelalterlichen Geschichte 25. Berlin, 1980.

Nash, Penelope. 'Adelheid's Travels During the Regencies'. Paper presented at the International Medieval Congress, University of Leeds, 7–10 July 2014.

Nash, Penelope. 'Empress Adelheid and Countess Matilda Compared'. PhD diss., University of Sydney, 2014.

Nash, Penelope. 'Maintaining Elite Households in Germany and Italy, 900–1115: Finances, Control and Patronage'. In *Elite and Royal Households in Later Medieval and Early Modern Europe*, edited by Theresa Earenfight. Leiden: Brill, forthcoming 2017.

Nash, Penelope. 'Reality and Ritual in the Medieval King's Emotions of *Ira* and *Clementia*'. In *Understanding Emotions in Medieval and Early Modern Europe*, edited by Michael Champion and Andrew Lynch, 251–71. Turnhout: Brepols, 2015.

Nash, Penelope. 'Shifting Terrain–Italy and Germany Dancing in Their Own Tapestry'. *JAEMA* 6 (2010): 53–73.

Neiske, Franz 'La tradition nécrologique d'Adélaïde'. In Corbet, *Adélaïde de Bourgogne*, 81–93.

Nelson, Janet. 'Aachen as a Place of Power'. In *Courts, Elites*, XIV.1–23.

Nelson, Janet, ed. *Courts, Elites, and Gendered Power in the Early Middle Ages: Charlemagne and Others*. Aldershot: Ashgate, 2007.

Nelson, Janet. 'Early Medieval Rites of Queen-Making and the Shaping of Medieval Queenship'. In Duggan, *Queens and Queenship in Medieval Europe*, 301–15.

Nelson, Janet. 'Legislation and Consensus in the Reign of Charles the Bald'. In *Ideal and Reality in Frankish and Anglo-Saxon Society*, edited by Patrick Wormald, 202–27. Oxford: Blackwell, 1983.

Nelson, Janet. 'Literacy in Carolingian Government'. In *The Uses of Literacy in Early Mediaeval Europe*, edited by Rosamond McKitterick, 258–96. Cambridge: Cambridge University Press, 1990.

Nelson, Janet. 'Medieval Queenship'. In *Women in Medieval Western European Culture*, edited by Linda Elizabeth Mitchell, 179–207. New York: Garland, 1999.

Nelson, Janet. 'Queens as Jezebels: The Careers of Brunhild and Balthild in Merovingian History'. In *Debating the Middle Ages: Issues and Readings*, edited by Lester K. Little and Barbara H. Rosenwein, 219–53. Malden, MA: Blackwell, 1998.

Nelson, Janet. 'Rulers and Government'. *NCMH* 3 (1999): 95–129.

Nelson, Janet. 'Symbols in Context: Rulers' Inaugruation Rituals in Byzantium and the West in the Early Middle Ages'. In *Politics and Ritual in Early Medieval Europe*, edited by Janet Nelson, 259–82. London: Hambledon Press, 1986.

Nelson, Janet. 'Tenth-Century Kingship Comparatively'. In *England and the Continent in the Tenth Century: Studies in Honour of Wilhelm Levison (1876–1947)*, edited by David Rollason, Conrad Leyser and Hannah Williams, 293–308. Turnhout: Brepols, 2010.

Nelson, Janet. 'The Wary Widow'. In *Courts, Elites*, II.82–113.

Niermeyer, J. F., C. van de Kieft, G. S. M. M. Lake-Schoonebeek. *Mediae Latinitatis lexicon minus: abbreviationes et index fontium*. In Niermeyer. *Mediae latinitatis lexicon minus*, vol 2, 1–83.

Niermeyer, J. F., C. van de Kieft, and J. W. J. Burgers. *Mediae latinitatis lexicon minus*. 2nd ed. 2 vols. Leiden: Brill, 2002.
Nobili, Mario. 'L'ideologia politica in Donizone'. In *SM III*, 263–79.
Nobili, Mario. 'La cultura politica alla corte di Mathilde di Canossa'. In *Le sedi della cultura nell'Emilia Romagna. L'alto-medioevo*, edited by Ovidio Capitani, 217–36. Milan: Silvana, 1983.
Nordenfalk, C. 'Milano e l'arte ottoniana: problemi di fondo sinora poco osservati'. In *Il millennio ambrosiano. La città del vescovo dai carolingi al Barbarossa*, edited by C. Bertelli, 102–23. Milan: Electa, 1988.
Novikoff, Alex. 'Licit and Illicit in the Rhetoric of the Investiture Conflict'. In *Law and the Illicit in Medieval Europe*, edited by Ruth Mazo Karras, Joel Kaye and E. Ann Matter, 183–96. Philadelphia: University of Pennsylvania Press, 2008.
Odegaard, Charles E. 'The Concept of Royal Power in Carolingian Oaths of Fidelity'. *Speculum* 20, no. 3 (Jul., 1945): 279–89.
Odegaard, Charles E. 'The Empress Engelberge'. *Speculum* 26, no. 1 (Jan., 1951): 77–103.
Oxford Dictionary of Popes. Edited by J. N. D. Kelly. Oxford: Oxford University Press, 1986.
Old High German (ca. 750–1050) English Dictionary online, http://glosbe.com/goh/en/.
Olson, Lynette. *The Early Middle Ages: The Birth of Europe*. Basingstoke: Palgrave Macmillan, 2007.
Olson, Lynette. 'Women and Gender in Europe at the End of the *First* Millennium'. unpublished paper: University of Sydney, Australia, 2000.
Oxford English Dictionary Online. Oxford: Oxford University Press, 2000. http://www.oed.com.ezproxy1.library.usyd.edu.au/
Overmann Alfred. *Regesten* in *Gräfin Mathilde von Tuscien. Ihre Besitzungen, Geschichte ihres Gutes von 1115-1230 und ihre Regesten*, 123–90. Innsbruck, 1895; repr. Frankfurt am Main: Minerva, 1965.
Pac, Grzegorz. 'Crowned Mary, Crowning Mary. Queen of Heavens and Queenship Ideology in Art from 10th and 11th c. England and Empire'. Paper presented at the International Medieval Congress, University of Leeds, July 2013.
Pächt, Otto. 'The Illustrations of St. Anselm's Prayers and Meditations'. *Journal of the Warburg and Courtauld Institutes* 19, no. 1/2 (1956): 68–83.
Paulhart, Herbert. 'Zur Heiligsprechung der Kaiserin Adelheid'. *MIöG* 64 (1956): 65–67.
Peroni, Adriano. 'La plastica in stucco nel S. Ambrogio di Milano: arte ottoniana e romanica in Lombardia'. In *Kolloquium über spätantike und frühmittelalterliche Skulptur*, edited by V. Milojcic, Vol. 3, 59–119. Mainz, 1972.

Perroy, Edouard. 'Carolingian Administration'. In *Early Medieval Society*, edited by Sylvia L. Thrupp, 129–46. New York: Appleton-Century-Crofts, 1967.

Pohl, Walter. 'Gender and Ethnicity'. In Brubaker, *Gender in the Early Medieval World*, 23–43.

Poupardin, René. *Le royaume de Bourgogne, 888–1038: Étude sur les origines du royaume d'Arles*. Paris: Champion,1907, repr. Geneva: Slatkine, 1974.

Pratt, David. *The Political Thought of King Alfred the Great*. Cambridge: Cambridge University Press, 2007.

Previté-Orton, Charles William. *The Early History of the House of Savoy, (1000–1233)*. London: Cambridge University Press, 1912, reprinted in Nabu Public Domain Reprints, 2011.

Puhle, Matthias, ed. *Otto der Große, Magdeburg und Europa*. 2 vols. Mainz: Philipp von Zabern, 2001.

Pullan, Brian S., ed. *Sources for the History of Medieval Europe: From the Mid-Eighth to the Mid-Thirteenth Century*. Oxford: Blackwell, 1966.

Ramseyer, Valerie. 'Territorial Lordships in the Principality of Salerno, 1050–1150'. *HSJ* 9 (1997): 79–94.

Reuter, Timothy. 'Contextualising Canossa: Excommunication, Penance, Surrender, Reconciliation'. In *Medieval Polities and Modern Mentalities*, edited by Janet Nelson, 147–66. Cambridge: Cambridge University Press, 2006.

Reuter, Timothy. '*Filii matris nostrae pugnant adversum nos*: Bonds and Tensions between German Prelates and Their *milites* in the High Middle Ages'. In *Chiesa e mondo feudale nei secoli X–XII*, 247–76. Milan: Vita e pensiero, 1995.

Reuter, Timothy. "Introduction: Reading the Tenth Century." In *NCMH, Volume III c. 900–c. 1024*, edited by Timothy Reuter, 1–24. Cambridge: Cambridge University Press, 1999.

Reuter, Timothy. 'Peace-Breaking, Feud, Rebellion, Resistance: Violence and Peace in the Politics of the Salian Era'. In *Medieval Polities and Modern Mentalities*, edited by Janet Nelson, 355–87. Cambridge: Cambridge University Press, 2006.

Reuter, Timothy. '*Regemque, quem in Francia pene perdidit, in patria magnifice recepit*: Ottonian Ruler-Representation in Synchronic and Diachronic Comparison'. In *Medieval Polities and Modern Mentalities*, edited by Janet Nelson, 127–46. Cambridge: Cambridge University Press, 2006.

Reyerson, Kathryn L., and Thomas Kuehn. 'Women and Law in France and Italy'. In *Women in Medieval Western European Culture*, edited by Linda Elizabeth Mitchell, 131–41. New York: Garland, 1999.

Reynolds, Brian K. *Gateway to Heaven: Marian Doctrine and Devotion Image and Typology in the Patristic and Medieval Periods. Volume 1. Doctrine and Devotion*. New York: New City Press, 2012.

Reynolds, Rosalind Jaeger. 'Reading Matilda: The Self-Fashioning of a Duchess'. *Essays in Medieval Studies* 19 (2002): 1–13.

Reynolds, Susan. *Fiefs and Vassals: The Medieval Evidence Reinterpreted*. Oxford: Oxford University Press, 1994.
Riley-Smith, Jonathan. *The First Crusaders, 1095–1131*. Cambridge: Cambridge University Press, 1997.
Roach, Levi. 'Hosting the King: Hospitality and the Royal *iter* in Tenth-Century England'. *JMH* 37, no. 1 (2011): 34–46.
Roach, Levi. 'Submission and Homage: Feudo-Vassalic Bonds and the Settlement of Disputes in Ottonian Germany'. *History* 97, no. 327 (2012): 355–79.
Robbie, Steven. 'Can Silence Speak Volumes? Widukind's *Res Gestae Saxonicae* and the coronation of Otto I reconsidered'. *EME* 20, no. 3 (2012): 333–62.
Robinson, I. S. *Authority and Resistance in the Investiture Contest: The Polemical Literature of the Late Eleventh Century*. Manchester: Manchester University Press, 1978.
Robinson, I. S. 'The Friendship Circle of Bernold of Constance and the Dissemination of Gregorian Ideas in Late Eleventh-Century Germany'. In *Friendship in Medieval Europe*, edited by Julian Haseldine, 185–98. Stroud, UK: Sutton, 1999.
Robinson, I. S. 'Gregory VII and the Soldiers of Christ'. *History* 58, no. 193 (1973): 169–92.
Robinson, I. S. *Henry IV of Germany, 1056–1106*. Cambridge: Cambridge University Press, 1999.
Robinson, I. S. *The Papacy, 1073–1198: Continuity and Innovation*. Cambridge: Cambridge University Press, 1990.
Rosenwein, Barbara H. *To Be the Neighbor of Saint Peter: The Social Meaning of Cluny's Property, 909–1049*. Ithaca, NY: Cornell University Press, 1989.
Rough, Robert H. *The Reformist Illuminations in the Gospels of Matilda: Countess of Tuscany. (A Study in the Art of the Age of Gregory VII)*: Nijhoff, 1973.
Russo, Giuseppe. 'Modena nel 1106'. In *SM I*, 130–33.
Saxon, Elizabeth. 'Carolingian, Ottonian and Romanesque Art and the Eucharist'. In *A Companion to the Eucharist in the Middle Ages*, edited by Ian Christopher Levy, Gary Macy and Kristen Van Ausdall, 251–324. Leiden and Boston: Brill, 2012.
Schetter, Rudolf. 'Die Intervenienz der weltlichen und geistlichen Fürsten in den deutschen Königsurkunden von 911–1056'. PhD diss., Friedrich-Wilhelms-Universität, 1935.
Schieffer, Rudolf. 'Das "Italienerlebnis" Ottos des Großen'. In Puhle, *Otto der Große*, Vol. I, 446–60.
Schramm, Percy Ernst, and Florentine Mütherich. *Die deutschen Kaiser und Könige in Bildern ihrer Zeit 751–1190*. Munich, 1983.
Schumann, Reinhold. *Authority and the Commune, Parma, 833-1133*, Fonti e studi 2nd ser. 8. Parma: Deputazione di storia patria per le province parmensi, 1973.

Sergi, Giuseppe. 'I poteri dei Canossa: poteri delegati, poteri feudali, poteri signorili'. In *I poteri dei Canossa*, edited by Paolo Golinelli, 29–39.

Sergi, Giuseppe. 'The Kingdom of Italy'. *NCMH* 3 (1999): 346–71.

Settia, Aldo A. 'Castelli e villaggi nelle terre canossiane tra X e XIII secoli'. In *SM III*, 281–307.

Shepard, Jonathan. 'Marriages Towards the Millennium'. In *Byzantium in the Year 1000*, edited by Paul Magdalino, 1–34: Brill, 2003.

Shoemaker, Stephen J. 'Mary at the Cross, East and West: Maternal Compassion and Affective Piety in the Earliest Life of the Virgin and the High Middle Ages'. *JTS* 62, no. 2 (2011): 570–606.

Shopkow, Leah. 'Dynastic History'. In *Historiography in the Middle Ages*, edited by D. M. Deliyannis, 353–85. Leiden and Boston: Brill, 2003.

Sicardi, Giulia Petracco. 'La formula salica di investitura nell'età matildica e i suoi antecedenti storici'. In *SM III*, 255–62.

Simeoni, Luigi. 'Il contributo della contessa Matilde al Papato nella lotta per le investiture'. *SG* 1 (1947): 353–72.

Simeoni, Luigi. 'La Vita Mathildis di Donizone et il suo valore storicho-critiche'. *Atti e memorie della Deputazione di storia patria per le antiche provincie modenesi* 7, no. 4 (1927): 18–64.

Skinner, Patricia. *Women in Medieval Italian Society, 500–1200*. Harlow, UK: Pearson Education, 2001.

Smith, Julia M. H. *Europe after Rome: A New Cultural History 500–1000*. Oxford: Oxford University Press, 2005.

Smith, Julia M. H. 'Introduction: Gendering the Early Medieval World'. In Brubaker, *Gender in the Early Medieval World*, 1–19.

Smith, Julie Ann. 'The Earliest Queen-Making Rites'. *Church History* 66, no. 1 (March, 1997): 18–35.

Smith, L. M. 'Cluny and Gregory VII'. *EHR* 26, no. 101 (1911): 20–33.

Southern, R. W. *The Making of the Middle Ages*. London: Cresset Library, 1987.

Southern, R. W. *Western Society and the Church in the Middle Ages*. Vol. 2. London: Hodder and Stoughton, 1970.

Squatriti, Paolo. *Water and Society in Early Medieval Italy, AD 400–1000*. Cambridge: Cambridge University Press, 1998.

Squatriti, Paolo. *The Complete Works of Liudprand of Cremona*. Washington, DC: University of America Press, 2007.

Staab, Franz. 'Liste der Äbte und Pröpste'. In *Adelheid: Kaiserin und Heilige, 931 bis 999*, edited by Maria Pia Andreola Panzarasa and Liliane Obreiter, 196–98. Karlsruhe: INFO, 1999.

Stafford, Pauline. "The Annals of Æthelflæd': Annals, History and Politics in Early Tenth-Century England'. In *Myth, Rulership, Church and Charters: Essays in Honour of Nicholas Brooks*, edited by Julia Barrow and Andrew Wareham, 101–16. Aldershot: Ashgate, 2008.

Stafford, Pauline. 'Emma: The Powers of the Queen in the Eleventh Century'. In Duggan, *Queens and Queenship in Medieval Europe*, 3–26.
Stafford, Pauline. '*La Mutation Familiale*: A Suitable Case for Caution'. In *The Community, the Family, and the Saint: Patterns of Power in Early Medieval Europe*, edited by Joyce Hill and Mary Swan, 103–25. Turnhout: Brepols, 1998.
Stafford, Pauline. *Queen Emma and Queen Edith: Queenship and Women's Power in Eleventh-Century England*. Oxford: Blackwell, 1997.
Stafford, Pauline. *Queens, Concubines and Dowagers: The King's Wife in the Early Middle Ages*. London: Batsford Academic and Educational, 1983.
Stahl, Alan M. 'Coinage in the Name of Medieval Women'. In *Medieval Women and the Sources of Medieval History*, edited by Joel Thomas Rosenthal, 321–36. Athens, GA: University of Georgia Press, 1990.
Story, Joanna. *Carolingian Connections: Anglo-Saxon England and Carolingian Francia, c. 750–870*. Aldershot: Ashgate, 2003.
Struve, Tilman. 'Matilde di Toscana – Canossa ed Enrico IV'. In *I poteri dei Canossa*, edited by Paolo Golinelli, 421–54.
Tabacco, Giovanni. 'Northern and Central Italy in the Eleventh Century'. *NCMH* 4, Part 2 (2004): 72–93.
Tabacco, Giovanni. *The Struggle for Power in Medieval Italy: Structures of Political Rule*. Translated by Rosalind Jensen Brown. Cambridge: Cambridge University Press, 1989.
Tincani, Arnaldo. 'Le corti dei Canossa in area Padana'. In *I poteri dei Canossa*, edited by Paolo Golinelli, 253–78.
Uhlirz, Karl. *Jahrbücher des Deutschen Reiches unter Otto II. und Otto III. Otto II. 978–983*. 2 vols. Vol. 1. Leipzig and Berlin: Dunker and Humblot, 1902, repr. 1967.
Uhlirz, Mathilde. *Jahrbücher des Deutschen Reiches unter Otto II. und Otto III. Otto III. 983–1002*. Edited by K. Uhlirz and M. Uhlirz. 2 vols. Vol. 2. Leipzig and Berlin: Dunker and Humblot, 1954.
Uhlirz, Mathilde. 'Die rechtliche Stellung der Kaiserinwitwe Adelheid im deutschen und im italischen Reich'. *ZSRGA* 74 (1957): 85–97.
Uitz, Erika, Barbara Pätzold, and Gerald Beyreuther, eds. *Herrscherinnen und Nonnen: Frauengestalten von der Ottonenzeit bis zu den Staufern*. Berlin: Wissenschaften, 1990.
Urbańczyk, Przemysław. *Europe around the Year 1000*. Warsaw: Polish Academy of Sciences Institute of Archaeology and Ethnology, 2001.
Vaughn, Sally N. *Anselm of Bec and Robert of Meulan: The Innocence of the Dove and the Wisdom of the Serpent*. Berkeley: University of California Press, 1987.
Vaughn, Sally N. *St. Anselm and the Handmaidens of God: A Study of Anselm's Correspondence*. Turnhout: Brepols, 2002.

Vecchi, Giuseppe. 'Temi e momenti di scuola nella "*Vita Mathildi*" di Donizone'. In *SM I*, 210–17.
Verzar, Christine B. 'Picturing Matilda of Canossa: Medieval Strategies of Representation'. In *Representing History, 900–1300: Art, Music, History*, edited by Robert A. Maxwell, 73–90. University Park: Pennsylvania State University Press, 2010.
Vogel, Cyrille, William George Storey, Niels Krogh Rasmussen, and John Brooks-Leonard. *Medieval Liturgy: An Introduction to the Sources*. Washington, DC: Pastoral Press, 1986.
Vogelsang, Thilo. *Die Frau als Herrscherin im hohen Mittelalter: Studien zur 'consors regni' Formel*. Göttingen, Frankfurt, Berlin, 1954.
Vollrath, Hanna. 'The Western Empire under the Salians'. *NCMH* 4, Part 2 (2004): 38–71.
Wallace-Hadrill, J. M. *The Long-Haired Kings*. Toronto: University of Toronto Press in association with Medieval Academy of America, 1962, repr. 1982.
Ward, Benedicta. *The Prayers and Meditations of St. Anselm*. Harmondsworth: Penguin, 1973.
Ward, John O. 'After Rome: Medieval Epic'. In *Roman Epic*, edited by A. J. Boyle, 261–93. London: Routledge, 1993.
Warner, David A. 'Ideals and Action in the Reign of Otto III'. *JMH* 25, no. 1 (1999): 1–18.
Warner, David A. 'The Representation of Empire: Otto I at Ravenna'. In Weiler, *Representations of Power*, 121–40.
Warner, David A. 'Thietmar of Merseburg on Rituals of Kingship'. *Viator* 26 (1995): 53–76.
Warner, G. *Gospels of Matilda, Countess of Tuscany, 1055–1115. Nineteen Plates in Gold and Colour, and 12 in Monochrome from the Manuscript in the Library of John Pierpont Morgan*. Vol. 172: [Oxford]: Privately printed for presentation to the Roxburghe Club, 1917.
Waßenhoven, Dominik. 'Swaying Bishops and the Succession of Kings'. In *Patterns of Episcopal Power: Bishops in 10th and 11th Century Western Europe*, edited by Ludger Körntgen and Dominik Waßenhoven, 89–110. Berlin and New York: De Gruyter, 2011.
Webb, Dians. *Pilgrimage in Medieval England*. London: Hambledon and London, 2000.
Weiler, Björn and Simon MacLean, eds. *Representations of Power in Medieval Germany, 800–1500*. Turnhout: Brepols, 2006.
Weinfurter, Stefan. 'Kaiserin Adelheid und das ottonische Kaisertum'. *FMSt* 33 (1999): 1–19.
Weinfurter, Stefan. *The Salian Century: Main Currents in an Age of Transition*. Translated by Barbara M. Bowlus. Philadelphia: University of Pennsylvania Press, 1999.

Wemple, Suzanne Fonay. *Women in Frankish Society: Marriage and the Cloister, 500 to 900.* Philadelphia: University of Pennsylvania Press, 1981.
Wickham, Chris. *Early Medieval Italy: Central Power and Local Society 400–1000.* London: Macmillan, 1981.
Wickham, Chris. 'European Forests in the Early Middle Ages'. In *Land and Power*, 155–99.
Wickham, Chris. *Land and Power: Studies in Italian and European Social History, 400–1200.* London: British School at Rome, 1994.
Wickham, Chris. *The Inheritance of Rome: A History of Europe from 400 to 1000.* London: Penguin, 2010.
Wickham, Chris. 'Italy and the Early Middle Ages'. In *Land and Power*, 99–118.
Wickham, Chris. 'La signoria rurale in toscana'. In *Strutture e trasformazioni della signoria rurale nei secoli X–XIII*, edited by Gerhard Dilcher and Cinzio Violante, 343–409. Bologna, 1996.
Wickham, Chris. 'Land Disputes and their Social Framework in Lombard-Carolingian Italy, 700–900'. In *Land and Power*, 229–56.
Wickham, Chris. 'Lawyers' Time: History and Memory in Tenth- and Eleventh-Century Italy'. In *Land and Power*, 275–93.
Wickham, Chris. *The Mountains and the City: The Tuscan Appennines in the Early Middle Ages.* Oxford: Oxford University Press, 1988.
Wickham, Chris. 'Pastorialism and Underdevelopment in the Early Middle Ages'. In *Land and Power*, 121–54.
Wickham, Chris. *Sleepwalking into a New World: The Emergence of Italian City Communes in the Twelfth Century*, The Lawrence Stone Lectures. Princeton, NJ: Princeton University Press, 2015.
Wilson, David M. *The Bayeux Tapestry: The Complete Tapestry in Colour.* London: Thames and Hudson, 1985.
Wilson, Katharina M. 'The Saxon Canoness: Hrotsvit of Gandersheim'. In *Medieval Women Writers*, 30–63. Manchester: Manchester University Press, 1984.
Witt, Ronald G. *The Two Latin Cultures and the Foundation of Renaissance Humanism in Medieval Italy.* New York: Cambridge University Press, 2012.
Wolf, Gunther. 'Das Itinerar der Prinzessin Theophano/Kaiserin Theophanu 972–991'. In *Kaiserin Theophanu: Prinzessin aus der Fremde - des Westreichs Grosse Kaiserin*, 5–18. Cologne: Böhlau, 1991.
Wolf, Gunther. 'Wer war Theophanu?'. In von Euw, *Kaiserin Theophanu*, vol. 2, 385–96.
Wolfram, Herwig. *Conrad II 990–1039: Emperor of Three Kingdoms.* Translated by Denise A. Kaiser. University Park: Pennsylvania State University Press, 2006.
Wollasch, Joachim. 'Cluny und Deutschland'. In *SMGB*, 7–32. St. Ottilien, 1992.
Wollasch, Joachim. 'Das Grabkloster der Kaiserin Adelheid in Selz am Rhein'. *FMSt* 2 (1968): 135–43.

Wollasch, Joachim. 'Les obituaires, témoins de la vie clunisienne'. *CCM* 22, no. 86 (1979): 139–71.
Wormald, Patrick. '*Lex Scripta* and *Verbum Regis*: Legislation and Germanic Kingship, from Euric to Cnut'. In *Early Medieval Kingship*, edited by P. H. Sawyer and I. N. Wood, 105–38. Leeds: University of Leeds, 1977.
Wormald, Patrick. *The Making of English Law: King Alfred to the Twelfth Century*. Vol. I. *Legislation and its Limits*. Oxford: Blackwell Publishers, 1999.
Wright, F. A. *The Works of Liudprand of Cremona*. New York: Dutton, 1930.
Zanarini, Marinella. 'I Canossa'. In *Lanfranco e Wiligelmo. Il duomo di Modena*, edited by E. Castelnuovo, Vito Fumagalli, Adriano Peroni and S. Settis, 46–65. Modena: Panini, 1984.
Zielinski, Herbert. 'Konrad'. *LMA* 5: 1342.

Index

A

Aachen, battle (978), 177
Adalaxia, ctss, dau of mgv Amaifredus, of uncertain identity, 118
Adalbert Atto (d. 988), sn of **Siegfried of Lucca**, 1–2, 4, 5, 105, 108, 113–14, 119, 123n56, 180
Adalbert Azzo II, mgv of Este (d. 1097), 46–7, 50, 61
Adalbert, mgv of Ivrea (d. 929) [**Ermengard**], 189

Adelaide, mgvne of Turin (d. 1091) (Adelaide of Susa) [Hermann IV; Henry, mgv of Montferrat; **Otto I, ct of Savoy**], Table 2, 35, 45–7, 118
Adelaide of Auxerre (d. 929), dau of **Waldrada** and **Conrad, ct of Auxerre**; sis of **Rudolf I, k of Burgundy**; great-aunt of EA [**Richard le Justicier**], 20, 78n127

Notes: EA in the body of the index stands for Empress Adelheid; CM for Countess Matilda. The names of concubine(s), quasi-husband(s) and spouse(s) are enclosed in square brackets. A name in bold indicates that the person has their own entry in the index. The following abbreviations are used: abp = archbishop, abss = abbess, abt = abbot, aft = after, bef = before, bp = bishop, br = brother, cb = concubine, ct = count, ctss = countess, dau = daughter, d. = died, dk = duke, emp = emperor, empss = empress, f = father, grandau = granddaughter, grandf = grandfather, grandm = grandmother, k(gs), = king(s), LL = Lower Lotharingia, m = mother, mgv = margrave/marquis/marquess, mgvne = margravine/marchioness, OT = Old Testament, q = queen, qh = quasi-husband, qw = quasi-wife, r = reigned, sis = sister, sn = son, UL = Upper Lotharingia Except for genealogical charts (Table 1 and Table 2), this index refers neither to the material in the Frontmatter before Chapter 1 nor to the material in the Epilogue and in other Backmatter after Chapter 4.
Page numbers followed by "n" refer to notes.
Publisher's style is to make consecutive page numbers into page ranges

© The Author(s) 2017
P. Nash, *Empress Adelheid and Countess Matilda*,
DOI 10.1057/978-1-137-58514-1

Adelaide, q (d. 1004) [Hugh Capet], 134
Adela of Flanders (d. 1079), 182
Adelasia, dau of **Adalbert Azzo II**, 61–2
Adelhard (Adalardo), bp of Reggio (d. 952), 1, 113
Adelheid, abss of Quedlinburg (d. 1043), dau of **Theophanu** and **Otto II**, grandau of EA, 21, 156, 197n15, 198n29. *See also dominae imperiales*
Adelheid of Burgundy, empss (d. 999), dau of **Bertha of Swabia** and **Rudolf II, k of Italy** [**Lothar, k of Italy; Otto I**]. *See also dominae imperiales*; **Gerbert of Aurillac** (d. 1003), abt of Bobbio; Pope Sylvester II from 999; law(s); **Maiolus, abt of Cluny** (956–994); **Mathilda of Ringelheim**, q of the East Franks (d. 968), m-in-law of **EA**; **Odilo, abt of Cluny** (994–1049); **Otto I, emp** (d. 973), second husband of EA; reverse dowry
a brief life of, 3–4
and Alsace, 4, 31, 40, 98, 100–2, 112, 117
ancestry and fine lineage, 3, 18–20, 33–5, 66, 97, 137
appearance, images and iconography, 1, 135, 141, 154–6, 189–93
authority of/as ruler, 3, 7, 28, 32, 35, 67, 97, 99, 102, 109, 133, 142–7, 149, 157, 159–61, 174–9, 184, 194
as bearer of the Italian kingdom, 2, 139–42
birth and early life, 20, 23, 32–3, 66

and brothers **Rudolf (d. 986)** and **Burchard (d. 956/7)**, 20–1, 70n37 (*see also* **Conrad I the Pacific, k of Burgundy** (d. 993), br of EA)
and Canossa, 4, 5, 105, 114–15, 119
ceremonies, ritual and display, 136, 147, 153–4
and children, 3
and the church, 24–32, 99, 136, 146, 150, 153–6, 190, 193
and Cluny, 21, 22, 26, 28–30, 55, 57
coins and seals, 155–6, 193–4
control of the roads, 164, 166, 168
coronations, 2, 7, 141, 153, 161, 190
criticism of, 25, 32, 99
and dau **Emma**, 3, 22, 32, 33, 35
and dau **Mathilda, abss of Quedlinburg**, 22, 32, 101, 145, 146, 156
disagreements and their resolution, 32, 33, 99–100, 117, 145–6, 156, 159
documents, charters and diplomata, 3, 27, 28, 40, 116–18, 136, 142, 174, 185–6
donations, endowments and gifts by, 4, 40, 99, 102, 109, 111, 137, 150, 203n113
donations, endowments and gifts to, 98–100, 112, 116–19, 129, 148
followers and personal connections, 23–8, 32, 36, 119, 137–8, 147, 149
and grandau **Adelheid, abss of Quedlinburg**, 21, 32
and husbands (*see* **Lothar, k of Italy** (d. 950), sn of Alda

(Hilda) and **Hugh, k of Italy**; first husband of EA; **Otto I, emp (d. 973)**, second husband of EA)
as intervener in diplomata, 21–2, 28, 41, 99, 109, 142–9
imprisonment and escape from Garda, 1, 3, 97, 114
Italian interests, 4, 21, 28, 32, 66, 146, 149
kin, 18–22
lands and other property, 96–100, 102–5, 109–14, 116–19, 148, 157, 185
last years, death and burial, 4, 29, 31, 66, 103, 147, 156, 157
letters to and from, 22, 25–7, 36, 164, 176, 178, 182, 184
Marriage Charter, 153–4
marriage to **Otto I**, 2, 3, 19, 21, 23, 24, 33, 66, 97, 104, 115, 129, 139–41
military involvement, 175, 177–9
miracles, 29, 31
name, history of, 19–20
as negotiator and peacemaker, 23, 32, 159–60, 179, 186
and **Otto II**, 21–2, 33, 99, 143–4
and **Otto III**, 26, 33, 99, 100, 155, 156
path to canonization, 4, 28–32
as regent, 4, 33, 99, 102, 103, 135, 145–6, 149, 174, 178, 185
and the Rhine route, 100–2
and San Salvatore, Pavia, 116
self-fashioning and public persona, 141, 153–5, 162, 164, 176, 185
and Selz, 67, 102
and sexual sinfulness, 33
and sis-in-law (*see* **Mathilda of West Francia**, q of Burgundy

(d. 981–90/992), dau of **Gerberga (d. 969)** and **Louis IV d'Outremer**)
spiritual advisors, 28–32, 59, 60
spiritual life, 67, 185, 193
and succession crisis, 4, 27, 33, 66, 157
travel, itinerary, progresses, *iter*, 3, 32, 67, 136, 138, 140, 142–6, 159
and **Theophanu**, 22, 32, 33, 117, 143–6, 149, 155, 156
titles and epithets: *consors regni*, 19, 139, 150; *domina*, 184; *imperatrix*, 29, 151, 152; *inclita*, 19, 152, 184; as 'mother of kingdoms', 33; as 'mother of the Ottos', 30; *regina*, 152, 184; *pietas*, 26, 138, 152; *virago*, 182; *virtus*, 136–7
as widow and dowager, 1, 3, 25, 66, 97–100, 117, 119, 137, 139, 145–6, 150, 178
Adige, river, 167
administration, domain and civil, 4, 10, 133, 142, 184
Æthelflæd, lady of the Mercians (d. 918), 182
Æthelstan, k of Wessex (d. 939), half-br of **Edith of Wessex (d. 947)**, 19, 190
Æthelwulf, k of Wessex (d. 858) (Æthelwuld) [**Judith, dau of Charles the Bald**], 153
Agilulf, k (d. 616) [**Theudelinda**], 134, 141
agnate, agnatic, agnatio, 17, 19–20, 34, 187. *See also* cognate, cognatic, *cognatio*; kin, kinship, kinship terminology

Agnes of Poitou, empss (d. 1077) [**Henry III, emp**], 35, 36, 44, 45, 57, 64, 100, 104, 107, 112–13, 118. *See also* 'senate of women'
abdication, 103
Aistulf (d. 756), 166
Alexander II, pope (1061–73). *See* Anselm (I) the Elder, bp of Lucca (d. 1073), uncle of Anselm the Younger; Pope Alexander II from 1061
Alfred the Great, grandf of **Edith of Wessex (d. 947)**, 19, 160, 175
Alps, Alpine passes, 2, 5, 6, 38, 45, 51, 102, 106–7, 140, 153, 158, 163, 166–7, 179, 184
Althoff, Gerd, 17, 18, 125n90
Angelberga, q of Italy, empss (d. 896/901) (Angilberga, Engelberga) [**Louis II, k of Italy, Carolingian emp (d. 875)**], 41, 141
Anjou, cts of, 163, 168, 175
Annales Quedlinburgenses, 22, 136, 151–2, 178, 184
Anno II, abp of Cologne (d. 1075), 57, 103
Anselm (I) the Elder, bp of Lucca (d. 1073), uncle of Anselm the Younger; Pope Alexander II from 1061, 59–60
Anselm (II) the Younger, bp of Lucca (d. 1086), 46, 52–5, 58, 60–2, 83n195, 173, 181
  as confessor and spiritual director of CM, 46, 59–61
  and Hugh, abp of Lyons, 61, 64, 91n203
  and miracle, 61–2
  Collectio canonum, 53
  Liber contra Wibertum, 53, 181

Anselm (III), abp of Milan (d. 1093), 55
Anselm, abp of Canterbury (d. 1109), 55, 58–9
Antapodosis. *See* Liudprand, bp of Cremona (d. 972) (Liutprand), historian, diplomat
Apennine(s), mountains, Italy, 167, 169, 171–2
Ardennes (Verdun), house of, 34, 37, 38
Arduinid family, 118. *See also* **Adelaide, mgvne of Turin** (d. 1091) (Adelaide of Susa)
Arduinus de Palude (d. aft 1116), follower of **CM**, 192
aristocrat(s) and *nobiles*, 9, 15–16, 26, 36, 39, 66, 96, 163, 188
Arrernte people of Central Australia, 15–16
Attoni/Attonids (Canossans), Table 1, Table 2, 2, 33–4, 38–9, 50, 106, 108, 113–14, 119, 163
Augsburg, Bavaria, 3, 44, 166
Austin-Broos, Diane J., 15
Authari, k of the Lombards (d. 590) [**Theudelinda**], 141

B
ban, bannum, 42, 59, 64, 110, 115, 130, 171. *See also* excommunication
battle(s), battlefield, battle strategy, 32, 164, 167, 175, 179, 181. *See also under* individual locations of battles
Bavaria, Bavarian people, 72n56, 134, 137, 141, 142
Beatrice (d. 1053–55), sis of **CM**, 4, 37–9, 108
Beatrice (d. 1071), dau of **CM** and **Godfrey the Hunchback**, 4, 50

Beatrice of Bar, ctss of Tuscany (d. 1076) (Beatrice of Lotharingia, Beatrice of Tuscany, Beatrice of Canossa), dau of **Mathilda of Swabia** and **Frederick II of UL**; m of **CM** [**Boniface of Tuscany**; **Godfrey the Bearded**], 192. *See also* CM, **Leo IX**, pope (1049–54); 'senate of women'
a brief life, 4–5
and Cadalus, 167, 179
documents, charters and diplomata, 39–41, 43, 50, 171
children, **Frederick (d. 1053–55)** and **Beatrice (d. 1053–55)**, 38, 108, 124n68
as *comitissa, dux, ducatrix* and *marchionessa*, 7, 171, 187
foundation and endowment of monasteries, 50
and **Gregory VII**, 56, 57, 60
and **Henry III, emp**, 37–8, 106–7
and husband, **Boniface**, 4, 34, 36–7, 39, 106–7, 110, 161–2, 181, 187, 188
and husband, **Godfrey the Bearded**, 4, 34, 36–9, 106–7, 124n74
inheritance, wealth and property, 34, 106, 107, 110, 118–19
and law, 40, 187
lineage and connections, 34, 36, 77n121, 77n122, 77n133, 79n137, 187
as 'Magna Beatrix', 190
and marriage within the prohibited degree, 36–7
as ruler, 7, 39–40, 161–2, 171, 172, 187
signature, 193–4
as war leader, 167, 179

Berengar II, k of Italy (d. 966), mrv of Ivrea [**Willa of Tuscany (d. aft 966)**], 97
and Adalbert Atto, 105
captures and imprisons **EA**, 1, 21, 33, 97
and Otto I, 2, 160–1
and kingship of Italy, 3, 160
pursues **EA**, 1, 177
Bernard of Clairvaux (d. 1153), two swords theory, 53
Bernard of Vallombrosa (d. 1133), later bp of Parma, confessor to **CM**, 60
Bernward, bp of Hildesheim (d. 1022), 166
Bernold of Constance (d. 1100), monk of St Blasien, chronicler, 51, 53, 55, 180, 183
Bertholdi et Bernoldi Chronica, 51, 52, 55, 85n232, 86n243, 89n266, 179–80, 183, 211n199
Berta, abss of San Sisto (d. 1100), 41
Bertha of Swabia, q of Burgundy, q of Italy (d. 966), dau of **Reginlind** and **Burchard of Swabia (d. 926)**; m of **EA** [**Rudolf II, k of Italy; Hugh, k of Italy**], 3, 20
date of death, 121n20
Hugh sends her back to Burgundy, 20
lineage and connections, 137
inheritance, wealth and property, 98, 100
Bertha of Turin, empss (d. 1087), dau of **Adelaide of Turin** and **Otto, ct of Savoy** [**Henry IV**], 35, 46, 167
accompanies **Henry IV** to Canossa, 35

Bertha of Turin, empss (*cont.*)
    as counsellor and negotiator, 35, 44–6
    lineage, 46
Berthold of Reichenau (d. c. 1088), monk, chronicler
Bertholdi et Bernoldi Chronica, 64, 93n322
Bertholdi et Bernoldi Chronica. *See* Bernold of Constance (d. 1100), monk of St Blasien, chronicler; Berthold of Reichenau (d. c. 1088), monk, chronicler
Bertrada the Younger, q of the Franks (d. 783) [**Pippin III**], 153
bishop(s), 2, 30, 39, 44–6, 55, 59, 66, 103, 136, 137, 150, 166, 175–6, 186–7
    and 'senate of women', 44
Bisson, Thomas N., 7
Bloch, Marc, 16
Bologna, 98, 108
Boniface, mgv of Tuscany (d. 1052), sn of **Guillia** and **Tedaldo**; f of CM [**Richilda, Beatrice of Bar**], 106. *See also* Attoni/Attonids (Canossans)
    death, 4, 37, 106, 108
    dress as marker of status, 192
    as father, 4, 36, 162, 171, 181, 184–5, 187
    inheritance and wealth, 4, 34, 105–6, 188
    and law, 105–6
    and Mantua, 161
    marriages, 34
    and property, 105, 107, 110
    as ruler, 34, 124n74, 167, 185
    woos Beatrice with fine display, 188
Bonizo, bp of Sutri (d. aft 1090), polemicist, 52–4
    Liber ad amicum, 53–5

Liber de vita Christiana, 53–5
    turns against CM, 54–5
Bormida, river, 98
Boso I, the Elder, ct (d. c 855) [Engeltrude], 20
Boso, k of Provence (d. 887) (k of Burgundy), br of **Richard le Justicier** [Ermengard, dau of **Louis II, k of Italy, Carolingian emp (d. 875)**], 20
Bosonids, 20
Bougard, François, 7
Brescello, monastery, 43, 49, 51, 85n233
Burchard, dk of Swabia (d. 926), f of **Bertha of Swabia**; grandf of EA [**Reginlind**], 69n35, 137
Burchard, dk of Swabia (d. 973), [**Hadwig (d. 994)**], 100
Burchard (I), abp of Lyons (d. 956/7), br of **EA**, 20–1, 70n37
Burchard (II), abp of Lyons (d. 1031), son of cb Aldiud and **Conrad I, k of Burgundy**, 70n37
Burgundian Rudolfings, Table 1, 3, 20–1, 100, 118
Burgundy, 3, 4, 20–2, 29, 67, 75n97, 100–2, 117, 137, 139, 146, 147, 149, 159, 161

C
Cadalus, b of Parma (d. 1071/72), antipope 28 Oct 1061–31 May 1064, 167, 179
Canossa (Reggio Emilia), 34, 35, 37, 47, 60, 104, 108, 115
    castle, fortress, rock of, 1, 2, 4, 5, 104, 105, 108, 110, 113–14, 119, 162–4, 166, 168, 172–3
    confrontation at (1077), 43–7, 61, 62, 64, 188, 191

monastery and church of Sant'Apollonio, 61, 62, 114, 157
siege of and battle at (1092), 6, 47, 62, 157–8
house of (*see* Attoni/Attonids (Canossans))
Capetians, French royal line, beginning with **Hugh Capet**, dynasty, 987–1328, Table 2, 18, 33, 162
capitanei, 176
Capua, 109
Capo Colonne, near Crotone, battle (982), defeat of Otto II at, 177
Carpineta, 172
Carpineti, 48, 158, 164, 173
castellan(s), 1, 8, 16. *See also* knight(s), miles, *milites*; warrior
Charlemagne, emp (d. 814), 24, 34, 133, 140, 155, 162
  dress and appearance as iconography, 189, 192
Charles, dk of LL (d. c 992), sn of **Gerberga (d. 969)** and **Louis IV d'Outremer**, 22, 32
Charles the Bald, West Frankish k (d. 877), [**Ermentrude (d. 869);** Richildis], 97, 78n126
  dress as display and iconography, 153
Charles III the Fat, Carolingian emp, set aside 887 (d. 888) [**Richgard**], 97
charter, charters. *See* documents under Adelheid of Burgundy, empss (d. 999); Matilda, ctss and mgvne of Tuscany (d. 1115)
the church, 95–6, 98, 99, 103, 108, 132, 136, 150, 153–6, 160, 173, 179, 181, 183, 186–7, 193, 194

Clement III, antipope (1080, 1084–1100) (Wibert), 47, 53, 63, 83n202, 183
Cluny, abbey, 30, 160. *See also* names of individual abbots
  support of EM's canonization, 28–9
cognate, cognatic, *cognatio*, 17, 19–20, 34, 35, 132. *See also* agnate, agnatic, agnatio; kin, kinship, kinship terminology
commune(s), *commune*, 115, 160, 163, 168, 176–7
community, communities, 7, 15–16, 36, 41, 61, 102, 132, 146, 195
Conrad I, East Frankish k (d. 918), 131
Conrad I the Pacific, k of Burgundy (d. 993), br of EA [cb Aldiud; first wife; **Mathilda of West Francia**], 4, 20–1, 26, 29, 33–4, 70n37, 77n2, 79n137, 146, 159
  'long shadowy reign', 21
  loyalty to the Ottonians, 21
  as maternal uncle, 22
  as peacemaker, 21–2
Conrad II, emp (1024–39), sn of **Henry II, emp [Gisela of Swabia]**, 34, 36, 46, 117, 124n74, 162, 163
  Constitutio de feudis, 9
Conrad, k (d. 1101), sn of **Bertha of Turin** and **Henry IV**, 45, 47, 66, 167, 169
  initially the heir, 5, 45
  defects to CM's side, 6, 31, 47, 51–2, 158, 167, 169
Conrad, ct of Auxerre (d. 876) [**Waldrada**], 20
Conrad the Red, dk of Lotharingia (d. 955) [**Liudgard**], 138
consanguinity, *consanguinei*, 17–18, 33, 37, 66, 79n135

Corbie, abbey, 96
Cortenuova, 41
council(s) and synod(s) of the church, 6
  Guastalla (1106), 63
  Lateran (1057), 36–7
  Lenten Synods (1076), (1080), (1097), (1099), 2, 4, 5, 44, 47, 59, 172
  Mantua (1064), 179
  Worms (1076), 2, 44, 46
court life and politics, 3, 9, 20–1, 23, 25–9, 32, 35, 42–3, 45, 52, 57, 62, 66, 99–100, 106, 109, 111–13, 116, 130–6, 145–50, 153–4, 159, 161–4, 184–5
Creber, Alison, 83n202
Cremona, 176, 190
Crotone. *See* Capo Colonne, near Crotone, battle (982), defeat of Otto II at
Cunegund (d. aft 923), dau of **Ermentrude, dau of Louis the Stammerer [Wigeric of Bidgau]**, 34
Cunigunde, empss. *See* Kunigunde, empss (d. 1040)
curtis, manor, estate, 98, 102, 104, 105, 107, 110, 119. *See also mansus(i)*, manse
  definition, 85n227

D
Daimbert, bp and abp of Pisa (d. 1105) (Dagobert), Latin Patriarch of Jerusalem, 55
Deborah, OT warrior, prophet and judge, 183
Desiderius, abt of Monte Cassino. *See* Victor III, pope (24 May 1086, 1087) (Desiderius, abt of Monte Cassino)

Deusdedit, cardinal (d. c. 1100), 53
diploma, diplomata. *See* documents *under* **EA, CM**
Doda (d. bef 1054), m of **Godfrey the Hunchback [Godfrey the Bearded]**, 38
Dodo, bp of Modena (d. 1136), 63–4
Donizo, abbot of Sant'Apollonio (d. aft 1133) (Donizone), 33–4, 47, 50, 52, 55, 62, 64, 113–15, 158, 159, 162, 167, 185, 188, 190–2
  Vita Mathildis (*De principibus canusinis*), 36, 62, 64, 114, 162, 191–2
dominae imperiales, 27, 134, 136, 145, 177–8, 184, 198n29
dos, 96, 100, 120n5. *See also* dowry; Morgengabe; lands and other property; reverse dowry
dowager(s), 3, 25, 32, 35, 96–7, 99–100, 109, 111, 119, 139, 145, 146, 149, 150, 178
dower, 96, 97. *See also* dowry; Morgengabe; lands and other property; reverse dowry
dowry, 95, 97, 106. *See also* Morgengabe; lands and other property; reverse dowry
  definition, 96
Duby, Georges, 8

E
Eberhard, archbp of Bamberg (d. 1170), 10
Eberhard, Frankish duke (d. 939), br of **Conrad I, k (d. 918)**, 137
Eberhard, ct of Nellenburg (probably d. 1078/1079), 112

Edith of Wessex, East Frankish q (d. 947) (Eadgyth, Otwith), dau of Ælfflaed and **Edward the Elder** [**Otto I**], 18, 137, 152, 153, 156, 157, 190
  appearance, 189
  as dowager, 32
  interventions in the diplomata, 148
  lineage, 18–19
  and Queen Mathilda, 32, 135, 149
Edith of Wessex, q of England (d. 1075), dau of Godwin of Wessex [**Edward the Confessor**], 149
Edward the Confessor, k of England (d. 1066), sn of **Emma of Normandy, q of England (d. 1052)** [**Edith of Wessex (d. 1075)**], 149, 220n335
Edward the Elder, Anglo-Saxon k (d. 924), f of **Edith of Wessex (d. 947)**; br of **Æthelflæd** [Ælfflæd; dau of Ealdorman Ælelhelm], 19
Ekkeman, monk, abt of Selz and confessor of **EA**, 29, 59, 60
Emma, East Frankish Carolingian q (d. 876) [**Louis the German**], 35
Emma of Normandy, q of England (d. 1052), m of **Harthacnut** and **Edward the Confessor** [Æthelread the Unready; Canute], 97, 151
  commissioned *Encomium Emmae Reginae*, 192
Emma, West Frankish q (d. aft c. 989), only child of **EA** and **Lothar, k of Italy** [Lothair], 3, 22, 32, 33, 35
  vicissitudes of widowhood, 22
empress(es). *See also* kings, kingship; queen(s), queenship
  crowning and anointing, 141, 153, 155

Encomium Emmae Reginae. *See* Emma of Normandy, q of England (d. 1052), m of **Harthacnut** and **Edward the Confessor**
Epitaphium domine Adalheide auguste. *See* Odilo, abt of Cluny (994–1049)
Ermengard, dau of Berta and Adalbert II, the Rich, mgv of Tuscany (d. 915) [**Adalbert, mgv of Ivrea**], 189–90
  and 'carnal trafficking', 190
Ermingarda, ctss [ct Rainer], 118
Ermentrude, q (d. 869) [**Charles the Bald**], 96–7
Ermentrude, dau of **Louis the Stammerer**, m of **Cunegund**, 34–5
Erstein (Alsace), 40, 98, 100–2, 109, 116–17, 143
Este family and lands, 5–6, 46, 47, 50, 61
Eupraxia, Evpraksia. *See* Praxedis, empss (d. 1109) (Prassede, Adelheid)
Eustace II of Boulogne (d. c 1087) [**Ida of LL (d. 1113)**], 38
excommunication, 5, 44–7, 64–5, 115, 172, 180, 186, 191

F
Ferrara, 43, 172
fief(s), fiefdoms, 9, 107, 108
Folkold, bp of Meissen (d. 992), 27
Frassinoro, monastery (Modena), 43, 50, 187
Frederick (d. 1053–55), son of **Beatrice of Bar** and **Boniface**; br of **CM**, 4, 37–9, 106–8
Frederick, ct of Mömpelgard (now Montbéliard) (d. 1091), sn of **Sophie of Bar**, 52–3, 167

Frederick of Lotharingia (d. 1058), br of **Godfrey the Bearded**; abt of Monte Cassino; Pope Stephen IX from 2 August 1057, 39

Frederick I Barbarossa, emp (d. 1190), 10, 166

Frederick II, d. of UL (d. 1026/1033), maternal grandf of **CM [Mathilda of Swabia]**, 106, 171, 187

Frederick, follower of **CM**, 148

Fried, Johannes, 178

G

Gandersheim, royal monastery, 19, 138

Garda, castle and lake, 1, 3, 5, 181

Garibald (d. 591), Bavarian ruler, 134

Garigliano, river, 180

Geilo, abt of St Peter, Weißenburg, 142

Geminianus, saint, early Christian bp, martyr, 63, 92n315, 185, 192

gendered terms, 179–83

Geoffrey of Mayenne (d. 1098) [qw **Gercendis**], 168

Gerald, saint and ct of Aurillac (d. 909), 160

Gerberga (d. 969), dau of **Mathilda of Ringelheim** and **Henry the Fowler** [**Giselbert, dk of Lotharingia**; **Louis IV d'Outremer**], 21, 34, 77n121, 78n133

Gerberga of Burgundy (d. aft 1016), dau of **Mathilda of West Francia** and **Conrad I, k of Burgundy** [**Hermann II of Swabia**], 44–5

Gerberga (II), abss of Gandersheim (d. 1002), dau of Judith (d. aft 985) and **Henry (I), dk of Bavaria (d. 955)**, 23, 138

Gerbert of Aurillac (d. 1003), abt of Bobbio; Pope Sylvester II from 999, 24–7, 29, 134, 157, 177–8, 184

Gercendis (active in the late eleventh century) (Gersendis), dau of **Herbert 'Wake the Dog'** [Theobald III, ct of Blois; **Adalbert Azzo II**; qh **Geoffrey of Mayenne**], 61–2, 168

Gesta Ottonis. See Hrotsvitha(d. c. 1002), canoness of Gandersheim

Gisela (d. aft 874), dau of **Louis the Pious** and **Judith (d. 843)**, 20

Gisela (d. 918), greatgrandm of **EA**, 34

Gisela of Burgundy (d. 1006), dau of **Conrad I, k of Burgundy** and his first wife [**Henry the Wrangler**], 22

Gisela of Swabia, empss (d. 1041), dau of **Gerberga of Burgundy** and **Hermann II of Swabia** [**Conrad II, emp**], 34, 36, 45, 46

Giselbert, dk of Lotharingia (d. 939), 137

Giselbert II, ct palatine of Bergamo (d. 993–1010), f of **Richilda**, 106

Godfrey (II) the Bearded of Verdun (d. 1069) (aka Godfrey III), sn of Gozelo II, mgv of Tuscany, d of LL [**Doda; Beatrice of Bar**], 4–5, 34, 36–9, 78n133, 79n138, 80n146, 106–8, 181, 184, 187, 215n266

Godfrey (III) the Hunchback (d. 1076) (aka Godfrey IV), sn of **Doda** and **Godfrey the Bearded** [first husband of **CM**], 4–5, 38–9,

INDEX   281

44, 50, 51, 66, 80n146, 104, 106–8, 118, 187, 215n266
Godfrey IV of Bouillon (d. 1100), nephew of **Godfrey the Hunchback**; mgv of Antwerp, dk of LL, 'Advocate of the Holy Sepulchre' = k. of Jerusalem, 44, 107
Goez, Elke and Werner, 168
Golinelli, Paolo, Foreword, 84n218, 85n233
governance, 3, 9–10, 23, 101, 115
Gozelo II, dk of UL and LL (d. 1044) (aka Gozelo I), 79n133, 79n138
Gozelo III, dk of LL (d. 1046) (aka Gozelo II), sn of **Gozelo II**, br of **Godfrey the Bearded**, 37, 79n138
Gozpert, abt of Tegernsee (r. 982–1001), 164
Gratian, 53
 Decretum, 53
Greeks, 149, 177
Gregory V, pope (996–999), grandsn of **Liudgard** and **Conrad the Red**, 156
Gregory VII, pope (1073–85) (Hildebrand), 2, 5, 36, 44, 46, 53, 56–8, 60, 61, 64, 65, 114, 156, 166, 172–3, 180, 186, 191, 194
Guastalla, 63, 174. *See also under* council(s) and synod(s) of the church
Guelf. *See* Welf IV, dk of Bavaria (Welf the Elder) (d. 1101) (Guelf IV), sn of **Adalbert Azzo II**; Welf V, dk of Bavaria (d. 1120) (Guelf V), eldest sn of Judith of Flanders and **Welf IV**
Guidi, 51

Guido V 'Guerra' of the Guidi (d. c. 1124), sn of ct Guido IV of the Guidi, adopted sn of **CM**, 49, 51, 67, 84n218
Guillia (d. by 1007) (Willia) [**Tedaldo**], 34

H
Hadwig (d. aft 965) (Hathui), dau of **Mathilda of Ringelheim** and **Henry the Fowler**; sis of **Otto I** [**Hugh the Great**], 33–4, 77n121, 77n133
Hadwig (d. 994), dau of Judith and **Henry (I), dk of Bavaria (d. 955)** [**Burchard, dk of Swabia (d. 973)**], 100
Hathui of Saxony (d. 903), m of **Henry the Fowler** and **Oda (d. aft 952)** [**Otto, dux (d. 912)**], 37
Harthacnut (d. 1042), sn of **Emma of Normandy**, 192
Henry I, k of England (d. 1135) [**Mathilda of Scotland (d. 1118)**], 59
Henry I, the Fowler, k of the East Franks (d. 936), br of **Otto I** [Hatheburg; **Mathilda of Ringelheim**], 28, 34, 36, 37, 97, 103, 129, 131, 134, 137, 141, 149, 175
Henry II, k and emp (d. 1024) [**Kunigunde**], 25, 26, 28–31, 117, 134, 157, 162, 182
Henry III, k and emp (d. 1056) [**Agnes of Poitou**], 4, 36–8, 45, 64, 104, 106–7, 112
Henry IV, k and emp (d. 1106) [**Bertha of Turin**; **Praxedis**],

282 INDEX

Henry IV, k and emp (*cont.*)
2–3, 5–6, 31, 35, 36, 44–7, 50–5, 60–2, 64–7, 103–4, 107, 108, 110, 112–13, 115, 157–8, 160, 163, 166–9, 171–3, 175, 179–80, 182, 183, 185, 186, 188, 191, 192. *See also* battle(s) under the names of their locations
illegitimate son of, 182
kidnapping, 45, 57
Henry V, emp (d. 1125) [Mathilda, dau of **Mathilda of Scotland (d. 1118)** and **Henry I, k of England**], 6, 35, 52, 62, 67, 110, 114. *See also* Matildine lands
Henry (I), dk of Bavaria (d. 955), br of **Otto I** [**Judith of Bavaria (d. aft 985)**], 2, 22–5, 97, 134, 137–8, 141–2, 156, 157, 189
Henry (II) the Wrangler, dk of Bavaria (d. 995) (Henry the Quarrelsome) [**Gisela of Burgundy**], 22, 25–8, 33, 121n33, 136, 145–6, 159–60, 177
Henry, abt of San Salvatore dell'Isola, 174
Henry, dk, unidentified, 131
Herbert 'Wake the Dog' (d. 1035), ct of Maine, 168
Hermann, bp of Metz (d. 1090), 56, 60
Hermann I, the Frank, dk of Swabia (d. 949), of Conradine family, f of **Ida (d. 986)**, 134, 138
Hermann II, dk of Swabia (d. 1003) [**Gerberga of Burgundy**], 44–5
Hildebrand. *See* Gregory VII, pope (1073–85) (Hildebrand)
Hildegard (d. mid-/late tenth century), great-grandm of **CM** [**Adalbert Atto**], 34

Hildegundis, abb of Geseke (Westphalia), 17
Hildibald, bp of Worms (d. 998) (Hildebald), 27
Hincmar, abp of Reims (d. 882), 133, 153
Hitda, abss of Meschede, 192, 219n333
Hochfelden (Alsace), 98, 104, 108, 112–13
Honorius (II), antipope. *See* Cadalus, b of Parma (d. 1071/72), antipope 28 Oct 1061–31 May 1064
Hrotsvitha (d. c. 1002), canoness of Gandersheim, 21, 33, 35, 97, 141, 152, 178, 184
on appearance and demeanor, 189–90
Gesta Ottonis, 23, 115, 130, 137–9, 152
privileges female ancestry, 19–20
on queenship, 141, 152
sensitivity to family ties, 23–4, 137
Hubert (d. c 864), son of **Boso I, the Elder (d. c 855)**, 20
Hugh, abt of Cluny (d. 1109), 2, 46–7, 55, 61, 64–5, 191
Hugh, abt of Flavigny (d. betw. 1114 and late 1140s), 65, 182–3
Hugh, abp of Lyons (d. 1106) bp of Die, papal legate, 55, 61, 64–6. *See also* **Anselm (II) the Younger (d. 1086)**
and quarrel with Pope Victor III, 65
Hugh the Great, West Frankish dux (d. 956), [**Hadwig**], 33
Hugh Capet, West Frankish k (d. 996) [**Adelaide (d. 1004)**], 32, 33, 105, 134
Hugh, k of Italy (d. 948) (Hugh of Arles), sn of Berta and Theobald;

INDEX 283

stepf of EA [Willa (d. before 925); Alda; **Bertha of Swabia**], 3, 20, 21, 23, 98, 118, 148
Hugh, ct at Le Mans (d. aft 1095), son of **Gercendis** and **Adalbert Azzo II**; half-br of **Welf IV** and of **Adelasia**, 50, 62, 168
Hugh, mgv of Tuscany (d. 1001), sn of **Willa, ctss of Camerino (d. aft 977/8)**, 32

I
iconography, 189–94
Ida (d. 986), dau of Hermann I of Swabia [**Liudolf (d. 957)**], 138
Ida of LL (d. 1113), dau of **Doda** and **Godfrey the Bearded**; stepsis of CM [**Eustace II of Boulogne**], 35, 38
interveners, interventions in diplomas/diplomata, 21–2, 41, 109, 113, 142–50, 203n108, 109
iron crown of the Lombards, 2
Isidore of Seville, 17

J
John Philagathos, abp (d. 1001), chancellor in Italy, antipope John XVI (997–8), 146
John of Mantua, 52–4, 182
Judith, OT warrior and prophet, 183
Judith, empss (d. 843), dau of ct Welf; m of **Charles the Bald** [**Louis the Pious**], 97
Judith (d. aft 870), dau of **Ermentrude (d. 869)** and **Charles the Bald** [**Æthelwulf**], 153
Judith of Bavaria, (d. aft 985), dau of Arnulf, dk of Bavaria (d. 937) [**Henry (I), dk of Bavaria, d. 955**], 189

K
kings, kingship, 129–30. *See also* empress(es); queen(s), queenship
crowning and anointing, 3, 132, 134, 153, 155, 162
display and iconography, 189, 190, 192
ideal, 129–32, 133
imperial coronations, 3, 5, 26, 141, 150, 172, 190
royal *iter*, 3, 132, 140, 142
regal authority, 220n335
treasury, 85n227
kin, kinship, kinship terminology
amici, 18
consanguinei, 17, 18, 33, 37, 66
kin, 16–18, 20, 23, 26, 35, 39, 44, 46, 47, 52, 64, 66–7, 95, 116
kinship, 8, 16, 22, 23, 26
familia, 17
parentes, 18
propinqui, 18, 52 (*see also* agnate, agnatio; cognate, cognatic, *cognatio*)
knight(s), 8, 9, 16, 54. *See also miles, milites*
Kunigunde, empss (d. 1040) [**Henry II, emp**], 46, 117, 134, 156, 182, 194

L
Lambro, river, 98
Lantbert, obscure ct, 37
law(s), 21, 38, 54, 100, 104, 106–7, 111, 113, 115–16, 118, 119
Lombard, 40, 97, 104, 111, 115–16, 118

law(s) (*cont.*)
  Salic, 39–40, 104, 111, 115–16, 118, 171, 187
  symbols and symbolic actions, 40, 116
lawful action and armed struggle, 22, 54, 97, 136, 141, 145, 159, 171–3, 177–8, 180–1
Lazzari, Tiziana, 38
Lech, battle (955), 141, 175
Le Mans, city, 61, 168
Leo, bp of Pistoia, 60
Leo IX, pope (1049–54), 106
Lenten Synod(s). *See* council(s) and synod(s) of the church
Leyser, Karl, 8, 16, 17, 20, 21, 139, 166
Liber ad amicum. *See* Bonizo, bp of Sutri (d. aft 1090), polemicist
Liber de vita Christiana. *See* Bonizo, bp of Sutri (d. aft 1090), polemicist
Liudgard (d. 953) (Liutgard), dau of **Edith of Wessex (d. 947)** and **Otto I [Conrad the Red]**, 156, 157
Liudolf (d. 866), East Saxon *dux* [Oda], 18
Liudolf (d. 957), dk of Swabia, sn of **Edith of Wessex (d. 947)** and **Otto I [Ida (d. 986)]**, 137–8, 140, 148, 190
Liudolfings, Table 2, 18, 24, 131–2, 197n15
Liudprand, bp of Cremona (d. 972) (Liutprand), historian, diplomat, 19, 141, 189–90
  Antapodosis, 190
  Relatio de legatione Constantinopolitana, 190
Liutharius, brother, prior at Melara, 109

Lothair IV, West Frankish Carolingian k (d. 986), sn of **Gerberga (d. 969)** and **Louis IV, d'Outremer [Emma (d. aft c. 989)]**, 21, 22, 32, 33, 119, 177
Lothar, k of Italy (d. 950), sn of Alda (Hilda) and **Hugh, k of Italy**; first husband of **EA**, 1, 3, 20–3, 33, 35, 66, 97, 98, 104, 118, 137, 141, 145, 148, 150, 153, 177
Louis the Pious, Carolingian emp (d. 840) [Ermengard (d. 818); **Judith of Bavaria (d. 843)**], 20, 34–5, 97
Louis II the German, East Frankish Carolingian k (d. 876), son of **Louis the Pious [Emma (d. 876)]**, 35
Louis II the Stammerer, k of the West Franks (d. 879), 78n126
Louis II, k of Italy, Carolingian emp (d. 875), sn of Lothar I (d. 855) [**Angelberga**], 41, 141
Louis IV, d'Outremer, West Frankish Carolingian k (d. 954) [**Gerberga (d. 969)**], 21, 33
Louis V (d. 987), sn of **Emma (d. aft c. 989)** and **Lothair IV**, 22, 32
Lucca, 4, 42, 46, 60, 98, 150, 163, 171, 187

M

Maiolus, abt of Cluny (956–994), 21–2, 29, 30, 99
Manegold of Lautenbach (d. c. 1103), polemicist, political theorist, 53
Mantua, 2, 4, 5, 39–42, 49, 53, 105, 106, 158, 161, 163, 169, 171–3, 186–7

mansus(*i*), manse, 98, 110, 123n59, 148. *See also curtis*, manor, estate definition, 148
Marcigny, a subsidiary Cluny house, 29
Marriage Charter, 153–4
Mathilda of Ringelheim, q of the East Franks (d. 968), m-in-law of **EA** [**Henry the Fowler**], 32, 34, 97, 135, 137, 149
Mathilda of West Francia, q of Burgundy (d. 981–90/992), dau of **Gerberga (d. 969)** and **Louis IV d'Outremer** [**Conrad I, k of Burgundy**], 4, 21, 33–4
Mathilda of Swabia (d. c 1030/4), dau of **Gerberga of Burgundy** and Hermann II of Swabia, grandm of **CM** [**Frederick II of UL**], 36, 45
Mathilda, abss of Quedlinburg (d. 999), dau of **EA** and Otto I, 3, 4, 22, 27, 98, 101, 117, 135, 136, 145–7, 149, 156, 159, 177–8
Matilda, ctss and mgvne of Tuscany (d. 1115) (Matilda of Canossa), dau of **Beatrice of Bar** and **Boniface** [**Godfrey the Hunchback**; **Welf V**]. *See also* **Geminianus**, saint, early Christian bp, martyr; **Gregory VII**, pope (1073–85) (Hildebrand); **Guido V 'Guerra'** of the Guidi (d. c. 1124), sn of ct Guido IV of the Guidi, adopted sn of **CM**; **Henry IV**, k and emp (d. 1106); **Henry V**, emp (d. 1125); **Paschal II**, pope (1099–1118); 'senate of women'; **Urban II**, pope (1088–99)
a brief life of, 4–6
acting like a king, 111, 195
and adoped son **Guido Guerra**, 51

ancestry and fine lineage, 2, 34–5, 66, 159, 161–2, 187–8
appearance, images and iconography, 34, 59, 63–4, 115, 190–4
and armor, 181
authority of/as ruler, 6, 44, 48–9, 57, 104, 107–8, 110–11, 118, 157, 159, 161–2, 165, 176–7, 184, 186, 191, 192, 194, 195
awareness of **EA**, 33, 114–15
birth and early life, 35–6, 66, 106
and Canossa, 2–3, 44–7, 114–15, 157–8, 166
chancery and bureaucratic organization, 48, 183–4
and the church, 6, 42, 47, 49, 51–66, 110, 115, 160, 173, 179, 181, 183, 186–7, 193, 194
control of the roads, 166–8
criticism of, 52, 54–5
and daughter **Beatrice**, 4, 50
death, burial and statue, 6, 49, 58–61, 67, 114, 173, 191, 195
dedication to reform, 5, 30, 39, 44, 47, 50–7, 60, 115, 160, 179
disagreements and their resolution, 5, 47, 50, 55, 159, 167, 175
documents, charters and diplomata, 39–43, 48–9, 51, 110–11, 118, 119, 159, 168–75, 187–8, 194
donations, endowments and gifts by, 6, 40, 42, 49, 51, 63, 107, 171, 186
donations, endowments and gifts to, 106–8
as female Old Testament model, 54, 183
and followers, 36, 40–3, 48–9
and husbands (*see* Godfrey(III) the Hunchback (d. 1076) (aka Godfrey IV), sn of **Doda** and

Matilda, ctss and mgvne of Tuscany (*cont.*)
    Godfrey the Bearded; and **Welf V, dk of Bavaria** (d. 1120) (Guelf V), eldest sn of Judith of Flanders and **Welf IV**)
    itinerary, 50, 169–75
    kin, 44–7, 52
    lands and other property, 40, 44, 46, 50, 60, 63, 64, 66, 100, 104–5, 107–11, 116, 167, 169, 184, 185
    largesse, 63
    letters to and from, 56–9, 61, 64–6, 168, 172, 185–7, 194
    lordship, 47, 66, 104, 110–11, 162, 173–5, 179, 184, 186
    loyalty, 43, 111
    and marriage, 50, 51, 66
    military initiatives and warfare, 5, 50–1, 67, 157–8, 163–4, 175–7, 180–3
    miracle, 61
    and mother **Beatrice**, 35–41, 43, 44
    as negotiator and peacemaker, 43, 47, 63, 65, 159
    and the papacy, 5–6, 36, 39, 44, 47, 53, 57, 64–5, 160, 173, 180–1, 186–7
    philosophical court, 52–5
    presence on the battlefield, 181–2
Matilda (*cont.*)
    self-fashioning and public persona, 59, 162, 179, 183, 185, 187, 192–4
    and siblings. *See* **Beatrice (d. 1053–55)**, sis of **CM**; **Frederick (d. 1053–55)**, son of **Beatrice of Bar** and **Boniface**; br of **CM**
    signature, seals and coins, 193–4
    spiritual family, 55–66
    spiritual life, 36, 58, 67, 160, 193, 194
    succession to, 49, 51–2, 66–7
    theft of her remains, 6
    titles and epithets: *comitissa* and *comes*, 159, 171, 187; 'daughter of St Peter', 181; *domina*, 179, 183, 184; *dux* and *ducatrix*, 159, 171, 179, 180, 184, 185, 187; *inclita*, 185; 'like another Deborah', 183; *marchionessa*, 159, 184; *miles*, 179, 180; *virago*, 179, 182–3; *virilis animi*, 183
    treasure, distribution in support of Gregory VII, 60
    as warrior, 160, 180, 182–3
Mathilda of Scotland, q (d. 1118) [**Henry I, k of England**], 59
Matildine lands, 67, 108
Melara, 104, 108–13, 116, 174
Milan, 2, 55, 108, 154, 193
miles, milites, 179–80, 182. *See also* knight(s), warrior
military strategy. *See* battle(s), battlefield, battle strategy
Modena, cathedral, 6, 63–4, 185, 192
Modena, location, 2, 50, 98, 105
Moore, R. I., 1, 103
Morgengabe, 96, 100. *See also* dowry; reverse dowry
Moselle, river, 102
Mouzay, 49
mundeburdium, 151

N
naming customs, 35
Nogara, 158, 167, 173
Notre Dame, cathedral (Lausanne), 147

O
Oda (d. 913) [**Liudolf (d. 866)**], 18

Oda of Saxony (d. aft 952), dau of
    Hathui of Saxony (d. 903) and
    Otto, East Saxon dk (d. 912),
    sis of **Henry the Fowler**, 37
Odilo, abt of Cluny (994–1049),
    21–2, 26, 29–32, 99, 141–2, 178,
    182
    *Epitaphium domine Adalheide
        auguste*, 57, 142, 151
Odo (Eudes), prior of Cluny, bishop
    of Ostia. *See* **Urban II**, pope
    (1088–99)
Orba, river, 98
Otto, East Saxon dk (d. 912), f of
    Henry the Fowler [**Hathui (d.
    903)**], 137–8
Otto I, emp (d. 973), second husband
    of EA [cb a Slav captive
    noblewoman; **Edith of Wessex
    (d. 947)**, EA], 1–3, 18–21, 23,
    26, 27, 29, 33, 41, 97, 98, 100,
    102, 104, 112, 115–18, 129,
    136, 141, 143, 145, 146, 148,
    152, 157
  appearance and depiction, 155
  authority, 159–61, 166, 177, 190
  and diplomata (charters), 148
  and **Adalbert Atto**, 105, 114
  and brother **Henry (I) of Bavaria**,
    137, 141, 142
  chancery, 183
  and **Edith of Wessex (d. 947)**, 18,
    148
  and epithets, 152
  and family relationships, 138
  imperial coronation, 141, 150, 161,
    190
  iter, 3, 143, 144
  as model for rulers, 130
  and mother **Mathilda of
    Ringelheim**, 134
  clementia, 131
  marriage to EA, 3, 156
  Marriage Charter and *Ottonianum*,
    153–4
  and son **Liudolf**, 138
  and son **Otto II**, 132, 134, 155
  tests **EA** with gold, 2, 129, 137
Otto II, emp (d. 983), sn of EA and
    Otto I [Theophanu], 3–4, 21–2,
    25–30, 33, 45, 99, 100, 109,
    116, 132, 135, 143, 145, 148,
    150, 151, 155, 164, 177
  at Capo Colonne and Taranto,
    177
  and **Theophanu**, 153–4
Otto III, emp (d. 1002), sn of
    Theophanu and **Otto II**, 24, 26,
    30, 32, 33, 37, 40, 100, 102–3,
    109, 116, 135, 146–7, 151,
    155–7, 166, 176
  minority, 4, 22, 27–8, 32, 33, 45,
    98–9, 102–3, 117, 134, 136,
    145–6, 149, 150, 160, 177–8,
    194
  coronations, 26
Otto, bp of Strasbourg (d. 1100), 31
Otto, ct of Savoy (d. by May 1060)
    [**Adelaide of Turin**], 46
Otto of Freising (d. 1158), bp,
    chronicler, 102
Ottonianum, 153–4
Ottonians, Ottonian dynasty, Saxon
    royal family, Henry I (d. 936)–
    Henry II (d. 1024), Table 2, 27,
    28, 34, 36, 131, 134, 162, 163,
    166, 167, 178, 192

P

Paganus of Corsena, follower of **CM**,
    41–2, 49, 84n220
papacy, papal, 3, 5, 6, 31, 39, 44, 45,
    47, 59, 64–5, 83n194, 103, 114,
    153, 154, 156–7, 159, 161, 173,
    179–81, 186, 194

Paschal II, pope (1099–1118), 6, 47, 49, 58–60, 63, 187
patrimony, 7, 8, 96, 97, 105, 107, 153
Pavia (Lombardy), 2, 3, 20, 40, 66, 98, 108, 109, 116, 129, 138, 146, 162, 163, 166
  ancient Lombard capital, 97, 139–40, 143
Payerne (Peterlingen), monastery, 147
Peter Damian, 37
Peterlingen. *See* Payerne (Peterlingen), monastery
Piacenza, 41, 55, 63
Piadena, 158, 167, 169, 173
Pippin III the Short, k of the Franks (d. 768) [**Bertrada**], 24, 166
Pippin, k of Italy (d. 810), 97
Po, plain, river system, valley, 2, 105–6, 108–10, 158, 159, 161, 162, 164, 166–8, 171, 176
power, private, 9
power, public, 9, 159, 183
Prangarda, sis of Tedaldo, 46
Praxedis, empss (d. 1109) (Prassede, Adelheid) [**Henry IV**], 6, 47, 51–2
precarial emphyteuse, 107. *See also* fief(s), fiefdoms
primogeniture, 8, 95, 134, 137

Q

Quedlinburg, royal palace and foundation for women, 3, 28, 32, 131, 136, 143, 147, 150, 156
Quedlinburg Annals. *See Annales Quedlinburgenses*
queen(s), queenship, 132–7, 141, 206n146, 152. *See also* EA; **Agnes of Poitou**, empss (d. 1077); empress(es); king, kingship; **Theophanu**, empss (d. 991) (Theophano)
  authority and role, 1, 35, 133–6, 141–2
  as counselor, 133
  crowning and anointing, 141, 153, 155
  as cupbearer, 134
  display and iconography of, 135, 153–5, 189
  as gift-giver, 133
  ideal, 132–6, 141, 152
  imperial coronation(s), 7, 26, 153, 161, 172, 190–1
  as intervener in charters, 142, 147–9
  as regent, 132, 134–5, 145–6, 156, 185
  royal *iter*, 3, 132, 140, 142
  and treasure, 97, 133

R

Rangerius, bp of Lucca (d. 1112), historian, 52, 53, 60
Rather, bp of Verona (d. 974), 194
Ravenna, 107, 108, 143, 166
Reggio, Reggio Emilia, 2, 41, 44, 48, 50, 64, 98, 105, 113, 114, 173, 180, 181, 186, 187
Reginlind (d. 958 or later), m of **Bertha of Swabia**; grandm of EA [**Burchard, dk of Swabia** (d. 926)], 20, 69n35, 137
Relatio de legatione Constantinopolitana. *See* Liudprand, bp of Cremona (d. 972) (Liutprand), historian, diplomat
Relatio translationis corporis sancti Geminiani, 63–4, 193
Res gestae Saxonicae. *See* Widukind of Corvey (d. aft 973), monk, historian
Reuter, Timothy, 45
Revere, 109–10, 174

Reynolds, Susan, 99
reverse dowry, 9, 41, 96, 98, 100, 112, 117, 154. *See also* dowry; *Morgengabe*; lands and other property
definition, 7, 96, 112
Rhine, river, 102, 143, 147
Richard le Justicier (d. 921), grandsn of **Boso I, the Elder; br of Boso, k of Provence (d. 887)** [**Adelaide of Auxerre**], 20, 78n127
Richard, abt of Saint-Victor, 65
Richilda (d. 1034/37), dau of **Giselbert II, ct palatine of Bergamo** [first husband, **Boniface**], 34, 106
Richgard, empss (d. betw 894 and 896) [**Charles III the Fat**], 97, 100
Robert the Pious, Capetian k (d. 1031) (Robert II, k of the Franks), sn of Hugh Capet, 30
Robert I, count of Flanders, 52
Robert Curthose, dk of Normandy (d. 1134), sn of **William the Conqueror** [**Sibyl of Conversano**], 50
Robert, k of the Franks, 30
Robinson, I. S., 38
Rome, 3, 5, 6, 40, 44, 46, 47, 56, 58, 59, 61, 64, 65, 106, 109, 113, 129, 142, 159, 161, 164, 166, 172, 178, 181
Rosvitha. *See* Hrotsvitha (d. c. 1002), canoness of Gandersheim
Rudolf I, k of Burgundy (d. 912), sn of **Waldrada** and **Conrad, ct of Auxerre** [Willa (d. before 925)], 20
Rudolf II, k of Italy (d. 937), sn of Willa (d. before 925) and **Rudolf I, k of Burgundy**; f of EA [**Bertha of Swabia**], 3, 21, 118, 137
Rudolf III (d. 1032), sn of **Mathilda of West Francia** and **Conrad I, k of Burgundy**; neph of EA, 22, 147
Rudolf, dk of Alsace, br of **Bertha of Swabia**, 100
Rudolf, dk of Burgundy (d. 986), br of **EA**, 20

S
San Benedetto Po (Mantua), monastery, 6, 49, 67, 193
San Colombano, monastery (Bobbio), 24–5. *See also* **Gerbert of Aurillac (d. 1003), abt of Bobbio; Pope Sylvester II from 999**
San Salvatore, monastery (Pavia), 30, 109–10, 116
San Sisto, monastery (Piacenza), 41, 63
Sant'Ambrogio, church and monastery (Milan) 193
Sant'Andrea, monastery (Mantua), 40
Sant'Apollonio, church and monastery (Canossa), 60, 62, 114
SS Felix and Regula, monastery (Zurich), 97
St Gerald, monastery (Aurillac), 25
St Maurice d'Agaune, monastery (Burgundy), 147
St Peter, monastery (Cavaillon/Chalon-sur-Saône), 30
St Peter, monastery (Weißenburg), 142
St Peter's Basilica (Rome), 6
St Victor, monastery (Geneva), 147

Salians (Conrad II (d. 1039)–Henry V (d. 1125)), 6, 8, 36, 45, 96, 112, 130, 148, 162–3
Saracens, 177
Selz, monastery, fortress, burial place of **EA** (Alsace), 4, 28–9, 31, 67, 98, 99, 102, 103, 117, 147
'senate of women', 44
Sibyl of Conversano (d. 1103) (Sybil, Sybilla) [**Robert Curthose**], 50
Sidonius Apollinaris (d. 489) (Gaius Sollius Apollinaris Sidonius), 164, 189
Siegfried of Lucca (d. c. mid-tenth century), 83n202, 105, 123n54
Siegfried, ct of Walbeck (d. c. 992), father of **Thietmar of Merseburg**, 178
Skinner, Patricia, 6
sn of **Henry IV** (d. 1092), illegitimate, 182
Sophie, abss of Gandersheim and Essex (d. 1039), grandau of **EA**, 100, 146, 198n29. *See also dominae imperiales*
Sophie of Bar (d. 1093), dau of **Mathilda of Swabia** and **Frederick II of UL**; maternal aunt of **CM**, 34, 77n122
Sorbara, battle (1084), 180
Stephen II, pope (752–757), 166
Stephen IX, pope (1057–58). *See* Frederick of Lotharingia (d. 1058)
Strasbourg (Alsace), 29, 31, 108
succession crisis(es), 8, 22, 27, 33, 51, 66, 95, 134–5, 145, 150
Sylvester II, pope (999–1003). *See* Gerbert of Aurillac (d. 1003), abt of Bobbio; Pope Sylvester II from 999
synod(s). *Se* council(s) and synod(s) of the church
Syrus of Cluny, 30, 99
Vita sancti Maioli, 30, 99

T

Taranto, battle (982), 177
Tassilo, dk in the eighth century, 24
Tedaldo (d. 1012), sn of **Hildegard** and **Adalbert Atto**; grandf of **CM** [**Guillia**], 4, 46, 105
Tegernsee (Bavaria), abbey, 164, 175–6
Theoderic (I), dk of UL (d. 1026/27), great-grandf of **CM**, 78n133
Theoderic (II), dk of UL (d. 1115), 186
Theodoric, k of Italy, k of the Ostrogoths (r 474–576), 131, 152, 189
Theodoric II, k of the Visigoths (r 453–456), 189
Theophanu, empss (d. 991) (Theophano) [**Otto II**], 3–4, 7, 22, 25, 27, 28, 32, 33, 45, 98–9, 102, 117, 134–6, 143, 145–6, 148–51, 153–6, 159–60, 174, 177–8, 184–5. *See also dominae imperiales*
mundeburdium, 151
Theudelinda, q of the Lombards (d. 628) (Theodelinda), dau of **Garibald** [**Authari, Agilulf**], 134, 141
Thietmar, bp of Merseburg (d. 1018), sn of Siegfried of Walbeck, chronicler, 26–7, 99, 136, 151–2, 178, 184, 188

Thietmari Merseburgensis episcopi chronicon, 151–2
treasure, 60, 97, 133
Tricontai, battle (1091), 50

U
Uhlirz, Mathilde, 99
Ulrich, bp of Augsburg (d. 973), (Udalrich, Uodalric, Odalrici), 166
Urban II, pope (1088–99), 4, 29, 31, 46, 51, 55, 59, 63, 173, 181, 186
Urban VIII, pope (1623–44), 6

V
vassal, vassalage, 1, 2, 5, 9, 17, 23–4, 36, 37, 54, 60, 104, 106, 113, 148, 151, 159, 167, 185
Vaughan, Sally, 78n130
Verdun, house of. *See* Ardennes (Verdun), house of
Verona, 1, 6, 28, 63, 132, 166, 169, 171, 172
Victor III, pope (24 May 1086, 1087) (Desiderius, abt of Monte Cassino), 65
Vita Mathildis reginae antiquior, 97
Vita Mathildis reginae posterior, 97, 135, 141–2
Volta, battle (1080), 181

W
Waldkirch, abbey, 100
Waldrada (d. ninth century) [**Conrad, ct of Auxerre**], 20
Warner, David, 142, 158
warrior, 23, 137, 160, 180, 182–3, 195

wealth, 1, 6–9, 16, 34, 42, 66, 95, 102, 103, 107–8, 113–14, 135, 139, 157, 161, 188, 195
Wedding Certificate. *See* Marriage Charter
Weinfurter, Stefan, 142
Welf IV, dk of Bavaria (Welf the Elder) (d. 1101) (Guelf IV), sn of **Adalbert Azzo II** [Judith of Flanders], 5–6, 50–1, 62, 167
Welf V, dk of Bavaria (d. 1120) (Guelf V), eldest sn of Judith of Flanders and **Welf IV** [second husband of CM], 5, 50–1, 62, 167, 169, 173, 180
Wibert. *See* Clement III, antipope (1080, 1084–1100) (Wibert)
Widukind of Corvey (d. aft 973), monk, historian, 19, 129–30, 134, 136–7, 139, 140, 152, 178, 189
Res gestae Saxonicae, 129–30, 152
Wigeric of Bidgau (d. bef 923) [**Cunegund (d. aft 923)**], 34, 37
Willa of Tuscany, q of Italy (d. aft 966), dau of Willa II of Burgundy (d. aft 936) and Boso, mgv of Tuscany [**Berengar II**]
as Jezebel and 'Lamia vampire', 190, 219n319
Willa, ctss of Camerino/Tuscany (d. aft 977/8), dau of Boniface of Spoleto, m of **Hugh, mgv of Tuscany (d. 1001)**, [Uberto, mgv of Tuscany, d. bef 977], 118
William the Pious of Aquitaine (d. 918), founder of Cluny, 160. *See also* Cluny, abbey
William, abp of Mainz (d. 968), sn of a captive Slav noblewoman and **Otto I**, 151

William, ct of Upper Burgundy (d. 1087), cousin of **Agnes of Poitou**, 45
William the Conqueror, 50, 168, 214n256

Willigis, abp of Mainz (d. 1011), chancellor, archchancellor, illegitimate son of Otto I, 26–8, 117, 146, 178, 185